BA

DURING THE

ABBASID CALIPHATE

FROM

CONTEMPORARY ARABIC AND PERSIAN SOURCES

BY

G. LE STRANGE

AUTHOR OF 'PALESTINE UNDER THE MOSLEMS,' 'CORRESPONDENCE OF PRINCESS LIEVEN AND EARL GREY,' ETC.

WITH EIGHT PLANS

Oxford

AT THE CLARENDON PRESS

M DCCCC

Oxford
PRINTED AT THE CLARENDON PRESS
BY HORACE HART, M.A.
PRINTER TO THE UNIVERSITY

TO

STANLEY LANE-POOLE

IN REMEMBRANCE OF WORK DONE AND

IN EXPECTATION OF WORK

TO BE DONE

THIS BOOK IS AFFECTIONATELY

DEDICATED

PREFACE

In the summer of the year 1883 it was my good fortune to make the acquaintance of the late Sir Henry Rawlinson, and the book which is now at length published is due to his suggestion. In the first place Sir Henry called my attention to the Ibn Serapion MS., of which the British Museum possesses an unique copy, and he urged on me the desirability, by its means, of working out the topography of mediaeval Baghdad; assuring me that, with the numerous articles on this subject contained in the great *Geographical Dictionary* of Yâḳût and other early authorities, a reconstruction of the old plan of the city was quite feasible. Ibn Serapion I published in the *Journal of the Royal Asiatic Society* (January, April, and October, 1895).

Other occupations hindered the conclusion of the present work; it took much longer than I had at first imagined to sift and set in order the mass of information scattered through the voluminous writings of the Arab geographers and historians;

and even now a good deal might be added from incidental notices, other than those which I have found, in the later volumes of the Annals of Ṭabarî, if the Index to that great chronicle had been available—but unfortunately this has not yet been published.

There is indeed no lack of material, as will be seen by glancing over the names of contemporary Arab Geographers given in the accompanying Chronological Table (which the bibliographical List of Authorities completes); but the real basis of the present reconstruction of the mediaeval plan is the description of the Canals of Baghdad written by Ibn Serapion in about the year A.D. 900. By combining the network of the water system, as described by this writer, with the radiating high-roads, as described by his contemporary Ya'ḳûbî, it has been possible to plot out the various quarters of older Baghdad, filling in details from the accounts of other authorities, which, taken alone, would have proved too fragmentary to serve for any systematic reconstruction of the plan.

As far as I am aware, no one has yet attempted to write a complete history and draw the plan of the great metropolis of the Abbasid Caliphs. A beginning was indeed made by the late A. von Kremer in his *Kulturgeschichte des Orients unter den Chalifen* (vol. ii. pp. 47–94); but unfortunately this went no further than a single chapter, giving an account (derived from Ya'ḳûbî) of the original burg, or Round City of Manṣûr, which was to later Baghdad much what the City of London has come to be in relation to greater London which now encompasses it for miles on every side.

The bibliographical list of original Authorities and Editions, given at the head of this work, is as complete as I can make it, being more especially intended to serve for the references in the notes; further, in the last three chapters some account will be found of these various authors and the nature of the description which each has left us of Baghdad.

The system of transliteration adopted is that now commonly used; but for the sake of brevity I have generally omitted the Arabic article, *Al*, before the names of the Caliphs, as also in many common place-names: and for so doing the sufficient authority of Silvestre de Sacy may be cited, who has followed this system in his *Religion des Druzes* (see vol. i. *Introduction*, p. v, note 2). It has the merit of brevity, and while rendering these names less uncouth to the English ear, makes them, I think, more easily distinguishable to the eye.

In many plural names, such as Bazzâzîn, Tustarîyîn, and the like, I have kept to the termination in *în* of the objective case (instead of writing Bazzâzûn, Tustarîyûn) to avoid a double transcription, since this *în*-form properly occurs in the full name—e. g. Nahr-al-Bazzâzîn, the Canal of the Cloth-merchants; Rabad-at-Tustarîyîn, the suburb of the people of

Tustar; further, this is the post-classical form and the one now in use. It has not been thought necessary to mark dotted letters and long vowels in the names of authors cited in the notes.

In mentioning dates, the years of the Hijrah are given, with the year A. D. following in brackets, which last is reckoned to be the year with which the major part of the Moslem year corresponds: thus A. H. 200 beginning on August 11, A. D. 815, is given as equivalent to A. D. 816.

The Map and Plans will serve to show what I conclude to be the disposition of the various quarters of the city as described in our authorities. Nobody can be better aware of the shortcomings of these Plans than I myself am, and they court criticism from any who will take the trouble of going through the evidence. The course of the Tigris has considerably changed during the last thousand years, of that there is ample proof, but it is not so easy to say where exactly, at any specified epoch, the bed of the river lay.

For modern Baghdad and its environs I have followed the great plan of the city published by Commander Felix Jones in his *Memoirs*, Bombay Government Records, No. XLIII, New Series, 1857; while the surrounding country and the course of the Tigris generally are given from the Map of Ancient Babylon, in six sheets, compiled by Mr. Trelawney Saunders from the surveys of Felix Jones, Bewsher, Collingwood, and Beaumont Selby, which was published by Stanford in 1885 on the scale of 4,000 yards to the inch.

My plans of mediaeval Baghdad are, to a certain extent, tentative; in the main lines of roads, and the relative positions of the various quarters, however, but little question is likely to arise, since the evidence is fairly complete. What is now more especially needed is excavation on the spot to show where, on the western side of the Tigris, the great Mosque of Manṣûr stood, and on the eastern bank what was the exact position of the Ruṣâfah Mosque. Both these buildings appear to have been standing in the middle of the fourteenth century of our era; and, since tiles or kiln-burnt bricks were largely used in their construction, some considerable vestiges of their foundation-walls would certainly be found were the mounds of rubbish, on either bank of the Tigris above modern Baghdad, to be carefully examined.

I have many to thank for aid in the carrying through of this work, and in the notes I have in all cases acknowledged more special obligations. For general bibliographical information, however, I may take this opportunity of expressing my thanks to both Professor Lane-Poole and to Mr. A. G. Ellis, Assistant-Keeper of Oriental Books and MSS. in the British Museum, and while recalling the names of Mr. A. A. Bevan and of Mr. E. G. Browne of Cambridge, who have always afforded me their friendly advice and assistance, I must not close my preface without recording how deeply I am indebted to Professor De Goeje of Leyden for his constant courtesy in answering many questions, and in affording me every kind of information, unstintedly, from his unrivalled knowledge of mediaeval Arab geography and history.

G. LE STRANGE.

ATHENAEUM CLUB, PALL MALL.
August, 1900.

CONTENTS

CHAPTER I

THE FOUNDATION OF BAGHDAD

Previous capitals of Islam. Medina and Kûfah. Damascus. The fall of the Omayyads. Need of a new capital for the Abbasid dynasty. The two Hâshimîyahs. The Râwandî insurrection. Courses followed by the Euphrates and Tigris during the Middle Ages. Manṣûr chooses the site of Baghdad. An Assyrian Baghdad; Etymology of the name. Az-Zawrâ and Ar-Rawḥâ. The legend of the name Miḳlâṣ; Sûḳ Baghdâd. The advantages of the situation of Baghdad . . . *pp.* 1–14

CHAPTER II

THE CITY OF MANṢÛR

The foundation of the Round City. Shî'ah insurrection: delays. No traces of the Round City now extant. Plan marked out in cinders; Abu Ḥanîfah. The Four Gates. Measurements. The Central Area, and the Palace of the Golden Gate. The Concentric Walls. Bricks used. The origin of the Gates. Description of thoroughfare going from outer Gate to Central Area. The original Markets and Arcades. The Prison, and the Central Area. The Water-conduits . . . . *pp.* 15–29

CHAPTER III

THE CITY OF MANSÛR (*continued*)

CHAPTER IV

THE CANALS OF WESTERN BAGHDAD

CHAPTER V

THE KÛFAH HIGHROAD AND THE KARKH SUBURB

CHAPTER VI

THE CANALS OF KARKH

CHAPTER VII

THE QUARTERS OF THE LOWER HARBOUR

CHAPTER VIII

THE QUARTER OF THE BASRAH GATE

CHAPTER IX

THE SHÂRI' QUARTER AND THE TRENCH OF ṬÂHIR

CHAPTER X

THE HARBÎYAH QUARTER

CHAPTER XI

THE QUARTERS OF THE MUHAWWAL GATE

CHAPTER XII

BARÂTHÂ, MUHAWWAL, AND THE KÂZIMAYN

CHAPTER XIII

EASTERN BAGHDAD IN GENERAL

CHAPTER XIV

RUSÂFAH

CHAPTER XV

THE SHAMMÂSÎYAH QUARTER

CHAPTER XVI

THE MUKHARRIM QUARTER

CHAPTER XVII

THE BUYID PALACES

CHAPTER XVIII

THE PALACES OF THE CALIPHS

CHAPTER XIX

THE PALACE GATES AND ADJOINING QUARTERS

CHAPTER XX

THE QUARTERS NORTH OF THE PALACES

CHAPTER XXI

THE QUARTERS EAST AND SOUTH OF THE PALACES

CHAPTER XXII

RECAPITULATION AND AUTHORITIES: EARLY PERIOD

CHAPTER XXIII

RECAPITULATION AND AUTHORITIES: MIDDLE PERIOD

CHAPTER XXIV

RECAPITULATION AND AUTHORITIES: FINAL PERIOD

LIST OF MAPS AND PLANS

BIBLIOGRAPHICAL LIST OF AUTHORITIES QUOTED IN THE NOTES

ABU-L-FARAJ, Gregorius Bar Hebreus: History. Beyrout. 1890.

ABU-L-FIDÂ: Geography. Arabic text, edited by Reinaud and De Slane. Paris, 1840.

—— Chronicle, edited by Reiske. 5 vols., Copenhagen, 1786.

ABU-L-MAḤÂSIN: Annals, edited by Juynboll. 2 vols., Leyden, 1855.

ABU SHÂMAH: Kitâb-ar-Rawḍatayn. Cairo edition, A. H. 1287 (1870).

ARÎB: Tabari Continuatus: M. J. De Goeje. Leyden, 1897.

BALÂDHURÎ: Edited by M. J. De Goeje. Leyden, 1886.

BENJAMIN OF TUDELA: Itinerary, in Hebrew and English, by A. Asher. London and Berlin, 1840.

DOZY, R.: Supplément aux Dictionnaires Arabes. 2 vols., Leyden, 1881.

FAKHRI: History. Arabic text, edited by Ahlwardt. Gotha, 1860.

FRÄNKEL, S.: Die Aramäischen Fremdwörter im Arabischen. Leyden, 1886.

GOLDZIHER, I.: Muhammedanische Studien. 2 vols., Halle, 1889.

GUZÎDAH: See next.

HAMD-ALLAH: Târîkh-i-Guzîdah (History), in MS., quoted by sections and reigns of Caliphs.

ḤAMD-ALLAH: Nuzhat-al-Ḳulûb (Geography). The section relating to Baghdad is printed by C. Schefer in his *Supplément du Siasset Nameh.* Paris, 1897. The text of the entire Nuzhat has been lithographed at Bombay in A.H. 1311 (1894). Excellent MSS. of both the Guzîdah and the Nuzhat will be found in the British Museum Library and in the Bibliothèque Nationale in Paris.

HOFFMANN, G.: Auszüge aus Syrischen Akten Persischer Märtyrer. Leipzig, 1880.

HOWORTH, Sir H.: History of the Mongols. 4 vols., London, 1888.

IBN BAṬÛṬAH: Travels, edited in Arabic with French translation by C. Defremery. 6 vols., Paris, 1877.

IBN-AL-FURÂT: MS. in the Vatican Library, No. 726 *Arab.*, and cf. Cat. Cod. Or. Bibl. Vat. edente Angelo Maio, Rome, 1831, p. 607.

IBN HAWKAL: Edited by M. J. De Goeje. Leyden, 1873.

IBN JUBAYR: Travels, edited by W. Wright. Leyden, 1852.

IBN KHALLIKÂN: Biographical Dictionary, the Arabic text edited by F. Wüstenfeld. Göttingen, 1837. The biographies are given under consecutive numbers (the pagination not being continuous). A useful translation, in 4 vols., was made by De Slane for the Oriental Translation Fund and published in 1871.

IBN ḲUṬAYBAH: History, edited by F. Wüstenfeld. Göttingen, 1850.

IBN MASKUWAYH: Edited by M. J. De Goeje in *Fragmenta Historicorum Arabicorum.* Leyden, 1871.

IBN RUSTAH: Edited by M. J. De Goeje. Leyden, 1892.

IBN SERAPION: See *Journal of the Royal Asiatic Society* for 1895, January, April, and October; 'Description of Mesopotamia and Baghdad,' edited and translated by Guy le Strange. London, 1895.

IDRISI: Description d'Afrique et de l'Espagne, R. Dozy et M. J. De Jong. Leyden, 1866.

IMÂD-AD-DÎN: Edited by M. T. Houtsma in *Recueil des Textes relatifs à l'Histoire des Seljoucides*, vol. ii. Leyden, 1889.

ISTAKHRÎ: Edited by M. J. De Goeje. Leyden, 1870.

JONES, Commander Felix: Report: Records of the Bombay Government, No. XLIII, New Series. Bombay, 1857. This Report includes a large plan of modern Baghdad and many maps of the surrounding country.

ḲAZWÎNÎ: Athâr-al-Bilâd, edited by F. Wüstenfeld (vol. ii of the Cosmography). Göttingen, 1848.

KER-PORTER: Travels. 2 vols., London, 1821.

KHÂḲÂNÎ: Tuhfat-al-'Irâḳayn. Lucknow edition; lithographed in A.H. 1294 (1877).

KHÂṬIB: History of Baghdad. References are to the MS. in the British Museum, Or. 1507. Other MSS. of this important work —which has never been printed—will be found in both the British Museum and the French Bibliothèque Nationale.

KITÂB-AL-AGHÂNÎ: In 20 vols. Cairo, A.H. 1285 (1868).

KITÂB-AL-FIHRIST: Edited by G. Flügel. Leipzig, 1871.

KITÂB-AL-'UYÛN: In *Fragmenta Historicorum Arabicorum*: M. J. De Goeje. Leyden, 1871.

KREMER, A. VON: Kulturgeschichte des Orients unter den Chalifen. 2 vols., Vienna, 1875.

MAFÂTIḤ-AL-'ULÛM: Edited by Van Vloten. Leyden, 1895.

MARÂṢID: The Epitome of Yâḳût's great Geographical Dictionary, called the Marâṣid-al-Iṭṭilâ', edited by T. G. Juynboll. 6 vols., Leyden, 1852.

MARCO POLO: See Yule.

MAS'ÛDÎ: The Golden Meadows, edited by Barbier de Meynard, with French translation. 9 vols., Paris, 1877.

—— Tanbîh. Edited by M. J. De Goeje. Leyden, 1894.

MÂWARDÎ: Edited by M. Enger. Bonn, 1853.

MIRKHWAND: Rawḍat-as-Ṣafâ; lithographed in 2 vols., folio. Bombay, A.H. 1266 (1850).

MUḲADDASI: Edited by M. J. De Goeje. Leyden, 1877.

MUSHTARIK: See Yâḳût.

NIEBUHR, C.: Voyage en Arabie. Amsterdam, 1776 and 1786.

NUZHAT: See Ḥamd-Allah.

PARSONS, A.: Travels. London, 1808.

RÂSHID-AD-DÎN: History of the Mongols. The first volume of the Persian text, with French translation, was published by E. Quatremere in 1836; it has never been completed.

RAWLINSON, Sir H. C.: The article on Baghdad in the ninth edition of the *Encyclopaedia Britannica.*

SHARAF-AD-DÎN: Histoire de Timur. Traduite par Petis de la Croix. 4 vols., Paris, 1722.

SHARÎSHÎ: Commentary on Ḥarîrî. Cairo edition, A.H. 1300 (1883).

SUYÛṬÎ: Lubb-al-Lubâb, edited by P. J. Veth. Leyden, 1840.

ṬABAḲÂT-I-NÂṢIRÎ, by Minhaj-ad-Dîn. The Persian text was printed at Calcutta in 1864, and an English translation has been published by Major H. G. Raverty in the *Bibliotheca Indica*, 1881.

ṬABARÎ: Chronicle: published in three parts and in thirteen volumes, under the editorship of M. J. De Goeje. Leyden, 1890.

TANBÎH: See Mas'ûdî.

TAVERNIER, J. B.: Les six Voyages de. Utrecht, 1712. 12mo.

THEOPHANES: Chronographia, edited by C. De Boor. 2 vols., Leipzig, 1883.

VAN VLOTEN, G.: Recherches sur la Domination Arabe sous le Khalifat des Omayades. Amsterdam, 1894.

WASSÂF: Edited in Persian, with German translation by Hammer-Purgstall. Vienna, 1856.

YA ḲÛBÎ: Geography, edited by M. J. De Goeje. Leyden, 1892.

—— History, edited by M. T. Houtsma. 2 vols., Leyden, 1883.

YÂḲÛT: Geographical Dictionary, called the Mu'jam-al-Buldân, edited by F. Wüstenfeld. 5 vols., Leipzig, 1866.

—— Mushtarik, edited by the same. Göttingen, 1846.

YULE, Col. Henry: Cathay and the Way thither. Hakluyt Society Publications. 1866.

—— The Travels of Marco Polo. 2nd edition. 2 vols., London, 1875.

Z. D. M. G.: Zeitschrift der Deutschen Morgenländischen Gesellschaft, vol. xxxix. Leipzig, 1885.

CHRONOLOGICAL TABLE

Year. A.H. (A.D.)	*Abbasid Caliphs.*	*Buildings and Events in Baghdad.*	*Contemporary Authorities.*
132 (750)	SAFFÂḤ.	Builds Hâshimîyah.	
136 (754)	MANSÛR.	(The First Period.) Foundation of Baghdad; the Round City.	
158 (775)	MAHDÎ.	Completion of Ruṣâfah.	
169 (785)	HÂDÎ.		
170 (786)	HÂRÛN-AR-RASHÎD.	Ja'farî Palace founded.	
193 (809)	AMÎN.	First Siege, 197 (813).	
198 (813)	MAMÛN.	Ja'farî Palace completed, and called the Ḥasanî.	
218 (833)	MU'TAṢIM.	Palace on Nahr Mûsâ. (The Second Period.) Caliphate removed to Sâmarrâ, 221 (836).	
227 (842)	WÂTHIḲ.	Sâmarrâ.	
232 (847)	MUTAWAKKIL.	Sâmarrâ.	
247 (861)	MUNTAṢIR.	Sâmarrâ.	
248 (862)	MUSTA'ÎN.	Returns to Baghdad. Second Siege, 251 (865).	
251 (866)	MU'TAZZ.	Sâmarrâ.	
255 (869)	MUHTADÎ.	Sâmarrâ.	
256 (870)	MU'TAMID.	Bûrân restores the Ḥasanî Palace. The Caliph returns to Baghdad, 279 (892).	*Ya'kûbî.*

Year. A.H. (A.D.)	*Abbasid Caliphs.*	*Buildings and Events in Baghdad.*	*Contemporary Authorities.*
279 (892)	MU'TAḌID.	The Caliph resides in East Baghdad. Palaces of the Thurayyâ and the Firdûs built. The Tâj Palace begun. The Ḥasanî Palace enlarged.	
289 (902)	'ALÎ MUKTAFÎ.	The Tâj Palace finished. Mosque of the Caliph built.	*Ibn Rustah.*
295 (908)	MUḲTADIR.	The Palace of the Tree and others. The Greek Embassy, 305 (917).	*Ṭabarî, Ibn Serapion.*
320 (932)	ḲÂHIR.	The wall of the Round City falls to ruin.	
322 (934)	RÂḌÎ.		
329 (940)	MUTTAḲÎ.	Palace of the Golden Gate ruined, 329 (941). The Round City inundated.	*Mas'ûdî.*
333 (944)	MUSTAKFÎ.		
334 (946)	MUṬÎ'.	(The Third Period.) Buyids: Palace of Mu'izz-ad-Dawlah and his Dyke. The Peacock Palace, the Octagon and Square Palaces.	*Iṣṭakhrî.*
363 (974)	ṬÂI'.	The 'Aduḍî Hospital.	*Ibn Ḥawḳal, Muḳaddasî.*
381 (991)	ḲÂDIR.		
422 (1031)	ḲÂIM.	(The Fourth Period.) Saljûḳs. Tughril Beg and Mâlik Shâh. The Nizâmîyah College. The inundation of 466 (1074).	*Khaṭîb.*
467 (1075)	MUḲTADÎ.	The Mosque of the Sultan. Suburbs of the Muḳtadîyah, &c.	

Year. A. H. (A. D.)	*Abbasid Caliphs.*	*Buildings and Events in Baghdad.*	*Contemporary Authorities.*
487 (1094)	MUSTAẒHIR.	Wall round lower East Baghdad, 488 (1095). The Rayḥânîyîn Palace.	
512 (1118)	MUSTARSHID.	The Bâb-al-Hujrah Palace.	
529 (1135)	MANṢÛR RÂSHID.	Third Siege, 530 (1136).	
530 (1136)	MUḤAMMAD MUḲTAFÎ.	The Tâj Palace burnt, 549 (1154), and in part rebuilt. Fourth Siege, 551 (1157). Inundation of 554 (1159).	*Khâḳânî.*
555 (1160)	MUSTANJID.	(The Fifth Period.)	*Benjamin of Tudela.*
566 (1170)	MUSTAḌÎ.	City Wall restored, 568 (1173). Inundation of 569 (1174). Older Tâj Palace demolished. The second Tâj and Dyke built.	
575 (1180)	NÂṢIR.	Inundation of 614 (1217). Talism Gate repaired, 618 (1221).	*Ibn Jubayr* *Yâḳût.*
622 (1225)	ẒÂHIR.	Restores the Bridge of Boats.	
623 (1226)	MUSTANṢIR.	Mustanṣiriyah College. Mosque restored.	
640 (1242)	MUSTA'ṢIM.	Library of the Rayḥânîyîn. Last Siege: Hûlâgû, 656 (1258).	*Ibn Khallikân.*

Map I To face page 1

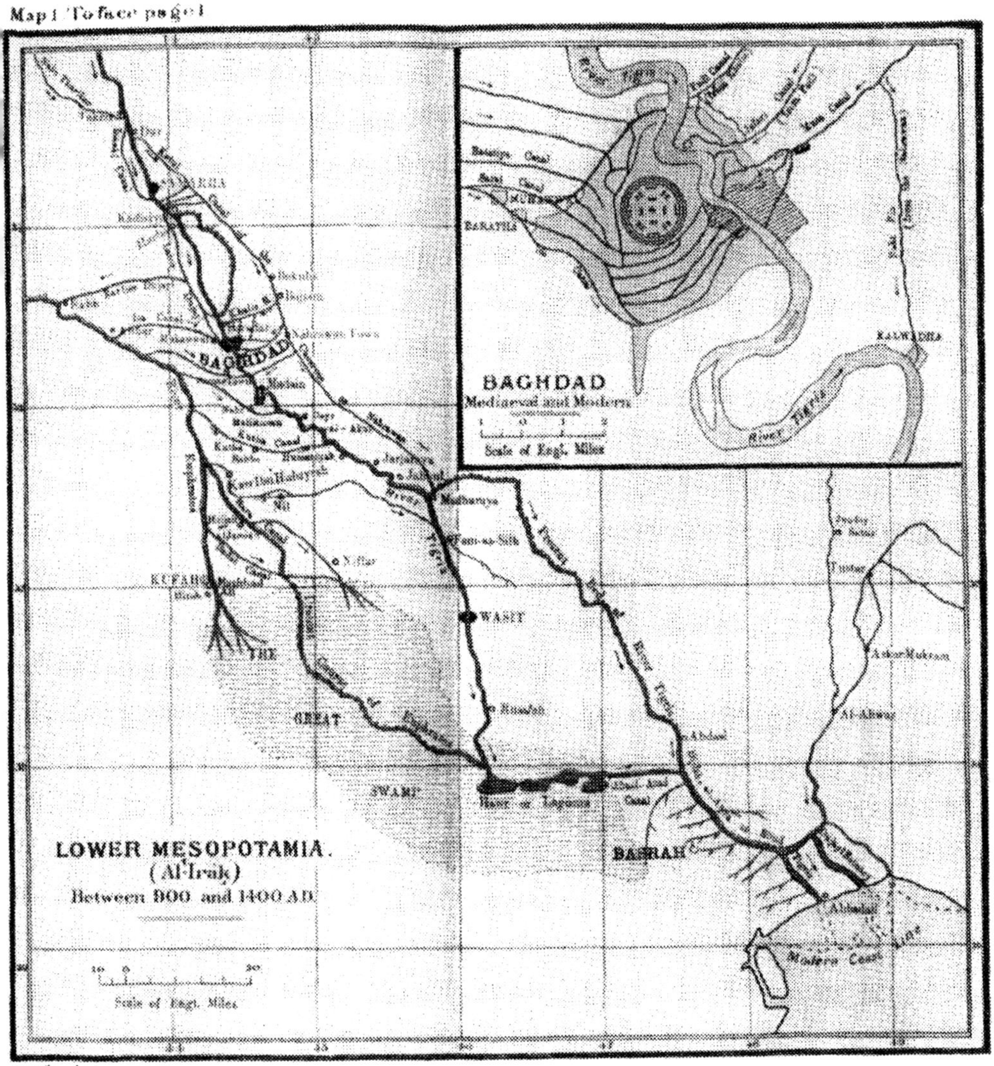

BAGHDAD
DURING THE CALIPHATE

CHAPTER I

THE FOUNDATION OF BAGHDAD

Previous capitals of Islam. Medina and Kûfah. Damascus. The fall of the Omayyads. Need of a new capital for the Abbasid dynasty. The two Hâshimîyahs. The Râwandî insurrection. Courses followed by the Euphrates and Tigris during the Middle Ages. Manşûr chooses the site of Baghdad. An Assyrian Baghdad; Etymology of the name. Az-Zawrâ and Ar-Rawḥâ. The legend of the name Miḳlâş; Sûḳ Baghdâd. The advantages of the situation of Baghdad.

THE history of Baghdad, as a metropolis, coincides with the history of the rise and fall of the Abbasid Caliphs, for in the East it would appear to be almost a necessity of the case that every new dynasty should found a new capital. In the earlier annals of Islam the Era of the Flight (or Hijrah) commemorates the date when the Prophet Muḥammad, being forced to leave Mecca, went to take up his abode in the little hamlet of Yathrib. This change shifted the political centre of Arabia from the older commercial city to Yathrib, now to be named Medina, 'the City of the Prophet,' and which, from a small provincial town, suddenly rose to be the capital of Islam, becoming in a few years' time the seat of the theocratic government that had imposed new laws on the desert tribes and transformed all Arabia into one nation. The first three successors (the Khalîfahs or Caliphs) of the Prophet, namely his companions Abu Bakr, 'Omar, and 'Othmân, continued to govern Islam from Medina; and among the secondary causes that brought about the fall of 'Alî, the next Caliph, is certainly to be counted his ill-advised abandonment of Medina and the Ḥijâz. In going to reside at Kûfah in Mesopotamia, 'Alî overset the balance of power among the Arab tribes, as established by his predecessors; also he was unable to found a strong administration in his new capital, discovering when too late that at Kûfah the majority of the population was unreliable, ever rebellious and inimical to his theocratic claims. Mu'âwiyah, who now became the rival of 'Alî in the Caliphate, had more than a score of years before this period been named governor of Syria by the Caliph 'Omar; and, foreseeing the struggle from the beginning, had made it his work to colonize Syria with relatives and dependants. The knife of a religious fanatic settled the question of who should be Caliph. 'Alî perished at Kûfah, inaugurating by his death the long line of Shî'ah martyrs, and Mu'âwiyah, first Caliph of the house of Omayyah, ruled Islam unquestioned, residing at Damascus, which thus from the capital of a province suddenly became the metropolis of the Commander of the Faithful.

Damascus was well situated to be the seat of government of the purely Arab Caliphate of the Omayyads. It lay in a most fruitful land; well within striking distance of the Ḥijâz, where Medina and Mecca still remained the double centre of religious power in Islam; further it was backed by the Arabian Desert, from whence the Caliphs drew their soldiers, and where such of their kinsmen as still clung to the nomad life roamed at pleasure, but close at hand in case of need. Damascus was also conveniently near the Byzantine frontier, and during the ninety years of the Omayyad Caliphate the Arab armies ever and again poured from the north of Syria into Eastern Asia Minor, making almost continuous raids against the unfortunate Christian subjects of the Greek Emperor. Finally, that Damascus did not stand on a navigable river was of little disadvantage during the infancy of Moslem commerce, when all the carrying trade followed the old caravan-routes over the desert, and was of such small amount as could still be borne on the backs of camels.

Of the many causes that led to the overthrow of the Omayyads, the two most potent factors would appear to have been the decay of the Arab tribal system on which the military power of the Damascus Caliphs depended, and the disaffection towards the government caused by the continued misrule of the New-Moslems, who were *not* Arabs—being mainly the subjects of the old Persian kingdom of the Chosroes—and who, both in numbers and in intellectual gifts, far surpassed their Bedawin conquerors. The Persians had accepted Islam cordially, but distinctly after a fashion of their own, which the Arab party regarded as heterodox; and the Abbasid claims to the Caliphate were made good, to no inconsiderable extent, by trading on the inborn hatred which the Persians, already Shî'ahs, nourished against the Sunnî Caliphs at Damascus, who, though lax in morals and given to wine-bibbing, were orthodox in faith, and, before all things, Arab in sympathy[1].

The last Omayyad Caliph, Marwân II, was routed and slain in the year 132 (A.D. 750), and the first Abbasid Caliph well merited his name of Saffâḥ—the 'Shedder of Blood'—he having been constantly occupied, during the four years of his reign, in hunting down and putting to death every male descendant of the house of Omayyah, save one youth only who, escaping to Spain, ultimately obtained rule there, and founded the dynasty which afterwards came to be known as the Caliphate of Cordova. In 136 (A. D. 754) Manṣûr succeeded his brother Saffâḥ on the throne, and during the twenty-two years of his reign built Baghdad, and there organized the government of the Abbasids, which first established in power, and then suffering a long decay, was destined to last for five centuries seated on the banks of the Tigris.

A new capital for the new dynasty was indeed an imperative need. Damascus, peopled by the dependants of the Omayyads, was out of the question; on the one hand it was too far from Persia, whence the power of the Abbasids was chiefly derived; on the other hand it was dangerously near the Greek frontier, and from here, during the troublous reigns of the last Omayyads, hostile incursions on the part of the Christians had begun to avenge former defeats. It was also beginning to be evident that the conquests of Islam would,

[1] The causes which led to the overthrow of the Omayyads, and the revolution of which the house of 'Abbâs skilfully profited to obtain the Caliphate, are discussed in a recent pamphlet (named in the List of Authorities) by the Dutch orientalist, G. Van Vloten.

in the future, lie to the eastward towards Central Asia, rather than to the westward at the further expense of the Byzantines. Damascus, on the highland of Syria, lay, so to speak, dominating the Mediterranean and looking westward, but the new capital that was to supplant it must face east, be near Persia, and for the needs of commerce have water communication with the sea. Hence everything pointed to a site on either the Euphrates or the Tigris, and the Abbasids were not slow to make their choice.

During the first Moslem conquest of Mesopotamia, two Arab cities had been founded there for the garrisoning of the troops—Baṣrah near the mouth of the twin rivers, and Kûfah on the Euphrates, where the desert caravan-road, from the Ḥijâz to Persia, entered the cultivated plain of Mesopotamia. The Caliph Saffâḥ, when not occupied in fighting and butchering, had lived at the Palace called Hâshimîyah (after the ancestor of his race), which he had built beside the old Persian city of Anbâr on the eastern side of the Euphrates, near to where the great canal, afterwards known as the Nahr 'Îsâ, branched off towards the Tigris. At this Hâshimîyah (of Anbâr) the first Abbasid Caliph died in 136 (A.D. 754); and his brother Manṣûr, shortly after succeeding to the throne, began to build for himself another residence called by the same name. This second Hâshimîyah, according to one account, was a town standing between the Arab garrison-city of Kûfah and the old Persian town of Ḥîrah; that is to say, on the Arabian side of the Euphrates, not far above the place where that river, in the tenth century A.D., spread out and became lost in the

Great Swamp. Another account places the later Hâshimîyah of Manṣûr near the town (Madînah) of Ibn Hubayrah, which last lay close by Kûfah, and therefore must not be confounded with the Castle (Ḳaṣr) of Ibn Hubayrah, a town of some importance lying higher up the Euphrates than Kûfah, and on its left or eastern bank[1].

The exact position, however, of this town of Hâshimîyah is of little importance, since Manṣûr very soon abandoned the site as most inconvenient for a capital. It was too near Kûfah, with its population of fanatical Shî'ahs, and its garrison of Arab tribesmen, who constantly rioted and otherwise gave trouble. Lastly, Manṣûr took a permanent dislike to Hâshimîyah after the insurrection of the Râwandîs, when a multitude of these Persian fanatics surging round his palace had insisted on worshipping him as the Deity. The indignant Caliph had repudiated their idolatrous homage, whereupon they began a riot, attacking the guards, and Manṣûr at last found himself in some danger of losing his life at the hands of those who had pretended to revere him as their God.

If the capital of Islam was to be shifted to

[1] Ya'kubi, 237; Tabari, iii. 271. This duplication of place-names, in the immediate neighbourhood one of the other, is one of the difficulties of mediaeval Arab geography. Dictionaries of homonyms exist—as, for instance, that of Yakut called *Al-Mushtarik*—and they are useful, though seldom affording sufficient information about places of minor importance. That there was a Hâshimîyah at Anbâr, as well as at Kûfah, is evident by the comparison of two such good authorities as the *Kitâb-al-'Uyûn*, pp. 211, 214, 236, with the passages in Tabari and Ya'kubi cited above. It is also evident from the passage in Tabari that the Madînah, or 'town,' of Ibn Hubayrah close to Kûfah, was not identical with his Ḳaṣr, or 'Castle,' a place which, however, afterwards rose to be a town of some importance standing on the high road from Baghdad to Kûfah.

Mesopotamia, the advantages of a site on the Tigris, rather than on the Euphrates, were conspicuous. The new capital would then stand in the centre of a fruitful country, and not on the desert border, as was the case with Kûfah and the neighbouring towns, for the barren sands of Arabia come right up to the western bank of the Euphrates. By a system of canals the waters of this latter river were used to thoroughly irrigate and fertilize all the country lying in between the two great streams, while the waters of the Tigris were kept in reserve for the lands on its left or Persian bank; and thus the whole breadth of the province, from the Arabian Desert on the one side to the mountains of Kurdistân on the other, was to be brought under cultivation, and converted into a veritable garden of plenty. Lastly, the Lower Tigris before its junction with the Euphrates was more practicable for navigation than this latter river, inasmuch as the great irrigation canals, by effecting the drainage of the surplus waters of the Euphrates into the Tigris, scoured the lower course of this river, and kept the water-way clear through the dangerous shallows of the Great Swamp immediately above the Baṣrah Estuary.

To understand the problem as presented to Manṣûr in his search after a suitable place for the new capital, it must also be borne in mind that during the period of the Abbasids, neither the Euphrates nor the Tigris followed the course marked on our modern maps. From the account given by Ibn Serapion, it is evident that the main stream of the Euphrates, at a short distance above the ruins of Babylon, took the right or western channel, and, very soon after passing Kûfah, discharged its waters into the Great Swamp, which is so important a feature in the political and physical geography of that day. The Tigris, on the other hand, when it reached the latitude of the present Ḳûṭ-al-'Amârah (about a hundred miles as the crow flies below Baghdad) turned due south, and passing down to Wâsiṭ by the channel now known as the Shaṭṭ-al-Hayy, shortly below this city, also entered the Great Swamp where, however, unlike the Euphrates, its course continued to be marked by a series of navigable lagoons, called *Hawr*. Finally the whole body of water collected in the Swamp, from both the great rivers, drained into a channel leading out immediately to the head of the tidal estuary, which, after passing Baṣrah, flowed into the Persian Gulf at 'Abbadân[1].

[1] At the present day the Tigris, below Ḳûṭ-al-'Amârah, instead of flowing down past Wâsiṭ, turns into the more easterly channel, and after making a great bend due east, takes its course south to Kurnah, where it joins the waters of the Euphrates to form the estuary of the Shaṭṭ-al-'Arab. It is still a question when this change of bed took place, for no direct evidence of the date is to hand; but the change doubtless was effected gradually, and probably during the course of the sixteenth century A.D. The western bed, going through Wâsiṭ, certainly continued to be full of water as late as the middle of the fifteenth century A.D. It is plainly thus described by all our Arabic and Persian authorities of the Middle Ages, to mention only the latest in date, by Ḥamd Allah Mastawfî in A.D. 1330, by 'Alî Yazdî, the historian of the campaigns of Timur, who took Wâsiṭ, 'on the Tigris,' in A.D. 1393, and by Ḥâfiẓ Abrû, who wrote about the year A.D. 1420. After this must have come the change, and our next authority, more than two centuries, however, later, is the Frenchman Tavernier. After visiting Baghdad in February, 1652, he describes his journey down the Tigris, which (he says) some distance below the city, divided into *two* branches, so as to enclose a great island that was traversed by numerous small canals. The western channel (the older course by Wâsiṭ) apparently was then already no longer navigable, and Tavernier did not travel by it, but describes the river here as running 'vers la

Manṣûr made many journeys in search of a site for his new capital, travelling slowly up the banks of the Tigris from Jarjarâyâ to Mosul. A site near Bârimmâ below Mosul was at first proposed, where the hills called Jabal Ḥamrîn are cut through by the Tigris, but the Caliph finally decided against this, it is said because of the dearness and the scarcity of provisions. The Persian hamlet of Baghdâd, on the western bank of the Tigris, and just above where the Ṣarât canal flowed in, was ultimately fixed upon, and in the year 145 (A.D. 762) Manṣûr began to lay the foundations of his new city.

From the discovery made by Sir Henry Rawlinson in 1848, during the low water in an unusually dry season, of an extensive facing in Babylonian brickwork, which still lines the western bank of the Tigris at Baghdad, it would appear certain that this place had already been occupied by a far more ancient city. The bricks are each stamped with the name and titles of Nebuchadnezzar, and it has since been found that in the Assyrian geographical catalogues of the reign of Sardanapalus a name very

pointe de la Mésopotamie.' The French traveller went by boat down the eastern (the present) channel, which took its course 'le long de l'ancienne Chaldée.' He was ten days going from Baghdad to Baṣrah, and after passing (Ḳûṭ-al-) 'Amârat, a clay-built fort, he mentions the villages of Satarat, Manṣûri, Magar, and Gazar, when he reached Gorno (Kurnah) 'where the Euphrates and Tigris come together.' (Tavernier, i. 240.) It is evident, therefore, that the Tigris has followed its present course from Ḳûṭ-al-'Amârah to Kurnah since the middle of the seventeenth century, some time before which, but after 1420, it began to change over from the Wâsiṭ channel that it had occupied during the Middle Ages. It is curious further to notice that this present eastern course, running from 'Amârah to Kurnah, is also the channel taken by the Tigris in pre-Islamic days, namely during the Sassanian period; as has been already pointed out in a note to my translation of Ibn Serapion (*J.R.A.S.*, 1895, p. 301).

like Baghdad occurs, which probably refers to the town then standing on the site afterwards occupied by the capital of the Caliphs.

Be this as it may, the name of Baghdâd in its more modern form is presumably Persian, for which Yâḳût and other Arab authorities give various fanciful etymologies. *Bâgh* in Persian means 'garden,' and the city, they say, had the name of the garden of a certain *Dâd* or *Dâdwayh*; or else *Bagh* was the name of an idol, and *dâd*, meaning 'given' or 'gift,' the name of the town would thus have signified 'the gift of the idol Bagh'—for the which reason, some pious Moslems add, its name was changed by the Caliph Manṣûr to Madînat-as-Salâm, 'the City of Peace.' This last was more especially the official name for the capital of the Caliphate, and as such Madînat-as-Salâm appears as a mint-city on the coins of the Abbasids. In common parlance, however, the older name, Baghdad, maintained its supremacy, and the geographical dictionaries mention several variations in the spelling, doubtless Persian or archaic forms, viz. Baghdâdh and Baghdân, also Maghdâd, Maghdâdh, and Maghdân. From an elegy quoted by Ṭabarî on the ruin which Baghdad had suffered during the great siege in the reign of the Caliph Amîn, it would seem that the pronunciation Baghdâdh was then held to represent what had been the name of this town in the Persian or infidel days, as against Baghdâd of the Moslems. The poem in question closes with these two lines:—

'And, in this present state of affairs, it will be well indeed,
If (Moslem) Baghdâd do not shortly relapse and again become (Infidel) Baghdâdh!'

The true etymology, however, of the name would

appear to be from the two ancient Persian words *Bagh*, 'God,' and *Dâdh*, meaning 'founded' or 'foundation'—whence Baghdad would have signified the city 'Founded by God.'

The western half of Baghdad in Moslem days was also known by the name of Az-Zawrâ, meaning 'the Bent' or 'the Crooked,' in allusion, it is said, to the Ḳiblah-point (or direction towards Mecca) not precisely coinciding here with any one of the cardinal points of the compass. Another explanation given is that Baghdad took the name Az-Zawrâ from the river Tigris, which was 'bent' as it passed by the city: while Eastern Baghdad is said to have received the name of Ar-Rawḥâ, 'the Widespreading,' or 'the Shallow,' from its position in a curve of the stream; and Mas'ûdî in mentioning these names adds that both Az-Zawrâ and Ar-Rawḥâ were in common use among the people in his day. It is to be remarked that the grammatical form of both these names is Arabic, but the explanation given for the use of the terms is in neither case very plausible; it is therefore noteworthy that Ḥamd-Allah the Persian geographer, writing in the eighth century (A. D. the fourteenth), states that while the Arabs always spoke of Baghdad as Madînat-as-Salâm, 'the City of Peace,' it was in preference named Zawrâ by the Persians, which almost looks as though this Arabic word *Zawrâ*, 'Crooked,' may have stood for some more ancient Iranian name, now long forgotten[1].

[1] Tanbih, 360; Nuzhat, 146; Tabari, iii. 273; Yakut, i. 677, 678; Rawlinson, Encycl. Brit., s. v. Baghdad. The verse quoted will be found in Tabari, iii. 872; and this reference I owe to Professor A. A. Bevan.

During the last period of the Sassanian dynasty, Persian Baghdad, on the western side of the Tigris, had been a thriving place, and at the period of the Moslem Conquest a monthly market was held here. It became famous in the early annals of Islam for the very successful raid of which it was the scene. During the Caliphate of Abu Bakr, Khâlid the general of the Arab army, after advancing some way into Mesopotamia, suddenly dispatched a body of troops against this Sûḳ Baghdâd, as the 'Market' held at the Ṣarât Point was then called; the raiders surprised the town 'and the Moslems filled their hands with gold and silver, obtaining also the wherewithal to carry away their booty,' for they promptly returned again to Anbâr on the Euphrates, where Khâlid lay encamped.

After this incident of the year 13 (A.D. 634) Baghdad appears no more in history until Manṣûr, seeking out a site for the new capital, encamped here in the year 145 (A.D. 762). We are told that the spot was then occupied by several monasteries (*Dayr*), chiefly of Nestorian monks, and from them Manṣûr learned that among all the Tigris lands this district especially was celebrated for its freedom from the plague of mosquitoes, the nights here being cool and pleasant even in the height of summer. These lesser advantages, doubtless, had no inconsiderable influence with Manṣûr in the final choice of this as the place for the new capital of the Abbasids in Mesopotamia; but the practical foresight shown by the Caliph has been amply confirmed by the subsequent history of Baghdad. This city, called into existence as by an enchanter's wand, was second only to Constantinople in size during the

Middle Ages, and was unrivalled for splendour throughout Western Asia, becoming at once, and remaining for all subsequent centuries, the capital of Mesopotamia. Wars, sieges, the removal for a time by the Caliphs of the seat of government to Sâmarrâ [1] (higher up the Tigris), even the almost entire destruction of the city by the Mongols in A.D. 1258, none of these have permanently affected the supremacy of Baghdad as capital of the Tigris and Euphrates country, and now, after the lapse of over eleven centuries, the Turkish governor of Mesopotamia still resides in the city founded by the Caliph Manṣûr.

It is related by the historian Ṭabarî that a prophecy was found in the ancient books of the Christian monks, foretelling of a great city to be built in course of time between the Ṣarât Canal and the Tigris, by one bearing the name of Miḳlâṣ. The Caliph Manṣûr hearing of this prophecy greatly encouraged his people by telling them that this very name had been given him as a boy by his nurse. The real Miḳlâṣ had been a celebrated robber of that day, and the young prince had earned this nickname for himself by stealing on one

[1] This city had already been a flourishing place under the Sassanian kings, and in Aramæan or Syriac the name was written Sâmarrâ. It became the capital of the Abbasids under Mu'taṣim, and from the year 221 to 279 (A.D. 836 to 892) seven Caliphs resided here, the name of the place being then (officially) changed to Surra-man-râa, meaning 'Who sees it, rejoices.' Under this form the name appears as a mint-city on the coins of the Abbasids, beginning with the Caliph Mu'taṣim. Six ways of pronouncing the name are cited by Ibn Khallikân, and Yâḳût quotes a variety of fanciful etymologies, giving, however, the pronunciation Sâmarrâ at the head of the article in his Geographical Dictionary. In Tabari, and the earlier authorities, the name is always spelt Surra-man-râa, but this form appears only to have been used officially. Yakut, iii. 14; Hoffmann, 188; Ibn Khallikan, No. 8, p. 15.

occasion his nurse's distaff and selling the thread from it to provide a banquet, all his companions having been invited to do honour to the collation.

The manifold advantages of the position of Baghdad are a theme on which Moslem geographers and historians fondly expatiate. Muḳaddasi, for instance, states that the Caliph took the advice of those who had had experience from living here both in summer and in winter, and all agreed in its praise, that geographer summing up in the following terms said to have been addressed to Manṣûr: 'We are of opinion that thou shouldst found the city here between the four districts of Bûḳ and Kalwâdhâ, on the eastern bank, and of Ḳaṭrabbul and Bâdurâyâ, on the western bank: thereby shalt thou live among palms and near water, so that if one district fail thee in its crops or be late in its harvest in another will the remedy be found. Also thy city being on the Ṣarât Canal, provisions will be brought thither by the boats of the Euphrates, and by the caravans through the plains, even from Egypt and Syria. Hither, up from the sea, will come the wares of China, while down the Tigris from Mosul will be brought goods from the Byzantine lands. Thus shall thy city be safe standing between all these streams, and thine enemy shall not reach thee, except it be by a boat or by a bridge, and across the Tigris or the Euphrates[1].'

[1] Baladhuri, 246; Tabari, iii. 274, 276; Mukaddasi, 119. The Miḳlâṣ story is also given, with amplifications, in Yakut, i. 68; and another summary of the advantages of the site will be found in Tabari, iii. 275, the speech in this account being put in the mouth of the Ṣâḥib, or Lord of the District, of Baghdâd.

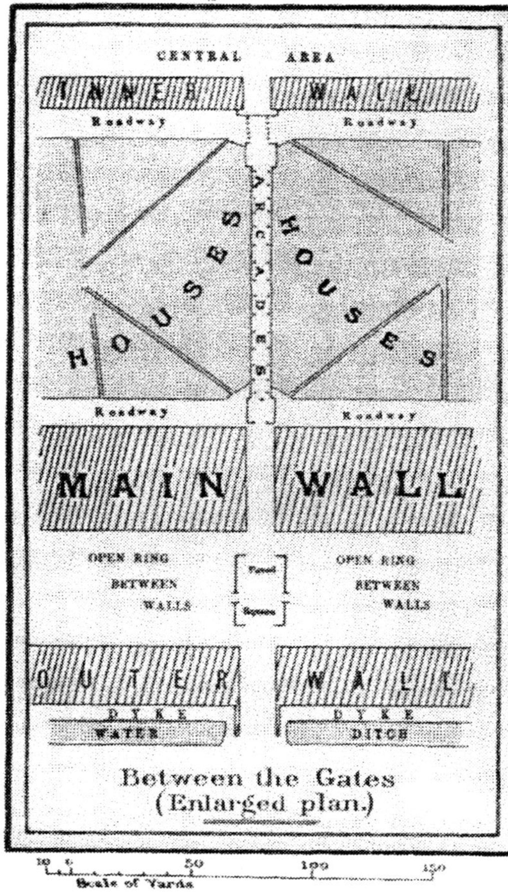

Between the Gates
(Enlarged plan.)

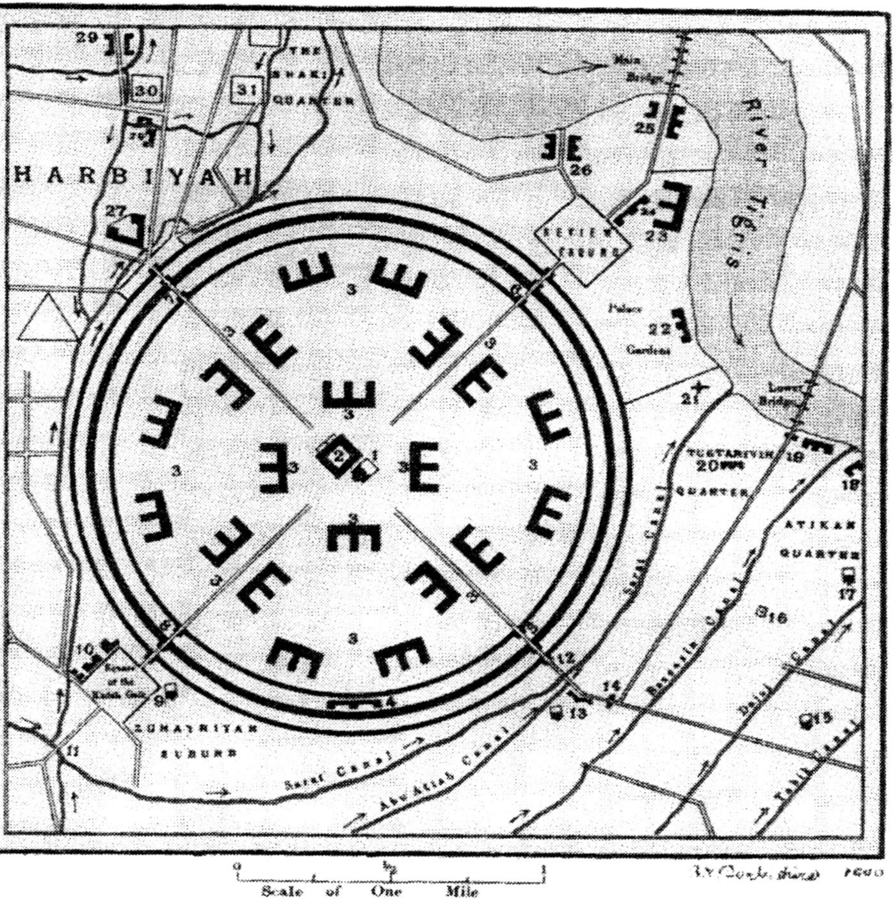

REFERENCES TO MAP No. II.

1. Mosque of Manşûr.
2. Palace of the Golden Gate with the two Galleries facing the Syrian Gate.

3. 3. 3. Various public offices, viz. Treasury, Armoury, Chancery, Land Tax Office, Public Bakery, Pay Office, Chamberlain's Office, and Palaces of the younger sons of the Caliph.

4. The Prison called Al-Maṭbaḳ.
5. The Başrah Gate.
6. The Khurâsân Gate.
7. The Syrian Gate.
8. The Kûfah Gate.
9. Mosque of Musayyib.
10. House of the Gate-keepers, Dîwân of the Şadaḳah (Poor Tax Office). The Stables and Dromedary House.
11. The Old Bridge.
12. The New Bridge.
13. Palace and Mosque of Waḍḍâḥ.
14. The Ḥarrânî Archway.
15. The Mosque of the Sharḳîyah Quarter.
16. The Tomb of Ma'rûf Karkhî.
17. Shrine of 'Alî, called Mashhad-al-Minṭaḳah.
18. Dâr-al-Jawz (the Nut-house).
19. Palace of Ḥumayd ibn 'Abd-al-Ḥamîd and the Barley Gate (Bâb-ash-Sha'îr).
20. Palace of 'Aḍud-ad-Dîn, the Wazîr.
21. The Old Convent at the Şarât Point.
22. The Ḳarâr Palace of Zubaydah.
23. The Palace of the Khuld.
24. The Royal Stables.
25. Office of the Bridge Works and Hall of the Chief of Police.
26. Palaces of the Princes Sulaymân and Şâliḥ.
27. Prison of the Syrian Gate.
28. Palace of Sa'îd-al-Khaṭîb and the Orphan School.
29. Dukkân-al-Abnâ (the Persian Shops).
30. Quadrangle of the Persians.
31. Quadrangle of Shabîb.

CHAPTER II

THE CITY OF MANṢÛR

The foundation of the Round City. Shî'ah insurrection: delays. No traces of the Round City now extant. Plan marked out in cinders; Abu Ḥanîfah. The Four Gates. Measurements. The Central Area, and the Palace of the Golden Gate. The Concentric Walls. Bricks used. The origin of the Gates. Description of thoroughfare going from outer Gate to Central Area. The original Markets and Arcades. The Prison, and the Central Area. The Water-conduits.

THE Round City in Western Baghdad which, as already said, was founded by Manṣûr in the year 145 (A.D. 762), formed the nucleus of the great metropolis which afterwards, radiating from this centre, spread itself over both banks of the Tigris. This burgh, generally referred to as Madînat-al-Manṣûr or the City of Manṣûr, was built with a double wall and four gates, it was exactly circular in outline, and stood close to the right bank of the river, at the angle formed by the inflowing of the Ṣarât Canal. Hardly, however, had Manṣûr begun to lay out the plan of his new city, when the work was stopped by reason of a Shî'ah rebellion in the Ḥijâz. A certain Muḥammad, grandson of the Caliph Ḥasan, son of 'Alî, rose in arms, at Medina, asserting the rights of his house to the Caliphate. He was before long defeated and slain by Ḥumayd ibn Kaḥṭabah and 'Îsâ ibn Mûsâ, a nephew of Manṣûr, who had been sent against him with an army. Then his brother Ibrahîm once more raised the standard of the Alids in Baṣrah, and immediately marched on Kûfah, where 'Îsâ, the nephew of the Caliph, opposing him with his victorious troops from the Ḥijâz, this Ibrahîm, too, was ultimately slain. Manṣûr, who had himself meanwhile crossed Mesopotamia to Kûfah, and superintended the dispatch of the troops, now returned to Baghdad, where his nephew 'Îsâ and Ḥumayd, the son of Ḳaḥṭabah, now joining him, they were both rewarded by a grant of fiefs in the new city as will be more particularly described in a later chapter.

It was, however, not until the year 146 (A.D. 763) that the buildings at Baghdad were sufficiently advanced to enable the Caliph to remove the Treasury and Public Offices (Dîwâns) from Kûfah, where they had been temporarily established, to his new capital. No further mishap occurring, the constructions were now rapidly pushed on, 100,000 craftsmen being constantly employed on the works, and by the year 149 (A.D. 766) the new burgh, the Round City of Manṣûr, was finished[1].

Of this Round City, apparently, no traces now exist; but the reason is not far to seek when it is remembered that the country where Baghdad stands being entirely wanting in stone quarries, the walls and houses were for the most part constructed of

[1] Ibn Kutaybah, 192. The following description of the Round City is derived mainly from Ya'kubi, who wrote about 130 years after the date of its foundation and when most of it was still standing. The historian Tabari, who wrote some twenty years after Ya'kubi, has given a detailed account in his Annals of the circumstances connected with the foundation of Baghdad.

those sun-dried mud bricks, which, with the lapse of centuries, are inevitably converted back into the clay from which they were originally moulded. Kiln-burnt bricks and tiles were indeed used to some extent, especially for facing the buildings, and fragments of these might still be found, marking the sites of ancient mosques and palaces, if suitable excavations could be made.

It is said that Manṣûr caused workmen to be brought together from Syria and Mosul, from Persia and from Babylonia, as also architects and land-surveyors; and over the craftsmen he appointed four chief overseers, one of these being the Imâm Abu Ḥanîfah, well known as the founder of the Ḥanifites, the earliest of the four schools of orthodox Sunnî theology. He is said to have been the first Moslem to discard the older method of counting the bricks prepared for building, and in its stead he measured the stacks with a graduated rod and then computed their number. The plan of the city was first traced out on the ground with lines of cinders, and, to mark it the better, all along the outline they set balls of cotton saturated with naphtha and then set these on fire. On the lines thus marked were dug the foundations of the double walls, with a deep ditch outside, filled with water, and a third innermost wall round the central area, the whole thus forming concentric circles, four equidistant gateways being left in each of the circuits of the walls. Of these gates two, the Kûfah Gate (SW.) and the Baṣrah Gate (SE.), both opened on the Ṣarât Canal; the Khurâsân Gate (NE.) was on the Tigris, leading to the Main Bridge of Boats, while the Syrian Gate (NW.) led to the highroad of

Anbâr, which came down along the northern or left bank of the upper Ṣarât Canal. As the Moslem writers remark, the main feature of the City of Manṣûr was that it was circular, with four equidistant gates, and this was a novelty in Islam, probably derived from Persia. Externally from gate to gate measured 5,000 ells, or about 2,500 yards, and this gives us a diameter for the outer circle round the ditch of nearly 3,200 yards[1].

In the centre of the city was a great circular area, at first only partially occupied by palaces and the mosque, but which in time came to be built over like the rest of Baghdad, and this area, which measured about 2,000 yards (over a mile) across, was enclosed by the innermost circular wall with its four gateways[2]. In the centre of this area stood

[1] Baladhuri, 295; Tabari, iii. 276, 277; Ya'kubi, 238. The ell used was the Hâshimite or Black Ell, which may be roughly estimated at half a yard. The measurement given above is from Ya'kubi, p. 238. Other and later authorities vary considerably. Thus Yakut, i. 683, says that from gate to gate measured an Arab mile, i. e. 4,000 ells or 2,000 yards, which agrees fairly well with Ya'kubi. On the other hand, Khatib (folio 65 b) states that the Caliph Mu'taḍid, who reigned from 279 to 289 (892 to 902 A. D.), used to point out the limits of the old city as covering an area two Arab miles across in every direction. Khatib also cites (folio 68 b) another tradition, namely, that while from the Khurâsân Gate to that of Kûfah measured 800 ells (400 yards), from the Syrian Gate to that of Baṣrah measured only 600 ells (300 yards). This tradition, however, appears to be untrustworthy, as it is supported by no other known authority, and would make the city oval, while all other accounts agree that it was circular in plan; Khatib himself later on implying this, when (folio 69 b) he asserts that the diameter of the city only measured 2,200 ells, that is 1,100 yards, though this last must certainly be an under estimate.

[2] There is an apparent confusion in the descriptions of the Round City, which speak of *two* walls and describe *three*. This is because the inner wall, round the central area, which was not a rampart, is not counted as a town wall. The double walls are the two outer ramparts, and these for clearness are in the following pages designated the outer

the Palace of the Caliph (called the Golden Gate), and beside it the Great Mosque; while from the four gates of the inner wall round the central area the four highroads led out, radiating like the spokes of a wheel, each in turn passing through the gateways in the double walls, and finally crossing the ditch. Apparently the gateways in the two outer walls had each double gates, for it is stated that from the outermost city gateway to the gateway leading into the central area there were in all five gates to pass. This system of concentric circular walls with a central palace was, as already said, an innovation in the plan of a Moslem city, first introduced by Manṣûr, who declared that the sovereign should thus live in the centre of all and equidistant from all.

The walls of Baghdad were built with sun-dried bricks of extraordinary size. It is stated that some bricks were cubical, and measured an ell (18 inches) every way, and these weighed 200 raṭls or pound weights. Others were half bricks, shaped square (somewhat like the Roman bricks), being 9 inches thick, with the surface measuring 18 inches by the like, and these were of the weight of 100 raṭls. That these weights, as reported by tradition, are not fictitious, but substantially correct, is shown by the fact that when part of the wall built by Manṣûr was afterwards demolished, an ancient brick was found on which was written in red paint, 'weight 117 raṭls,' and the trial then made proved that this was exact. We are told further that the courses of bricks in the city walls were not bonded together

and the main wall. The inner wall was merely a partition to enclose the area of the palace and mosque.

with wooden beams (as would seem to have been the common usage among the Arabs), but with bundles of reeds: and it is stated that 162,000 bricks were set in each course. Of the double walls the inner was the higher, and sufficiently broad to be of the nature of a rampart. According to one account this, the main wall, was 90 feet high, and at its foundations measured 105 feet across (another account giving the lower width at 90 ells, or 135 feet, but this appears to be a clerical error), while at the summit it narrowed to 37½ feet. The outer wall was, by all accounts, less massive in its construction, and apparently it is this wall whose dimensions are given by Ṭabarî as 75 feet across at the foundations, narrowing to 30 feet at the summit, with a height that may be set down at about 60 feet[1].

The doors of the four gateways in the main wall were of iron, and some curious details as to their origin are given us by Ṭabarî. It is said that King Solomon, the son of David, had founded a city in lower Mesopotamia called Zandaward; and near this ancient town, in the days of the Omayyad Caliphs, Ḥajjâj, their great viceroy in 'Irâḳ, had built the Moslem city of Wâsiṭ. Now by command of King Solomon the Shayṭâns of old had made five iron gates for Zandaward, and these, being such as no living man could have made, Ḥajjâj took from the old city, already then a ruin, and set them up

[1] Khatib (folio 69 b) gives other dimensions for the main wall: namely, height 35 ells (or 52½ feet), and width below 20 ells (or 30 feet). Ya'kubi, however, is the better authority, and his figures are those given above. To avoid needless repetition in the following pages, measurements in the Arab ell (*Dhirâ'*) are given in feet or yards, at the rate of two ells to three feet, which is a sufficiently exact estimate for all practical purposes.

in the gateways of Wâsiṭ. This was about the year 84 (703 A.D.), and half a century later Manṣûr ordered these famous gates to be carried away from Wâsiṭ, bringing them up the Tigris to adorn the rising walls of Baghdad. Ṭabarî states that in his day (say 300 A.H.) the five gates of Solomon were still to be seen, but what their subsequent fate was is nowhere recorded. Four out of the five closed the four gateways of the main wall of Baghdad, and the fifth was the gate of the Palace of Manṣûr in the central area. In the outer wall the four gates were of diverse origin: the Khurâsân Gate which had been brought from Syria, was said to be of Pharaonic workmanship; the Kûfah Gate had been made in that city by a certain Khâlid, son of 'Abd-Allah, a Moslem craftsman; the Syrian Gate, recognized as being the weakest of the four, was constructed in Baghdad by order of Manṣûr; lastly, where the Baṣrah Gate came from is not known [1].

Any one entering the City of Manṣûr would, after crossing the ditch which encircled the outer wall, pass in by one of these four gates, from each of which a thoroughfare led directly to the great central area. The ditch was kept filled with water brought by underground conduits from the Karkhâyâ Canal, which will be described later, and on the inner side of the ditch rose an embankment or dyke, leading in quarter-circles from gate to gate round the city, this dyke having its sides lined with kiln-burnt bricks, carefully cemented.

[1] Khatib, folios 68 b, 69 b; Ibn Serapion, 50, note 4; Tabari, iii. 277, 278, 321, 322; Ya'kubi, 238, 239; idem, *History*, ii. 449; Marasid, i. 454. Zandaward was also the name of a Nestorian monastery in East Baghdad, as will be seen later.

Above the dyke and the ditch rose the outer wall, crowned with battlements described as 'circular,' and this wall was flanked by bastions. Between the Kûfah Gate and that of Baṣrah there were twenty-nine bastions, while between each of the other gates there were only twenty-eight, which reckoned out would give a bastion for about every sixty yards of wall length.

It is to be noted that the four thoroughfares leading respectively from each of the outer gates to the central area were all exactly alike, and hence the following description will apply indifferently to the Kûfah roadway, or that entering by the Baṣrah, the Khurâsân, or the Syrian Gate.

Each of the four gateways of the outer wall was surmounted by a great gatehouse, the hall or passage-way of which was flanked by porticoes, both hall and porticoes being vaulted with burnt bricks set in mortar. The hall of the gatehouse measured 120 feet in length, and it therefore must have traversed not only the outer wall, which, as already said, was 75 feet in width at base, but also have extended over the dyke and part of the culvert crossing the ditch[1]. Passing in through this hall and thus traversing the outer defences, the thoroughfare from the gatehouse led to a small square, paved with flagstones, and enclosed by walls 30 yards long by 20 yards broad, occupying the space between the gatehouses respectively of the outer and the main wall. For purposes of defence, the ground, measuring 50 yards across, was left unoccupied

[1] Khatib, folio 70a, gives the dimensions of the gate-hall as only 30 ells by 20 (45 feet by 30); possibly this was the size of an outer portico.

between the two outer city walls, this forming a circular ring in four quadrants, and making a convenient roadway from gate to gate immediately within the outer line of defence, each quadrant of the ring being reached at either end from the paved squares within the outer city gates.

On the inner side of each paved square, aforesaid, rose the gatehouse of the main wall, surmounted by a great dome or cupola, with a portico before the gateway. The iron doors closing these four gateways have already been described, and it is reported that each of these was so ponderous that it took a company of men to open or to shut it; while the gateway was so lofty that, as Ya'ḳûbî writes, 'a horseman with his banner, or a spearman with his lance, could enter the same freely and without lowering the banner or couching the lance.' The main wall, as already stated, was a great rampart of sun-burnt bricks, 90 feet high and 12½ yards broad along the top, one account adding that it was surmounted by battlements and little turrets, these last being each 7½ feet high. The upper level of the main wall could be reached from each of the four gatehouses by a gangway, probably rising in gradients, for it is said that a horseman could ride up, and this gangway was carried over the vaultings which formed the roof of the portico in front of the gatehouse. Within, the portico was occupied by the horse and foot-guards of the Caliph, and the vaulted roof is described as of unequal height, part being constructed of great unburnt bricks and part of burnt brick set in mortar, the gangway (already mentioned) rising over the various levels of the vaultings to the summit of the wall, from whence the cupola crowning the gatehouse was reached. The various passages were all closed off by doors, and the top story of each gatehouse in the main wall was occupied by an upper chamber (*Majlis*) overlooking the city, that above the Khurâsân Gate, especially, having been a favourite resting-place of the Caliph Manṣûr. Masʿûdî relates an anecdote of how an arrow, bearing a warning, was shot up and fell at the feet of the Caliph as he was once seated here, and the historian takes occasion to remark that this Gate of Khurâsân was in old days often called Bâb-ad-Dawlah, the Gate of Good Fortune or the Gate of the Dynasty, because the Dynasty (*Dawlah*) or Good Fortune of the Abbasids had come to them out of Khurâsân.

The cupola over the upper chamber of each gatehouse was supported on columns of teak wood; it was green in colour outside, being probably covered with tiles, and within the ceiling was wrought in gold work, vaulted, the interior height being 75 feet above its flooring. Crowning the cupola was a figure which served as a wind-vane, 'the equal of which was not elsewhere to be seen.' Lastly, it is stated that the hall below the cupola of each gateway in the main wall was 18 feet broad and 30 feet long, and this hall apparently occupied part of the thickness of the wall.

Between the main wall and the third or inner wall enclosing the central area was another broad circular ring of ground, which (like the outer ring already described) was of course divided into four quadrants by the thoroughfares from the gates. Summing up the measurements given by Khaṭîb, it would appear that its width from the main wall to the inner wall must have been somewhat less than 150 yards across, while each of its four quadrants measured in length about a mile from gate to gate. Unlike the outer ring (which was vacant), these quadrants were occupied by houses forming streets and lanes, and though the space between the main and inner walls was somewhat narrow, the total area of the four quadrants was not inconsiderable, amounting to over a third of a square mile in the aggregate.

The thoroughfare between the gates of the main and the inner wall began and ended respectively in an outer and inner square—a double line of arcades connecting the two—and from these squares and the arcades access was obtained, right and left, to the streets and houses. Returning, therefore, to the gate in the main wall, after passing in through this, the outer square would be reached, measuring 10 yards in length and breadth, from which to right and to left gateways opened to the road which ran on the inner side of the main wall separating it from the houses; while straight on from the outer square, and leading to the inner square in front of each gateway of the central area, was the roadway flanked on either side by the arcades. This road was 7½ yards broad, being 100 yards in length from square to square; and the archways forming the arcades are stated to have numbered fifty-three, probably twenty-six on either hand, and one at the end, through which lay the entrance from the outer square. The archways were all alike, and at its entrance the road could be closed off by double doors of teak wood. The arcades were vaulted, being built of burnt brick set in mortar, and they had 'Grecian windows'

(*Kiwâ Rûmîyah*) opening on the roadway, these being probably of pierced tiles, which while letting in the sunlight kept out the rain; and rooms in the arcades were originally tenanted by the Ghulâms, the pages of the Caliph[1]. The markets, within the City of Manṣûr, had originally occupied the four roadways from the gates flanked by these arcades, but before many years had passed the Caliph ordered all the shops to be removed from within the city, and he then built the suburb of Karkh, as will be described in a following chapter, for the accommodation of the market people and the merchants, the arcades thus cleared of the shops being used as permanent barracks for the city police and the horse-guard. At the end of the arcades came the inner square, measuring 10 yards by the like, which fronted the gateway in the circular wall enclosing the central area, while close to the gateway stood a double row of small arcades, these probably being on either side of the portico before the gatehouse.

Between the main and the inner wall, as already said, the area of the four quadrants divided off by the thoroughfares from the gates, was in the earlier times built over by the houses of the immediate followers of the Caliph Manṣûr, to whom had been granted here plots of land, and before long the whole space had come to be covered by a network of roads and lanes. But the Caliph did not allow his people to build their houses close up against either the main wall or the wall of the central area, for immediately within the main wall an open ring 12½ yards broad was kept clear as

[1] Ya'kubi, 239; idem, *History*, ii. 449; Ibn Rustah, 108; Khatib, folios 68 a, 69 b, 70 a, b, 72 a; Mas'udi, vi. 171.

a roadway, while outside the wall of the central area there was also a clear space forming a road. The houses in the streets and lanes of each quadrant could also, at need, be closed off from these roads by strong gates.

The streets here in most cases continued to be called after the names of those who had become the owners of the houses and gardens when Manṣûr had first built the Round City: the full list is given in Ya'ḳûbî, but this being merely a catalogue of proper names, it is needless here to transcribe. In the quadrant of houses on the south side, that between the thoroughfares leading respectively to the Baṣrah and Kûfah Gates, the Caliph built his great prison called the Maṭbaḳ, standing in the street of the same name, 'constructing it with well-built walls and solid foundations;' and until the reign of Mutawakkil, grandson of Hârûn-ar-Rashîd, this remained the chief prison of Western Baghdad. One of the roads near here was called after the Sunnî Imâm Abu Ḥanîfah, who, as already mentioned, had aided the Caliph Manṣûr when laying out the plan of the city. In some of the quadrants also the streets were named after the trades of their inhabitants, thus for instance between the Baṣrah and the Khurâsân Gates was the Street of the Water-carriers, and in another quadrant we find the Street of the Mu'adhdhin (or Crier to prayer), and the Street of the Horse-guards.

The great central area of the Round City, as already stated, was enclosed by the inner wall, pierced by the four gates leading to the main thoroughfares, and its circle must have had a diameter of nearly 2,000 yards, being in other words over a mile across. The gatehouses, which thus opened into the central area from each of the four squares at the end of the arcades already described, were alike, and each gatehouse had a vaulted portico before it, built of burnt bricks set in mortar, leading into a great hall or passage-way closed by an iron door. It would appear that at first the wall of the central area had been pierced by many doorways leading directly to the houses and streets in the four quadrants immediately outside this wall; but these openings the Caliph Manṣûr, at an early period, caused to be walled up, only the four gates to the thoroughfares being kept open. Manṣûr further commanded that no one but himself should enter the central area riding, and everybody else had to leave his horse or mule at one of the four gatehouses. It is related that 'Îsâ ibn 'Alî, uncle of the Caliph, complained that he suffered so much from weakness as to be unable to walk the distance of about half a mile from the gatehouse across to the palace, and he petitioned to be allowed to ride in on his horse or else to make use of a sumpter mule. Manṣûr, however, bade him in that case betake himself to a woman's litter, and when 'Îsâ replied that he was ashamed before the people to appear thus, the Caliph declined to allow any exception to be made in his favour. On the other hand it is reported that Dâûd ibn 'Alî, another uncle of the Caliph, being very gouty, was for a time permitted to be carried to the palace in his litter, and the same privilege was also granted to the heir-apparent Mahdî. On another of the uncles of the Caliph, 'Abd-aṣ-Ṣamad by name, asking for a similar favour, the Caliph was induced to promise him the privilege of being carried by one of the pack-mules commonly employed for bringing in the filled water-skins for the use of the palace, so soon as he, 'Abd-aṣ-Ṣamad, should succeed in laying a conduit to bring water direct from outside the Khurâsân Gate into the palace tanks. This work 'Abd-aṣ-Ṣamad successfully accomplished, making the conduits of teak-wood (*Sâj*), and the Caliph afterwards improved on the invention by digging permanent watercourses from both the Dujayl Canal and from the Karkhâyâ, thus bringing a plentiful supply of water into the palace and other parts of the Round City. The beds of these new water-courses he laid in cement, and they were arched over throughout their whole length with burnt bricks set in mortar, so that both summer and winter (as it was said) in after-times water never failed in any of the streets or quarters of the City of Manṣûr[1].

[1] Tabari, iii. 322, 323, 324; Ya'kubi, 240, 241; Khatib, folios 72 a, b, 73 a, b; also Yakut, i. 284, where (line 9) read *Munaḳrisan* (gouty) for *Mutafarrisan*, which, in this context, has no sense. Ibn Khallikan, No. 9, p. 16; No. 128, p. 30.

CHAPTER III

THE CITY OF MANṢÛR (*continued*)

The Palace of the Golden Gate, and the Dîwâns or Public Offices. The history of the Great Mosque of Manṣûr. Khâlid the Barmecide and the Palace of the Chosroes. Sums spent. The Khuld Palace outside the Khurâsân Gate. The foundation of Ruṣâfah. Question how long the Round City remained standing: the siege in the reign of Amîn. The Main Wall. Inundations destroy walls and houses.

THE middle of the central area was occupied by the palace of the Caliph and the Great Mosque, the two standing side by side with a space kept free of houses all round, except on the north-west side, in the direction facing the Syrian Gate, where two buildings had been erected close up against the palace wall. One of these was the barrack for the horse-guards of the Caliph, and the other is described as standing adjacent, and probably stretching beyond the guardhouse; it consisted of a broad gallery, divided into two parts, and was supported on columns of brickwork set in mortar. This double gallery had originally been intended to serve, on the one side, as the audience hall for the chief of the city police, on the other for the audience hall of the captain of the horse-guards; but in later times, when Ya'ḳûbî wrote, they were, he says, for the most part used by the people as convenient places in which to say their prayers. Beyond the space which, as already stated, was kept clear all round the palace and mosque, and thence extending back to the limit of the encircling inner wall, were built the various palaces of the younger children of the Caliph Manṣûr and the houses of his servants, also the public offices, such as the Treasury and the Armoury, with the various buildings of the Chancery (or Secretariat), of the Office for the Land Tax, of the Privy Seal, of War and the Department of Public Works, of the Household of the Caliph and the Public Bakery, and finally of the Pay Office.

The great palace of Manṣûr, in the centre of his Round City, was known as the Golden Gate (Bâb-adh-Dhahab) or the Palace of the Green Dome (Al-Ḳubbat-al-Khaḍrâ); sometimes also it was named the Golden Palace. Its area covered a space originally measuring about 200 yards square, and its central building was crowned by a great dome, green in colour as already said, on the summit of which, at a height of 120 feet above the ground, and visible from all quarters of Baghdad, was the figure of a horseman. In later times this figure was credited with having been endowed originally with the magical power of pointing its lance in the direction from which the enemies of the Caliph were about to appear[1].

[1] The account of the Magic Horseman is apparently first mentioned by Khatib, who wrote in 450 (1038 A.D.). It is copied by Yakut (i. 683), who is very angry at his predecessor for relating such fables, 'only worthy of Balînâs,' i. e. Apollonius of Tyana, adding that 'the religion of Islâm is not glorified by such fables,' and assuring his readers that all this 'is but a cheat and a manifest lie.' It is seldom that Yakut shows so much common sense.

Under the dome, on the ground-floor of the palace, was an audience chamber measuring 30 feet square, with a vaulted ceiling that was 30 feet high at the summit; and above this was built a second chamber, of like dimensions to the first, and its ceiling was formed by the interior of the green dome. In front of the lower audience chamber was a great open alcove—after the Persian fashion and called the Aywân—surmounted by an arch, the key-stone of which was 45 feet above the pavement, and the width of this open Aywân was 30 feet.

This was the first palace that Manṣûr built himself; then, a few years afterwards he began laying out the celebrated palace of the Khuld (to be described later), which stood outside the Khurâsân Gate of the Round City, on the Tigris bank. The Palace of the Golden Gate, however, appears to have been the official residence of Manṣûr and his immediate successors. Hârûn-ar-Rashîd, it is true, preferred the Khuld and lived for the most part there when staying in Baghdad, but his son Amîn again held his court in the Palace of the Golden Gate, where he is said further to have added a building of his own invention, probably some sort of pinnacle or belvedere[1]. During the great siege of Baghdad in the year 198 (A.D. 814), when Amîn began to be hard pressed by the troops of his brother Mamûn, it was within the Golden Gate with the walls of the Round City for a bulwark that his partisans made their final stand. The great palace must

[1] The word used by Tabari is *Janâḥ*, literally 'a wing,' but apparently here not a 'wing' of a building as we use the term: cf. Dozy, s.v. *Janâḥ*.

then have suffered considerable damage, for during this siege the whole of the Round City was, for the space of several weeks, continuously bombarded by the catapults which Ṭâhir, the commander of the troops sent against his brother by Mamûn, had erected in the suburbs; and though the Green Dome stood intact for more than a century after this time, the palace itself does not appear to have been used as a royal residence after the death of Amîn. Three-quarters of a century later a considerable part of the Golden Palace was pulled down in order to enlarge the neighbouring mosque; the Green Dome, however, was left standing, and this only fell to ruin in the year 329 (A. D. 941). During the month of March of that year there were great storms in Baghdad with heavy rains, and finally, on the night preceding the eighth day of the month Jumâdî II, the Green Dome suddenly collapsed, having been just before struck by a thunderbolt and probably set on fire[1].

The Great Mosque, as already stated, was built by Manṣûr side by side with his palace of the Golden Gate. The mosque did not exactly face the Mecca point, as it should have done, the cause being that its plan having only been laid down after the palace was completed, the quadrangle of the mosque, for the sake of symmetry, had to conform to the already existing lines of the palace walls. Hence the Ḳiblah point was askew, the true direction of Mecca (it is said) bearing rather more towards the Baṣrah Gate than the compass-point, marked by the Nich (Miḥrâb) in the end wall of

[1] Ya'kubi, 240; idem, *History*, ii. 450; Tabari, iii. 326, 930; Khatib, folios 68 b, 69 a, 99 b; Yakut, i. 683, 684.

the mosque, would indicate. To the spectator who faced Mecca-wards, the Great Mosque must have stood on the left or south-eastern side of the Golden Palace—the guardhouses and halls it will be remembered were on the opposite, north-western, side—while the main fronts of both buildings, more or less in a line, looked towards the Khurâsân Gate. Assuming that this gate stood exactly to the north-east in the line of the circular walls, the back wall of the mosque, with the Ḳiblah point marked in its centre by the Nich or Miḥrâb, would thus have pointed due south-west, while the true direction of Mecca from Baghdad is found to lie about south-south-west, or as the Moslem writers have described it, 'more towards the Baṣrah Gate,' than due south-west.

When first planned, the mosque covered an area one-quarter that of the neighbouring palace, namely a square measuring 200 ells or 100 yards either way; and the original structure was of sun-dried bricks set in clay, with a roof supported on wooden columns. Most of these columns were constructed of two or more beams or baulks of timber, joined together endwise with glue, and clamped with iron bolts; but some five or six columns, those near the minaret, were formed each of a single tree-trunk. All the columns supported round capitals, each made of a block of wood, which was set on the shaft, like a drum. This was the first mosque built in Baghdad, and, as originally constructed by Manṣûr, it stood for about half a century, when it was pulled down by Hârûn-ar-Rashîd, who replaced its somewhat primitive structure by an edifice solidly built of kiln-burnt brick set in mortar. An inscription in honour of the Caliph Hârûn, mentioning also the names of the architects and master-masons, with the date—it was begun in 192 and finished a year later (A. D. 809)—was set up on the outer mosque wall, facing the Khurâsân Gate; and this inscription, apparently, was seen by Khaṭîb, who wrote in 450 (A. D. 1058). This mosque in subsequent times was commonly known as Aṣ-Ṣaḥn-al-'Atîḳ (the Old Court). However, before many years had elapsed, its precincts had come to be too narrow for the number of the worshippers who crowded thither to the Friday prayers, and a neighbouring house called the Dâr-al-Ḳaṭṭân, which had originally been erected by the Caliph Manṣûr for one of the Dîwâns or public offices, was pressed into service by the people, and used as an additional mosque. This place, being the more convenient, by the year 260 or 261 (A. D. 875) had come to be almost exclusively used for the Friday prayers, and the older mosque was left empty, a state of affairs which was considered uncanonical by the reigning Caliph Mu'taḍid, who was moved to remedy the case by ordering the restoration and enlargement of the Great Mosque. In the year 280 (A. D. 893), therefore, a part of the neighbouring palace of the Golden Gate was thrown down and its site added to the area of the mosque; and to this extension access was given by seventeen arches, pierced in the partition wall originally separating the two buildings—thirteen archways opening from the palace area into the Mosque Court, and four into the Riwâḳs, the aisles or porticoes. Further, and by order of the Caliph, the pulpit, the Mecca Nich (Miḥrâb), and the Maḳṣûrah or oratory, were all fully restored and beautified, while what still remained standing of the old mosque of the time of Hârûn-ar-Rashîd was thoroughly cleaned and set in order. Khaṭîb mentions that Badr, the celebrated Wazîr of Mu'taḍid, was more especially made responsible for carrying into effect these additions made to the mosque from the adjacent area of the old palace of Manṣûr, and Khaṭîb adds that, in his honour, these newer portions came afterwards to be known as the Badrîyah. Thus enlarged and restored, the mosque is described by Ibn Rustah, who wrote about the year 290 (A. D. 903), as a 'fine structure of kiln-burnt bricks well mortared, which is covered by a roof of teak wood supported on columns of the same, the whole being ornamented with (tiles the colour of) lapislazuli.'

During five centuries and more, while the Abbasid Caliphs ruled in Baghdad, this mosque of the City of Manṣûr continued in use for the Friday prayers, and its name frequently recurs in the chronicles. In the year 450 (A. D. 1058) the rebel Basâsîrî, when master of Baghdad, temporarily desecrated it by causing the heretical Fatimite Caliph of Egypt to be prayed for publicly on the Friday from its pulpit; but this was only a passing insult to Sunnî orthodoxy, and the mosque was, on the defeat of the rebels, restored to the true Commander of the Faithful. The Jew, Benjamin of Tudela, who visited Baghdad about a century after this, namely in A. D. 1160, relates how the Caliph, who now had come to be but rarely seen outside the walls of his great palace in East Baghdad, once a year, at the feast of the close of the Ramaḍân fast, visited in state 'the mosque of the Baṣrah Gate quarter,' as the

Jewish traveller names it, adding that this was still the metropolitan mosque of Baghdad. The building appears even to have passed unhurt through the great Mongol siege of the year 656 (A.D. 1258), for its name does not occur in the list of the mosques and shrines which were burnt and subsequently restored by order of Hûlâgû; and in the year 727 (A.D. 1327), when Ibn Baṭûṭah visited Baghdad, the mosque of Manṣûr is mentioned as still standing. At the present day, however, all traces of it have entirely disappeared, and no remains apparently were to be seen even in the last century, when Niebuhr visited Baghdad, though the exact date of its demolition is unknown[1].

As already remarked, the houses of Baghdad were for the most part built of sun-dried bricks, a fact which must account for there being now hardly any ruins of the ancient city. Kiln-burnt bricks were, of course, to some extent used in many of the public buildings, and at one time it would appear that the Caliph Manṣûr had even had some intention of taking the stones from the ruins of Madâin (the ancient Ctesiphon and Seleucia), a few leagues below Baghdad, on the Tigris bank, which lay, therefore, conveniently to hand as a quarry for building materials. In connexion with this matter an anecdote is given, in which Khâlid, the first of the Barmecides who rose to power at the Abbasid court, plays a prominent part: he representing

[1] Tabari, iii. 322; Khatib, folios 99a to 100b; Ibn Rustah, 109; Ibn-al-Athir, ix. 441; Benjamin of Tudela, i. 97; Ibn Batutah, ii. 107. Timur took Baghdad in the year 795 (A.D. 1393), and a year afterwards ordered the city to be rebuilt: the old mosque of Manṣûr may have disappeared at this time, though no mention of it is made by Sharaf-ad-Dîn.

the Persian influences which were later on to be supreme. This Khâlid, son of Barmak, was a native of Balkh, where his father, a Magian of some note, had become a Moslem at the time of the first Arab conquest. Khâlid himself had emigrated westward when the Abbasid armies had been raised, and had taken service under the first Caliph of the new dynasty, Saffâḥ, by whom he was appointed Wazîr, in which post Manṣûr had retained his services after his brother's death. When Baghdad was founded it became a question, as already said, whether the plentiful materials of stone and brick existing at Madâin might not be used with advantage for the buildings of the new city. There was in particular the great White Palace of the Chosroes, which Manṣûr now proposed to demolish, and he took counsel of Khâlid the Barmecide how the work should be carried out. The latter, however, immediately strove to hinder its execution, trying to persuade the Caliph to go elsewhere for his building materials: this ancient palace, said Khâlid, had become an abiding proof of the might of Islam; it was an enduring monument, for all who should behold it, of how the worldly glory of its builder, the great Chosroes, had come to naught before the religion of the Arabs, who had overthrown the Persian monarchy, and whose sovereign now ruled in its stead; and Khâlid is reported to have added, 'Further, O Commander of the Faithful, the Caliph 'Alî did make his prayer in this palace, wherefore indeed let it stand.' Manṣûr, however, was not to be turned from his purpose; he told Khâlid that, with all this specious reasoning, his real objection to the destruction of the palace of the Chosroes lay in his (Khâlid's) veneration for the ancient Persian monarchs and their monuments, and despite his advice the Caliph ordered the demolition of the White Palace to be begun. When in part this had been accomplished, it was found that the cost of breaking down the walls and then transporting the materials upstream was greater than the price that new material in Baghdad would come to; and Manṣûr without further loss of time put a stop to this extravagant demolition. Khâlid thereupon came forward and urged the Caliph for very shame to continue his work, and pull down the palace to its foundation; otherwise, as he pointed out, men would say that Manṣûr, the Successor of the Prophet, was impotent even to destroy what the Chosroes had built. The Caliph, however, with practical common sense declined to ruin himself on account of what men might say, and the work was permanently abandoned. At a later date, as will be mentioned in a subsequent chapter, part of this Madâin palace was pulled down to supply materials for building the Tâj, a palace in Eastern Baghdad begun by the Caliph Mu'taḍid. On this latter occasion, however, the work of demolition must have been only in part carried out, for the ruins of the White Palace still tower above the Tigris bank at Ctesiphon, the solid building of the Sassanian epoch having survived the palaces of the Caliphs, to be a record, if the anecdote be true, of the patriotic spirit displayed by the first of the Barmecides. This Khâlid, son of Barmak, it will be remembered, was the father of Yaḥyâ, who with his two sons, the Wazîr Ja'far and the courtier Faḍl, enjoyed the favour and contributed so much to the glory of Hârûn-ar-Rashîd: their ultimate disgrace and sudden downfall being the proverbial example in Oriental history of the change of fortune and the mutability of royal favour[1].

Some curious details are given by our authorities regarding the sums of money which the Caliph Manṣûr, who was noted for his parsimony, spent on the building of Baghdad. The sum total disbursed, when the Caliph came to take the accounts, for building the palace and the double walls, and for digging the ditch, is set down by Ṭabarî at 4,000,833 silver dirhams, and in addition of copper coins (*fils*) they had spent 100,023,000. These figures (with minor variations, probably due to the errors of copyists) are repeated by many subsequent authorities, and turned into modern currency the sum in dirhams is equivalent to about £160,000, while the copper coins come to some £200,000. Khaṭîb, and Yâḳût (following him), on the other hand, estimate the sum total at 18,000,000 gold dînârs, equivalent to about £9,000,000 sterling in our money, and some further variations in the figures are given by Khaṭîb in his history of Baghdad[2].

Such was the Round City, the building of which Manṣûr had completed by the year 149 (A.D. 766); and shortly after this date the great suburbs, which will form the subject of the following chapters, began to be laid out beyond the three gates of Baṣrah, Kûfah, and Syria.

At the Khurâsân Gate, opening on the Tigris and the Main Bridge of Boats, the Caliph, as already

[1] Tabari, iii. 320; Yakut, i. 426.

[2] Tabari, iii. 326; Mukaddasi, 121; Khatib, folio 65 b; Yakut, i. 683.

stated, built himself a second great palace which he called the Khuld, and the later history of this palace will be given in a subsequent chapter[1].

The opposite or eastern bank of the Tigris had hitherto been unoccupied by any buildings, when Manṣûr, the Round City being now completed, in the year 151 (A.D. 768) proceeded to lay the foundations of a mosque and palace on the Persian side of the river, and the new suburb took the name of Ruṣâfah (the Causeway), from the dyked road leading across the marsh-land in the bend of the Tigris. This causeway started from the further end of the bridge of boats; and the suburb of Ruṣâfah formed the nucleus of Eastern Baghdad, which afterwards came to be the main half of the metropolis when the Caliphs, after building the eastern palaces, took up their abode here, and transferred the government offices to the Persian side of the stream. Hence it came about that the Caliph Manṣûr was not only the founder of Western, but also of Eastern Baghdad,

[1] It is nowhere precisely stated what was the orientation of the four gates of the Round City; but they are known to have been equidistant, and a number of considerations tend to the conclusion that they must almost exactly have faced respectively the NE. and the NW., the SE. and the SW. points. Trial on the map shows that no other position will better suit the circumstances of the case, for, since the course of the Tigris going through Baghdad ran from north-west to south-east, (1) the Khurâsân Gate, which opened on the main bridge, must have faced north-east, being at right angles to the river, and (2) the Baṣrah Gate south-east, this opening on the road which went down parallel with the Tigris. Then, as will be seen in the next chapter, from outside (3) the Kûfah Gate two roads diverged, one south to Kûfah, the other turning westward to Muḥawwal and Anbâr—south-west, therefore, halfway between the two points, will suit the requirements for this gate; while (4) the Syrian Gate which faced north-west gave access both to the northern suburbs and to the Anbâr road, which last turned off at a right angle to the northern roads and ran due west from beyond this gate to the nearest point on the Euphrates.

which last in time totally eclipsed the glory of the Round City on the Arabian side of the Tigris. Eastern Baghdad will be described in later chapters: at present it is enough to note that the plan of Ruṣâfah having been laid out by Manṣûr in 151 (A.D. 768), Mahdî the son, and in after-times the successor of Manṣûr, arrived in the month Shawwâl of that year from Khurâsân, at the head of his troops, and the Caliph gave orders that these should remain encamped on the Persian side of the Tigris. The land round the new mosque and palace of Ruṣâfah being thus occupied by the troops, their leaders received grants of fiefs, and many houses were built, the new quarter taking the name of 'Askar-al-Mahdî, or the Camp of Mahdî[1].

In concluding this description of the Round City of Manṣûr, the question will be asked—how long, with the rapid growth of Western and then of Eastern Baghdad, this burgh or citadel with its four gates, triple concentric walls, and ditch, continued to exist intact. The chronicles nowhere definitely state when

[1] During the earlier centuries of the Abbasid period, the Tigris, within the limits of Baghdad, was crossed at three places by bridges of boats. These will be more particularly noticed in a later chapter; in the following pages, for the sake of brevity, and clearly to distinguish them, they are referred to as (1) the Upper Bridge, (2) the Main Bridge, and (3) the Lower Bridge. The second of these is the bridge of boats in front of the Khurâsân Gate of the Round City; the first being the bridge crossing about a mile above this point, immediately below the Upper Harbour, while the third was the bridge of boats crossing the Tigris probably at a point below the mouth of the Ṣarât Canal. As will be explained in chapter xiii, the single bridge of boats which in modern times connects Eastern Baghdad with its western suburb, cannot be identical in position with any one of the three above mentioned, but is that referred to by Yakut in the seventh century (the thirteenth A.D.), and which apparently was first moored opposite the palaces of the Caliphs, at about the close of the fifth century (the eleventh A.D..

the City of Manṣûr fell to ruin; but it is evident that of the triple walls, the innermost, namely that surrounding the central area, being merely an enclosing wall and not a rampart, must have disappeared before long, from the encroachment of the houses built in the ring beyond it. Except in the description of the first building of the Round City, this inner wall is indeed apparently never mentioned in the chronicles of Ṭabarî and his successors; neither does the ditch encircling the outer wall appear to have existed for long after the time of Manṣûr, for no reference to it occurs in the accounts of the (first) siege of Baghdad, in the time of Amîn. In the main, however, it appears that the Round City remained standing as Manṣûr had built it, till the death of Hârûn-ar-Rashîd, grandson of Manṣûr, in 193 (A.D. 809). Five years later, at the close of the civil war which immediately after the death of Hârûn had broken out between his two sons Mamûn and Amîn, the latter had as a last resort entrenched himself within the Round City, after garrisoning the Khuld Palace, on the western bank of the Tigris, with his troops. The siege of Baghdad at this time had already lasted for over a year; Ṭâhir and Harthamah, the two generals sent by the Caliph Mamûn against his brother, were blockading respectively Western and Eastern Baghdad, and Ṭâhir finally found himself obliged to storm the Round City, which was stubbornly defended to the last by the partisans of Amîn.

The first destruction of the double walls must have been in part the work of the soldiers of Ṭâhir during the assault which ended the first siege of Baghdad in the year 198 (A.D. 814), but throughout the succeeding century much of the Round City would appear to have remained standing. The palace of the Golden Gate in the centre, as has already been mentioned, only fell to ruin in 329 (A.D. 941), and the mosque was in use down to the eighth century (the fourteenth A.D.) after the Mongol siege. In regard to the main wall of the Round City, Ibn Serapion, writing about the year 300 (A.D. 913), states that a canal coming down the road outside the Kûfah Gate threw off a branch which entered 'part of the remains of the City of Manṣûr,' proving that the line of the main wall in this quarter must have been cut or tunnelled through at the date in question. On the other hand Khaṭîb reports that in the year 307 (A.D. 919) the populace of Baghdad, having risen in insurrection, broke open the prisons in the City of Manṣûr and set free their inmates. The prisoners, however, were promptly recaptured by the city police, who closed the iron gates of the City of Manṣûr, and at their leisure hunted down the malefactors, who were thus entrapped within the circuit of the walls; but this is apparently the last mention of these gates being closed. Inundations, both of the Tigris and of the Euphrates (the last coming down through the 'Îsâ Canal), were wont periodically to lay Baghdad in partial ruin—the waters having at all times been difficult to keep in check—and one such inundation is reported by Khaṭîb to have taken place in the year 330 and odd (about A.D. 942), which destroyed the arcades in the Round City near the Kûfah Gate. This inundation was caused by the bursting of the dams on the Euphrates at a place called Ḳubbîn, which regulated the waterflow of the 'Îsâ Canal. A volume of black water, it is reported, burst suddenly into the Round

City, and the flood destroyed many houses, among others the house of the narrator, from whom Khaṭîb had copied his account, who was forced to remove his family up stream to Mosul, where he had to remain for two years, until the damage done by the flood had been repaired. In regard to the four great gatehouses in the main wall, Mas'ûdî, writing in the year 332 (A.D. 944), alludes incidentally to these as still standing in his day, apparently with their upper chambers and vaulted cupolas still intact; further (and in this he confirms the account given by Khaṭîb), the same author speaks of the green dome of the Palace of the Golden Gate as having fallen 'in our own times,' evidently alluding to the ruin caused by the great storm of the year 329, which was just three years before Mas'ûdî finished his chronicle called the *Golden Meadows* (Murûj-adh-Dhahab).

With the close of the fourth century (the tenth A.D.) much of the older City of Manṣûr must have disappeared, and in the year 370 (A. D. 980), as will be described more fully in a later chapter, the site of the great palace of the Khuld outside its walls, which had remained for some decades an uninhabited ruin, was cleared, preparatory to the building of the New Hospital (Bîmâristân) by the Buyid Prince 'Aḍud-ad-Dawlah. From many incidental allusions in the chronicles, it would appear that various remaining portions of the Round City had gradually come to be absorbed among the buildings, forming the quarters of West Baghdad, which rose up beyond and round the four ancient gates of the City of Manṣûr. Thus the Great Mosque, down to the period of the Mongol invasion, was counted as forming part of the Quarter at the Baṣrah Gate; the Khurâsân Gate and its neighbourhood became incorporated into the market (Sûḳ) which had sprung up round the 'Aḍudî hospital, and was connected with the quarter along the river bank, known as the Shâri': while from the Mosque of Manṣûr to beyond the Syrian Gate ruins extending over nearly a mile existed in the time of Yâḳût, namely the seventh century (the thirteenth A. D.), and the inhabited houses of the older city, round this gate, were then considered to form part of the Ḥarbîyah Quarter, which had formerly extended to the northward beyond the gate. Lastly, the Kûfah Gate, which, as has been above described, had suffered much injury from the inundations, together with its adjacent streets and houses, would appear to have been absorbed into the Muḥawwal Gate Quarter on the west, or to have come to form part of Karkh on the south, which latter quarter having survived all its rivals is now the only relic left standing of the ancient city of Western Baghdad[1].

[1] See Plan, No. VII; Ibn Serapion, 25; Khatib, folios 71 b, 72 b; Mas'udi, vi. 171; Marasid, ii. 388, who mentions another bursting of the Ḳubbîn dam during the reign of Musta'ṣim, the last Abbasid Caliph.

Map III. To face page 47.

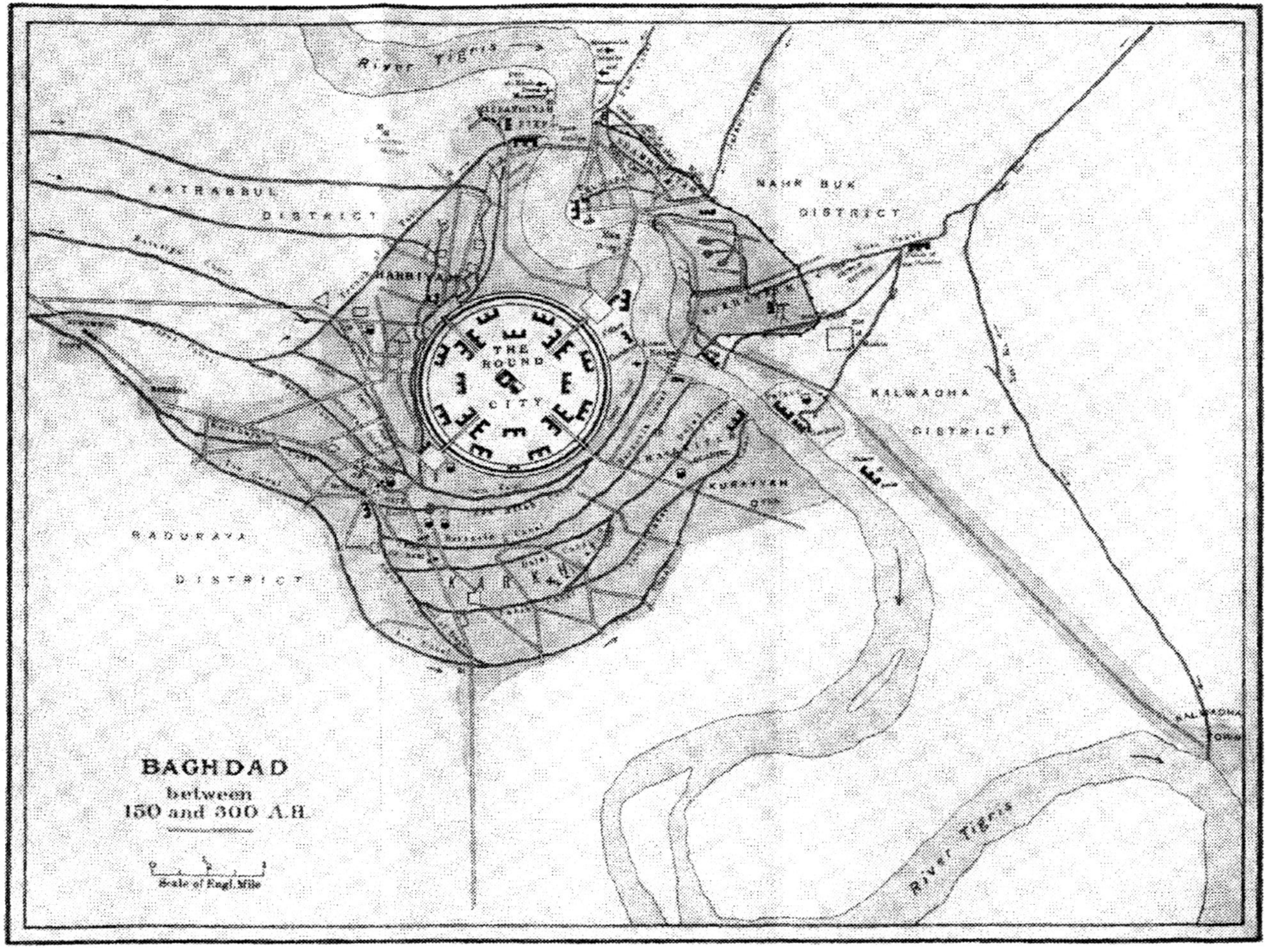

CHAPTER IV

THE CANALS OF WESTERN BAGHDAD

Ya'ḳûbî and Ibn Serapion. The older Dujayl Canal. The Nahr 'Îsâ and the Ṣarât Canal. The Ḳaṭrabbul and Bâdurâyâ districts. The Trench of Ṭâhir. The Karkhâyâ Canal and its branches. The Canal of the Syrian Gate. The Baṭâṭiyâ and the channels of the Ḥarbîyah Quarter. Comparative sizes of these various watercourses.

Our systematic knowledge of the topography of Baghdad is derived from two nearly contemporary sources, namely Ya'ḳûbî, who wrote near the end of the third century of the Hijrah, and Ibn Serapion, whose work dates from the beginning of the fourth, in other words, respectively a short time before and after the year 900 A. D. The first of these authorities, Ya'ḳûbî, describes the various quarters and buildings of the city as the traveller would pass them when riding, in turn, along one or other of the great highroads which radiated to the chief points of the compass from the four gates of the Round City. Ibn Serapion, on the other hand, chiefly occupies himself with tracing out the network of canals whose ramifications traversed the suburbs of the Round City, which in his time had come to form Western and Eastern Baghdad. In the following pages it is by the intersection of the various watercourses with the highroads that, combining the two descriptions, we are enabled to lay out a rough sort of triangulation, and thus remake the plan of the great city of the Caliphs, of which otherwise the few ancient ruins that still occupy the sites of its former buildings would hardly have afforded us sufficient data for the reconstruction of its topography.

As is well known, the Arabs had inherited from the Persians, their predecessors in Mesopotamia, the system of canalization which connected the lower course of the Euphrates with the Tigris, making the Sawâd—as the alluvial plain to the west and south of Baghdad was named—one of the most fruitful countries of the East. The system of canals thus adopted had for its object to employ the surplus waters of the Euphrates entirely for irrigating the lands lying between the two great rivers; while on the other hand the waters of the Tigris, being tapped by canals from its eastern bank, a portion of its stream was thus carried by irrigation channels through the lands which lay on the Persian or eastern side of the river. The greatest of the canals taken from the Tigris was the eastern offshoot called the Ḳâṭûl-Nahrawân channel, dating from the days of the Chosroes, from which directly or indirectly the lands of Eastern Baghdad were irrigated; but at a subsequent period a lesser system of canals was also derived from the western bank of the Tigris above Baghdad—namely the Isḥâḳîyah and the later Dujayl—from which, after the date when Ibn Serapion wrote, the lands to the north of Western Baghdad likewise came to receive their water supply from the Tigris. The four great irrigation canals, which in part drained the Euphrates into the Tigris, bore respectively the names of the Nahr 'Îsâ, the Nahr Ṣarṣar, the Nahr Mâlik, and the Nahr Kûthâ, of which the highest up, namely the 'Îsâ Canal, supplied water to a full moiety of the lands of Western Baghdad. Further, at the time when the Caliph Manṣûr was building the Round City, the older Dujayl Canal running from the Euphrates to the Tigris, with a course parallel to and above the Nahr 'Îsâ, was still in existence; and thus, during the first two centuries after the foundation of the city, Western Baghdad was irrigated solely by the waters of the Euphrates. At a date subsequent to this, namely by the close of the fourth century (the tenth A.D.), the Dujayl, by the silting in of its upper course, had ceased to receive the waters of the Euphrates; and a new, shorter channel was then dug connecting the lower Dujayl with the Tigris, from the right bank of which it continued to draw its waters, irrigating the district of Maskîn and supplying the needs of the Ḥarbîyah Quarter of Western Baghdad, during subsequent times[1].

In order to gain a general idea of the ground plan of Western Baghdad in mediaeval times it will be convenient to summarize in this chapter the account which Ibn Serapion has given of the canals which embraced the Round City of Manṣûr in a network of waterways. All these, as already remarked, were derived from one of two sources, namely, either from the Nahr 'Îsâ or from the Dujayl Canal.

[1] See *J. R. A. S.*, 1895, 'Notes on Ibn Serapion,' p. 747. The following description is from the Arabic text, pp. 14, 15, and pp. 24 to 28.

The point where the Nahr 'Îsâ left the Euphrates was almost on the same parallel of latitude as that occupied by Baghdad on the Tigris, and the 'Îsâ Canal flowed, speaking generally, due east. At what Ibn Serapion describes as 'a short distance'—say one mile—before coming to the township of Muḥawwal, which itself lay three miles distant from the City of Manṣûr, the 'Îsâ Canal bifurcated, and the left branch took the name of the Nahr-aṣ-Ṣarât. The main channel, to the right, still keeping its name of the Nahr 'Îsâ, curving first southward and then north-east almost through a semicircle, traversed the great southern suburb of Karkh, and finally flowed out into the Tigris at a spot some little way below the City of Manṣûr, which was known as Al-Farḍah or 'the (Lower) Harbour.'

The Ṣarât Canal (the branch to the left at the bifurcation of the Nahr 'Îsâ above Muḥawwal) followed a course almost parallel in direction with the parent channel, which ultimately brought it to the south-western side of the Round City at the Old Bridge, a short distance outside the Kûfah Gate. From here it curved round the city wall, passed up in front of the Baṣrah Gate, and continuing north-eastward for a short distance, flowed out into the Tigris below the gardens of the Khuld Palace, which, as already described, lay outside the Khurâsân Gate, and to the right of the road leading to the Main Bridge of Boats.

The line of the Ṣarât Canal formed the boundary dividing the two districts of Ḳaṭrabbul and Bâdurâyâ one from the other, which, occupying the western bank of the Tigris, lay opposite to the two districts of Nahr Bûḳ and Kalwâdhâ on the eastern side of the river; and hence the two halves of Baghdad, west and east, are described as standing on the ground where these four districts met. On the western side of the Tigris, with which we have now to deal, the land that lay on the left bank of the Ṣarât, and upstream as regards the Tigris, or as the Arabs deemed it, the 'western' side of the Ṣarât, was the Ḳaṭrabbul district; while from the right bank, or, as they wrote, to the 'east' of the Ṣarât, stretched the Bâdurâyâ district, downstream along the course of the Tigris. Hence, while the suburb of Karkh lay in Bâdurâyâ, the City of Manṣûr and its northern suburbs were situated in the Ḳaṭrabbul district.

The Ṣarât Canal, at a distance of one league from its point of origin (and therefore a mile or more before it reached the City of Manṣûr at the Kûfah Gate), bifurcated, and the left branch was called the Trench of Ṭâhir. This canal, turning sharp off to the north-east, almost at a right angle, flowed round the outer side of the northern suburb of Baghdad (called the Ḥarbîyah), and beyond this its waters joined the Tigris about a mile above the Round City, at a place which, like the mouth of the Nahr 'Îsâ, is known as 'the Harbour' (Al-Farḍah). In the following pages, however, in order clearly to distinguish between the two Farḍahs, they will be named respectively the Upper and the Lower Harbour.

At a short distance down its course the Trench of Ṭâhir threw out a branch canal to the right, which flowing south-east was known as the Little Ṣarât, and this after a comparatively short course curved back to join the main Ṣarât Canal at a point just before the latter reached the wall of the City of Manṣûr outside the Kûfah Gate.

From the foregoing description it will be seen that, upstream, the Round City and its northern suburb (the Ḥarbîyah) stood in the space embraced between the Ṣarât Canal and its left branch the Trench of Ṭâhir; and that, downstream, the great southern suburb of Karkh covered the tract of ground which lay enclosed between the lower reaches of the Ṣarât and the 'Îsâ Canal; while the right bank of the Tigris, in either case, formed the third side of these two triangular parcels of land on which Western Baghdad was thus built.

The water-channels which, flowing between the Ṣarât and the Nahr 'Îsâ, traversed the southern suburb of Karkh, were exclusively derived from the Karkhâyâ Canal, a stream which the Nahr 'Îsâ threw off from its left bank at a point about a mile below the Muḥawwal township. The Karkhâyâ, as its name implies, was in fact the 'Canal of Karkh'; and after sending out four branches to the left and one to the right, it finally discharged the remainder of its waters into the parent channel of the Nahr 'Îsâ, at a place close above the Lower Harbour, where the 'Îsâ Canal, as already noticed, itself disembogued into the Tigris.

Of the four left-hand branches of the Karkhâyâ, the first was called, in its upper reach, the Nahr Razîn, while lower down it became the Nahr Abu 'Attâb. It traversed Inner Karkh, passing through the Pool of Zalzal, and ultimately flowing out into the Ṣarât Canal just below the New Bridge outside the Baṣrah Gate of the Round City. The second left-hand branch was called the Nahr Bazzâzîn (the Canal of the Clothes-merchants). It passed through the Mart of the Clothes-merchants and other markets, finally flowing out direct into the Tigris after traversing the Sharkîyah or 'eastern suburb,' which lay outside the Başrah Gate on the river bank. The third branch, also to the left hand, was called the Nahr-ad-Dajâj (the Fowls' Canal), its banks being occupied by the poulterers, and this again ran out direct into the Tigris, following a nearly parallel course to the Nahr Bazzâzîn. The next branch from the Karkhâyâ was the single canal, which was taken from its right bank. This was called the Nahr-al-Kilâb (the Canal of the Dogs), and it carried a moiety of the waters of the Karkhâyâ back into the Nahr 'Îsâ, going to rejoin this last immediately below the Thorn Bridge (Kanṭarah-ash-Shawk), which will be spoken of later. The fifth branch of the Karkhâyâ (being the fourth to the left) was called the Nahr-al-Kallâyîn (the Canal of the Cooks who sold fried meats), and this after a short course flowed out into the third branch canal, already mentioned, namely that of the Poulterers or the Nahr-ad-Dajâj. Finally the Karkhâyâ fell into the 'Îsâ Canal, as before stated, and its lower course took the name of the Nahr Ṭâbiḳ, as will be noticed in its due place.

It has been already mentioned that the northern part of Baghdad, on this western bank of the Tigris, was called the Ḥarbîyah Quarter, and this neighbourhood was supplied with water from canals which branched from the Dujayl. Before, however, proceeding to describe these, we must give attention to the small watercourse into which two of these channels from the Dujayl ultimately flowed. This is called the Canal of the Syrian Gate, and it was a derivative of the first branch canal from the Karkhâyâ, namely the Nahr Razîn, from the left bank of which it was led off shortly after the Nahr Razîn had itself branched to the left from the parent stream of the Karkhâyâ.

This minor canal ran at a higher level than the neighbouring Ṣarât, and turning northwards from the Razîn, its waters were carried over and across the main stream of the Ṣarât by a conduit built in the masonry of the Old Bridge. Here the channel skirted the Kûfah highroad, and after going up some way towards the Kûfah Gate, it turned off to the left, and curved along outside the wall of the Round City (which lay to the right), flowing on towards the Syrian Gate. Before, however, reaching this, it sent off a branch to the right hand, which, as mentioned in the previous chapter, penetrated across the circular walls, disappearing among the remains of the City of Manṣûr. Immediately before and again after reaching the Syrian Gate, the main channel of the small canal which we are describing, received on its left bank the surplus waters of two of the Ḥarbîyah water-channels (as will be detailed in the next paragraph); it then finally turned northwards, and after flowing along the road leading from the Syrian Gate to the Upper Bridge of Boats, its stream ran dry in the quarter near this bridge, called the Zubaydîyah Fief.

Coming finally to the water system of the Ḥarbîyah Quarter, it is to be noted that the three small watercourses which were brought into this suburb from the north, by conduits crossing the Trench of Ṭâhir, all ran at the same high level as the small canal of the Syrian Gate, just described. These three Ḥarbîyah watercourses were all derivatives of the canal called the Nahr Baṭâṭiyâ, which finally gave its name more especially to the westernmost of the three branches, and which itself was taken from the right or western bank of the Dujayl Canal, some distance above Baghdad.

Of these three branches of the Nahr Baṭâṭiyâ, the first, from its left bank, and therefore that flowing most to the eastward and the nearest to the Tigris, passed into the Ḥarbîyah by the bridge crossing the Trench of Ṭâhir at the Ḥarb Gate, and after traversing the suburb by a somewhat serpentine course, finally poured its waters into the lower reach of the Canal of the Syrian Gate, as has been already mentioned. The next branch from the Baṭâṭiyâ Canal came into the Ḥarbîyah Quarter by a conduit specially built for the purpose, which spanned the Trench of Ṭâhir between the Ḥarb Gate and the next gate to the west, called the Iron Gate. This watercourse, like the first, also poured its overflow into the Canal of the Syrian Gate (after throwing off two minor channels, right and left), its point of junction being somewhat to the westward of the Syrian Gate. The third branch, called more particularly the Baṭâṭiyâ Canal, entered the northern suburbs by the bridge at the Anbâr Gate, the westernmost of the four gates on the line of the Trench. This canal then flowed down the Anbâr Road, but after a short course its waters failed, and it finally ran dry in branch-channels. It will thus be observed that all the water channels of the Ḥarbîyah Quarter sooner or later ran dry and failed, no water from them flowing out into the Tigris.

They were, indeed, mere water-conduits (Ḳanât) rather than canals, and we are told that within the limits of the Ḥarbîyah Quarter their courses were underground.

An estimate of the respective sizes of the various canals which we have above enumerated may be gained by noticing which of these needed to be spanned by bridges (Ḳanṭarah) of stone or brick at the points where they were crossed by the high-roads. By this criterion it becomes evident that the Nahr 'Îsâ, the Ṣarât, and the Trench of Ṭâhir, all three crossed by numerous bridges, were main streams, and the same term may be applied to the upper reach of the Karkhâyâ before it branched off among the numerous canals of Karkh. All the remaining canals—though each bore the title of *Nahr* (canal or river)—were mere watercourses, partly open and partly carried underground, but all of a size to be easily crossed on the level by the various thoroughfares, under which their waters must have been carried through culverts.

Map IV. To face page 57.

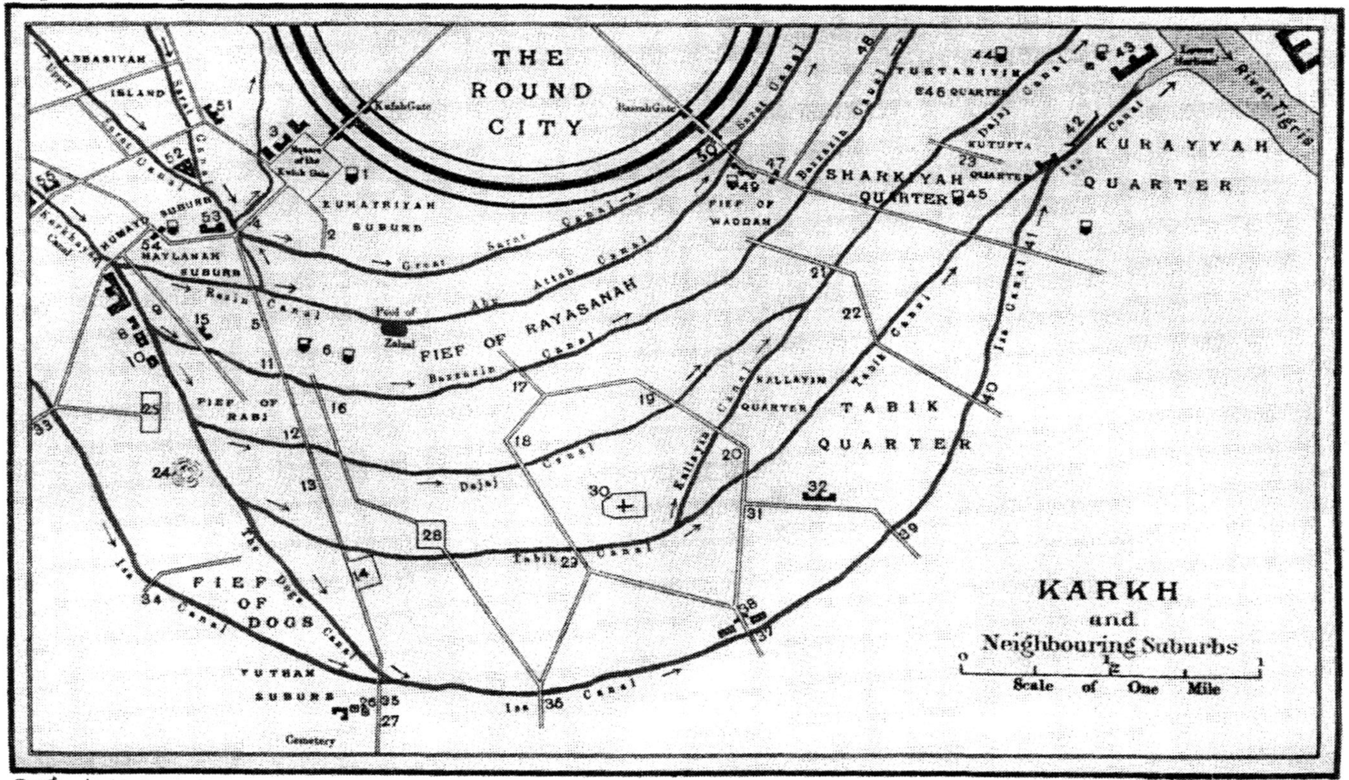

B.V. Darbishire 1900

REFERENCES TO MAP No. IV.

1. Mosque of Musayyib with the Tall Minaret.
2. Market of 'Abd-al-Wâhid.
3. Fief of the Gate-keepers, Dîwân of the Ṣadaḳah (Poor Tax Office). The Stables and Dromedary House.
4. The Old Bridge.
5. Market of Abu-l-Ward.
6. Mosque of Ibn Raghbân and Mosque of the Anbârites.
7. The Hospital Bridge and the Old Hospital (Bîmâristân).
8. The Darrabât and Mill of Abu-l-Ḳasim.
9. Quarter of men of Wâsiṭ.
10. Al-Khafḳah (the Clappers).
11. Gate of Karkh.
12. Gate of the Coppersmiths.
13. Market of Ghâlib.
14. Square of Suwayd.
15. Road of the Painter and House of Ka'b.
16. The Clothes-merchants' Market (Sûḳ-al-Bazzâzîn).
17. The Butchers' Quarter.
18. Market of the Poulterers.
19. Soap-boilers' Quarter.
20. Canal-diggers' Quarter.
21. Reed-weavers' Quarter.
22. Road of the Pitch-workers.
23. The Cookmen's Quarter.
24. Mound of the Ass.
25. Quadrangle of the Oil-merchant.
26. Shrine of Junayd and of Sarî-as-Saḳaṭî: the Sûfî Convent.
27. The Tuesday Market.
28. Quadrangle of Ṣâliḥ.
29. The Sawwâḳîn.
30. Fief of the Christians and Monastery of the Virgins.
31. The Road of Bricks.
32. The Cotton House.
33. Bridge of the Oil-merchants.
34. The Alkali Bridge.
35. The Thorn Bridge.
36. The Pomegranate Bridge.
37. Maghîd Bridge and Mills.
38. Gate of the Mills.
39. The Garden Bridge.
40. The Ma'badî Bridge.
41. The Banî Zurayḳ Bridge.
42. The Myrtle Wharf and the Melon House (Fruit-market).
43. Palace of 'Îsâ, Mosque of Ibn-al-Muṭṭalib, and Tomb of the Caliph Mustaḍî.
44. Shrine of 'Alî called Mashhad-al-Minṭaḳah.
45. Great Mosque of the Sharḳîyah Quarter.
46. The Shrine of Ma'rûf Karkhî and the Cemetery of the Convent Gate.
47. The Ḥarrânî Archway.

47–41. The Baṣrah Gate Road.

47–48. Road to the Lower Bridge, called the Barley Street.

49. Palace and Mosque of Waḍḍâḥ.
50. The New Bridge and the Booksellers' Market.
51. Palace and Market of 'Abd-al-Wahhâb.
52. The Patrician's Mill.
53. Palace in Fief of 'Îsâ.
54. The Muḥawwal Gate and Mosque.
55. Bridge of the Greeks and House of the Farrâshes.

CHAPTER V

THE KÛFAH HIGHROAD AND THE KARKH SUBURB

Square at Kûfah Gate and various Fiefs. The Old Bridge and bifurcation of Muḥawwal and Kûfah Roads. Market of Abu-l-Ward: the Ibn Raghbân and Anbârite Mosques. Pool of Zalzal. The Old Hospital and buildings on the 'Amûd. The Karkh Suburb and Gate. The story of the Greek Envoy. The Fief of Rabî'. Warthâl and Bayâwarî. The Gate of the Coppersmiths; the Square of Suwayd and the Tuesday Market.

In describing the suburbs which stretched beyond the gates of the City of Manṣûr—which suburbs, after a brief lapse of time, through the levelling of the circular walls, became the western half of the metropolis of Baghdad—it will be found convenient to follow in turn the lines of the chief highroads which began at each of the four gates of the Round City. This is the method pursued by Ya'ḳûbî, and, taking him for guide, the present account begins at the Kûfah Gate, from which went the great southern highway, namely the Pilgrim-road to Mecca and Medina. Bearing next to the eastward, and then north up the river bank, the description will follow of the various roads and suburbs lying respectively beyond the gates of Baṣrah and of Khurâsân; the quarters to the north beyond the Syrian Gate will come next; from whence turning to the westward by the suburb of the Muḥawwal Gate with its highroad, and then south, we come once more to our starting-point at the Kûfah Gate.

In the accompanying plans it has been possible only to mark the main thoroughfares, and these though here, for the sake of clearness, drawn straight and broad, must certainly, in point of fact, have been both crooked and narrow, as any one who has visited an eastern city will know. Further, it is to be remarked that many of the original fiefs (Ḳaṭî'ah) and palaces (Ḳaṣr or Dâr), granted by Manṣûr to his nobles, became in the lapse of time minor suburbs and quarters, which, still preserving the old name of the Ḳaṭî'ah, Ḳaṣr or Dâr (itself long fallen to ruin), came to be occupied by a congeries of small houses and narrow lanes. Thus for instance the Ḳaṣr Waḍḍâḥ, originally the palace of that noble, before many years have elapsed is found to be no longer his palace, but the general name of the quarter which, occupying the site of its courts, stretched for a considerable distance along both banks of the Abu 'Attâb or Razîn Canal; similarly the Fief of Rabî' was in later times celebrated as one of the most populous quarters of the suburb of Karkh, the family of Rabî' having presumably died out, and their inheritance here having passed into other hands.

To one coming out of the Kûfah Gate of the Round City and facing south-west, there lay, fronting the gate, a square, from the further side of which started the great Kûfah highroad. After passing out from the gate, on the left-hand side of this square, towards the south-east, the land was occupied, originally, by the Fief of Musayyib, chief of the city police under the Caliph Manṣûr, and a mosque, 'with the tall minaret,' stood here close to the palace of Musayyib. Behind this came in succession a number of other fiefs, occupying the strip of ground going from the Kûfah to the Baṣrah Gate, along the line of the Ṣarât Canal as it here converged to the wall of the Round City. In this space also, but lying nearer to the highroad of the Kûfah Gate, mention is made of the market called Sûḳ 'Abd-al-Wâḥid, after its founder, also the Zuhayrîyah, or Rabaḍ (suburb of) Zuhayr, probably so called after Zuhayr the father of both Musayyib (already mentioned) and Azhâr, who possessed fiefs in this neighbourhood. On the right-hand side of the square at the Kûfah Gate, towards the north-west, came first the fief of the Sharawî family, who had been the original gate-keepers in the time of Manṣûr; and behind this fief lay the palace of 'Abd-al-Wahhâb in the suburb bearing the same name, its market street extending along the Little Ṣarât, as will be described in a later chapter. Next to the fief of the Sharawî gate-keepers, and likewise on the right side of the square outside the Kûfah Gate, stood the Dîwân-aṣ-Ṣadaḳah—the Office of the Poor Tax—beside which was the fief of Muhâjir, its chief clerk during the reign of Manṣûr. Beyond or facing this Dîwân was the so-called Khân-an-Najâib (the Dromedary House), with the house of the Overseer next to it, while on the nearer side stood the Iṣṭabl-al-Mawlâ (the Freedmen's Stables).

From the Square of the Kûfah Gate the highroad led immediately to the Old Bridge crossing the Great Ṣarât, as Ya'ḳûbî names this canal from below the point of junction of its upper reach with the waters of the Little Ṣarât. The Old Bridge (Al-Ḳanṭarah al-'Atîḳah) was a solid structure, with arches built of kiln-burnt bricks set in mortar, which according to Ya'ḳûbî came to be called 'old' merely because it was the first piece of building executed by the Caliph Manṣûr; Ṭabarî, on the other hand, states that the bridge was more ancient than this and dated from Persian times, which may indeed have been the case, since the Sassanian kings are credited with having dug the Ṣarât Canal[1].

Shortly after crossing this bridge the road bifurcated. That to the right, westward, was the highroad of Muḥawwal, leading ultimately to the township of that name, one league distant from Baghdad, and this road will be described later on. To the left at the bifurcation, and running almost straight south, the great Kûfah road turned off, leading to the gate of the Karkh Suburb, and traversing on its way the market called the Sûḳ of Abu-l-Ward. This market took its name from one of Manṣûr's nobles, to whom the fief here had been originally granted. He was at one time Chief Clerk of the Public Treasury (Bayt-al-Mâl), and during the reign of the Caliph Mahdî was Judge in the Court of Appeal and Superintendent of the Briefs. This market is described as having been well supplied with wares of all kinds, and beyond it eastward towards the river bank various fiefs are named. Here stood two mosques, one

[1] Tabari, iii. 280; Ya'kubi, 243; Ibn Serapion, 24; Yakut, ii. 964; iii. 194.

named after a certain Ibn Raghbân, the other called the mosque of the people of Anbâr, who originally were the scribes of the Dîwân-al-Kharâj (the Office of the Land Tax), and who lived with their families in the streets round this mosque. We are told that the site of the neighbouring mosque of Ibn Raghbân had in ancient times been a dungheap, and it was named after Ibn Raghbân, freedman of Ḥabîb ibn Maslamah, who had been governor of these districts in the days of the Caliphs 'Othmân and Mu'âwiyah. In later times the Ibn Raghbân Mosque became celebrated for the assemblies of learned men which took place here. It must have stood at some distance to the eastward of the Abu-l-Ward market, and the fief of Rayasânah occupied the land close to this mosque, at some distance beyond which was the Barley Gate, apparently not far from the river bank, as will be described on a later page.

Through and across the Abu-l-Ward market passed the canal called the Nahr Abu 'Attâb, the name given to the lower reach of the Nahr Razîn (the first branch canal, it will be remembered, from the Karkhâyâ), and this ultimately joined the Ṣarât below the New Bridge at the Baṣrah Gate of the Round City. On the course of the Abu 'Attâb Canal, and just beyond the market, came the pool called after Zalzal the lute-player, 'whose playing had passed to a proverb for its grace;' this Zalzal being the brother-in-law of the even more celebrated musician Isḥâḳ of Mosul, whose orchestra and choir of singers were the delight of the court of Hârûn-ar-Rashîd. Zalzal dug the pool, and, at his death, left it to the people of Baghdad for the public use, with a sufficient endowment to keep it in repair. It is said that in the days before Baghdad was built, a village called Sâl, which had at one time given its name to a suburb here, occupied the ground between where the pool was dug and the site of the Palace of Waḍḍâḥ, which lay beyond this towards the New Bridge, but after the time of the celebrated lute-player, this quarter took the name of the Birkat (or Pool of) Zalzal, and the name Sâl fell completely into disuse [1].

Turning to the western side of the Kûfah highroad, the Nahr Razîn or Abu 'Attâb Canal, as described above, was the left branch at that bifurcation of the Karkhâyâ which occurred immediately after this canal had passed under the Hospital Bridge—Ḳanṭarah-al-Bîmâristân. Here the right branch was considered the main channel of the Karkhâyâ, and locally was known as Al-'Amûd, a name which in Arabic signifies 'the Trunk canal.' After flowing under the bridge, the canal passed beside the buildings of the (old) Hospital, the prototype in early Baghdad of the great Bîmâristân, or Mâristân [2] of 'Aḍud-ad-Dawlah, which the Buyid prince (half a century later than the time of Ibn Serapion) built on the Tigris bank. This older Bîmâristân is presumably the institution where the celebrated Rhazes—as westerns called the Physician Muḥammad ibn Zakarîyâ-ar-Râzî—gave his lectures, thus founding the Baghdad medical school. Rhazes died in 320 (A.D. 932), and half a century later the

[1] Ya'kubi, 244, 245; Ibn Serapion, 25; Ibn Kutaybah, 299; Khatib, folios 82 b, 84 a; Yakut, i. 592; ii. 795; iii. 201; iv. 142, 524.

[2] This last is the shortened Arabic form of the Persian word, which means 'a place for the sick.' For Rhazes see Abu-l-Faraj, 274.

'Aḍudi Hospital (above named) was built, where the work he had begun was ably continued. Below the (old) Hospital the Karkhâyâ or 'Amûd Canal, before it again bifurcated at the Clothes-merchants' Market to form the Nahr Bazzâzîn, had, upon one or other of its banks, the following places, of which however nothing but the names are known:—first, Ad-Darrâbât, meaning 'the house of the female musicians,' standing next to which was the mill of a certain Abu-l-Ḳasim: then came the place or street inhabited by the men of Wâsiṭ, and lastly a building called Al-Khafḳah, meaning 'the Clappers,' from some craft or trade (possibly connected with cloth-fulling) which was carried on here upon the bank of the stream.

Ibn Serapion tells us that it was from the 'Amûd section of the Karkhâyâ that all the canals were taken which ran through the quarters of the inner Karkh suburb; while Outer Karkh was the quarter traversed by the various ramifications which started from the lower reach of the Karkhâyâ Canal. At the southern end of the market of Abu-l-Ward, and on the Bazzâzîn Canal which branched from the 'Amûd, stood the gate called the Bâb-al-Karkh, opening into this great suburb. It would appear that Karkh, as a separate township, had existed before the times of Islàm, and the Persian writer Ḥamd-Allah asserts that it was founded by the Sassanian king Shâpûr II, surnamed by the Arabs Dhu-l-Aktâf, who reigned from A.D. 309 to 379[1].

[1] Nuzhat, 146. According to Yakut (iv. 252) Karkh is a Nabathaean, as we should say an Aramaean or Syriac word, derived from a verb in that language, meaning 'to collect water in any place'; and Yakut adds that the word was still in use among the Aramaean population of

Be this as it may, Moslem Karkh, the great suburb when planned by the Caliph Manṣûr, occupied those lands to the southward of the Kûfah and Baṣrah Gates, which were included between the Ṣarât Canal and the Nahr 'Îsâ. Before the century had elapsed, however, Karkh began to overpass the limit of the 'Îsâ Canal, and by the time of Hârûn-ar-Rashîd this suburb extended far to the southward of the great canal, covering ground along both sides the Kûfah highroad for a considerable distance out from Baghdad. Thus Ya'ḳûbî says that Karkh measured two leagues in length, the upper limit being at the Palace of Waḍḍâḥ, outside the Baṣrah Gate, and the lower at the Tuesday Market; while in its breadth Karkh measured a league across, reckoning from the Tigris bank on the east to the Fief of Rabi' on the west, this last lying immediately on the right hand of one coming down the Kûfah highroad, after passing through the Bâb-al-Karkh. After describing the extent of Karkh, Ya'ḳûbî, the contemporary of its prime, then continues: 'Here every merchant, and each merchandise, had an appointed street: and there were rows of shops, and of booths, and of courts, in each of those streets; but men of one business were not mixed up with those of another, nor one merchandise with merchandise of another sort. Goods of a kind were only sold with their kind, and men of one trade were not to be found except with their fellows of the same craft. Thus each market was kept single, and the merchants

Mesopotamia in his day. The name of Karkh appears in Syriac under the form *Karka*; and the name of the Karkhâyâ Canal, which traversed it, is the Syriac form of the corresponding relative noun or adjective. See Fränkel, p. xx; Hoffmann, p. 43.

were divided according to their merchandise, each craftsman being separated from others not of his own class.'

Karkh, which thus before long became the great commercial centre of Western Baghdad, though founded by Manṣûr, was an afterthought on the part of the Caliph, no such suburb being included in his original plan of the Round City. As already described, the markets had been at first placed within the city walls, in the arcades which radiated from each of the four gates of the inner wall to the outer gates of Kûfah, Baṣrah, Khurâsân, and Syria (see above, p. 26). The cause of the removal of the markets from the arcades is thus related by Ṭabarî (and he has been copied by many later authorities): The Emperor of the Greeks had sent one of his Patricians on an embassy to Manṣûr, and before the envoy was dismissed back to Constantinople, the Caliph ordered his chamberlain Rabî' to conduct the Greek over his new capital, namely the Round City, then recently completed. So the envoy was shown over all the new buildings and palaces, and was taken up on the tops of the walls and into the domes above the gateways. At the farewell audience, the Caliph inquired what the Greek had thought of the new city, and he received these words in reply: 'Verily (said the envoy), I have seen handsome buildings, but I have also seen that thy enemies, O Caliph, are with thee, within thy city.' For explanation he added that the markets within the city walls, being always full of foreign merchants, would become a source of danger, since these foreigners would not only act as spies for carrying information to the enemy, but also, being domiciled in the markets, they would have it in their power traitorously to open the city gates at night to their friends outside. Pondering over this answer, the Caliph Manṣûr—as the chronicle says—ordered the markets to be removed to form suburbs outside the various gates: and in Karkh the new market street, as originally laid out, along the main thoroughfare measured 40 ells or 20 yards in width.

From the time of Manṣûr onwards this great market suburb continually increased in extent, and a great fire which occurred here about a century after its foundation, during the reign of the Caliph Wâthiḳ (then residing at Sâmarrâ), was not allowed to become a permanent damage, for Karkh was promptly rebuilt, the Caliph contributing, it is reported, a million dirhams (some £40,000) from his private purse towards the expenses of laying out the new roadways. After the building of Karkh and of the other suburbs of Western Baghdad,—but more especially as a consequence of the rise of the new quarters on the eastern river bank, to which the seat of government before the close of the third century (the ninth A.D.) came to be transferred,—the old City of Manṣûr fell more and more to decay, and before long all the business still left in Western Baghdad had come to centre in Karkh. Extending a mile and more along the pilgrim highroad, Karkh retained a considerable population even after the remainder of West Baghdad had become a complete ruin; indeed, it finally appears to have given its name to the whole of the region which continued to be habitable of this western side, for down to the present day Karchiaka is what the

Turks call the more ancient quarter of Baghdad, namely that which stands on the Arab side of the Tigris.

Within the limits of Karkh (as laid out in the time of Manṣûr) was the Fief of Rabî‘, a plot of ground which had been granted to the favourite chamberlain of the Caliph, and who, as just described, had been commissioned to show the Greek envoy over the new capital. The original fief must have been of considerable extent, for it occupied all the land near the Bazzâzîn and Dajâj Canals, and it extended from the line of the Kûfah highroad westward as far as the Karkhâyâ Canal. It is stated that the whole of this tract had, in former days, been taken up by the arable lands of the ancient village of Bayâwarî (or Banâwarî), which had stood here before Baghdad was founded; while more to the southward, and nearer the Tigris bank, had been the lands of another ancient village of this neighbourhood called Warthâl (or Warthalâ, according to the spelling given by Khaṭîb), which were afterwards occupied in part by the Rabî‘ Fief, and in part taken up by the road of the subsequent market called the Suwayḳah Ghâlib. When Muḳaddasi wrote in the year 375 (A.D. 985), the Fief of Rabî‘ is mentioned as being already the most populous part of Karkh, and even before a hundred years had elapsed since the date of the foundation of the city, the fief had become completely built over by the houses of the merchants. This suburb afterwards came to be divided into the Inner and the Outer Fief of Rabî‘; and the Inner, it is said, had originally alone been granted by Manṣûr to his chamberlain, while the Outer Fief dated from a grant made by the Caliph

Mahdî to Faḍl the son of Rabî', who served Mahdî for a time as his Wazîr.

Immediately after passing the Karkh Gate and entering the quarter, the highroad came to another gate called the Bâb-an-Nakhkhâsîn, or Naḥḥâsîn (for the MSS. vary), signifying either the gate of the slavedealers, or of the coppersmiths, and a square lay beyond this, called the Raḥbah Suwayd, after one of the freedmen of Manṣûr, who had granted him a fief here. From this point onward the market streets followed one after the other, bordering the roadway on either hand, as far as the utmost limit of Karkh beyond and to the south of the 'Îsâ Canal, where the great suburb at length came to an end in the district known as the Sûḳ-ath-Thalâthâ, or the Tuesday Market of West Baghdad[1].

[1] Ibn Serapion, 25; Mukaddasi, 120; Ya'kubi, 245, 246; Kitab-al-'Uyun, 265; Tabari, iii. 279, 323; Yakut, iv. 142, 245, 254, 919. Khatib, folio 83 a, where the MSS. give Banâwarî, Nabâwarî, and other readings. See also Guzîdah, under the reign of Caliph Wâthiḳ, for the fire in Karkh.

CHAPTER VI

THE CANALS OF KARKH

The Karkhâyâ and the Rufayl Canal. The 'Îsâ Canal and its Bridges. The Butchers' and the Poulterers' Markets. The Bazzâzîn and Dajâj Canals, with the Quarters of the Soap-boilers and others. The Fief and Canal of Dogs. The Shûnîzîyah Cemetery and its shrines; the Tûthah Suburb.

A SUMMARY account of the canals which traversed Karkh has already been given in chapter iv. It will be remembered that the Karkhâyâ—from which these were derived—was a great loop-canal taken from the Nahr 'Îsâ, a short distance below Muḥawwal Town, which in part discharged its waters back into the 'Îsâ Canal by the two streams of the Nahr-al-Kilâb and the Nahr Ṭâbiḳ. A moiety of the waters of the Karkhâyâ, however, were carried off above this to the Tigris, either directly by the two channels of the Bazzâzîn and Dajâj Canals, or indirectly, by the Nahr Razîn (otherwise the Canal of Abu 'Attâb), which joining the Ṣarât, poured its waters into the Tigris at a point above the mouths of the Bazzâzîn and Dajâj Canals.

The Karkhâyâ Canal is said to have been dug at the time of the foundation of Baghdad by 'Îsâ (the uncle of the Caliph Manṣûr), he being then occupied in building the famous mills at the junction of the

Great Ṣarât and the Little Ṣarât, which will be described in the sequel.

The Karkhâyâ, below the Hospital Bridge (as already said), was divided up into many channels, and further we have seen that while in its upper, single course, the Karkhâyâ was a broad canal that needed to be crossed by arched stone bridges (Ḳanṭarah), the lower branch canals, with the channels of the ʿAmûd and the Ṭâbiḳ (as the Karkhâyâ below the Hospital Bridge came to be called), were evidently much smaller watercourses, since no such bridges were needed for the highroads to cross them. This will perhaps explain why, before many centuries had elapsed, most of these lower channels had fallen into disuse, for being shallow they had easily become silted up. At the time when Yâḳût wrote, namely in the early part of the seventh century (the thirteenth A.D.), it is indeed asserted that no one then could point out what had been the course originally followed by the Karkhâyâ Canal; this statement, however, the epitomist of Yâḳût (the author of the *Marâṣid*) denies, for writing a century later than Yâḳût, he affirms that the course of the old canal still existed in his day, and that water flowed along it, which was used for the irrigation of the neighbouring fields. What, indeed, had by this date—A.H. 700 (A.D. 1300)—for the most part disappeared, were the lower ramifications which in the earlier times had traversed Karkh, as also the branch canal that had formerly crossed the Ṣarât by the Old Bridge, and flowed through the Ḥarbîyah beyond, to the north of the Syrian Gate[1].

[1] Ibn Serapion, 24 to 26; Yakut, iv. 252; Marasid, ii. 485; and compare Plan, No. VII.

The Nahr 'Îsâ, the parent stream from which the Ṣarât and the Karkhâyâ were both derived, was one of the great navigable canals connecting the Euphrates with the Tigris, which (as has been noticed in a former chapter) dated from times long antecedent to Islam, having been dug by one of the Sassanian kings of Persia. It was by the Nahr 'Îsâ that Baghdad received the produce of the west and provisions from the Euphrates lands. Great boats and barges were loaded at Raḳḳah, 'the port' (as it was called) of the Syrian desert on the Upper Euphrates, there taking over from the land-caravans the corn of Egypt and the merchandise from Damascus, and these boats coming down the great river, and then along the 'Îsâ Canal, discharged their cargoes at the wharves on the Tigris banks at the Lower Harbour in Karkh.

The chronicles relate that at the time of the first Arab conquest of Mesopotamia in the reign of the Caliph 'Omar, one of the canals in this district had received from the Moslems the name of the Nahr Rufayl, after a certain Persian noble who had turned Moslem. He, coming one day before 'Omar in a robe of brocade that trailed on the ground, the Caliph inquired as to who was the little man 'in the trailing skirt' (in Arabic *Rufayl*), and this nickname ever afterwards clinging to him, the canal which he had owned came likewise to be so called. This ancient Nahr Rufayl was, according to one account, the lower part of the 'Îsâ Canal—namely from the Thorn Bridge down to the Lower Harbour—while, according to another version, it was the upper reach of the Karkhâyâ. Whichever it may have been originally, the Nahr Rufayl in later days had come to be rather a poetical name than one in common use, and it apparently fell into desuetude as early even as the time when 'Îsâ made the great navigable waterway that took his name. This Abbasid Prince 'Îsâ is stated by Ibn Serapion (our earliest authority) to have been the nephew of Manṣûr, being the son of Mûsâ his brother. Almost all other authorities, however, assert that this 'Îsâ was the son of 'Alî, grandfather of that Caliph; hence that it was the uncle of Manṣûr who redug the great canal. In the conflict of our authorities, it may perhaps be surmised that both 'Îsâs had a hand in the undertaking. Other buildings, however, dating from the early days of the foundation of Baghdad and ascribed to Prince 'Îsâ, all undoubtedly have reference to 'Îsâ ibn 'Alî, the uncle of Manṣûr, who held the governorship first of Medina and next of Baṣrah, where he died during the Caliphate of Mahdî his grand-nephew. 'Îsâ ibn Mûsâ, on the other hand, the nephew of Manṣûr, was in turn governor of Ahwâz and of Kûfah, and at one time he had been declared heir-apparent to the Caliphate. It will be remembered how, at the time when Manṣûr was engaged in the building of Baghdad, this 'Îsâ was dispatched in command of the Abbasid forces against the two 'Alid pretenders, Muḥammad and Ibrâhîm—the grandsons of the Caliph Ḥasan—who had raised the standard of revolt. 'Îsâ ibn Mûsâ defeated the rebels and returned in triumph; but at a later date he was ousted from his rights to the succession by Manṣûr, who proclaimed his own son, Mahdî, heir-apparent, and 'Îsâ ibn Mûsâ subsequently died at his governorship of Kûfah[1].

[1] Yakut, iv. 117, 190, 839; Marasid, iii. 247; Ibn Kutaybah, 190, 192. Of later authorities the only writer who states the digger of the great

The 'Îsâ Canal left the Euphrates just below the town of Anbâr, and passing under the great arched bridge called Ḳanṭarah Dimmimâ, flowed eastward till it came to the township of Muḥawwal, which lay about a league distant from the suburbs of the Round City. It will be remembered that a short distance before the Nahr 'Îsâ reached Muḥawwal, the Ṣarât Canal—which likewise dated from Sassanian times—branched from it to the left, while equally a short distance below Muḥawwal the Karkhâyâ (already described) flowed off also to the left hand. Iṣṭakhrî particularly notes that while barges could pass freely down the 'Îsâ Canal all the way from the Euphrates to the Tigris, the Ṣarât, on account of its weirs, dams, and water-wheels, was not navigable for large boats. The word *Muhawwal* signifies a place where bales are 'unloaded,' and the town appears to have received this name from the unloading of the river barges which took place here, when the cargoes were carried over to the small skiffs that plied on the Ṣarât and Karkhâyâ in the reaches between the weirs. Further, it would appear that the waters of the Karkhâyâ and its subsidiary canals were kept, by these weirs, to a higher level than the stream that flowed down the Ṣarât, for, as we have already seen, a branch from the Karkhâyâ was carried across, above the Ṣarât, by the arches of the Old Bridge, passing thence to

canal to have been 'Îsâ ibn Mûsâ is Hamd-Allah, the Persian author of the eighth century (the fourteenth A.D.): he however in another passage speaks of the canal as that of 'Îsâ ibn Maryam, in other words, of Jesus son of Mary, this apparently being the popular Persian ascription of his time. Hamd-Allah is, of course, no authority in this matter, and he further makes a mistake in stating that this Mûsâ (the father of 'Îsâ) was uncle to the Caliph Manṣûr, he in fact having been his brother. See Nuzhat, 148, 164.

the northward into the Ḥarbîyah Quarter. It is especially mentioned by early writers that the waters of the Nahr 'Îsâ never failed, nor was its channel liable to become silted up. They describe it as flowing in a fine stream through the midst of the city, reaching the Tigris at the Lower Harbour, which, as will be shown later, must have been situated immediately below the later, single, bridge of boats, the position of which very nearly corresponded with the present pontoon bridge of modern Baghdad[1].

On the line between Muḥawwal Town and the Tigris bank, the waterway of the Nahr 'Îsâ was crossed by ten arched bridges, the great Kûfah high-road probably passing over it by that known as the Thorn Bridge (Ḳanṭarah-ash-Shawk), which spanned the canal immediately above where the Nahr-al-Kilâb (or Dogs' Canal from the Karkhâyâ) flowed in. Below this there were five bridges across the 'Îsâ Canal before it reached the Lower Harbour on the Tigris, and above the Thorn Bridge, four, the highest up being the Ḳanṭarah Yâsirîyah. This bridge took its name from the Yâsirîyah Quarter, which, as will be seen later, was reckoned the westernmost of Baghdad along the Muḥawwal road; it was surrounded by fine gardens, and lay on the canal bank, one mile below the town of Muḥawwal, and two miles (according to Yâḳût) distant from Old Baghdad. The bridge below this was the Ḳanṭarah-az-Zayyâtîn, the Bridge of the Oil-merchants;

[1] Compare Plan No. III with No. VII. In the sketch-plan of Baghdad given in my paper on Ibn Serapion (*J. R. A. S.*, 1895, facing p. 275), the whole western quarter is put too low down in regard to the eastern; and the course of the Nahr 'Îsâ should be as shown in the accompanying maps.

the next was the Ḳanṭarah-al-Ushnân, the Alkali Bridge, the word *Ushnân* being explained as the stuff used for washing clothes, and which was sold at the market adjacent to the bridge.

The Ḳanṭarah-ash-Shawk (already mentioned) came next, at the Market of the Thorn-sellers, *Shawk* being the thorns used for kindling ovens and heating the Ḥammâms or hot baths; and near here lived the clothes-merchants and hucksters. Below this, on the canal, and therefore probably between the great Kûfah highroad and the river bank, came the Ḳanṭarah-ar-Rummân, where pomegranates (from which it took its name) were sold; then the Ḳanṭarah-al-Maghîd—where the mills stood—near the spot called Maghîd, meaning 'the place which lacks water,' and after this came the Garden Bridge, Ḳanṭarah-al-Bustân. The two lowest bridges on the 'Îsâ Canal were the Ḳanṭarah-al-Ma'badî and the Ḳanṭarah-Banî-Zurayḳ. The first of these took its name from a certain 'Abd-Allah ibn Muḥammad al Ma'badî[1], who, possessing fiefs here, built for himself a palace (*Dâr*) and a mill, also this bridge over the great canal, these all being called after his name. When Al Ma'badî flourished is not stated, but it must have been in the early days of the Abbasids, before the reign of the Caliph Mu'taṣim, since we learn that all his lands subsequently passed into the possession of the celebrated Muḥammad-az-Zayyât, who was Wazîr of that Caliph between the years 218 and 227 (A.D. 833 to 842). The lowest of the bridges, and that over which must have passed the highroad coming down from the Baṣrah Gate, was called after

[1] This is almost certainly the right spelling: some MSS. give the reading *Ma'îdî*, as is printed in the Marasid, iii. 249.

the Banî Zurayḳ, a family of architects, of Persian origin, and this bridge was built of marble.

The preceding enumeration of the ten bridges over the Nahr 'Îsâ is taken from the description of this canal written by Ibn Serapion at the beginning of the fourth century (the tenth A.D.). Yâḳût, who copies all this, adds that originally at each of these bridges a market had been held, but that in his day, namely at the beginning of the seventh century (the thirteenth A.D.), through the ruin of Karkh and the transference of its population in greater part to East Baghdad, all this region had come to be deserted, and of these ten bridges over the Nahr 'Îsâ only two then remained standing, namely that of the Oil-merchants (Ḳanṭarah-az-Zayyâtîn) and the Garden Bridge (Ḳanṭarah-al-Bustân), also known as the Bridge of the Traditionists (Ḳanṭarah-al-Muḥaddithîn). The author of the *Marâṣid*, however, writing about the year 700 (A.D. 1300), and three-quarters of a century after Yâḳût, contradicts most of this statement, asserting that both the bridges which his predecessor mentions as still standing must have gone to ruin already long before his time, seeing that the only ones remaining when he (the author of the *Marâṣid*) wrote were three: namely, the Yâsirîyah Bridge, lately rebuilt by a certain Sa'îd, the Thorn Bridge, and that of the Banî Zurayḳ—in other words the bridges crossed respectively by the two highroads southward, from the Baṣrah and the Kûfah Gates, and the uppermost bridge of all, where the Yâsirîyah road crossed the 'Îsâ Canal, turning off due west from the Muḥawwal highroad [1].

[1] Ya'kubi, 250; Ibn Serapion, 14; Istakhri, 83; and Ibn Hawkal, 164; Yakut, i. 284; iv. 191, 842, 843, 1002; Marasid, iii. 249, 250.

Returning once more to the description of Karkh after this digression on its canals, it will be remembered that while Inner Karkh occupied the land between the Ṣarât and ʻÎsâ Canals, Outer Karkh lay to the south of this last; most of the bridges above named thus affording communication between Inner and Outer Karkh in the line of its breadth, while in its length Karkh extended along both sides of the great pilgrim highroad southward. The upper part of Karkh was inhabited by the Khurâsân merchants who traded in stuffs (Bazzâzîn), and these gave their name to the first of the canals (the Nahr-al-Bazzâzîn) which crossed Inner Karkh, flowing off from the Karkhâyâ. Taken likewise from the Karkhâyâ was the Nahr-ad-Dajâj (the Fowls' Canal), so called because the poulterers had their stalls on its banks; and both the Bazzâzîn and Dajâj Canals flowed out directly into the Tigris, their lower reaches passing through the Sharḳîyah or Eastern Suburb, which will be described presently. At the beginning of the fourth century (the tenth A. D.) when Ibn Serapion wrote, the Bazzâzîn Canal, near the Market of the Clothes-merchants, passed a street which ran to the westward of the Karkh Gate, and probably led into the Rabîʻ Fief; this was called the Road of the Painter (Shâriʻ-al-Muṣawwir), and in it was the house (Dâr) of Kaʻb. Next to the Market of the Clothes-merchants, but lower down the canal, and probably to the eastward of the Karkh Gate, was the Market of the Cobblers or of the Butchers (for the MS. of Ibn Serapion by the addition of the diacritical points, which are lacking, may read either *Kharrâzîn* or *Jazzârîn*), the latter being the more probable reading, since Khaṭîb tells us that the Caliph Manṣûr, when laying out Karkh, set the butchers to dwell in the outermost part, 'since they be shedders of blood, and have ever sharp iron in their hands,' and this would have been in early days the outer part of Karkh. Further down along the Bazzâzîn Canal came the quarter of the soap-boilers; and the various other markets on the lower canals doubtless here formed lines of streets, with shops on either hand, which led to one or other of the bridges (already mentioned) crossing the Nahr 'Îsâ into Outer Karkh.

On the section of the Karkhâyâ, or 'Amûd as it was here called, between the two canals of the Clothes-merchants and the Poulterers, opened the Quadrangle of the Oil-merchant (Murabba'at-az-Zayyât), this probably lying adjacent to the Oil-merchants' Bridge over the Nahr 'Îsâ, already described. Below here the Poulterers' Canal turned off, and on its course to the Tigris traversed a number of other quarters and markets, namely those inhabited by the canal-diggers and the reed-weavers, beyond which lay the Street of the Pitch-workers and the Market of the Sellers of Cooked Meats. The Karkhâyâ Canal meanwhile, after passing a place known by the curious name of the Mound of the Ass (Dawwârat-al-Ḥimâr), sent off its single branch to the right, called the Nahr-al-Kilâb, or the Dogs' Canal, which flowed out directly into the Nahr 'Îsâ, just below the Thorn Bridge. On the banks of the Dogs' Canal lay the Fief of the Dogs (Ḳaṭî'at-al-Kilâb), and it is said this was so named in jest by the Caliph Manṣûr, from the number of dogs that lived here[1].

[1] Ibn Serapion, 26; Khatib, folios 76 a, 83 b.

Across the 'Îsâ Canal, immediately beyond the Thorn Bridge, came the cemetery called the Great Shûnîzîyah [1], and lower down this probably occupied both banks of the Nahr 'Îsâ, for it is spoken of as lying adjacent to the Ḳallâyîn and Ṭâbiḳ Canals; beyond was the suburb on the Nahr 'Îsâ, called At-Tûthah. In the thirteenth century A.D., Yâḳût speaks of a Khânḳah, or Ṣûfî convent, which existed here in his time, also the tomb, covered with blue tiles, of a well-known saint called Al-'Abbâdî, who had died in 547 (A.D. 1152). In the Persian history called the *Guzîdah*, it is mentioned that in the time of the Caliph Mustaḍî (who reigned from 566 to 575, A.D. 1170 to 1180) one of his slave women, called Banafsah (Violet), who was renowned for her generosity, had built, or restored, a bridge near the Shûnîzîyah Quarter (probably the Thorn Bridge), and founded this Khânḳah or convent. The cemetery further possessed many other celebrated tombs, among the rest that of the Ṣûfî saint Sirrî, or Sarî-as-Saḳaṭî (the dealer in old clothes), who died about the year 256 (A.D. 870), having been the disciple of Ma'rûf-al-Karkhi, whose shrine will be mentioned in a following chapter.

In the thirteenth century A.D. (according to Yâḳût), At-Tûthah was still a populous suburb, though standing solitary like a village apart, opposite the Thorn Bridge. Ibn Khallikân, who wrote in the same century, also speaks of the tomb of Saḳaṭî as being in his day a conspicuous and well-known object standing close beside the grave of the celebrated Ṣûfî ascetic Al-Junayd, who was the nephew

[1] The Lesser Shûnîzîyah, as will be mentioned below, was the name given to the cemetery lying round the Kâẓimayn Shrine.

of Sakaṭî on the sister's side. At the present time, however, all trace of these shrines has apparently vanished, though as late as the middle of the fourteenth century A.D., when Ḥamd-Allah wrote, the tombs of Junayd and of Sarî-as-Sakaṭî were still objects of veneration in Baghdad[1].

[1] Yakut, i. 889; iii. 338, 599; iv. 843; Khatib, folio 113 a; Guzidah, reign of Caliph Mustaḍî, and Nuzhat, 149; Ibn Khallikan, No. 255, p. 65.

CHAPTER VII

THE QUARTERS OF THE LOWER HARBOUR

The Ṭâbiḳ and Ḳallâyîn Canals. Chickpea Broth. The Monastery of the Virgins. The Street of Kiln-burnt Bricks and the Cotton House. The Melon House, or Fruit Market, and the Myrtle Wharf. The Lower Harbour. The Palace of 'Îsâ and the Ḳaṣr 'Îsâ Quarter. The later Bridge of Boats. The Ḳurayyah Quarter. The Highroad of the Baṣrah Gate. The Sharḳîyah Quarter and the 'Atîḳah. The Ḥarrânî Archway. The Palace and Fief of Waḍḍâḥ. The Booksellers' Market and the New Bridge.

THE Karkhâyâ Canal, after passing the place known as the Mound of the Ass, took the name of the Nahr Ṭâbiḳ (or Ṭâbaḳ), and began to curve round to the eastward and north-east in its final reach before flowing out into the 'Îsâ Canal, not very far above where this last itself joined the Tigris. Before the Karkhâyâ, however, changed its name to Ṭâbiḳ, a branch was taken from its left bank at a place known as the Quadrangle of Ṣâliḥ. This branch or loop canal was the Nahr-al-Ḳallâyîn, so called from the shops of those who sold fried meats, and after passing a place named As-Sawwâḳîn—from the sellers of parched-pea broth called *Sawîḳ*—the Ḳallâyîn Canal flowed round to join the Poulterers' Canal (or Nahr Dajâj, already described) in the quarter of the reed-weavers.

The Sawîķ, from which the Sawwâķîn took their name, forms the subject of a curious note by Khaţîb. He relates that Sawîķ-al-Ḥimmâş—a broth or ptisan of chickpeas—was about the year 360 (A.D. 970) sold in great quantities throughout the markets of Baghdad, a certain cookman making it after a special receipt, and giving it an uncommon name, though what the name was Khaţîb had forgotten. This man, in the beginning of each year, was wont to import for the demands of his business the immense quantity of 280 *Kurrs*—a dry measure, each *Kurr* equivalent to six ass-loads—of the chickpeas called Ḥimmâş, and at the close of the season he would have none left in store, so that for the next year a like quantity had to be obtained. This broth of parched peas was more especially the food eaten by the poor in Baghdad during the two or three months when no fresh fruit was to be obtained; it was not, however, very savoury, and many could not stomach it. In time the dish went completely out of fashion, and Khaţîb remarks that in his day—about the year 450 (A.D. 1058)—the broth had come to be no longer in demand, so little so that, as he adds, 'were a single Makûk (half-bushel) of these chickpeas to be sought for now, in both East and West Baghdâd, this small quantity could hardly be obtained.'

One of the many churches of the Nestorians in Baghdad appears to have been situated near this market where the chickpea broth had been sold; for Yâķût writes that in the space between the Nahr-ad-Dajâj (the Poulterers' Canal) and the Nahr Ţâbiķ was the Ķaţî'at-an-Naşârâ (the Fief of the Christians), where stood the Monastery of the Virgins

(Dayr-al-'Adhârâ). It was, he reports, a magnificent shrine, and here the Christians in Baghdad were wont to celebrate the Holy Communion at the conclusion of the three days' Lesser Fast, called the Fast of the Virgins, which preceded their Great Fast, by which presumably Lent is to be understood[1].

The quarter of the Nahr-al-Ḳallâyîn occupied part of the ground where, as has already been mentioned, in earlier days had stood the village of Warthâl; and Yâḳût adds that in the seventh century (the thirteenth A.D.) this canal had by that date come to mark the southernmost limit of Karkh, so much had the great suburb then shrunk in extent from the six-mile length of when it had been first laid out. The Nahr Ṭâbiḳ, as already explained, was the designation of the last reach of the Karkhâyâ before it flowed out to the 'Îsâ Canal. The name is given by Ṭabarî as the Nahr Ṭâbiḳ-al-Kisrawî (Ṭâbiḳ of the Chosroes), being originally the canal of the Sassanian Pâpak (or Bâbak), son of Bahrâm, son of Bâbak, who had first dug it and founded a palace[2] on the site where the Ḳaṣr 'Îsâ ibn 'Alî afterwards stood. Ya'ḳûbî, however, declares that the canal took its name from a certain Ṭâbaḳ-ibn-Ṣamyah. Yâḳût, who in part copies his predecessors, seems to imagine that this word Ṭâbaḳ or Ṭâbiḳ was merely a variant for Bâbak; but adds that in his opinion the name of the canal was really derived, not from a man, but from the great tiles called *Ṭâbaḳ* made on its banks, which were in use throughout Baghdad for paving the houses. Since the year

[1] Yakut, ii. 680; iv. 143; Khatib, folio 110 b.

[2] The word used is 'Aḳr, which Yakut (iii. 695) explains to mean 'a castle (Ḳaṣr) to which the villagers may flee for safety.'

488 (A. D. 1095), Yâḳût continues, the quarter of the Ṭâbiḳ Canal had become an area of rubbish mounds, the result of a conflagration following on the riots which had broken out between the people of this quarter—who were Sunnîs—and those of the neighbouring Bâb-al-Arḥâ (the Gate of the Mills), near the Maghîd Bridge over the 'Îsâ Canal, who were Shî'ahs. The same authority states that on the Ṭâbiḳ Canal were also two minor quarters, namely that of the Darb-al-Ajurr (the Street of Kiln-burnt Bricks), which was a ruin at the time when Yâḳût wrote (thirteenth century A. D.), and the Dâr-al-Ḳuṭn (the Cotton House), which is elsewhere spoken of as lying between the 'Îsâ Canal and Karkh [1].

Near where the Ṭâbiḳ Canal joined the Nahr

[1] Ibn Serapion, 26; Ya'kubi, 250; Tabari, iii. 280; Yakut, i. 58; ii. 517, 523; iii. 486; iv. 254, 838, 841, 843; Marasid, iii. 249; Ibn-al-Athir, x. 162, gives the year of the insurrection as A.H. 487, and the Bâb-al-Arjâ mentioned in this passage is apparently a mistake for Bâb-al-Arḥâ, namely the quarter of the Gate of the Mills.

The account which Yakut, iv. 255, gives of the relative positions of Karkh and the surrounding suburbs is in complete contradiction with all that is known from other sources, and inconsistent with many other passages in his own works. Hence either the MSS. are here corrupt or he, writing from memory at Merv, had forgotten how the points of the compass lay. Thus he says that the Ṣarât Canal ran on the Ḳiblah or south-west side of Karkh, while the quarter of the Baṣrah Gate lay to the south-east. Further, he puts the quarter of the Nahr-al-Ḳallâyîn to the south of Karkh, and to the south-west of it (he says) was the quarter of the Muḥawwal Gate; while to the eastward of Karkh lay the boundaries of Baghdad and the other great quarters of the western city. Again, while in one passage (iv. 841) he states that the Ṭâbiḳ Canal lay to the east of the Ḳallâyîn, in another article (iv. 843) the Ṭâbiḳ is described as flowing to the south of the Ḳallâyîn, having the Shûnîzîyah Cemetery on its western side. Some confusion evidently must have existed as to the relative positions of these canals, for Khatib states (folio 25 b of the Paris MS.) that he had been told on good authority, in 450 A. H., that the Nahr-al-Ḳallâyîn flowed out into the Tigris *below* the Farḍah or Lower Harbour.

'Îsâ was the building known as the Melon House (Dâr-al-Baṭṭîkh), a name commonly given to the town fruit-markets; and to this spot these markets, which had been kept within the Round City by the Caliph Manṣûr, were finally removed during the reign of Mahdî. The actual point of junction of the Ṭâbiḳ with the 'Îsâ Canal was marked by a place known as the Myrtle Wharf (Mashra'at-al-Âs), which doubtless formed the northern strand of the Farḍah, or Lower Harbour, where the 'Îsâ Canal disembogued into the Tigris. This, as already said, was the Port of Karkh, and in early days it lay in the very midst of West Baghdad, where (as Ibn Hawḳal writes) the ships from the Euphrates were moored to discharge their cargoes, all along the harbour side standing the warehouses of the merchants, with many great markets near[1].

This Lower Harbour—as we have named it to distinguish it from the Upper Harbour at the mouth of the Ṭâhir Trench—was known as the Farḍah of Ja'far, son of the Caliph Manṣûr, and to him his father had granted the lands here in fief. On its upper strand and near the Tigris bank was the Ḳaṣr 'Îsâ, the palace that gave its name to the surrounding quarter, and which is commonly stated to have been built by that Abbasid prince 'Îsâ (whether uncle or nephew of the Caliph Manṣûr is uncertain)[2] who dug the 'Îsâ Canal. By another account, how-

[1] Ibn Serapion, 28; Fakhri, 299; Ibn Hawkal, 165. I translate *Mashra'ah* by 'wharf,' tentatively; it may signify 'ford' or 'passage,' but in the modern dialect of Baghdad the cognate term *Sharî'ah* means 'wharf,' and is in frequent use (see Jones, 312); further, this signification appears to suit the context where the word *Mashra'ah* occurs in Tabari and other early authorities.

[2] See above, p. 72.

ever, this Ḳaṣr took its name from ʻÎsâ, son of Jaʻfar, after whom the harbour was called, hence a grandson of Manṣûr; and this ʻÎsâ is stated to have had a brother called Jaʻfar, after his father, and he had owned the neighbouring palace called the Dâr Jaʻfar. On the other hand Yâḳût, who quotes a long anecdote in illustration of the well-known avarice of the Caliph Manṣûr, showing how he once tried to inveigle his kinsman into giving up his palace, states that it was built by Prince ʻÎsâ, son of ʻAlî (that is to say the uncle of the Caliph Manṣûr), who Yâḳût asserts dug the ʻÎsâ Canal. This he adds was the first palace (Ḳaṣr) which any Abbasid prince built in Baghdad; and it stood on the upper strand of the Rufayl Canal, otherwise called the Nahr ʻÎsâ, where this last joined the Tigris, and on the further side this palace overlooked the river. It apparently had the good fortune to escape the destruction which overtook so many of the houses in this quarter during the two great sieges of Baghdad (in the reigns respectively of Amîn and Mustaʻîn), for the Continuator of Ṭabarî mentions that the maternal uncle of the Caliph Muḳtadir, named Gharîb (or Ghurayb)—who died in 305 (A.D. 917)—was buried in the Ḳaṣr ʻÎsâ. Apparently lying opposite to this palace there was, at about the same period, an island in the Tigris stream, for in the year 313 (A.D. 925) the Wazîr of the Caliph Muḳtadir, Aḥmad Ibn-al-Khaṣîb, was molested by arrows shot at him while riding up to the Ḳaṣr ʻÎsâ, by some insurgent troops who had landed on this island.

As late as the beginning of the seventh century (the thirteenth A.D.), in the time of Yâḳût, the populous suburb and markets known as the quarter of the Ḳaṣr 'Îsâ still existed, though the palace itself had long since entirely disappeared. The quarter was celebrated for the mosque called the Jâmi' of Ibn-al-Muṭṭalib, and it was probably in the neighbourhood of this mosque that the tomb of the Caliph Mustaḍî, who died in 575 (A.D. 1180), had been erected. The Caliphs for the most part were buried at Ruṣâfah (as will be described later); but the chronicle specially states that this Caliph was buried 'in a tomb apart outside the quarter of the Ḳaṣr 'Îsâ in Western Baghdad.'

From a topographical point of view, the Ḳaṣr 'Îsâ with its surrounding quarter, lying on the Tigris immediately above the harbour where the 'Îsâ Canal flowed out, is a position of much importance, for Yâḳût informs us that the Bridge of Boats in his day, which crossed the Tigris to the palaces of the Caliphs, began 'in front of the Ḳaṣr 'Îsâ Quarter.' The precise epoch when this bridge was first laid down is not known, but it can only date, at the earliest, from the latter half of the fifth century (the eleventh A.D.), and the first notice of it occurs under the year 568 (A.D. 1173), as will be shown in a later chapter. This bridge, the position of which Yâḳût describes, is the same of which Ibn Jubayr speaks, who visited Baghdad in 580 (A.D. 1184), as lying immediately above the Ḳurayyah Quarter; and there seems no reason to doubt that in position it represents the Bridge of Boats of the present day. On the other hand, as will be seen in the sequel, it cannot be identified with any one of the three bridges (upper, main, or lower) which existed from the time of the Caliph Manṣûr till the middle of the fourth century (the tenth A.D.), when the Buyid princes became masters of Baghdad, for the lowest of these must have crossed the Tigris considerably above the mouth of the harbour and to a point within, or above, the gate of the Tuesday Market in the wall of the Mukharrim Quarter of Eastern Baghdad[1].

On the south side of the harbour, and stretching from here for a considerable distance along the Tigris bank, was the quarter called Al-Ḳurayyah (the Little Village). This must have been one of the latest built of the outlying suburbs, for it is mentioned neither by Ibn Serapion nor by Ya'ḳûbî, and it probably only came into existence about the middle of the fifth century (the eleventh A.D.), during the earlier years of the Saljûḳ supremacy, when the suburbs of both East and West Baghdad were considerably enlarged, and the Niẓâmîyah College came to be built on the eastern river bank, immediately opposite to the Ḳurayyah on the western side. Ibn Jubayr, who visited Baghdad in 580 (A.D. 1184), found the Ḳurayyah to be the largest of the quarters of West Baghdad. He lodged here on his first arrival, 'in a district thereof that is called Al-Murabba'ah (or the Quadrangle), lying on the bank of the Tigris, very near to the Bridge of Boats.' Yâḳût describes this same suburb in the year 623 (A.D. 1226) as like a town apart, having its separate Friday mosque and numerous markets; while across the river opposite the Ḳurayyah was the wharf at the market of the Niẓâmîyah College. The com-

[1] Tabari, iii. 280; 'Arib, 69, 127; Ya'kubi, 245, 250; Yakut, ii. 484; iv. 117, 839; Mushtarik, 350; Ibn Jubayr, 226; and compare Plan No. VII with No. III.

manding position of this suburb made it a point of importance when half a century later, in the year 656 (A.D. 1258), the Mongols laid siege to Baghdad; and the chronicles state that Hûlâgû then ordered the chief part of his army that was sent across to besiege Baghdad from the west side to pitch their siege camp 'over against Al-Ḳurayyah, which lies opposite the palaces of the Caliphs.' This incident, however, will be more fully discussed at a later page, when we come to deal with the events of the last great siege.

From another passage in Yâḳût it would further appear that the Ḳurayyah Quarter must also have stretched across and to the north of the 'Îsâ Canal along its left bank; for part of the Ḳurayyah is described as occupying ground between the canal and the Ḳuṭuftâ suburb at the Baṣrah Gate, at the time when all these quarters suffered damage by a great inundation of the Tigris in the year 614 (A.D. 1217)[1].

The Ḳurayyah was the lowest, downstream, of the suburbs of Karkh which lay on the Tigris bank, and it communicated directly with the City of Manṣûr by the highroad of the Baṣrah Gate. In its lower portion this thoroughfare on leaving the Ḳurayyah passed, on the right, the quarter of the Ḳaṣr 'Îsâ (already described), immediately after crossing the 'Îsâ Canal by the Bani Zurayḳ Bridge, and from the highroad at this point must have diverged the

[1] Ibn Jubayr, 226; Yakut, iv. 85, 137; Mushtarik, 344; Chronicle of Abu-l-Fida, iv. 552; Ibn-al-Athir, xii. 217. In the edition by W. Wright of Ibn Jubayr, the name of Al-Ḳurayyah is given without points and is misprinted. There can be no doubt, however, as to the true reading, for the passage is copied by Sharîshî in his *Commentary on Ḥarîrî*, i. 216. For this reference I am indebted to Professor De Goeje.

street to the (later) Bridge of Boats, mentioned by Ibn Jubayr and Yâḳût. Further up, and before reaching the Ḥarrânî Arch, the Baṣrah Gate highroad skirted the quarter called the Sharḳîyah, which lay between it and the Tigris, immediately above the quarter of the Ḳaṣr 'Îsâ; and part of the Sharḳîyah Quarter, namely that portion more immediately on the river bank, bore the name of an older suburb known as Al-'Atîḳah.

The Sharḳîyah, meaning 'the Eastern Quarter' (and not to be confounded with Eastern Baghdad on the further side of the Tigris), was so called from its position to the eastward of the City of Manṣûr. Originally it had its special Friday mosque, and a Ḳâḍî or judge appointed to settle the disputes of the people in the Karkh markets; but this Friday mosque was afterwards disestablished. The 'Atîḳah, meaning 'the ancient' suburb, is described as situated between the Ḥarrânî Arch and the Barley Gate, on the land contiguous to the river bank. It was also known as the Ancient Market (As-Sûḳ-al-'Atîḳah), and before Baghdad was built a village had existed here that went by the name of Sûnâyâ, the black grapes from its vineyards being very celebrated. In later times a shrine dedicated to the Caliph 'Alî, and much frequented by the Shî'ahs, stood in this quarter, being known as the Mashhad-al-Minṭaḳah (the Shrine of the Girdle), probably from some relic here preserved. The Shî'ahs asserted that 'Alî had prayed at this shrine, a fact mentioned as doubtful by Khaṭîb, and when Yâḳût wrote in the beginning of the seventh century (the thirteenth A.D.), this shrine had already disappeared.

The Sharkîyah Quarter must have been traversed by the lower reaches of both the Bazzâzîn and Dajâj Canals, already described. The latter of the two, after passing the Street of the Pitch-workers, flowed out to the Tigris among the Cookmen's Quarter; while the Bazzâzîn Canal had its exit immediately below the building known as the Nut-house (Dâr-al-Jawz), after passing through the Soap-boilers' Quarter[1].

On the highroad coming down from the Başrah Gate, the upper limit of the Sharkîyah Quarter was at the archway of the Harrânian (Ţâk-al-Harrânî). This archway stood between the lowest part of the Abu-'Attâb Canal—immediately above where its waters flowed out into the Şarât—and the lower reach of the Nahr Bazzâzîn, spanning the roadway where it crossed a plot of ground that had been included in the limits of the ancient village of Warthâl, which, as already mentioned, had existed here before Baghdad was founded. According to one authority the arch was built by a man of Harrân in Upper Mesopotamia, named Ibrâhîm, son of Dhakwân, once the freedman of the Caliph Manşûr, and who, becoming in later times a chief favourite of the Caliph Hâdî, had served him at the close of his short reign in the capacity of Wazîr. Ya'kûbî on the other hand states that the Harrânian who built the archway, and had his fief here, was not Ibrâhîm, but a certain 'Amr ibn Sim'an[2].

Between the Harrânî Archway and the New Bridge over the Şarât Canal at the Başrah Gate

[1] See Plan, No. II.

[2] Ya'kubi, 245; Khatib, folios 76 a, 84 b; Yakut, iii. 197, 279, 489, 613; Marasid, ii. 70; Ibn Serapion, 25, 26.

the highroad traversed the parcel of land originally granted in fief to Waḍḍâḥ by the Caliph Manṣûr. Waḍḍâḥ was a native of Anbâr and freedman of the Caliph; he had been one of the superintendents appointed for the building of the Round City, and he was afterwards chief of the armoury. His palace, known as the Ḳaṣr Waḍḍâḥ, with the adjoining mosque, at one time gave its name to this part of Karkh, of which great suburb, further, he drew the ground plan by order of the Caliph, being also made superintendent of the funds set apart for the building of the neighbouring Sharḳîyah Quarter. At a somewhat later date, this palace in the fief or suburb (Ḳaṭî'ah or Rabaḍ, as it was indifferently called) of Waḍḍâḥ was, for a time, the residence of Mahdî, the heir-apparent, while the Caliph Manṣûr, his father, was completing the Ruṣâfah Quarter and the new Palace of Mahdî across the river.

From the Ḥarrânî Archway up to the New Bridge over the Ṣarât Canal both sides of the roadway were occupied by the shops of the papersellers and booksellers, whose market was in this quarter, as also on the bridge itself; and this market was called after them the Sûḳ-al-Warrâḳîn, more than one hundred booksellers' shops being found here.

It is said that the New Bridge (Al-Ḳanṭarah al-Jadîdah or Al-Ḥadîthah) took this name from the fact that it was the last of those built by the Caliph Manṣûr over the Ṣarât Canal; and Yâḳût, while remarking that in his day (thirteenth century A.D.) it was no longer entitled to its designation of *new*, says that though it had been many times restored, it had now come to be a complete ruin. It must indeed have been rebuilt after the first siege of Baghdad, that of the Caliph Amîn in 198 (A.D. 814), when both this New Bridge opposite the Baṣrah Gate and the Old Bridge (already described) higher up the Ṣarât, at the foot of the square opposite the Kûfah Gate, were destroyed. On this occasion after occupying the Sharḳîyah Quarter and the line of the Ṣarât Canal, Ṭâhir, the general of Mamûn's troops, forced Amîn to retreat within the City of Manṣûr, and stubborn fighting took place round the Palace of Waḍḍâḥ, and again at the Karkh Gate, before the partisans of Amîn were finally driven in[1].

[1] Ya'kubi, 245; Baladhuri, 295; Tabari, iii. 906; Yakut, iv. 123, 188.

CHAPTER VIII

THE QUARTER OF THE BAṢRAH GATE

The Lower Bridge of Boats and the Barley Gate. The Palace of Ḥumayd. The Ḳuṭuftâ Quarter and the Palace of 'Aḍud-ad-Dîn. The Tustarîyîn. Later Baṣrah Gate Quarter. The Shrine of Ma'rûf Karkhî and the Old Monastery of the Ṣarât Point. The Convent of the Foxes. The Khuld Palace and the Ḳarâr. The Great 'Aḍûdî Hospital. The Review Ground and the Stables of the Caliph.

THE name of Sharḳîyah, to denote the suburb beyond the Baṣrah Gate, appears to have gone out of use during the course of the third century (the ninth A.D.); probably because this same name Sharḳîyah, meaning the Eastern Quarter, had come more and more to be used exclusively for East Baghdad, across the Tigris, to which, after the return of the Caliphs from Sâmarrâ in 279 (A.D. 892), the seat of government had finally been transferred. The area of this Sharḳîyah of the Baṣrah Gate was, in later times, occupied by the Quarter of the Tustarîyîn, and that called Ḳuṭuftâ, within which also a part of the suburb of the Ḳaṣr 'Îsâ was included; for this latter suburb had originally gone all along the Tigris bank from the mouth of the 'Îsâ Canal to the mouth of the Ṣarât, where it met the lower part of the gardens of the Khuld Palace.

At this point was moored the Lower Bridge of Boats, which from the time of Manṣûr till the middle of the fifth century (the eleventh A.D.) connected the quarters of West Baghdad outside the Baṣrah Gate with the Tuesday Market within, or above, the gate of that name in the city wall of the Mukharrim Quarter in East Baghdad. This bridge of boats, with others, will be more particularly noticed in a later chapter; it is spoken of by Ya'ḳûbî under the name of the First (or Lowest) Bridge (Al-Jisr-al-Awwal), and near its western end must have stood the Barley Gate, and subsequently the Palace of Ḥumayd. The exact position of the Barley Gate (Bâb-ash-Sha'îr) is not easy to fix, but it appears to have shut off the lower part of the branch road called the Darb-ash-Sha'îr (the Barley Street), leading from the Ḥarrâni Archway to this Lower Bridge, which last is described as having been first moored across the Tigris by the Caliph Manṣûr when he was building the Khuld Palace in the year 157 (A.D. 774) 'at the Barley Gate.' Further, it is stated that some of the markets were set near this Barley Gate when these came to be removed from within the Round City to the suburbs of Karkh; and the Rayasânah Fief (as already mentioned) is described as lying between this gate and the Mosque of Ibn Raghbân. The chronicles also frequently mention this Quarter of the Bâb-ash-Sha'îr in connexion with Karkh, the Ḳallâyîn, and other neighbouring suburbs, as for example on the occasion of the insurrections which broke out and devastated the greater part of Western Baghdad in the years 406, 422, and 447 (A.D. 1015, 1031, and 1055); and Yâḳût refers to the Barley Gate as standing near the 'Atîḳah suburb (which has been already described), near the Minṭaḳah Mosque and not far from the Ṭâḳ-al-Ḥarrânî, adding that in his time, at the beginning of the seventh century (the thirteenth A.D.), the gate might still be seen, standing solitary in the midst of the surrounding ruins.

Another building which serves to fix the position of this Lower Bridge of Boats is the Palace of Ḥumayd, which the chronicle speaks of as standing on the Tigris bank at the lower end of the semicircle of wall which was built to defend West Baghdad in the year 251 (A.D. 865), when the Caliph Musta'în was about to be besieged by the troops sent against him by his rival the Caliph Mu'tazz from Sâmarrâ. This wall must have included the Lower Bridge of Boats in its circuit, and it formed the continuation of the wall round the three northern quarters of East Baghdad (as will be described later), which came down to the river at the gate of the Tuesday Market. The Palace of Ḥumayd had been built half a century before this date, receiving its name from a general of the time of the Caliph Mamûn, Ḥumayd ibn 'Abd-al-Ḥamîd, who died in 210 (A.D. 825). He took a prominent part in suppressing the revolt of Ibrâhîm, uncle of Mamûn, whom the Arab party had sought to establish as Caliph in Baghdad after the death of Amîn; and Ḥumayd was for some time viceroy of 'Irâḳ, being the friend and supporter of the Wazîr Ḥasan ibn Sahl, whose daughter Bûrân the Caliph Mamûn had married. Khaṭîb writes as though the Ḳaṣr Ḥumayd were still existing in his day (A.H. 450), and it must have stood on the Tigris bank, as is evident from the description of it in a panegyric on Ḥumayd, written by the poet 'Alî ibn Jabalah, in which he praises the beauty of the palace grounds lying on the river[1].

The Ḳuṭuftâ Quarter is frequently mentioned in the chronicle of Ibn-al-Athîr subsequent to the year 512 (A.D. 1118). In the sixth century (the twelfth A.D.) it is described as a great suburb with many markets; from south to north it stretched from the 'Îsâ Canal, where its houses were coterminous with the upper part of the Ḳurayyah, to the Şarât, near the cemetery, in which was the shrine of Ma'rûf Karkhî; while from west to east it extended from the highroad of the Başrah Gate down to the Tigris bank, being here rather less than one mile across. In the year 569 (A.D. 1174) 'Aḍud-ad-Dîn, the Wazîr of the Caliph Mustaḍi, had his palace in the Ḳuṭuftâ Quarter, and here he died in 573 (A.D. 1177), slain by the knife of a fanatic. In 601 (A.D. 1205) this quarter suffered much damage during the riots which broke out between its inhabitants and those of the neighbouring Ḳurayyah Quarter, and the great inundation of the Tigris in 614 (A.D. 1217) completed the ruin of those streets and houses which the rioters had spared.

The other quarter lying between the Başrah Gate and the Tigris was that of the Tustarîyîn, namely of the people of Tustar, otherwise called Shustar, the celebrated town in Khûzistân on the Kârûn River. The Baghdad quarter was so called, being inhabited by settlers from Khûzistân, who

[1] Ya'kubi, 245, 306; Tabari, iii. 324, 1551; Kitab-al-Aghani, xviii. 106 (for this reference, which to a certain extent fixes the position of the Ḳaşr Ḥumayd, I am indebted to Professor De Goeje); Khatib, folios 71 a, 75 a, 76 b, 80 b, 87 a, 107 a; Ibn-al-Athir, ix. 184, 285 *bis*, 422; Yakut, iii. 301, 613; Mushtarik, 274.

manufactured here the Tustarî stuffs for which their native city was celebrated.

The ruin that had overtaken the Round City during the siege in the time of the Caliph Amîn was completed by the subsequent demolition of its circular walls, and the quarter of the Baṣrah Gate appears to have incorporated within its area most of the houses that still remained habitable of the old City of Manṣûr, its Great Mosque becoming more specially the Friday mosque of this quarter. When Ibn Jubayr visited Baghdad in 580 (A.D. 1184), he describes the quarter of the Baṣrah Gate as like a small city standing by itself, with the Mosque of Manṣûr, 'a great Jâmiʿ and an ancient edifice very firmly built'; and this suburb of the Baṣrah Gate, traversed by the Ṣarât Canal, was one of the four chief quarters into which West Baghdad had then come to be divided[1].

Between the Baṣrah Gate and the Tigris bank, and probably along the lower course of the Ṣarât, lay the Cemetery of the Convent Gate (Maḳbarah Bâb-ad-Dayr), of which the most celebrated tomb was that of the Moslem saint Maʿrûf Karkhi. The position of this shrine is of importance topographically, since it is one of the few existing places in Western Baghdad dating from the days of the Caliphs, for Maʿrûf of Karkh has never ceased to be honoured by the people as one of the chief patron saints of Baghdad. The shrine and cemetery occupied the upper limit of the Ḳuṭuftâ Quarter, already described;

[1] Ibn Jubayr, 227; Yakut, i. 850; iv. 137; Ibn-al-Athir, x. 383; xi. 270, 296; xii. 133, 217. Ḳuṭuftâ is said by Yakut to be a foreign word. It is presumably the Aramaean or Syriac word 'Ḳaṭûftâ,' meaning 'cut-off.' Cf. Fränkel, p. xx.

but in regard to the exact situation of the original convent (*Dayr*), from which the cemetery took its name, Yâḳût confesses ignorance. It is not, however (he writes), to be confounded with the Dayr-ath-Tha'âlib (the Convent of the Foxes), as has so often been done, for this last lay more than a mile distant from the shrine of Ma'rûf, and two miles from Baghdad. In the absence of more direct evidence, it may be conjectured that this Cemetery of the Dayr took its name from the ancient convent which had existed at the Ṣarât Point (as the place was called where that canal disembogued to the Tigris) from times anterior to the building of Baghdad, and where, as the chronicles relate, the Caliph Manṣûr temporarily took up his residence when he came to lay out the plan of his new capital.

In regard to Ma'rûf, the son of Al-Fîrûzân, much is recorded, for he was the contemporary of Hârûn-ar-Rashîd, and celebrated as 'the ascetic of his age and the Imâm of his time.' He died about the year 200 (A.D. 816), and Khaṭîb names him as one of the four saints, the guardians of Baghdad, whose intercession will ever prevent the approach of evil to the City of Peace. He was by birth a Christian, but professed Islam at the hands of the Imâm 'Alî-ar-Riḍâ, whose freedman he became, and his merits were further perpetuated by the fame won by his great disciple Sarî-as-Saḳaṭî, the celebrated Ṣûfî saint, whose tomb has already been mentioned as standing in the Shûnîzîyah Cemetery on the Kûfah highroad. The shrine which had originally been built over the grave of Ma'rûf was accidentally burnt in 459 (A.D. 1067), but was rebuilt by order of the Caliph Ḳâim, under the superintendence of the Ṣûfî Shaykh of Shaykhs

Abu-Sa'd of Nîshâpûr, and in 479 (A.D. 1086), when Mâlik Shâh, the Saljûḳ, and his Wazîr Niẓâm-al-Mulk came to Baghdad, they visited this among other celebrated shrines of the capital. In 580 (A.D. 1184) the traveller Ibn Jubayr mentions the tomb of Ma'rûf, 'a man of righteousness, and one of the most celebrated of saints'; and in 611 (A.D. 1214) the younger son of the Caliph Nâṣir, dying before his father, was buried near this shrine. Apparently on this occasion the tomb was rebuilt, for at the present day it still bears an inscription recording the year A.H. 612 as the date of its latest restoration. It evidently suffered but little during the Mongol siege (in A.D. 1258), for Ibn Baṭûṭah, who visited Baghdad in A.D. 1327, speaks of the tomb of Ma'rûf of Karkh as standing in the quarter of the Baṣrah Gate, and a few years later, about 740 (A.D. 1339), Ḥamd-Allah also mentions it among the notable shrines of West Baghdad. There can be little doubt, therefore, that the present shrine of Ma'rûf covers the site of his tomb in the Convent Cemetery, where he was buried during the reign of Hârûn-ar-Rashîd.

In regard to the so-called tomb of Zubaydah, which is a large building standing at the present day a short distance to the south of this shrine of Ma'rûf, more will be said in the sequel, all that need be noted here is that there is no authority for this ever having been the tomb of the celebrated wife of Hârûn-ar-Rashîd, she having been buried in the Kâẓimayn, as will be mentioned in a subsequent chapter[1].

[1] Khatib, 112 b, 113 b; Yakut, ii. 650; iv. 137; Tabari, iii. 280; Ibn-Khallikan, No. 739; Ibn-al-Athir, vi. 225; x. 37, 103; xii. 201; Ibn Jubayr, 227; Ibn Batuta, ii. 107; Nuzhat, 149; Niebuhr, ii. 243; Rawlinson, *Encycl. Brit.*, s.v. Baghdad.

The course of the Ṣarât Canal must have curved round through almost a semicircle, following the walls of the City of Manṣûr; but it is to be remarked that while at the Kûfah Gate this canal was separated from the wall by a considerable space (occupied by the square of the Kûfah Gate), at the Baṣrah Gate it ran close under the city wall, for this last gateway is described as opening immediately on the Ṣarât, overlooking it at the point crossed by the New Bridge. Ḳurn-aṣ-Ṣarât (the Ṣarât Point) was the name given to the spit of land where the canal ran out to the Tigris, and here in Persian times had been held the market called Sûḳ Baghdâd, where, as already stated, in the early days of the Caliph Abu Bakr, the Moslems had made their first successful raid into Mesopotamia. Near the Ṣarât Point also, later on, had stood the Christian convent where Manṣûr sojourned when planning Baghdad, and this probably, as already mentioned, had given its name to the neighbouring cemetery.

From the Ṣarât Point upstream to the Main Bridge of Boats opposite the Khurâsân Gate, a plot of ground nearly a mile in length but much less in width, lay between the wall of the Round City and the Tigris. Judging from the curve of the river and the quarter circle of the wall between the Baṣrah and the Khurâsân Gates, this piece of land was probably broader in its upper than in its lower part; and it was occupied in the earlier period chiefly by the Palace of the Khuld and its gardens. The Ḳaṣr-al-Khuld (the Palace of Eternity) was so called from its gardens being supposed almost to rival those of Paradise mentioned in a verse of the Ḳurân (xxv. 16), which speaks of 'the Palace of

Eternity which is promised to the God-fearing'; and it was built as already stated by the Caliph Manṣûr, who took up his abode here in the year 158 (A.D. 775). The palace itself stood on the Tigris bank opposite the Khurâsân Gate and a short distance below the Main Bridge of Boats. According to one account, Manṣûr chose this spot for his palace because the site was of all that neighbourhood the highest above the Tigris bed, and hence the place was almost free from the plague of gnats which swarmed elsewhere. It is also asserted by one of our authorities that the Christian Convent, where the Caliph had lodged, was near here, and not at the Ṣarât point lower down, as is more generally said.

Both Manṣûr and Mahdî spent much of their time in the Khuld — though the latter usually preferred living in his own palace at Ruṣâfah—but the Ḳaṣr-al-Khuld is more especially connected with the memory of Hârûn-ar-Rashîd, who kept his state here, enjoying its magnificent gardens, which, bordering on the river, gave easy access to the distant quarters of the city. After the death of the great Caliph, his son, the luckless Amîn (as has been already mentioned), entrenched himself in the Khuld and the neighbouring Round City, when outer Baghdad (East and West) was finally occupied by the armies of Mamûn: and from the palace wharf, called the Mashra'ah of the Khurâsân Gate, he embarked, seeking to escape, but finding his death at the hands of Ṭâhir.

Below the Khuld, but some distance above the Ṣarât Point, was another palace, called Al-Ḳarâr, a name signifying 'the stagnant waters,' or 'the pool.' It is frequently mentioned in the accounts of this famous siege, and is the palace otherwise called the Ḳaṣr of Zubaydah, being so named after the widow of Hârûn-ar-Rashîd, and the mother of Amîn, who through all his disasters shared the fortunes of her favourite son. The palace was also known as the Ḳaṣr Umm Ja'far, that being the surname of Zubaydah. Both the Khuld and the Ḳarâr suffered so severely by the stones shot from the catapults which Ṭâhir had erected for bombarding Baghdad, that after the siege they appear to have been almost in a state of ruin, though according to one account, when Mamûn finally reached Baghdad in 203 (A.D. 818), he at first held his court in the Khuld, while the Wazîr Ḥasan Ibn Sahl was preparing the Ḥasanî Palace (in East Baghdad) for his master's reception.

The next Caliph Mu'taṣim, as history relates, removed the seat of government from Baghdad to Sâmarrâ, and during the sixty odd years that his successors made this latter city their capital, the Khuld must have fallen completely to ruin. When finally in 279 (A.D. 892) the Caliphate was re-established in Baghdad, Mu'taḍid took up his residence in the palaces of the eastern bank, and the Khuld thus continued an unoccupied ruin till the year 368 (A.D. 979), when the Buyid Prince 'Aḍud-ad-Dawlah appropriated its site for the buildings of his great Bîmâristân or hospital[1].

The New Hospital of Western Baghdad is reported by Yâḳût to have stood somewhat higher up the river bank than the spot where the Khuld had been, and this confirms the contemporary notice in Mu-

[1] Ibn Serapion, 24; Baladhuri, 246; Tabari, iii. 384, 848, 906, 954; Mas'udi, vi. 475, 477; Yakut, i. 807; ii. 459.

ḳaddasi, who, writing about the year 375 (A.D. 985), describes it as having been recently built by 'Aḍud-ad-Dawlah, close beside the Main Bridge of Boats, from which the Khuld had been separated by outlying buildings. According to one account, the hospital was only completed in A.H. 371, a year before 'Aḍud died. Nearly a century later, in the year 466 (A.D. 1074), it suffered some damage at the time of a great inundation of the Tigris, when the waters are reported to have entered by its windows and the whole building was flooded. A like misfortune occurred in the year 554 (A.D. 1159), and again in 569 (A.D. 1174), when, during the spring-time, after forty days of ceaseless rain upstream in the Mosul district, the Tigris rose as it had never done before. On this occasion the whole of Baghdad was flooded and many houses fell in. The shutters of the windows in the Hospital had, it appears, been removed, and the flood rose so high that boats entered the building through the empty doorways and window-openings, floating about in the interior. The damage done by this inundation must, however, have been promptly repaired; for when, in 580 (A.D. 1184), Ibn Jubayr came to Baghdad, the great hospital was again in full working order. He describes it as an immense palace, situated on the Tigris bank, with many chambers and separate wards furnished like a royal abode. Every Monday and Thursday, he says, the city physicians attended there to visit patients, for whom both food and medicine were gratuitously prepared by servants especially appointed for this office. The building, he adds, was plentifully supplied with water from the river.

This Hospital, further, in later times, gave its

name to the market, called Sûḳ-al-Mâristân, which, like a small city, was one of the great suburbs of West Baghdad, lying between the suburb of the Baṣrah Gate and the Shâri' Quarter, which will be described in the next chapter. With the lapse of time houses and streets had sprung up round the hospital buildings, occupying much of the ground where the gardens of the Khuld Palace had formerly been, and the district formed the populous Suburb of the Hospital, which is described by Yâḳût in the beginning of the thirteenth century A.D.

When, in 656 (A. D. 1258), Hûlâgû besieged Baghdad, he made the Quarter of the Bîmâristân 'Aḍudi (as it was called) the upper point of his attack on the western side, and the hospital probably suffered much during the siege operations; for, less than a hundred years after this time, when Ibn Baṭûṭah visited Baghdad, in 730 (A. D. 1330), he found the place a complete ruin, and of its former buildings only traces of walls could be seen. It is probable, however, that though the houses remained standing, the hospital had been dismantled even before the Mongol siege, namely at some time prior to the year 630 (A. D. 1233), when the Caliph Mustanṣir (as will be described in a later chapter) founded his Bîmâristân of the Mustanṣirîyah College in East Baghdad[1].

Once more to return, however, to the Round City as this was left by its founder, the Caliph Manṣûr: we are told by Ya'ḳûbî that originally between the Khurâsân Gate and the Main Bridge of Boats, where

[1] Mukaddasi, 120; Ya'kubi, 249; Ibn Khallikan, No. 543, p. 33; Abu-l-Faraj, 299, 474; Ibn-al-Athir, x. 62; xi. 164, 270; Ibn Jubayr, 227; Rashid-ad-Din, 282; Ibn Batutah, ii. 107.

the great highroad into Persia crossed the Tigris, lay the Review Ground, immediately adjacent to the Khuld Palace. Next to this were the Royal Stables; and at the bridge-head itself there was again an open space or square flanked by the workshops of the bridge, and the Office of the Shurṭah or chief of police. Beyond, to the left of this and upstream, came the quarter of the Shâri', which will be spoken of in the following chapter: but it will be understood that this review ground and the stables, with other buildings of the days of the Caliph Manṣûr, must all have entirely disappeared long before the time when 'Aḍud-ad-Dawlah began to build his hospital, their sites coming afterwards to be occupied by the markets and streets which formed the new quarter of the Bîmâristân.

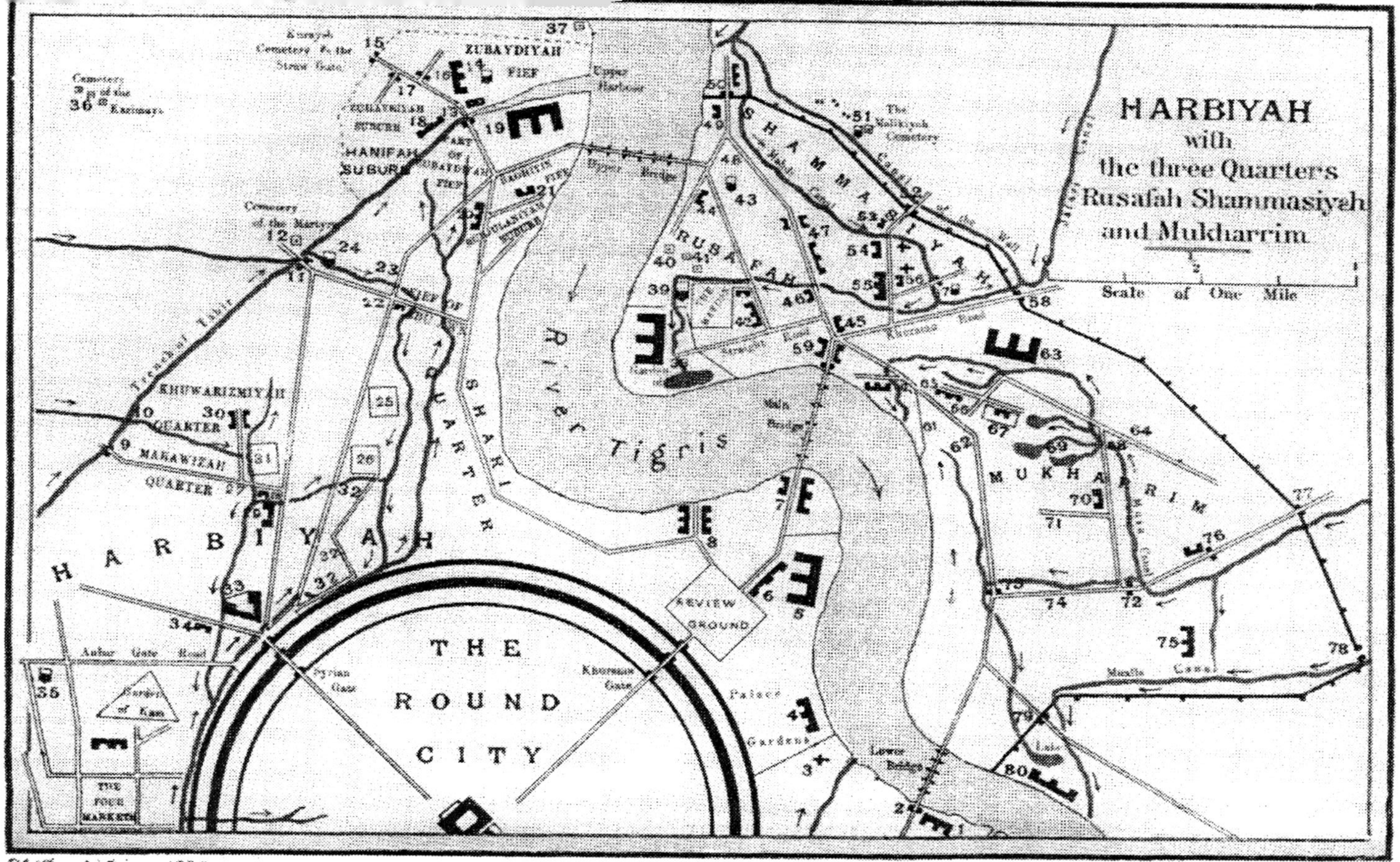

B.V. Darbishire 1900.

REFERENCES TO MAP No. V.

Palace of Ḥumayd ibn 'Abd-al-Ḥamîd.
Barley Gate (Bâb-ash-Sha'îr).
Old Convent at the Ṣarât Point.
ce of Zubaydah, called the Karâr.
Khuld Palace (site afterwards occupied by
e 'Aḍudî Hospital).
Royal Stables.
e of the Bridge Works and Hall of the
hief of Police.
ces of the Princes Sulaymân and Ṣâliḥ,
ns of Manṣûr, on the Street called Darb
ılaymân.
Iron Gate and Bridge, leading to the
ujayl Road.
Water-conduit called 'Abbârat-al-Kûkh.
Ḥarb Gate and Bridge, leading to the
arb Gate Road.
b of Ibn Ḥanbal the Imâm.
abbul Gate and Bridge of the Mill of
mm Ja'far.
ce and Mosque of Zubaydah (Umm Ja'far).
Straw Gate (Bâb-at-Tibn).
of the Fief.
aṣ-Ṣaghîr (the Little Gate).
ce of 'Umârah.
ce of the Ṭâhirid Ḥarîm.
Slaves' House (Dâr-ar-Raḳîḳ) and Fief of
e Ghulâms (Pages).
ce of Ḥafṣ ibn 'Othmân in Darb Siwâr
Street of the Bracelet).
ce of Ibn Abi 'Awn.
Bridge of the Straw-merchants (Ḳanṭarah-
-Tabbânîn).
Ḥarbîyah Mosque.
drangle of Abu-l-'Abbâs.

27. The Abu-l-Jawn Bridge.
28. The Palace of Sa'îd-al-Khaṭîb.
29. The Orphan School.
30. Dukkân-al-Abna (the Persian Shops).
31. Quadrangle of the Persians, with Suburbs of Rushayd, of Zuhayr, and of 'Othmân ibn Nuhayk.
32. The Three Arcades of 'Akkî, Ghiṭrîf, and Abu Suwayd.
33. The Prison of the Syrian Gate.
34. Road and Palace of Hânî.
35. The Bukhariot Mosque.
36. The Kâẓimayn Shrines; Tombs of Zubaydah, the Caliph Amîn, and the Buyid Princes.
37. Tomb of 'Abd-Allah, son of Ibn Ḥanbal.
38. Palace of Mahdî in Ruṣâfah.
39. The Ruṣâfah Mosque.
40. Shrine of Abu Ḥanîfah in the Khayzurân Cemetery.
41. The Tombs of the Caliphs.
42. Palaces of Umm Ḥabîb and of Faḍl on the Road of the Maydân.
43. The Khuḍayrîyah Quarter and Mosque; the Khuḍayr Market.
44. Palace of Waḍḍâḥ on Road of Skiffs.
45. Market of Yaḥyâ and Road of the Bridge.
46. Palace of Faraj.
47. Palaces of Dûr; Palace of Ja'far the Barmecide.
48. Market of Ja'far and Road of the Mahdî Canal.
49. Market of Khâlid and Ḳaṣr-aṭ-Ṭîn (the Clay Castle).
50. The Shammâsîyah Gate and the Palace of Mûnis.
51. Three Gates Suburb, the Place of Vows, and the Chapel of the Festival.
52. The Baradân Gate.

54. The Ḥuṭam Palace.
55. The Barmecide Fief and Palaces.
56. Dâr-ar-Rûm (House of the Greeks), the Nestorian and Jacobite Churches of the Christian Quarter, with the House of the Patriarch.
57. Market of Naṣr, the Mosque and the Iron Gates.
58. The Khurâsân Gate of East Baghdad.
59. The Bâb-aṭ-Ṭâḳ (Gate of the Archway), Palaces of Khuzaymah, of Prince 'Ubayd-Allah, and of Princess Asmâ.
60. The Street of 'Amr the Greek.
61. The Garden of Ẓâhir at the mouth of the Mûsâ Canal, and Palace of Ibn Muḳlah.
62. The Great Road.
63. The Palace of Mu'taṣim.
64. The Long Street.
65. The Palace of Ibn-al-Furât and the Street of the Vine Tendril.
66. The Thirst Market (Sûḳ-al-'Aṭsh).
67. Palace, Quadrangle, and Market of Ḥarashî.
68. The Anṣâr Bridge.
69. The Three Tanks of the Anṣâr, of Haylânah, and of Dâûd.
70. Palace of Ibn-al-Khaṣîb in the Road of Sa'd Waṣîf.
71. Market of Ḥajjâj.
72. The Great Pitched Gate.
73. The Mukharrim Gate and the Bridge of 'Abbâs.
74. The Hay Market and the Booths.
75. The Palace of Banûjah.
76. The 'Ammâr Gate and the Palace of 'Umârah.
77. The Gate of the Horse Market.
78. The Abraz Gate.
79. The Gate of the Tuesday Market.

CHAPTER IX

THE SHÂRIʿ QUARTER AND THE TRENCH OF ṬÂHIR

The Shâriʿ Quarter and Fiefs. The Baghîyîn and Burjulânîyah Suburbs. The Ḥarbîyah Quarter and the Trench of Ṭâhir. The Anbâr Gate and Highroad: the Garden of Ṭâhir. The Iron Gate. The Ḥarb Gate. The Ḳaṭrabbul Gate. The Zubaydîyah Fief and its Mosque. The Straw Gate. The Zuhayrîyah Suburb. The Bâb-aṣ-Ṣaghîr. The Ḥanîfah Suburb and the Palace of ʿUmârah. The Durtâ Monastery and the Dayr-al-Ḳibâb. The Ṭâhirid Palace and its history.

UPSTREAM, running along the Tigris bank, between the Main Bridge of Boats and the Upper Bridge, lay the highroad (Ash-Shâriʿ) which gave its name to the adjacent quarter; the Shâriʿ here forming the eastern boundary of the Ḥarbîyah, which was the great suburb stretching to the northward of the City of Manṣûr, and balancing the Karkh Quarter on the south. In the year 580 (A.D. 1184), when Ibn Jubayr visited Baghdad, the Ḥarbîyah having fallen in great part to ruin, the Shâriʿ had risen to be one of the four main quarters of West Baghdad; but as originally laid out by Manṣûr, this consisted of the highroad only, which traversed a number of fiefs lying along the river bank. The first of these, near the Main Bridge, after passing the Offices of the Bridge Works, was the fief of Prince Sulaymân, and next it came that of Prince Ṣâliḥ, two sons of the Caliph Manṣûr. The street called Darb Sulaymân also took its name from the first of these princes—who, according to another account, died in 199 (A. D. 815), and was the grandson of Manṣûr—his palace standing in the street immediately opposite the bridge-head. Prince Ṣâliḥ, whose fief came next, is known by the surname of Al-Maskîn (the Poor Man), for unlike the other Abbasid princes he preferred piety and poverty to riches, and lived the saintly life of an ascetic.

Many other fiefs followed these along the river bank, and the Shâri', or highway, before coming to the road which led off to the Upper Bridge of Boats, passed through the great fief or suburb known as that of the Baghîyîn, who were the descendants of a certain Ḥafṣ ibn 'Othmân, the Palace of Ḥafṣ, which ultimately passed to the Ṭâhirids, standing in this district. The Baghîyîn Fief is described by Khaṭîb as lying between the Darb Siwâr[1] (the Street of the Bracelet) and the Rabaḍ or suburb of the Burjulânîyah—otherwise the Burjulânîyîn—so called from the people from Burjulân, a village near Wâsiṭ, who had come to settle here. Beyond this, and further upstream, came the market which occupied the south side of the Farḍah or Upper Harbour, where stood the Palace of the Ṭahirids in the midst of their fiefs.

The Ḥarbîyah, the name given to the great quarter of the town lying west of the Shâri' and north of the Syrian Gate of the City of Manṣûr, took its name from a certain Ḥarb, son of 'Abd-

[1] Pronunciation uncertain, as also the meaning here given.

Allah, a native of Balkh, who became a favourite of the Caliph Manṣûr, and was by him made chief of the Baghdad Police. Later on Manṣûr transferred Ḥarb to be Chief of Police in Mosul, when Ja'far, the son of the Caliph, was appointed to that governorship, and finally Ḥarb was sent to Tiflis, in Georgia, where he met his death in the year 147 (A. D. 764), at the hands of certain Turks who had rebelled in the neighbouring province of Darband on the Caspian. As described by Ya'ḳûbî towards the end of the third century (the ninth A. D.), the population of the Ḥarbîyah Quarter was then chiefly made up of Persian or Turk immigrants who had originally come to Baghdad in the train of the Abbasids, namely of people from the lands that are now generally known as Central Asia. Its broad markets and numerous streets were occupied by fiefs which Manṣûr had originally granted to men from Balkh, Merv, and Bukhârâ, to the countrymen of the Kâbul-Shâh, and to people from Khuwârizm (Khiva) or from Sughd—and each company had been placed under its head man and captain[1].

In general terms the Ḥarbîyah of West Baghdad (taken to include the Shâri') is described as lying opposite the Shammâsîyah Quarter of the eastern bank. The Ḥarbîyah had thus the Tigris to the east of it, the Syrian Gate and the semicircle of the adjacent wall belonging to the City of Manṣûr for its southern boundary, while the Trench of Ṭâhir occupied the north side. The western boundary was formed by the great Anbâr highroad, beyond

[1] Ibn Jubayr, 227; Baladhuri, 295; Ya'kubi, 249, 258; Istakhri, 83; Yakut, i. 550; ii. 234, 563; Khatib, folio 80 b.

which lay the Little Ṣarât, a minor canal (as already described), which flowed from the Trench of Ṭâhir back into the Great Ṣarât a short way above the Kûfah Gate. The Trench of Ṭâhir must have carried a considerable body of water—to judge by the masonry bridges needed for the roads to cross it—and it will be remembered that the Trench was the left arm at the bifurcation of the Upper Ṣarât, which occurred at a point less than one league down the course of this last, and at a distance of more than a mile above Baghdad. Not far from the point of its bifurcation the Trench, after throwing off the Little Ṣarât to the right, curved up round the Ḥarbîyah, and finally flowed out into the Tigris at the Farḍah or Upper Harbour[1]. By whom the Trench was first dug is not apparently recorded, but by its name it may be taken to have been the work of Ṭâhir, the founder of the Ṭâhirid dynasty, and general-in-chief of the army dispatched by Mamûn against his brother Amîn. The Trench must already have been in existence at the time of this siege of Baghdad, of the year 198 (A.D. 814), for Ṭâhir is then described as having his headquarter camp in a garden of the suburb beyond it.

The positions of places in the Ḥarbîyah Quarter can be approximately fixed by the courses of the three small canals—or water-conduits—which entered this suburb from the north-west across the Trench. Four gates here gave exit from the Ḥarbîyah to the Ḳaṭrabbul district; and the highroads, passing

[1] Yakut (iii. 378) by an oversight states that the Khandaḳ or Trench of Ṭâhir falls into the Tigris 'before the Baṣrah Gate of the City of Manṣûr': he is evidently here thinking of the Ṣarât, and he has been duly corrected by his epitomist, the author of the Marasid (ii. 151).

out through these gates, crossed the Trench by arched bridges of masonry (Ḳanṭarah) which bore respectively the names of the gates. Taking these in their order down the course of the Trench, the first was the Anbâr gate and bridge, by which the highroad coming from the Syrian Gate of the Round City went out to the town of Anbâr on the Euphrates, skirting the left or northern bank of the Ṣarât Canal, and then along the Nahr 'Îsâ. On the Trench outside the Anbâr Gate lay the garden where Ṭâhir had fixed his headquarter camp during the great siege, and here mention is made of a second gateway called the Garden Gate (Bâb-al-Bustân). The Anbâr Gate at the bridge is stated to have been set on fire by the people of Baghdad when Ṭâhir stormed the Round City; and according to one account it was in the garden outside this gate that the unfortunate Caliph Amîn was summarily put to death by Ṭâhir, after the failure of his attempt to escape from Baghdad. According to the description given by Ibn Serapion, a watercourse from the Nahr Baṭâṭiyâ crossed the Trench by the bridge at the Anbâr Gate, and entering the Ḥarbîyah passed down the Street of the Anbâr Gate to the Street of the Ram, where its waters failed, as will be more particularly described in the next chapter.

The next gate and bridge on the Trench was the Bâb-al-Ḥadîd (the Iron Gate)[1], opening within the Ḥarbîyah on the road of the Dujayl (Shâri' Dujayl). The second water-channel, from the Nahr Baṭâṭiyâ coming into Baghdad, passed down this road, but did not cross the Trench by the bridge at the Iron

[1] Often written in the MSS., in error, Bâb-al-*Jadîd*, 'the New Gate.'

Gate; for this watercourse had a separate bridge to itself, called the 'Abbârat-al-Kûkh (the Conduit at the Cabin or Reed-hut), which spanned the Trench between the Iron Gate and that of Ḥarb, the next below. The subsequent course of this, the Dujayl Road, Canal will enable us to plot out the positions of many buildings in the Ḥarbîyah existing at the time when Ibn Serapion wrote; and, after following a sinuous course, its surplus waters ultimately joined the little canal of the Syrian Gate, which, it will be remembered, flowed up northward from the Razîn Canal. In the account of the first siege of Baghdad the Iron Gate is celebrated for having served as the gibbet on which the head of the Caliph Amîn was exposed to public view, before being dispatched by Ṭâhir to Mamûn in Khurâsân, as indubitable proof of the death of his rival.

The next gate (and bridge) was that called the Bâb Ḥarb, which took its name from the founder of the Ḥarbîyah; and the third water-channel from the Baṭâṭiyâ, after crossing the Trench by this bridge, passed down the Street of the Ḥarb Gate, and ultimately discharged its waters also into the canal of the Syrian Gate. This third watercourse, as will be seen later, is an important factor for plotting out the eastern side of the Ḥarbîyah Quarter, being connected by a branch transversely with the Dujayl Road Canal. Beyond the Ḥarb Bridge, and on the northern side of the Trench, lay the Ḥarb Cemetery, in which among other celebrated shrines was the tomb of the Imâm Ibn Ḥanbal. In later times, when the Ḥarbîyah Quarter had shrunk to a moiety of its former size, the small suburb which still kept the old name of the Ḥarbîyah, centered round the old Ḥarb Gate, and, for the most part, lay only along the southern side of the Trench.

The lowest of the gates on the Trench was the Bâb Ḳaṭrabbul, and its bridge was known as the Ḳanṭarah Ruḥâ Umm Ja'far, namely the Bridge of the Mill of Umm Ja'far or Zubaydah, the wife of Hârûn-ar-Rashîd. Ḳaṭrabbul, from which the gate took its name, as already stated, comprised the whole of the great district in which the upper part of Western Baghdad was situated; and technically speaking this also included all the lands on the left or northern bank of the Ṣarât Canal, so that both the site occupied by the City of Manṣûr and the Ḥarbîyah were within the Ḳaṭrabbul district. The Ḳaṭrabbul Gate, as is evident from the accounts of the second siege of Baghdad (in the time of the Caliph Musta'în), must have stood at no great distance from the Tigris bank. Not far from it, but beyond the Trench, stood another gate known as the Bâb-al-Ḳaṭî'ah, or the Gate of the Fief. This fief had belonged to the Princess Zubaydah (whose mills near this have just been mentioned), and it was known indifferently either as the Zubaydîyah or as the Fief of Umm Ja'far. The more important moiety of the fief lay on the upper bank of the Trench, near where this last flowed out into the Tigris at the Upper Harbour, and the angle of land enclosed between the Tigris and the Trench was presumably shut off by a wall in which stood the Gate of the Fief. When originally granted, and possibly during later times also, the Zubaydîyah Fief extended some distance across the Trench to the southward, as is made evident from the description given by Ibn Serapion, and it must then have curved down almost to the Tigris bank at the Baghîyîn Fief below the Ṭâhirid Palace.

At the period of the second siege of Baghdad in the year 251 (A. D. 865), the great wall, which had been constructed in haste by order of the Caliph Musta'în, began in West Baghdad at the river bank, close to the gate of the Zubaydah Fief, and in the accounts of the siege operations we learn that the chief camp of the army from Sâmarrâ was pitched between this gate and the Bâb Ḳaṭrabbul on the Trench. The bridge outside the Ḳaṭrabbul Gate was the one on the Trench that withstood the longest the ruin which gradually overtook the whole of the Ḥarbîyah Quarter. When the author of the Marâṣid wrote, in about the year 700 (A. D. 1300), all the bridges and gates along the Trench, except this one, had completely disappeared. He states that he himself had seen the Bridge of Ḳaṭrabbul, as it was then called, adding that it was only pulled down a short time after the beginning of the eighth century (the fourteenth A. D.), and that when he saw it the bridge had consisted of two great arches constructed of kiln-burnt bricks, which, after the demolition, it was found worth while to carry away to be used again in other buildings [1].

The land afterwards occupied by the Zubaydîyah Fief had originally been granted by the Caliph Manṣûr to his son Ja'far (the same whom Ḥarb, the founder of the Ḥarbîyah, had served as Chief of Police when Ja'far was named Governor of Mosul), and from Ja'far the fief had passed to the Princess Zubaydah, who built herself a palace in the fief,

[1] Tabari, iii. 934, 1558, 1562; Ibn Serapion, 24, 27; Mas'udi, vi. 482; Yakut, i. 460; Marasid, ii. 432.

which last came to be known as the Ḳatî'iyah or the Zubaydîyah Quarter, being chiefly inhabited by the servants and followers of the princess during the years when her power was at its height. Later on the fief must have become the property of the reigning Caliph, for about a century after her time, in the year 306 (A.D. 918), the Zubaydîyah was occupied by the Caliph Muḳtadir, who bringing part of his Ḥarîm over to this side of the Tigris, temporarily established his residence here, the officials and his courtiers living in tents that were set up in the grounds of the fief.

As already stated, the Zubaydîyah Fief must originally have occupied both sides of the Trench, but its more important lands, in later times, lay on the north or left bank, coming down as far as the Tigris on the east, and stretching upstream to the gate leading out from the suburbs to the shrine of the Kâẓimayn, which was known as the Bâb-at-Tibn [1], or the Straw Gate. Canonically speaking this gate was the northern limit of Western Baghdad, for the doctors of the law held that the city proper occupied the land along the Tigris 'from the Bâb-at-Tibn to the Ṣarât Canal,' Karkh being ruled to form a suburb. The Zubaydîyah Fief became in later times a very populous quarter, and as such possessed its own Friday mosque. This, according to the account given by Khaṭîb, was first erected in the year 379 (A.D. 989), in consequence of a vision vouchsafed to a certain pious woman of this quarter.

[1] *Tibn* is the broken straw, reduced almost to powder, and used for fodder, which is left after the treading out of the corn; it presents therefore a totally different appearance to our sheaf of long straw-stalks.

She declared that in her dream she had seen the Prophet Muḥammad praying in the little oratory which at this date stood in the fief, and that a celestial voice had foretold to her the day of her death. Subsequent miracles confirmed the authenticity of her statements, the mark of the Prophet's hand was found on the wall of the building, and the woman died at the date named by the voice. With the special permission of the reigning Caliph, Ṭâi', the little oratory was therefore rebuilt on an enlarged plan, an Imâm was appointed to conduct the Friday prayers, and the new Jâmi' was counted as one of the chief congregational mosques of Baghdad[1].

Both the mosque and the adjacent Quarter of the Zubaydîyah must have fallen somewhat early into ruin, for by the year 700 (A.D. 1300), when the author of the *Marâṣid* wrote, this mosque had entirely disappeared, though he states that the ruins of the quarter might still be traced along the river bank in the upper part of the city. Twice during the preceding centuries this region had suffered severely from the inundations of the Tigris, and it

[1] Ibn-al-Athir (ix. 48), under the year 379, mentions the building of this mosque, which he names the Jâmi'-al-Ḳaṭî'ah. It is to be noted that in West Baghdad *Al-Ḳaṭî'ah*, 'the Fief,' always refers to the Zubaydîyah, while in Eastern Baghdad *Al-Ḳaṭî'ah* was more especially the 'Ajamî or Persian Fief. On the occasion of describing the Zubaydîyah, Yakut (iv. 141) mentions a second Ḳallâyîn Canal—as of the Zubaydîyah—the name being identical with that of the better known stream in Karkh (see p. 81). The author of the Marasid, however (ii. 432), corrects the name to Nahr *Ḳallâtîn*; and this second Ḳallâyîn Canal would seem to be a pure invention, on the part of Yakut, who misread the MS. of Khatib, where the name given is not Ḳallâyîn, but *Ḳâfilâyîn*, or some such name (compare the British Museum MS. of Khatib, folio 102 a, with the Paris MS., folio 34 b, for the reading of the MSS. vary). This last canal, if it really ever existed, was probably a minor offshoot of the Trench of Ṭâhir.

would further appear that by the changing of its bed (as will be mentioned when we come to speak of the disappearance of the so-called tomb of Ibn Ḥanbal) the river may ultimately have come to flow over part of the site of the former Fief of Zubaydah. Adjacent to the Zubaydîyah Quarter had been the Zuhayrîyah, with the Fiefs of the Mawlas or Freedmen of the Princess Zubaydah. This Zuhayrîyah (for there was another near the Kûfah Gate, as already mentioned on p. 59) was the fief of a certain Zuhayr ibn Muḥammad of Abiward in Khurâsân, and it stretched along the old wall of the Zubaydîyah between the Straw Gate (Bâb-at-Tibn) and the Ḳaṭrabbul Gate. Into it had opened the Bâb-aṣ-Ṣaghîr (the Little Gate), but when Yâḳût wrote in 623 (A.D. 1226) both this gate and the fief of Zuhayr had long since disappeared, so that no one then knew what had been their exact positions. The great cemeteries beyond the Tibn and Ḥarb Gates, with the adjacent Shrine of the Kâẓimayn, will be described in a following chapter, but occupying ground between these graveyards and the Zubaydîyah Quarter, in early times there had existed a suburb called the Rabaḍ of Ḥanîfah, or of Abu Ḥanîfah (for the authorities differ as to the name), so named after one of the nobles of the court of Manṣûr, who must not be confounded with the more celebrated Imâm, Abu Ḥanîfah. This suburb is described as having stretched from the Ḳuraysh Cemetery to the Tibn Gate and the Ṭâhirid Ḥarîm; and in it was the Palace (Dâr) of 'Umârah ibn Ḥamzah, freedman of the Caliph Manṣûr, the spot where his palace came to be built having of old been a garden planted, report said, by one of the

Persian kings who had reigned before the days of Islam. At the period when the *Marâṣid* was written, namely about the year 700 (A. D. 1300), all the houses here had already fallen to ruin, and the waste land was cultivated for cornfields, but in the earlier times of the Caliphate this region had been as densely populated as Karkh and the southern quarters of West Baghdad.

To the north of the Zubaydîyah, and lying on the river bank opposite the Shammâsîyah Gate in East Baghdad, stood the great Christian monastery of Durtâ, which is frequently mentioned in the earlier chronicles. It is described as having been at one time crowded with monks, and it possessed a stately well-built church. Near by was also another similar establishment called Dayr-al-Ḳibâb (the Monastery of the Cupolas), and in the year 334 (A.D. 946) the Durtâ Monastery was a place of sufficient importance to have become for a time the residence of the Caliph Mustakfî, showing that it must have been a building of no inconsiderable extent. By the year 700 (A.D. 1300), however, through the changes in the course of the river, both these monasteries had been swept away, no trace of them remaining when the author of the Marâṣid wrote his epitome of Yâḳût[1].

Partly enclosed by the older and lower part of the Zubaydîyah Fief, and standing on the southern bank of the Trench so as to overlook the Tigris and the Upper Harbour, was the great Palace of

[1] See Plan, No. III; Ya'kubi, 250; Khatib, folios 67 a, 102 a, b; Baladhuri, 296; 'Arib, 71; Yakut, ii. 521, 565, 659, 685, 750, 964; iv. 132, 141, 142; Mushtarik, 200; Marasid, i. 429, 459; ii. 151, 432; Mas'udi, viii. 391.

Ṭâhir, already frequently mentioned, at one time general of the armies of Mamûn, and afterwards independent ruler of Khurâsân, who bore the surname of Dhû-l-Yamînayn or Ambidexter. This palace was one of the most notable buildings in West Baghdad, and during many years was the residence of the Governor of the City. Hence it came to be considered in a certain degree as a royal palace, and had the rights of sanctuary granted to it, where offenders might gain a safe refuge, and on this account was known as the Ṭâhirid Ḥarîm or Precinct.

The Ṭâhirid family was one of the most important of the semi-independent princely houses that rose to power under the shadow of the Caliphate in the third century (the ninth A.D.). The direct descendants of Ṭâhir 'Ambidexter,' above mentioned, became independent rulers of Khurâsân, and a cousin, Isḥâḳ ibn Ibrâhîm, was made Governor of Baghdad during the reigns of Wâthiḳ and Mutawakkil, when the seat of the Caliphate had been removed to Sâmarrâ. This Isḥâḳ had previously been Chief of Police under Mamûn, and he died in the year 235 (A.D. 850). Later on another member of the same house, Muḥammad ibn 'Abd-Allah, was Governor of Baghdad in 251 (A.D. 865), during the short reign of Musta'în, and it was he who organized the defence of the older capital during the second of its great sieges, when the Caliph Musta'în, having fled from Sâmarrâ to Baghdad, was pursued thither, besieged, and finally deposed by the Turk bodyguard who had espoused the cause of his cousin Mu'tazz.

A generation later, at the time of the final return

of the Caliphs to Baghdad, in the reign of Mu'taḍid, the Ṭâhirid family having died out, their Ḥarîm or palace became a secondary residence of the Caliphs—who by this date had already established their more permanent abode in the new palaces of East Baghdad—and Mu'taḍid dying in 289 (A.D. 902), his body was brought across the Tigris and buried in the celebrated Marble House (the Dâr-ar-Rikhâm) of the Ṭâhirid Ḥarîm. 'Alî Muktafî, the next Caliph, who died in 295 (A.D. 908), was likewise buried here, probably also Muḳtadir, his successor, who was slain in 320 (A.D. 932) at the Shammâsîyah Gate of East Baghdad by the bodyguard, when his corpse was left for a time unburied, till at last the people by night carried it away and gave it decent sepulture. During the next few years puppet Caliphs were set up and deposed, one after another, at the pleasure of the Captain of the Bodyguard, and the Ṭâhirid Ḥarîm became a state prison where the deposed Caliph and his probable successor in the Caliphate lived together side by side. Thus in 333 (A.D. 944) Mustakfî was brought from the Ṭâhirid Palace to ascend the throne of Muttaḳî, who had been blinded and deposed; both Muttaḳî and the Caliph Ḳâhir, who had suffered the fate of Muttaḳî in 322 (A.D. 934), remaining to end their days within the Ḥarîm of Ṭâhir, where they were buried with other members of their house.

A couple of centuries later, in 530 (A.D. 1136), the Ṭâhirid Ḥarîm was plundered by the populace of Baghdad at the close of the two months' siege which the Caliph Manṣûr Râshid suffered as the penalty for defying the power of the Saljûḳ Sultan Mas'ûd. Much wealth is said then to have been carried off from the great palace, and its devastation was before long completed by the inundation of the Tigris, which occurred in the year 614 (A.D. 1217). Yâḳût, writing in 623 (A.D. 1226), states that the Ṭâhirid Ḥarîm in his day stood ruined and deserted amongst the remains of former houses and palaces. The adjacent quarter, however, was still in part inhabited, and a market was held in some of the streets, these forming as it were a separate township which stood solitary, apart from the other quarters of West Baghdad, surrounded by its own wall[1].

[1] Khatib, 87 b; Mas'udi, viii. 212, 288, 351, 379, 383; Yakut, ii. 255, 783; Ibn-al-Athir, ix. 26; xii. 217.

CHAPTER X

THE ḤARBÎYAH QUARTER

Road to the Upper Bridge of Boats. The Canal of the Syrian Gate. The Slaves' House. The Ḥarb Gate Road and the Suburb of Abu 'Awn. The later Ḥarbîyah and its Mosque. The Quadrangles of Abu-l-'Abbâs and Shabîb. The Dujayl Road. The Persian Quarters of the Ḥarbîyah. The Abnâ and the Dihḳâns. The Abu-l-Jawn Bridge and the Market of the Syrian Gate. The three Arcades near the highroad to the Upper Bridge of Boats. The Syrian Gate, the Prison, and the Cemetery. The Garden of Ḳass and the Anbâr Gate Road. The Quarter of the Lion and the Ram. The Shrine of Ibrâhîm-al-Ḥarbî. The Bukhariot Mosque and the Ramalîyah.

IMMEDIATELY below the Ṭâhirid Ḥarîm the Upper Bridge of Boats crossed the Tigris, to which led the highroad from the Syrian Gate of the City of Manṣûr, passing through the Ḥarbîyah Quarter diagonally. This great road to the Upper Bridge, Ya'ḳûbî at the close of the third century (the ninth A.D.) describes as having markets along its whole length, both to the right hand and the left, and from his contemporary, Ibn Serapion, we learn that a small canal ran more or less parallel with this road, in the space between it and the river bank, from the Syrian Gate to 'the outskirt of the Zubaydîyah,' where its waters finally disappeared in irrigation channels. This is known as the Canal of the Syrian Gate, and as already mentioned, it was derived from the Razîn Canal, at a point near where this last was crossed by the Kûfah highroad, being carried over the Ṣarât by the Old Bridge, whence it flowed round outside the wall of the Round City from the Kûfah Gate, past the Syrian Gate, up to the Zubaydîyah Fief. This channel, it will be noticed, flowed from south to north (from the Old Bridge to near the western end of the Upper Bridge of Boats), and into it drained the two canals from the Baṭâṭiyâ, which, as already described, entered the Ḥarbîyah, the one by the road of the Ḥarb Gate, and the other by the Dujayl highroad.

Entering the Ḥarbîyah Quarter from the Upper Bridge of Boats, and taking the highroad to the Syrian Gate, the Ḥarîm of Ṭâhir was on the right hand, while on the left lay the congeries of buildings called the Slaves' House (Dâr-ar-Raḳîḳ)[1], to which the thoroughfare of the Shâri' Dâr-ar-Raḳîḳ went crosswise, coming påst the Ṭâhirid Ḥarîm from the Ḳaṭrabbul Bridge, this being the direct road from the Tibn Gate beyond the Trench. The Slaves' House had been originally used in the days of Manṣûr as barracks for his domestic slaves, who were bought and imported from the Turk borderlands, to be placed on their arrival in Baghdad under the superintendence of his chamberlain Rabi'; and also near the Slaves' House Ya'ḳûbî mentions the fief where the pages (Ghulâms) of the chamberlain had their lodgings. In course of time the

[1] In the MSS. of Khatib this name is generally written Dâr-ad-Daḳîḳ, which would mean 'the Flour House'; but from numerous passages in Ya'kubi and Yakut, this is evidently a clerical error.

Dâr-ar-Raḳîḳ gave its name to the surrounding suburb, and the name continued in use down to the seventh century (the thirteenth A. D.), for when Yâḳût wrote a market was still held in this quarter, though many of the neighbouring houses had then fallen to ruin. Further, it would appear that the portion of the Zubaydîyah Fief which lay on the south side of the Trench had come to be more commonly known by the name of the Dâr-ar-Raḳîḳ, as early as the fifth century (the eleventh A. D.), when Khaṭîb was living in Baghdad.

Next to the quarter of the Slaves' House, and connected with it by the crossroad from the Ṭâhirid Ḥarîm, was the fief of Abu 'Awn, which Ya'ḳûbî describes as lying nearer the river bank and the quarter of the Shâri'. The palace of Ibn Abu 'Awn, son of the original owner of the fief, is stated by Ibn Serapion to have stood on the road named after him, along which passed the canal from the Ḥarb Gate. The road of Ibn Abu 'Awn, therefore, would appear to have been a side street leading to this fief and turning off the highroad which went from the Upper Bridge to the Syrian Gate. This crossroad of Ibn Abu 'Awn must further have been the continuation of the road coming from the Ḥarb Gate, down which the canal, above mentioned, passed, and the highroad from the Syrian Gate to the Upper Bridge of Boats appears to have crossed this Canal by the arched masonry bridge which Ya'ḳûbî speaks of as the Ḳanṭarah-at-Tabbânîn (the Straw-merchants' Bridge)[1]. Abu 'Awn, from whom the fief and the subsequent suburb received their name, was a native

[1] Ya'kubi, 248, 249; Ibn Serapion, 25, 27, 28; Yakut, ii. 750; ii. 231; Marasid, ii. 85; Khatib, 79 a, 103 a.

of Jurjân in Khurâsân, a freedman of the Caliph Manṣûr, and Ibn Abu 'Awn, his son, was twice Governor of Egypt, namely in the years 134 and 138 (A.D. 751 and 755). In the following century another member of this family, Muḥammad ibn Abu 'Awn, commanded a body of troops in the service of the Caliph Musta'în during the second siege of Baghdad, namely in the year 251 (A.D. 865).

The highroad from the Upper Bridge of Boats to the Syrian Gate of the Round City crossed diagonally the eastern part of the great northern suburb, the whole of which in early times had been known as the Ḥarbîyah. In later times, however, the name Ḥarbîyah came to be used in a more restricted sense, and was applied solely to that part of the northern suburb lying immediately below the Ḥarb Bridge, and which was traversed by the road of the Ḥarb Gate. This quarter by the fourth century (the tenth A.D.) came to possess its own Friday mosque, which had originally been built for an oratory by one of the Abbasid princes during the Caliphate of Muṭî', who had had some scruple in allowing congregational prayers to be said here. It was, therefore, only in the reign of Ḳâdir, namely in the month Rabî' II of the year 383 (A.D. 993), that a decree was obtained erecting this minor mosque into a Jâmi' (as a great mosque for the Friday prayers is termed); and Khaṭîb, writing in the following century, adds that he himself had frequently attended the Friday prayers here. When Yâḳût wrote in 623 (A.D. 1226), though many of the surrounding quarters had in greater part then fallen to ruin, the later Ḥarbîyah, namely the suburb of the Ḥarb Gate, remained a populous quarter, shut in by its own wall, with the Friday mosque and many well supplied markets. It stood, he adds, 'like a township in the midst of the waste,' and a distance of almost two miles, covered by ruins, separated it from the quarter of the Baṣrah Gate, to which belonged the great Mosque of Manṣûr. In the previous century, when Ibn Jubayr visited the Ḥarbîyah, it is described as the highest up of the then inhabited quarters of West Baghdad, and beyond it there were only to be seen some villages that were considered as outside the city limits[1].

The Canal of the Ḥarb Gate Road, as already stated, was crossed at the Straw-merchants' Bridge by the highroad going from the Upper Bridge of Boats to the Syrian Gate, and after passing the suburb of Abu 'Awn, this canal reached the two quadrangles (Murabba'ah) named respectively after Abu-l-'Abbâs and Shabîb, through which it took its course before finally discharging its waters into the Canal of the Syrian Gate. Abu-l-'Abbâs of Ṭûs, or of Abiward (both well-known cities of Khurâsân), after whom the first quadrangle took its name, was one of the nobles who attended the Caliph Manṣûr; and his quadrangle occupied land where, before the foundation of Baghdad, the ancient village of Wardânîyah had stood. Shabîb, a native of Marv-ar-Rûdh[2], from whom the neighbouring quadrangle took its name, is variously given by our authorities as Ibn Wâj or Ibn Râḥ (the latter name, however, is probably only a clerical error); he was a favourite

[1] Khatib, 102 b; Yakut, ii. 234; Ibn Jubayr, 227.

[2] A couple of hundred miles south of Great Merv, and on the upper stream of the Merv river.

officer of Manṣûr, and is known to history as the slayer of the too powerful general Abu Muslim—to whom the Abbasids had mainly owed their accession to the Caliphate—Shabîb thus giving his master a signal proof of devoted zeal for the new dynasty[1].

Another thoroughfare, which ran parallel with the Ḥarb Gate Road, went across the older Ḥarbîyah, coming down from the Iron Gate (Bâb-al-Ḥadîd). This was known as the Dujayl Road (Shâri' Dujayl), from the canal of that name which flowed along it, having crossed the Ṭâhirid Trench by a small aqueduct known as the Conduit of the Cabin or Hut ('Abbârat-al-Kûkh), which spanned the Trench near the Iron Gate on the side towards the Ḥarb Gate. After passing for some distance down the Dujayl Road the watercourse reached the Quadrangle of the Persians (Murabba'at-al-Furs), where a branch canal went off to the place known as the Shops of the Persian Nobles (Dukkân-al-Abnâ); but whether this minor canal struck off to the right or to the left is not known, and before long it ran dry, having no exit from the quarter. The Ḥarbîyah, as has already been said, was originally for the most part settled by the Persian followers of the Abbasids, and both the places just named recall this fact. The Persian Quadrangle is described as having been situated at no great distance from the Quadrangle of Abu-l-'Abbâs, already described, and it was so called in memory of certain Persians, to whom the Caliph Manṣûr had here granted fiefs. The quarter round it was known as the Suburb of the Persians (Rabaḍ-

[1] Yakut, iii. 489; iv. 485; Khatib, folio 79 a, b; Baladhuri, 296; Ibn-al-Athir, v. 363.

al-Furs), and adjacent thereto was the Khuwârizmîyah Suburb, where the troops from Khuwârizm (the modern Khiva) had been settled by Manṣûr, while the quarter of the men of Merv (called Al-Marâwizah) lay next to this.

The suburb called the Rabaḍ 'Othmân ibn Nuhayk, which was included in the quarter of the Khuwârizmians, took its name from a certain 'Othman who was captain of the Horse Guards in the reign of Manṣûr; and Rushayd, another of the freedmen of this Caliph, gave his name to the adjacent Rabaḍ Rushayd. In addition to these, Yâḳût gives the names of various other suburbs of this quarter, which were called after the nobles, to whom the lands here had originally been granted in fief by Manṣûr and his successors. The Abnâ, from whom the shops (Dukkân) above mentioned took their name, are said to have been Persian nobles who had adopted Arab nationality, for the term *Abnâ* (the plural in Arabic of *Ibn*) is explained as meaning the 'sons of the Dihḳâns.' These Dihḳâns were the old territorial Persian chiefs who were already settled in Mesopotamia at the time of the Moslem conquest, many of whom having accepted Islam were left in peaceable possession of their lands, and under the Abbasid Caliphs were employed in the various offices or government Dîwâns[1].

The Dujayl Road Canal, after traversing these various Persian fiefs, turned off at right angles, flowing down towards the Syrian Gate, and first passed under the bridge called the Ḳanṭarah-Abu-l-Jawn. This took its name from the Dihḳân or Persian noble who

[1] Ibn Serapion, 27; Yakut, ii. 750, 751; iv. 480, 485; Mas'udi, iv. 188; Mafatih-al-'Ulum, 119.

had owned the village of Sharafânîyah that had occupied this site before Baghdad was built; and some palms which had belonged to the old village were still standing near this bridge in the year 450 (A.D. 1058), close to which stood the palace (Dâr) of a certain Sa'îd-al-Khaṭîb. The Abu-l-Jawn Bridge in all probability was on the Dujayl road, near where it joined the highroad which ran direct from the Syrian Gate up into the Harbîyah Quarter. Ya'ḳûbî names this the Market of the Syrian Gate, and here all kinds of wares and merchandise were to be found exposed for sale in the shops, both to right and to left, along the thoroughfare, from which also numerous streets branched into neighbouring courts and alleys, each being named after the people of the province from which its inhabitants had originally come. Near the Abu-l-Jawn Bridge stood the Orphan School (Kuttâb-al-Yatamâ); and here a transverse watercourse struck off from the canal of the Dujayl highroad, flowing into the canal of the Ḥarb Gate highroad (already described), which latter it joined at the Quadrangle of Shabîb. This connecting branch canal, therefore, must have crossed under both the Market of the Syrian Gate and the highroad running from the Upper Bridge of Boats to the Syrian Gate, probably by culverts near the Shabîb Quadrangle[1].

On or near the highroad to the Upper Bridge of

[1] Ibn Serapion, 27; Khatib, 79 b; Ya'kubi, 248; Tabari, iii. 279; Yakut, iii. 277. In the MSS. of Khatib the name of Abu-l-Jawn is often incorrectly written Abu-l-*Jawz*. In my translation of Ibn Serapion (*J. R. A. S.*, 1895, p. 294) for 'Scribes' read *School* of the Orphans. The word *Kuttâb*, as Professor De Goeje has pointed out to me, has evidently here this meaning, and is not to be taken as the plural of *Kâtib*, 'scribe.'

Boats, and in a line between the Quadrangle of Shabîb and the Syrian Gate, stood three Ṭâḳât—archways or arcades—which were called after their several builders. The nearest of these to the Quadrangle of Shabîb, into which it led by a thoroughfare, was the Ṭâḳât-al-'Akkî, which gave its name to the street called Sikkat-al-'Akkî, having been built by a certain Muḳâtil, of the Yamanite tribe of 'Akk, one of the generals of the Caliph Manṣûr, from whom Muḳâtil had received the grant of a fief in this quarter. This is said to have been the first of the arcades to be built in Baghdad, and next to it came the Ṭâḳât-al-Ghiṭrîf. Ghiṭrîf was at one time governor of the Yaman province, he being brother of the Princess Khayzurân, mother of the two Caliphs Hâdî and Hârûn-ar-Rashîd, to whom therefore Ghiṭrîf stood in the relationship of maternal uncle. The Ghiṭrîf archways were the second of those built in Baghdad, and adjacent to them were the Ṭâḳât Abu Suwayd, the latest to be built. These occupied the fief and suburb of Abu Suwayd, surnamed Al Jârûd, and they traversed part of the cemetery which lay immediately outside the Syrian Gate.

The Syrian Gate of the City of Manṣûr gave egress to the three principal highroads traversing the northern suburbs of West Baghdad, two of which have already been mentioned. On the right went the road to the Upper Bridge of Boats with the archways just described; and next this came the road into the Ḥarbîyah Quarter, which is known as the Market of the Syrian Gate; while on the left was the highroad going towards the Anbâr Gate on the Trench of Ṭâhir. Fronting the Syrian Gate stood the great jail, built by the Caliph Manṣûr, and known as the Prison of the Syrian Gate. Down to the latter half of the third century (the ninth A.D.) this continued to be the chief jail of West Baghdad, for in the year 255 (A.D. 869), when Sulaymân the Ṭâhirid was governor of Baghdad (the Caliphs then being resident at Sâmarrâ), the chronicle relates how this prison was broken open by the mob during an insurrection, and much trouble ensued in the recapture of the malefactors who had escaped. The adjacent Cemetery of the Syrian Gate is stated to have been the earliest of the burial grounds in West Baghdad, having been laid out by Manṣûr after he had finished the Round City. In course of time much of its area came to be built over by the houses of the Ḥarbîyah and adjacent quarters, though as late as the beginning of the fourth century (the tenth A.D.) mention is made of this cemetery as a place where personages of note were still buried.

In front of the Syrian Gate, and across the cemetery, ran the small canal so often mentioned, which came up from the Kûfah Gate and ultimately lost itself in the lower limits of the Zubaydîyah Fief to the northward. Into this canal, at some distance to the right of the gate towards the Tigris bank, flowed the surplus waters of the Canal of the Ḥarb Gate Road, while to the left of the gate flowed in the discharge of the Canal of the Dujayl Road. The lower portion of the Canal of the Dujayl Road, after turning down past the Orphan School (already described), must have crossed through culverts under both the highroad of the Market of the Syrian Gate and the road leading to the Anbâr Gate, after passing behind (to the north-west of) the prison.

Near here must have been the Road of the Palace of Hânî (Shâri' Ḳaṣr Hânî), mentioned by Ibn Serapion, next to which on the canal came the Garden of Al-Ḳass in the suburb of that name, said to have been called after a freedman of the Caliph Manṣûr[1].

The highroad from the Syrian Gate to the Anbâr Gate would appear to have passed to the north of the Garden of Ḳass, and it probably ran between this and the Palace of Hânî above mentioned. The great triangular space of ground lying between the three points marked by the Kûfah, the Syrian, and the Anbâr Gates—and which was bounded by the Little Ṣarât and part of the Syrian Gate Canal on two sides, with the Ḥarbîyah Quarter on the third—was occupied by a number of roads and crossroads, which appear to have come in the following order. Beginning from the Trench of Ṭâhir at the Anbâr Gate, the Anbâr highroad, as already stated, led direct to the Syrian Gate of the City of Manṣûr, and along its upper part ran the water-channel which retained the name of the Baṭâṭiyâ Canal, and which had crossed the Trench by the Bridge of the Anbâr Gate. This channel, after passing some short way

[1] Ibn Serapion, 27; Ya'kubi, 241, 247, 248; 'Arib, 47; Khatib, folio 111 b; Yakut, iii. 488, 489; Ibn-al-Athir, vii. 137. The name is also written *Al-Ḳuss*, and it is somewhat puzzling to find that according to Tabari (iii. 274) there was already a 'Bustân-al-Ḳass,' near Baghdad, before the Moslem city was founded. Further, there was a Dayr or monastery, the head of which gave the Caliph Manṣûr advice in the matter of the site for the projected capital. In this passage *Bustân-al-Ḳass* would appear to mean simply 'the Priest's Garden,' the last word not being taken as a proper name, and this recalls a former passage in Tabari (iii. 273), where mention is made of the *Bay'ah Ḳass* (without the article), presumably the 'Priest's Church.'

down the Anbâr Road, turned off and finally lost itself in what is known as the Road of the Ram (Shâri'-al-Kabsh), which appears to have been a thoroughfare branching from the Anbâr Road, immediately within the gate, and running down towards the bank of the Little Ṣarât Canal.

The quarter here was known as Al-Kabsh-wa-l-Asad (the Ram and the Lion), and as late as the beginning of the fifth century (the eleventh A.D.) the houses and streets of the suburbs of West Baghdad, on the highroad towards Anbâr, extended as far as this line. Soon after that date, however, the region came to be deserted, for Khaṭîb states that while in his youth this region had still been occupied by many houses, and had even possessed a crowded market, yet when in later life, namely about the year 450 (A.D. 1058), he had come to visit the place, only arable fields were then to be seen lying at a considerable distance from the nearest houses of the suburb. In explanation of its curious name, Yâḳût writes that the Ram and the Lion originally represented two separate streets leading into the neighbouring suburb of the Naṣrîyah, but which in his day had long since disappeared. The tomb of Ibrâhîm-al-Ḥarbî stood in this quarter, on the highroad at no great distance from the Anbâr Gate, and it is spoken of by Mas'ûdî in the fourth century (the tenth A.D.) in connexion with these streets of the Ram and the Lion, when mentioning a burial which took place in the cemetery near the Anbâr Gate. Ibrâhîm-al-Ḥarbî (that is of the Ḥarbîyah Quarter) had been a celebrated traditionist, and became a saint, whose shrine was a notable place of visitation. He had been one of the most famous of the pupils of Ibn Ḥanbal, the great Sunnî Imâm, and dying in the year 285 (A.D. 898) was buried in his own house, which stood on the Anbâr Road[1]. His tomb still existed as late as the year 700 (A.D. 1300), but at that date, as was to be expected from the account of this quarter already quoted from Khaṭîb, the author of the *Marâṣid* states that it had come to stand solitary in the midst of the fields, all the neighbouring houses having long ago disappeared.

Among the fiefs of this suburb, detailed by Ya'ḳûbî, two other roads are mentioned, namely the Road of the Cages (Darb-al-Aḳfâṣ) and the Fullers' Road (Darb-al-Ḳaṣṣârîn), and adjacent thereto stood the Bukhariot Mosque (Masjid-al-Bukhârîyah), celebrated for its green minaret. According to Ṭabarî, the Road of the Cages occupied the site of a village called Al-Khaṭṭâbîyah, that had existed here before the Caliph Manṣûr began to build the Round City, the site of which originally stretched as far as the neighbouring gate of the Darb-an-Nûrah (the Chalk Road). Some of the ancient palm-trees of the village were still growing here at the close of the second century (the eighth A.D.) in the reign of Amîn; and from the author of the *Marâṣid* we learn that the Khaṭṭâbîyah had stood on the bank of the Little Ṣarât, near where the Ram and Lion Quarter, with the tomb of Ibrâhîm-al-Ḥarbî, afterwards came to be built. Finally, beyond this, and probably on the northern side of the Anbâr Road, lay the open space known as the Ramalîyah (the Sandy Place), for this

[1] In Marasid, ii. 85, line 8, the words 'Bâb-al-Anbâr of the City of Al-Manṣûr' must undoubtedly be a mistake for *Bâb-ash-Shâm*, the Syrian Gate, of the Round City.

was the boundary of the Ḥarbîyah in the direction of the Anbâr Gate, at the time when Ya'ḳûbî wrote, namely at the close of the third century (the ninth A.D.)[1].

[1] Ibn Serapion, 27; Khatib, folio 67a; Ya'kubi, 247, 248; Yakut, ii. 235; iv. 233; Marasid, i. 358; ii. 85; Mas'udi, viii. 184; Tabari, iii. 279.

CHAPTER XI

THE QUARTERS OF THE MUḤAWWAL GATE

The Four Markets. The Naṣrîyah Quarter. The 'Attâbîyah Quarter; its watered silks and papermakers. The Dâr-al-Ḳazz or the Silk House. The Upper Barley Gate. The 'Atîkîyah Suburb: the Ḳaḥṭabah Road and Suburb. The Palace of 'Abd-al-Wahhâb and his Suburb. The 'Abbâsîyah Island. The Patrician's Mill. The story of the Greek Patrician. The Muḥawwal Road. The Fief of 'Îsâ and the Muḥawwal Gate. The Suburb of Haylânah. The Suburb of Ḥumayd, son of Ḳaḥṭabah. Bridges of the Mills, of China, and of 'Abbâs, leading to the 'Abbâsîyah Island. The Bridge of the Greeks and the Fief of the Farrâshes. The Old Tank. The Bridges on the Great Ṣarât and Karkhâyâ. The Kunâsah and the Market for Beasts of Burden. The Yâsirîyah Quarter.

THE Garden of Ḳass, on the lowest reach of the Dujayl Road Canal, has already been mentioned, and near this stood the Four Markets, which was the centre of one of the most populous quarters of West Baghdad.

These Four Markets were known under the Persian-Arabic name of the Shâr Sûḳ, or the Shahâr Sûj—the first word being the Persian numeral *Chahâr*, 'four,' with *Sûj* for *Sûḳ*, in Arabic meaning 'a market'—and they had been built by a certain Al-Haytham, a native of Khurâsân, a captain of troops in the days of the Caliph Manṣûr, after whom the place was also called by the Arabs the Sûḳ

Map VI. To face page 136.

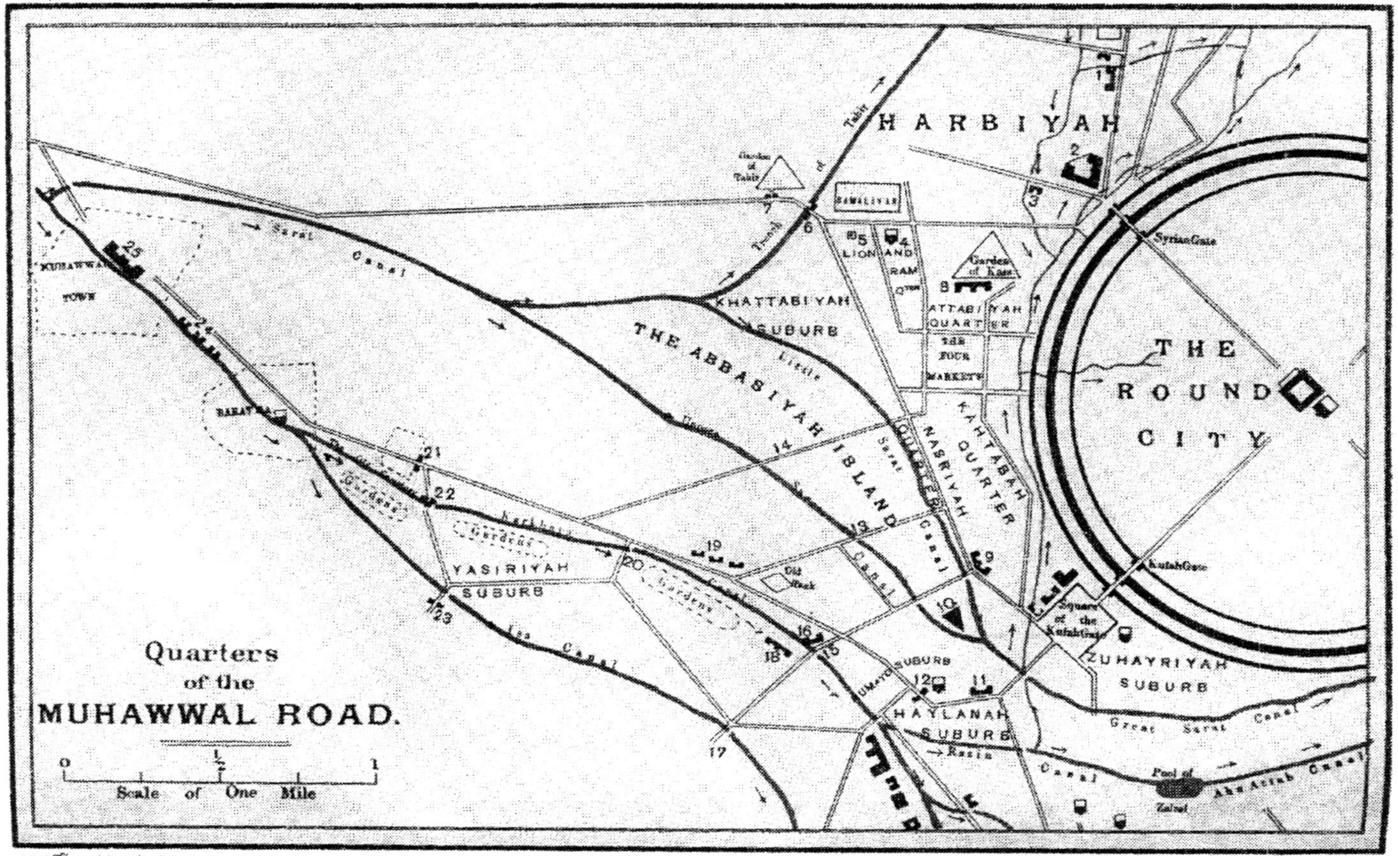

H. V. Darbishire 1900

REFERENCES TO MAP No. VI.

1. Palace of Sa'îd-al-Khaṭîb and the Orphan School.
2. The Prison of the Syrian Gate.
3. Road and Palace of Hânî.
4. The Bukhariot Mosque.
5. The Shrine of Ibrâhîm-al-Ḥarbî.
6. The Anbâr Gate and Bridge.
7. The Garden Gate.
8. Dâr-al-Ḳazz (the Silk House) and the Street of Ghâmish.
9. Palace and Market of 'Abd-al-Wahhâb.
10. The Patrician's Mill and Bridge of the Mills.
11. Palace in Fief of 'Îsâ.
12. The Muḥawwal Gate and Mosque.
13. The China Bridge.
14. Bridge of 'Abbâs.
15. Bridge of the Greeks.
16. House of the Farrâshes.
17. Bridge of the Greek Woman
18. Palace of Ka'yûbah.
19. Houses of the Persians.
20. Bridge and Street of Rocks.
21. The Kunâsah Gate and Place of the Sweepings, the Tying-place for beasts of burden.
22. Gate of Abu Ḳabîsah and the Jews' Bridge (Ḳanṭarah-al-Yahûd).
23. The Yâsirîyah Gate, Bridge, and Quarter.
24. Place of the Tanners.
25. Palace of Mu'taṣim at Muhawwal Town.

(or Market of) Al-Haytham. From the time of its foundation it became a great emporium of merchandise, being soon surrounded by streets and lanes with warehouses, forming a quarter by itself. In the middle of the fourth century (the tenth A.D.) the Four Markets were apparently rebuilt, for they are mentioned by Ḥamd-Allah as among the celebrated constructions undertaken by the Buyid Prince 'Aḍud-ad-Dawlah. Near the Four Markets stood a minaret which Khaṭîb mentions as having been built here by Ḥumayd ibn 'Abd-al-Ḥamîd, who owned the Ḳaṣr Ḥumayd on the Tigris bank, near the Lower Bridge of Boats, which has already been described. The suburb of the Four Markets stood at some little distance to the south-west of the older Ḥarbîyah, and round it, connected by market streets, lay three other quarters, which are frequently mentioned in the later history of Baghdad, namely the Naṣrîyah, the 'Attâbîyah, and the Dâr-al-Ḳazz (the Silk House). At the time when Yâḳût wrote—namely in 623 (A.D. 1226)—these were still very populous quarters, being then chiefly celebrated for the manufacture of an excellent kind of paper; but all round them lay the ruins of former suburbs marked by the lines of deserted streets and fallen houses.

The Naṣrîyah, otherwise called the Suburb of Naṣr ibn 'Abd-Allah, must have occupied a considerable extent of ground. A thoroughfare led thence towards the Dujayl highroad, but there is some question as to its exact position. The 'Attâbîyah or 'Attâbîyîn Quarter, which lay to the north of the Four Markets, was famous for the manufacture of the 'Attâbî stuffs, woven of mixed silk and cotton in variegated colours, which were celebrated throughout all Moslem countries. The 'Attâbîyah Quarter perpetrated the name of 'Attâb, great-grandson of Omayyah (the ancestor of the Omayyad Caliphs), and 'Attâb, who was a contemporary of the Prophet, had been named by Muḥammad to be Governor of Mecca, a post which he also continued to hold during the reign of the Caliph Abu Bakr. The quarter of Baghdad which bore his name appears to have been occupied by his descendants who had settled here at an unknown period, and the name of the 'Attâbîyîn afterwards obtained a world-wide renown by reason of the silk stuffs which were first manufactured in this suburb [1]. Ibn Jubayr in 580 (A.D. 1184) mentions the 'Attâbîyîn as one of the most flourishing parts of West Baghdad in his day; and a street called the Shâri'-

[1] This name has had a long life. The 'Attâbî silks became famous throughout the Moslem world, and were imitated in other towns. Idrisi in 548 (A.D. 1153) describes Almeria in Southern Spain as in his time possessing eight hundred looms for silk-weaving, and the 'Attâbî stuffs are particularly mentioned among those that were there manufactured. The name passed into Spanish under the form *attabi*, and thence to Italian and French as *tabis*. The name *taby* for a rich kind of silk is now obsolete in English, but in the seventeenth and eighteenth centuries the word was in common use. In February, 1603, when Elizabeth received the Venetian envoy Scaramelli, the Queen is described as wearing 'a dress of silver and white taby' (*vestita di tabi d' argento et bianco*). The diary of Samuel Pepys records how on October 13, 1661, he wore his 'false-taby waistecoate with gold lace'; and a century later Miss Burney, on the occasion of the birthday of the Princess Royal at Windsor, September 29, 1786, appeared in a gown of 'lilac tabby.' Dr. Johnson gives the spelling *tabby* in his dictionary, and explains it as 'a kind of waved silk,' adding that the tabby cat is so named from the brindled markings of the fur. It is certainly curious that the common epithet applied to a cat in modern English should be derived from the name of a man who was a Companion of the Prophet Muḥammad and governor of Mecca in the seventh century A.D.

al-Ghâmish connected this quarter with the neighbouring Dâr-al-Ḳazz, in which thoroughfare had stood a mosque for the Friday prayers, but this in the year 700 (A.D. 1300) had already fallen to ruins.

The quarter of the Dâr-al-Ḳazz or Silk House is described by Yâḳût as a large suburb which in his day stood a league distant from the quarters of West Baghdad at the Baṣrah Gate. In the seventh century (the thirteenth A.D.) it was surrounded by mounds of rubbish and ruins; but the paper manufactured here continued to be famous throughout the East. Apparently in early times a second or Upper Barley Gate (Bâb-ash-Shâ'ir)[1] had stood in the neighbourhood of the Silk House, on the side towards the Ṭâhirid Ḥarîm. There is, however, evidently some confusion in the accounts. Yâḳût, who says that this gate had completely disappeared in his time, describes it as having been the centre of a quarter lying on the Tigris above the City of Manṣûr, at the place where the ships from Mosul and Baṣrah came to their moorings—in other words, at the Upper Harbour. The shifting of the river bed may account for some of the difficulty in fixing the position of the Upper Barley Gate, but it is not easy to understand how, if indeed this gate had been near the Silk House of the 'Attâbîyah Quarter, it could have stood on the Tigris bank and adjacent to the Ṭâhirid Ḥarîm.

Another quarter, the position of which cannot be very clearly defined, but which appears to have been of this same neighbourhood, was that known as the 'Atîkîyah, which when Yâḳût wrote was

[1] For the other Barley Gate, near the Lower Bridge of Boats, see p. 95.

already in ruin. He describes it as having stood between the Ḥarbîyah and the later Quarter of the Baṣrah Gate—possibly within the ruins of what had originally been the City of Manṣûr—and it was named after a certain 'Atîk ibn Halâl the Persian[1].

From the neighbourhood of the Garden of Ḳass, and doubtless communicating directly with the Four Markets, thence leading down to the square in front of the Kûfah Gate, ran the thoroughfare known as the Ḳaḥṭabah Road (Shâri'-al-Kuḥâṭibah, for the plural form of the name is used), which traversed the suburb of Ḥasan ibn Ḳaḥṭabah. The Ḳaḥṭabah family had taken a prominent part in the events which led to the accession of the Abbasids, and fiefs were granted by the Caliph Manṣûr to more than one member of this house. Ḳaḥṭabah, father of Ḥasan and Ḥumayd, had been one of those zealous partisans or missionaries who, in Omayyad days, had publicly preached the right of the house of 'Abbâs to the Caliphate; but he lost his life before the time came for the full realization of his hopes, being drowned while crossing the Euphrates at the head of his troops in the year 132 (A.D. 749). His son Ḥasan succeeded to the command of the Abbasid army, and in time effected the conquest of Mesopotamia for his masters. He stood in high favour with Manṣûr, and only died in the year 181 (A.D. 797), under the reign of Hârûn-ar-Rashîd. The fief in West Baghdad that had been granted him, and through which the

[1] Ya'kubi, 247; Khatib, folio 80 b; Yakut, i. 445; ii. 167, 522, 751; iii. 614; iv. 786; Ibn Jubayr, 227; Marasid, i. 112; ii. 85; Suyuti, 175; Guzidah, book iv, section 5, reign of 'Aḍud-ad-Dawlah. This 'Atîkîyah must not be confounded with the 'Atîḳah suburb, mentioned p. 90.

Ḳaḥṭabah Road lay, stretched along a quadrant of the wall of the Round City from outside the Kûfah Gate to near the Syrian Gate. Up this road and parallel with the line of the wall ran the Canal of the Syrian Gate, already so often mentioned, which, at the beginning of the fourth century (the tenth A.D.), according to Ibn Serapion, threw off a channel to the right, that passed 'in among the remains of the City of Manṣûr,' showing that at this date the wall of the Round City had already fallen to ruin.

On the other side of the Ḳaḥṭabah Road, and lying along the lower part of the Little Ṣarât Canal, was the Palace and Fief of 'Abd-al-Wahhâb, nephew of the Caliph Manṣûr. Near by stood the Market of 'Abd-al-Wahhâb (as already mentioned, p. 59), at no great distance from the Square of the Kûfah Gate, and the market street appears to have connected the Ḳaḥṭabah Road with the Kûfah Gate Square. The whole of this suburb must have fallen to ruin at an early date, for Ibn Abi Mariyam—who died in 224 (A.D. 839)—writes that when passing across it he found all the houses fallen in and deserted, and Ya'ḳûbî, half a century later, states that both palace and market had in his time almost entirely disappeared[1].

The channel of the Little Ṣarât, along the lower course of which the 'Abd-al-Wahhâb Fief stretched, was, as already stated, a loop canal of the Great Ṣarât, and compared with it must have been an insignificant stream, as is shown by the fact that no bridges were needed for the roads to cross it. The Little Ṣarât began at the Ṭâhirid Trench (a

[1] Ya'kubi, 242, 246, 247; Ibn Serapion, 25; Khatib, folio 80 a.

short distance below where this last left the parent stream of the Great Ṣarât), and took its course through the garden lands on the outskirts of Baghdad, flowing back finally into the Great Ṣarât not far above the Old Bridge in front of the Kûfah Gate Square. The island thus included between the Great and the Little Ṣarât was known as the 'Abbâsîyah, and immediately above where the two streams ultimately came together lay the water-mills called Ruḥâ-al-Batrîḳ, or the Patrician's Mill. The 'Abbâsîyah Island took its name from Al-'Abbâs, brother of the Caliph Manṣûr, to whom it had been granted in fief. He laid it out in gardens and corn-lands, which became celebrated for their fertility, for, in the words of a contemporary account, 'at no time, neither by summer nor by winter, did its crops ever fail.'

The great mill which stood at the junction of the two Ṣarâts is said originally to have possessed one hundred millstones, and produced in yearly rent the fabulous sum of one hundred million dirhams (say £4,000,000). The mill had received its name, according to the earlier authorities, from a certain Byzantine Patrician who had come to Baghdad as ambassador from the Greek Emperor, and who, having a knowledge of engineering, had built it to please the Caliph. Such is the account given by Ya'ḳûbî, written in 278 (A.D. 891), but the building is also sometimes referred to as the Mill of Abu Ja'far, that is to say of the Caliph Manṣûr; and occasionally, though apparently in error, we find it named the Mill of *Umm* Ja'far, who is the princess Zubaydah, the celebrated wife of Hârûn-ar-Rashîd [1].

[1] Yakut, iv. 522; Marasid, ii. 485.; and compare Tabari, iii. 887.

This confusion in the name is probably accountable for the assertion by Khaṭîb in one place that it was the Abbasid Prince 'Îsâ (uncle of the Caliph Manṣûr), and according to the generally received account the digger of the 'Îsâ Canal, who had been the founder also of these mills. In another passage, however, Khaṭîb (and Yâḳût copies both statements from him) gives a long anecdote, in which the building of the mills is attributed to the Greek Patrician who came as ambassador from Constantinople to Baghdad.

The name of the Greek envoy is here stated to have been Târâth, fifth in descent from Marûḳ, who had been Emperor of the Greeks in the days of the Caliph Mu'âwiyah (in point of fact Constans II and Constantine IV were the contemporaries of Mu'âwiyah), and this Târâth had come to Baghdad to convey to the Caliph Mahdî, on his accession, the congratulations of the Byzantine Caesar. The date, therefore, must have been about the year 158 (A.D. 775), when Mahdî succeeded his father Manṣûr. The anecdote begins by relating how in former days the Caliph Manṣûr had granted a garden on the Ṣarât Canal to his chamberlain Rabi' (already mentioned in connexion with another Greek ambassador, see p. 65), and how this garden, which produced most excellent dates and other fruits, had in due time come to be inherited by Faḍl, son of Rabi', who, succeeding to his father's honours, served the Caliph Mahdî as Wazîr. The Greek envoy

There was also a Mill of Umm-Ja'far, or Zubaydah, on the Ṭâhirid Trench in the Zubaydîyah Fief (see above, p. 113). Khatib, folio 86 a, from whom Yakut gets his information, gives the name as *Abu* Ja'far, i.e. the Caliph Manṣûr.

having duly presented his message of congratulation remained for some time in Baghdad as the guest of the Caliph Mahdî, and ultimately being much pleased with his reception, offered in gratitude to build a great mill on the Ṣarât. By order of the Caliph the Wazîr Faḍl supplied the sum of half a million dirhams (say £20,000) for building expenses, and it was promised that the mills would produce this same sum yearly in clear profit from the rents paid by the millers. This proving to be the case, the Caliph was so much gratified that he ordered the whole of this rent to be paid over in free gift to the envoy; and even after the latter had returned to Constantinople the sum was year after year transmitted to him there, down to the date of his death, which occurred in 163 (A.D. 780), after which time, by order of the Caliph, the rent was kept back and expended in the maintenance of the estate.

Whatever may be the grain of truth in this anecdote, there can be no doubt that the mills existed in the year 197 (A.D. 813), for they are mentioned as having suffered some damage during the first siege of Baghdad, when Ṭâhir, after driving the unfortunate Caliph Amîn within the walls of the Round City, demolished and burnt many of the houses in this and the neighbouring quarters. Apparently, however, the mills were then not permanently injured, for they were in working order down to the close of the third century (the ninth A.D.), when Ya'ḳûbî and Ibn Serapion wrote their descriptions of Baghdad. When, indeed, the mills fell to ruin does not seem to be mentioned in the chronicles, but in the year 700 (A.D. 1300) the author of the

Marâṣid in writing his epitome of Yâḳût, remarks that no trace of them was then to be seen.

As militating against the story that it was the Greek envoy of the days of Mahdî who first built these mills, it must be stated that Ṭabarî, when narrating the events which led to the foundation of Baghdad by Manṣûr, particularly mentions a certain Baṭrîḳ as among those who offered the Caliph advice in the matter of the site, and Ṭabarî adds that this was the builder of the mill of the Baṭrîḳ. From the context, however, where mention is made of the Christian monastery (*Dayr*) on the Tigris bank, near the site of the later Palace of the Khuld, it is evident that in this passage *Baṭrîḳ* has the signification not of 'Patrician' but of 'Patriarch[1],' and the mills would therefore appear to have dated from times previous to the Abbasid Caliphate, and to have been the work of Nestorian Christians.

Immediately below the junction of the Little Ṣarât with the Great Ṣarât, the Old Bridge carried the highroad from the Kûfah Gate across the canal, and here, a short distance beyond the bridge, the way bifurcated. That to the left was the great Kûfah highroad leading south through the Karkh Quarter, which has been described in chapters v and vi: we have now to deal with the road to the right, which, turning westward and passing through the lands lying between the upper reach of the

[1] According to the dictionaries, 'Patriarch' ought to be rendered by *Baṭrak* or *Baṭrik* (with the *un*dotted *k*), this being the proper Arabic equivalent of the Greek Πατριάρχης; while 'Patrician' is in Arabic *Baṭrîḳ* (with the dotted *ḳ*), this standing for Πατρίκιος. Ibn Serapion, 24; Ya'kubi, 243; Yakut, ii. 759; Khatib, folios 86 a, b, 87 a, b; Marasid, i. 463; Tabari, iii. 274, 887.

Great Ṣarât and the Karkhâyâ Canal, was the first portion of the highroad from Baghdad to Anbâr on the Euphrates. This was known as the Muḥawwal Road, from the name of the first town on it, called Al-Muḥawwal, which lay one league out from Baghdad on the banks of the 'Îsâ Canal.

Near the bifurcation from the Kûfah Road, the Muḥawwal Road at first skirted the Fief and Palaces of Prince 'Îsâ, uncle of the Caliph Manṣûr, who, according to the usually accepted account, had dug the 'Îsâ Canal, and these buildings with their grounds occupied the space between the road and the Ṣarât Canal. Beyond lay other fiefs, and then the road passed under the great vaulted gateway, known as the Bâb-al-Muḥawwal, which gave its name to the whole of the neighbouring quarter. The Muḥawwal Gate appears to have stood uninjured for fully five centuries, for it existed in the time of the last Abbasid Caliph, and long after the neighbouring Kûfah Gate of the City of Manṣûr had disappeared with the ruin of West Baghdad. Yâḳût and the author of the *Marâṣid*, as late as the year 700 (A.D. 1300), both speak of it as the centre of the great quarter, then inhabited entirely by Sunnîs, which stood like a separate township with its own mosque, and its markets that were still much frequented. Forming part of this quarter and towards Karkh—probably on the opposite side of the Muḥawwal Road to the 'Îsâ Fief just mentioned—came the suburb of Haylânah, called after the Greek slave named Helena, who is said to have been a favourite concubine of Hârûn-ar-Rashîd, and the stewardess of the Harîm. A tank also called after her will be mentioned in a later chapter when East Baghdad comes to be described.

After passing through the Muḥawwal Gate the highroad came to the suburb of Ḥumayd, which extended for some distance beyond the gate, going across from the upper reach of the Great Ṣarât on the right hand down to the Karkhâyâ Canal on the left, where this last was spanned by the Hospital Bridge; and the Razîn Canal, which here branched from the Karkhâyâ, is described as having traversed the lower part of the Ḥumayd Suburb. This suburb took its name from Ḥumayd, son of Ḳaḥṭabah, whose brother Ḥasan has already been spoken of as possessing the fiefs along the Ḳaḥṭabah Road between the Kûfah and the Syrian Gates. Ḥumayd, like his brother, was a favourite noble of Manṣûr, and as has been mentioned on a former page, he was the general dispatched by the Caliph to crush the Alid insurrection which had broken out in Medina at the time when Baghdad was being founded. Having successfully disposed of the rebels, Ḥumayd returned to Baghdad, where he was rewarded by the gift of this fief, and afterwards, in the year 143, the Caliph appointed him Governor of Egypt, though he kept the post for little more than a year (A.D. 760 to 762). Ḥumayd at a later date was named Governor of Khurâsân[1], and died in the year 159 (A.D. 776). The Ḥumayd Suburb

[1] He resided at Ṭûs—the ruins of which exist at the present day, not far from Meshed—in the neighbourhood of which he built his great palace. It is described as having covered a square mile of ground; and here at a later date, in part of its gardens, the Caliph Hârûn-ar-Rashîd was buried, also the Imâm of the Shî'ahs, 'Alî-ar-Riḍâ, whose shrine is still the most venerated sanctuary in modern Persia, being the chief mosque in Meshed, the capital of Khurâsân.

is described as having its principal thoroughfare lying along the upper reach of the Great Ṣarât, and it must have extended over and across the lower part of the Island of the 'Abbâsîyah, for on the northern side it was coterminous with the Naṣrîyah and the Four Markets in the Suburb of Haytham, both of which quarters lay on the further side of the Little Ṣarât. Unlike these, however, which continued to be flourishing and populous quarters down to a late time, the Ḥumayd Suburb had fallen to ruin, probably before the close of the fourth century (the tenth A. D.)[1].

The 'Abbâsîyah Island, the lower part of which was occupied by the Ḥumayd Suburb, on the one side was bounded by the Little Ṣarât, a watercourse, as has already been described, so small as to need no bridges for the roads to cross it. On the other side, however, where the upper reach of the Great Ṣarât formed the boundary, three bridges gave access to the island from the quarters along the Muḥawwal highroad. The lowest of these stood close to the Patrician's Mill, from which it took its name (Ḳanṭarah Ruḥâ-al-Baṭrîḳ), being also known as Ḳanṭarah-az-Zubd (the Butter Bridge), but there is some doubt about the pronunciation and meaning of this name. The next bridge above this was the Ḳanṭarah-aṣ-Ṣînîyât, which may signify the Porcelain Bridge, *Ṣîn* being the Arab name for China, both the country and its most notable ware. Possibly, however, the name is of Aramaic origin, in which case it would signify the Bridge of the Date-palms, and Aṣ-Ṣîn with this sense is a name common to other

[1] Ya'kubi, 244; Ibn Serapion, 25; Yakut, i. 451; ii. 750, 752; iii. 201, 560; iv. 255; Marasid, i. 113.

places in Lower Mesopotamia[1]. The highest up of the three bridges was the Ḳanṭarah-al-'Abbâs, doubtless so called after the brother of the Caliph Manṣûr, from whom the 'Abbâsîyah Island took its name; and from each of these three bridges streets must have gone down from the island to the Muḥawwal Road.

This last, as soon as the Muḥawwal Gate had been passed, had on the left hand and lying between the roadway and the Karkhâyâ Canal, the Fief of the Farrâshes or Carpet-spreaders (Ḳaṭî'at-al-Farrâshîn), otherwise known as the House of the Greeks (Dâr-ar-Rûmîyîn). This is the account given by Ya'ḳûbî in 278 (A.D. 891), who adds that the Karkhâyâ was here crossed by the Bridge of the Greeks (Ḳanṭarah-ar-Rûmîyîn), a name recalling the Bridge of the Greek Woman (Ḳanṭarah-ar-Rûmîyah), which Ibn Serapion mentions as lying on the Nahr 'Îsâ; and it seems probable that this Bridge of the Greek Woman on the parallel canal was connected by a road with the Bridge of the Greeks on the Karkhâyâ. After traversing the Ḥumayd Suburb, and leaving the Fief of the Farrâshes or of the Greeks on the left, the Muḥawwal Road approached the bank of the Karkhâyâ Canal; and all along this part of the highway there were shops to right and left, forming a market that was plentifully supplied with wares of all kinds. At the further end of this (probably lying on the right-hand side, for the canal was to the left) the Muḥawwal Road

[1] Yakut (iii. 378) in place of 'Aṣ-Ṣînîyât' gives *Aṣ-Ṣabîbât*, and he copies the whole of this passage from Ibn Serapion. His reading, however, is probably a clerical error, for all the MSS. of Khatib give the first reading.

came to the Old Tank (Al-Ḥawḍ-al-'Atîḳ), round which were grouped the houses belonging to certain Persians, the followers of Shâh ibn Sahl, killed in 223 (A.D. 838), who had been a favourite noble of the Caliph Mu'taṣim.

Near this point the Karkhâyâ Canal was crossed by the Bridge of the Street of Rocks (Ḳanṭarah Darb-al-Ḥijârah), where a branch road must have turned off to the left, while beyond this came the highest up of the bridges which crossed the Karkhâyâ, namely the Ḳanṭarah-al-Yahûd or the Jews' Bridge (some MSS. of Khaṭîb add 'of the Jews' Fief'), near to which stood the gate called the Bâb Abu Ḳabîsah[1]. This gate and bridge on the canal were near an open space on the Muḥawwal Road, known as Al-Kunâsah, where, as the name implies, lay great rubbish-heaps (*Kunâsah* in Arabic means 'a sweeping'); here it was customary for those who came in to the markets of Baghdad to tie up their beasts of burden, and in the adjacent quarter a market was held for the sale of camels, horses, mules, and asses[2].

At the time of the first siege of Baghdad, a great battle extending over many days took place during the latter part of the year 197 (A.D. 813) near the Kunâsah, between the partisans of the Caliph Amîn and the troops of Ṭâhir, who had his siege camp, as already mentioned, outside the Anbâr Gate on the Trench, at the further side of the 'Abbâsîyah

[1] This is the right pronunciation of the name, which in my translation of Ibn Serapion (p. 286) is incorrectly given in the diminutive form—'Abu-Ḳubaysah.'

[2] Ibn Serapion, 14, 24, 25; Ya'kubi, 244; Yakut, ii. 914; iii. 378; De Goeje in *Z. D. M. G.*, xxxix, p. 9, note 4.

Island. During the fight many of the neighbouring quarters were set on fire, and in the account given by Ṭabarî mention is frequently made of the Kunâsah Quarter, with the Street of the Rocks (Darb-al-Ḥijârah), and the battle raged all along the line of the Karkhâyâ Canal down to the Suburb of Ḥumayd and the Muḥawwal Gate. In connexion with these events Mas'ûdî refers to the gate called the Bâb-al-Kunâsah, which must either have stood on the Muḥawwal Road, or possibly may have been identical with the Bâb Abu Ḳabîsah (of Ibn Serapion), already mentioned.

The houses in the outskirts of the Baghdad suburbs extended as far as this point on the Karkhâyâ Canal, which last is described as entering the city limits at the Abu Ḳabîsah Gate. On the 'Îsâ Canal, near here, was the Yâsirîyah Suburb, which gave its name to the bridge called the Ḳanṭarah-al-Yâsirîyah, noted in chapter vi as the highest up of those which crossed the Nahr 'Îsâ. The gate of this suburb, called the Bâb-al-Yâsirîyah, is mentioned by Ibn Hawḳal in 367 (A.D. 978) as the limit of Baghdad in his time on the west, and he adds that five miles of streets separated this point from the limit of the houses on the other side, namely at the Khurâsân Gate of East Baghdad. Yâḳût, three centuries later, speaks of the Yâsirîyah as having come to be a village, in his day very famous for its gardens, which lay on the 'Îsâ Canal, one mile below the town of Muḥawwal, and about two miles from Baghdad, the latter distance being probably reckoned from the Suburb of the Muḥawwal Gate. As late as the year 700 (A.D. 1300) the Yâsirîyah still existed, and the author of the *Marâṣid* writes of the fine bridge which, as of old, here spanned the 'Îsâ Canal. It is added that the place had originally received its name from a man called Yâsir, of whom, however, no details are given[1].

[1] Tabari, iii. 865, 883 to 893; Mas'udi, vi. 445, 446; Ibn Hawkal, 165; Ibn Serapion, 14; Yakut, iv. 1002; Marasid, iii. 332.

CHAPTER XII

BARÂTHÂ, MUḤAWWAL, AND THE KÂẒIMAYN

Barâthâ and its Mosque: the Old Cemetery and the Gardens of Ka'yûbah. The Dyers' Garden. The Muḥawwal Township and the Palace of Mu'taṣim. The Cemetery of the Martyrs and the Tomb of Ibn Ḥanbal. The Cemetery of the Ḳuraysh and of the Straw Gate. The Kâẓimayn Shrines and the Buyid Tombs. Tombs of Zubaydah and the Caliph Amîn. Tomb of 'Abd Allah Ibn Ḥanbal.

On the banks of the 'Îsâ Canal, immediately above the point where the Karkhâyâ branched off, lay the township of Barâthâ. This is described as situated at but 'a short distance'—say half a mile—from Muḥawwal; while, coming out from Baghdad, it was immediately beyond the burial ground of the Kunâsah, otherwise called the Old Cemetery (Al-Maḳbarah-al-Ḳadîmah), which stretched from the rubbish heaps on the Muḥawwal Road down to as far as the 'Îsâ Canal above the bifurcation. On the further side of the Karkhâyâ Canal and running down its right bank from Barâthâ as far as the Bridge of the Greeks, Ya'ḳûbî describes a succession of gardens, which ended at the Palace (Dâr) of Ka'yûbah, a native of Baṣrah and surnamed 'the Gardener,' which lay opposite the bridge. This

Ka'yûbah was celebrated for his plantations of date-palms, young trees being brought up the river from Baṣrah to Baghdad, where after being thus transplanted they became acclimatized, ultimately producing most excellent fruit.

The township of Barâthâ was celebrated for its mosque, which to the Shî'ahs was a much venerated shrine. The tradition was that the Caliph 'Alî had halted here in the year 37 (A.D. 657), when on his march to fight the Harûrî rebels at Nahrawân, and it was said that 'Alî had prayed on the spot where the mosque was subsequently built. Baghdad of course was only founded a century after this date, but Barâthâ was already a flourishing hamlet, and after his prayers 'Alî bathed in the Ḥammâm or hot bath of the village. From this period onwards Barâthâ obtained celebrity as a holy place among the Shî'ahs, many ascetics coming to live in the reed cabins that were built on the canal side, and in connexion with these people Yâḳût tells an edifying story of a man and woman who each had lived at Barâthâ a long life of pious renunciation. In course of time a mosque was built, where the Shî'ahs used to assemble and perform what the Sunnîs looked upon as heretical rites. Matters continued in this wise down to the beginning of the fourth century (the tenth A.D.), but in the reign of the Caliph Muḳtadir the orthodox party would no longer tolerate the scandal, the Shî'ahs were finally accused of compassing rebellion, and one Friday, the mosque having been surrounded by troops, those found there were, by order of the Caliph, carried off to prison and severely punished. The Shî'ah Mosque was then pulled down, and its site included in the grounds of the neighbouring Cemetery of the Kunâsah.

The heterodox services of the Shî'ahs having been thus suppressed, the needs of the Sunnî population had to be supplied, and hence about a quarter of a century later, namely in the year 328 (A. D. 940), the Caliph Râḍî gave permission to the Governor of Baghdad, who was the Amir Bajkam the Turk, to rebuild the old mosque for orthodox worship. The original plan was now greatly enlarged, many neighbouring houses having been bought in, and the new walls were strongly built of kiln-burnt bricks set in mortar, the roof being constructed of teak beams painted or carved, and the name of the Caliph Râḍî was inscribed over the entrance. The next Caliph Muttaḳî completed the work, giving orders that the pulpit which Hârûn-ar-Rashîd had originally bestowed on the great mosque of the City of Manṣûr—and which being out of use had been temporarily stored in the mosque treasury—should be taken thence, and set up in the new Barâthâ Mosque. Further, he appointed the Imâm of the Ruṣâfah Mosque to serve in the new establishment, and the Caliph himself in great pomp led the Friday prayers when said here for the first time—the people of both East and West Baghdad crowding to attend—on the second Friday of the month Jumâdî I of the year 329 (A. D. 941). The Barâthâ Mosque after this date was counted as one of the great mosques of Baghdad, and continued in use as such down to the year 451 (A. D. 1059), when Khaṭîb visited it. Subsequently it was again dismantled, and when Yâḳût wrote in 623 (A. D. 1126), it had long fallen into ruin, and though some traces of the walls still remained, these were then fast disappearing, for the people constantly carried off bricks from them to be used in other newer buildings.

Such is the account given by Khaṭîb and Yâḳût; it is to be remarked, however, that at first it appears not to have been considered as one of the Baghdad mosques. Iṣṭakhri, who wrote his description of Baghdad in 340 (A. D. 951), more than ten years, therefore, after the date when the Caliph Muttaḳî is said to have completed the restoration of the Barâthâ Mosque, omits all mention of it. He says that in his day there were only three great mosques for the Friday prayers in Baghdad, namely that of the City of Manṣûr on the western side, with the Ruṣâfah Mosque and that of the Palace for East Baghdad. Ibn Hawḳal, who wrote in 367 (A. D. 978), is the first to mention the Barâthâ Mosque, adding it as a fourth to those already named by his predecessor Iṣṭakhri, and he mentions that it had originally been an oratory dedicated to the Caliph 'Alî, which account confirms that given above from Khaṭîb and Yâḳût[1].

The Muḥawwal Road, after leaving the Kunâsah Cemetery and passing Barâthâ, came on to the town of Muḥawwal, and the only places mentioned here as lying along the highroad are the Tanners' Yards (Ad-Dabbâghîn), which on the further side stretched down to the 'Isâ Canal. The name of Muḥawwal, as already mentioned, signified the Place of Unloading, the cargoes of boats that came down the Nahr

[1] The name of Barâthâ is derived from the Syriac word *Broitâ*, meaning 'the outermost'; cf. Fränkel, p. xx; Ya'kubi, 244, 251; Khatib, folios 101 a, b, 102 a, b, 113 a; Yakut, i. 532; Istakhri, 84; Ibn Hawkal, 165.

'Îsâ being here disembarked for subsequent transport into Baghdad. Yâḳût describes Muḥawwal in the seventh century (the thirteenth A. D.) as a fine township, a league distant from Baghdad, surrounded by many gardens where abundance of fruit was grown, and it had also excellent markets. According to Ḥamd-Allah, the Persian author of the following century, Muḥawwal was then two leagues distant from the capital, and lay for the most part on the western (or as we should count it, the northern) bank of the 'Îsâ Canal. Its gardens were continuous with those of West Baghdad, and he adds that many of the Abbasid Caliphs had built palaces here. Among the rest had been a celebrated pleasure-house (*Kûshk* or *Kiosk*) built in the early part of the third century (the ninth A. D.) for the Caliph Mu'taṣim in the highest part of the town, so as to be above the reach of the mosquitoes which swarmed among the low-lying gardens: these insects, it is reported, having been 'bound by an incantation, whereby they could not come into that building.'

To distinguish this town from other places of the like name, it was called Al-Muḥawwal-al-Kabîr or Great Muḥawwal, and though all traces of it have apparently now disappeared, Muḥawwal was still a populous place after the year 700 (A. D. 1300), when the author of the *Marâṣid* wrote his epitome of Yâḳût, and as late as the year 740 (1339), when Ḥamd-Allah the Persian appears to have visited it[1].

To complete the survey of Western Baghdad, some account remains to be given of the grave-

[1] Ibn Serapion, 14; Ya'kubi, 244; Tabari, iii. 890; Yakut, iv. 252, 432; Marasid, iii. 53; Nuzhat, 161.

yards which lay on the river bank above the northern suburbs, in which the shrines of the Kâẓimayn, still existing, mark the site of the older Cemetery of the Ḳuraysh, so named after the celebrated Arab tribe from which the Prophet and the Abbasids alike traced their descent.

It is a Moslem custom to bury the dead near the city gates, and beyond the Ṭâhirid Trench the cemetery which lay outside the Ḥarb Gate on the road leading to the Kâẓimayn was celebrated for possessing the tomb of the Imâm Ibn Ḥanbal, founder of the Ḥanbalites, the latest of the four orthodox Sunnî sects. This was the Cemetery of the Martyrs (Muḳâbir-ash-Shuhadâ), though why this graveyard especially should have been so called Yâḳût confesses ignorance. The Imâm Ibn Ḥanbal took his name from his grandfather (for to be exact, he was Aḥmad ibn Muḥammad Ibn Ḥanbal), and he died at Baghdad during the reign of the Caliph Mutawakkil, in the year 241 (A. D. 855), being buried in this cemetery at the Ḥarb Gate in presence of an immense concourse of mourners, his steadfastness under persecution, in the cause of orthodoxy, having won him the unbounded veneration of the people of Baghdad. In the next century, Muḳaddasi, writing in 375 (A. D. 985), mentions his tomb as that of a most holy man, and Khaṭîb in 451 (A. D. 1059) speaks of the shrine of Ibn Ḥanbal at the Ḥarb Gate as a place of pious visitation. Close by stood the tombs of two other saints, namely of the ascetic Bishr-al-Ḥâfî, surnamed 'Barefoot,' who was the friend of Ibn Ḥanbal and died in 226 (A. D. 841), and of Manṣûr ibn 'Ammâr the Traditionist, who died in 225 (A. D. 840). And these were three out of the four saintly guardians of Baghdad — Ma'rûf Karkhi, already mentioned as having his tomb beyond the Baṣrah Gate, making up the quartette—whose tombs sanctified the city.

The tomb of Ibn Ḥanbal as time elapsed became a noted holy place, and among other pious visitors the chronicles mention that both the Saljûḳ Sultan Mâlik Shâh and his Wazîr the famous Niẓâm-al-Mulk, when they were in Baghdad in 479 (A.D. 1086), made their devotions here. During the three great inundations of Baghdad, namely in the years 466 (A.D. 1074), 554 (A.D. 1159), and 614 (A.D. 1217), the shrine of Ibn Ḥanbal suffered much damage, which was, however, repaired. Both Yâḳût in 623 (A.D. 1226), and his epitomist the author of the *Marâṣid* in 700 (A.D. 1300), mention the tomb of Ibn Ḥanbal as still standing at the Ḥarb Gate; and Ibn Khallikân, who is of the same century, repeats the substance of the foregoing in his biography of the Imâm. Ibn Baṭûṭah, who visited Baghdad in 727 (A.D. 1327), especially describes this shrine as one that was still highly venerated by the inhabitants of the metropolis. He adds that the cupola over the grave of the Imâm, though many times restored, had been, as often again, demolished by a supernatural power, lest (as the Berber traveller explains it) against the will of Ibn Ḥanbal his tomb should become the object of a devotion savouring of idolatry[1].

[1] A similar miracle is related by Hamd-Allah of the tomb of the saint named Ṭâûs-al-Ḥaramayn, who is buried near Abarḳûh in Northern Fârs; see Nuzhat (Bombay Lithograph), p. 174; Ibn Batutah, ii. 113, and compare with this Goldziher, i. 257. Mas'udi, vii. 229; Mukaddasi, 130; Yakut, i. 444; iv. 586, 587; Marasid, i. 112; iii. 129; Khatib, folios 112 a, b; Ibn Khallikan, No. 19, p. 29; Ibn-al-Athir, x.

To the north of the Cemetery of the Martyrs at the Ḥarb Gate, and towards the river bank, stretched the great Ḳuraysh Cemetery, the eastern part of which was more especially known as the Cemetery of the Straw Gate (Muḳâbir Bâb-at-Tibn), this having opened from the Zubaydîyah Fief near here. The graveyard in this region had originally been laid out by the Caliph Manṣûr, and one of the first to be buried here was his own son Ja'far-al-Akbar (the elder), who died in the year 150 (A.D. 767). This cemetery not long afterwards came to be known as that of the Shrine of Kâẓim, or of the Two Kâẓims (Kâẓimayn), a name which it still

62, 103; xi. 164; xii. 216. Ibn Jubayr (p. 228), and Ibn Batutah, who merely copies the account of his predecessor, both speak of the tomb of Ibn Ḥanbal as lying 'close to the quarter of the tomb of Abu Ḥanîfah,' and from the context it would appear at first sight as though Ibn Jubayr put the shrine of Ibn Ḥanbal on the *eastern* or left bank of the Tigris. Ibn Jubayr and Ibn Batutah, however, mention it among other tombs that undoubtedly lay on the *west* bank, and the confusion may have arisen either from a mistake in the MS. or from Ibn Jubayr confounding the tomb of Ibn Ḥanbal at the Ḥarb Gate with that of 'Abd-Allah, son of Ibn Ḥanbal, which, as will be mentioned below, was situated close to the west bank of the Tigris, immediately opposite the shrine of Abu Ḥanîfah in Ruṣâfah. Further, Ibn Jubayr states that Ibn Ḥanbal lay buried in the immediate neighbourhood of the tombs of the two Sûfî saints—Ḥallâj, who was put to death in 309 (A.D. 921), and Shiblî his contemporary, who died in 334 (A.D. 946)—while Hamd-Allah, writing in 740 (A.D. 1339), speaks of both of these tombs in conjunction with that of Ibn Ḥanbal as situated in Western Baghdad (Nûzhat, 149). Ibn Batutah, describing the holy places in Western Baghdad, adds that near the tomb of Ibn Ḥanbal stood the shrine of Bishr, surnamed 'Barefoot,' also that of Sarî-as-Saḳaṭî and Junayd. Hamd-Allah also mentions the tomb of Ibn Ḥanbal in his history called the *Guzîdah*, and there speaks of it as lying 'above' (in Persian *bâlâ*) the shrine of Abu Ḥanîfah, which seems to point again to a confusion between the graves of Ibn Ḥanbal and of his son 'Abd-Allah on the Tigris bank. See the fifth book of the *Guzîdah*, 'On the Imâms,' under heading 'Life of Ibn Ḥanbal.'

bears, in honour of the two Shî'ah Imâms who had been buried here; while near by were the graves of Zubaydah, the widow of Hârûn-ar-Rashîd, and of her son the Caliph Amîn, also the tombs of the two Buyid princes, Mu'izz-ad-Dawlah, who died in 356 (A.D. 967), and Jalâl-ad-Dawlah, who died in 435 (A.D. 1044).

In regard to the two Shî'ah Imâms who gave their names to the Kâẓimayn shrines, these were: Mûsâ, surnamed Al-Kâẓim, 'He who restraineth his anger,' grandson of the grandson of Ḥusayn, son of the Caliph 'Alî; and Muḥammad, surnamed Al-Jawâd or At-Taḳî, 'the Generous' or 'the Pious,' grandson of Mûsâ-al-Kâẓim aforesaid. The two were respectively the seventh and the ninth Shî'ah Imâms, Mûsâ having been put to death by Hârûn-ar-Rashîd in 186 (A.D. 802), while Muḥammad-at-Taḳî died, poisoned, it is said, in 219 (A.D. 834), during the Caliphate of Mu'taṣim. These shrines of the Kâẓimayn are also sometimes spoken of as standing in the Shûnîzîyah, which is here therefore taken to be synonymous with the Ḳuraysh burial ground, the explanation given by Khaṭîb being that there were two brothers of the name, and that while the Ḳuraysh Cemetery was called after Shûnîzî the Less, his elder brother had given his name to the graveyard down the Kûfah highroad, already described in chapter vi. In later times, however, the great northern graveyard of West Baghdad was exclusively known as the Cemetery of the Bâb-at-Tibn, but, from the position of the Straw Gate, this would appear to have been a name more properly applied to the eastern part only [1].

[1] The anonymous epitomist of Ibn Hawkal, who wrote in 630

Who first built the Kâẓimayn shrines is unknown, but Yâḳût describes these in 623 (A. D. 1226) as forming a separate walled suburb, inhabited by a considerable population, the houses at that date lying at a distance from the Tigris bank which might be estimated at a good horse gallop, or about a thousand yards. The Persian writer Ḥamd-Allah, a century later than Yâḳût, also speaks of the Kâẓimayn as forming a township by itself, measuring six thousand paces in circumference, the centre point of which was occupied by the tombs of the Imâms. In the earlier centuries, during the constantly recurring riots between the Sunnî and the Shî'ah factions of Baghdad, the suburb of the Kâẓimayn naturally became the rallying-place of the heterodox party, and when these last were discomfited the orthodox mob would plunder the shrines. On the other hand, princes of Shî'ah tendencies like the Buyids, frequently enriched the sanctuary with gifts, and the Caliph Ṭâi', who reigned from 363 to 381 (A. D. 974 to 991), is stated to have acted as Imâm of the Friday prayers on more than one occasion in the great mosque of the Kâẓimayn.

In 443 (A. D. 1051), as will be described in the following paragraph, the shrines were plundered and burnt, but the buildings must have been shortly afterwards restored, for in 479 (A. D. 1086) they were visited by Mâlik Shâh the Saljûḳ, and in 580 (A. D. 1184) again are honourably mentioned by the traveller Ibn Jubayr in his description of Baghdad.

(A.D. 1233), apparently transfers the name of the Ḳuraysh Cemetery to the quarter round the tomb of Abu Ḥanîfah in Eastern Baghdad; see Ibn Hawkal, 164, note *e*.

In 622 (A. D. 1225), during the short reign of the Caliph Ẓâhir, the dome over the shrine of the two Imâms was destroyed by fire, and the Caliph began to rebuild it, but dying in the following year it was his son and successor Mustanṣir who completed the work. During the great Mongol siege in 656 (A. D. 1258) the shrines are stated to have been plundered and burnt by order of Hûlâgû, but subsequently rebuilt; and in the year 700 (A. D. 1300), when the author of the *Marâṣid* wrote, the mosque was still standing near the Tigris bank, though from having been twice flooded in the recent inundations it had come for the most part to be a ruin [1].

Of the many plunderings which the Kâẓimayn suffered, perhaps the worst was that consequent on the riots of the year 443 (A. D. 1051), and it is on this occasion that the chronicle first mentions the tombs of Zubaydah and of her son the Caliph Amîn, which are described as standing in immediate proximity to the Shî'ah shrines. It will be remembered that after the tragic death of Amîn, his head was cut off and sent to Mamûn in Khurâsân, while his body was hurriedly buried in a garden near the Iron Gate (Bâb-al-Ḥadîd) on the Ṭâhirid Trench. Zubaydah, with her grandsons, the sons of Amîn, was at first deported to Humânîyah down the Tigris, but subsequently appears to have been allowed to return to Baghdad, where she died in 216 (A. D. 831), some seventeen years after the great siege, and two years before the death of the Caliph Mamûn. Ṭabarî (copied by all succeeding chroni-

[1] Khatib, folios 111 b, 113 a; Mas'udi, vi. 330; vii. 215; Ibn-al-Athir, viii. 425; Fakhri, 379; Yakut, iv. 587; Marasid, ii. 432; Rashid-ad-Din, 302, 308; Nuzhat, 149.

cles), who gives the date of her death, says nothing in regard to where she was buried, but it will be remembered that the Zubaydîyah Fief, which was occupied by her people, lay close to the Straw Gate, which opened towards the Kâẓimayn, and hence there is every likelihood of her having been buried in this cemetery.

In the year 443 (A. D. 1051) a dispute broke out between the Sunnîs and Shî'ahs of West Baghdad in the matter of a gate in Karkh, the Shî'ahs having wished to set above this an inscription in praise of the Caliph 'Alî, which inscription the Sunnîs held to savour of rank idolatry. The leader of the Sunnîs was killed in the riot which attended the discussion of this thorny matter, and when his friends assembled to bury him in the Cemetery of the Martyrs near the tomb of Ibn Ḥanbal, the riot of the previous day was purposely renewed, the orthodox party wishing to avenge his death. In pursuance of this intention they proceeded to break open the neighbouring shrines of the Kâẓimayn and plunder the tombs of the Shî'ah saints. After carrying off the gold and silver lamps and the curtains which adorned these sanctuaries, the rioters on the following day completed their work by setting fire to the buildings. The great teak-wood domes above the shrines of the Imâms Mûsâ and Muḥammad were entirely burnt, and the fire spreading to the neighbouring tombs of the two Buyid princes, Mu'izz and Jalâl-ad-Dawlah, first consumed these structures, together with the tomb of Ja'far, son of the Caliph Manṣûr, and next attacked the tomb of the Caliph Amîn and of his mother the Princess Zubaydah, the mob meanwhile perpetrating many horrible and impious acts. Ibn-al-Athir, who gives us these details, is apparently the first authority to record the place of burial of Zubaydah, but since there would appear to be no reason for doubting the accuracy of his information, and that therefore the tomb of Zubaydah near the Kâẓimayn existed here in the middle of the fifth century (the eleventh A. D.), this entirely invalidates the attribution of the present, so-called, tomb of Zubaydah, a comparatively modern structure standing near the tomb of Ma'rûf Karkhi, some three miles to the south of the Kâẓimayn, which will be more particularly noticed in the concluding chapter of the present work.

In the Ḳuraysh Cemetery, or rather in its eastern half near the Straw Gate, another celebrated grave remains to be mentioned, namely that of 'Abd-Allah, the son of the Imâm Ibn Ḥanbal. He died in 290 (A. D. 903), and was a famous traditionist, emulating also the reputation of his father for sanctity. By the terms of his will he had enjoined that his body should not be buried in the shrine of Ibn Ḥanbal, but outside in the cemetery beyond the Straw Gate. Here, according to a well authenticated tradition, a prophet (*nabî*) of some former dispensation had been given sepulture, and 'Abd-Allah Ibn Ḥanbal was of opinion that to rest in the neighbourhood of a prophet's bones was even better than to be buried in the grave of his father the Imâm. The tomb, therefore, was made at a place between the Kâẓimayn and the Zubaydîyah Fief, where it continued for many centuries to be a place of visitation, and in the seventh century (the thirteenth A. D.), when Yâḳût wrote, was still standing, though much in ruin, the surrounding plain being already used for arable land, on which corn crops were grown.

In later times a confusion arose between the tomb of Aḥmad ibn Ḥanbal and that of his son 'Abd-Allah; and when the former shrine fell to ruin with the disappearance of the quarter round the Ḥarb Gate, the latter tomb must have taken its place in the popular veneration. This is first indicated by Mîrkhwând, who, when describing the occupation of Baghdad by Timur in 695 (A. D. 1296), states that 'the shrine of the Imâm *Aḥmad*,' having recently become ruined by the rebellious floods of the Tigris, Timur gave orders that it should be rebuilt; but the tomb in question, from its position on the river bank, can only have been that of 'Abd-Allah, son of Aḥmad Ibn Ḥanbal. The confusion would easily have come about from the names, for as has already been mentioned, Ibn Ḥanbal the Imâm was not in reality the son of Ḥanbal (as the form of name would imply), but his grandson, and Ibn Ḥanbal thus coming to be used as a sort of patronymic, the traditionist 'Abd-Allah, his son, naturally also came to be sometimes called Ibn Ḥanbal. When, therefore, the tomb of Ibn Ḥanbal the Imâm at the Ḥarb Gate had disappeared, the tomb of his son 'Abd-Allah took its place, and came to be called the tomb of Ibn Ḥanbal. As such it existed, after having been restored by Timur, down to about the year A. D. 1750, when Niebuhr in describing Baghdad mentions this shrine on the Tigris bank (opposite the tomb of Abu Ḥanîfah in East Baghdad); and he also incorrectly speaks of it as the tomb of Aḥmad Ibn Ḥanbal. It, however, then was a complete ruin, the building for the most part having been recently carried away by the river floods; hence at the present day nothing remains of either the tomb of 'Abd-Allah, or of that of his father the more celebrated Aḥmad Ibn Ḥanbal, which in former times had been among the most illustrious shrines of Western Baghdad[1].

[1] Mas'udi, vi. 482; Tabari, iii. 934, 1105; Ibn-al-Athir, ix. 395; Yakut, i. 443; Khatib, folio 112 a; Mirkhwand, part vi. 66; Niebuhr, ii. 248.

CHAPTER XIII

EASTERN BAGHDAD IN GENERAL

East and West Baghdad and Sâmarrâ. The three northern quarters of East Baghdad: Ruṣâfah, Shammâsîyah, and Mukharrim. The Eastern Palaces and modern Baghdad. The second Siege: Musta'în and the walls on the western and eastern sides. Ya'ḳûbî and Ibn Serapion: the highroads of the three northern Quarters. The Canals of the eastern side: from the river Khâliṣ and from the Nahr Bîn. The three Bridges of Boats. The Main Bridge. The Upper Bridge and Lower Bridge. The Zandaward Bridge. Executions on the Bridges. Upper Bridge dismantled. Later Bridge of the Palaces. Numbers of skiffs. Bridge of Ḳaṣr Sâbûr. The modern Bridge.

THE rule of the Abbasids in Baghdad lasted for rather more than five centuries—from 146 (A.D. 763), when Manṣûr founded the city, to 656 (A.D. 1258), when, after the Mongol invasion, the last Caliph Musta'ṣim was put to death by Hûlâgû—and these five centuries are divided into two periods of unequal length by an interval of fifty-eight years, during which the Caliphs, abandoning Baghdad, lived at Sâmarrâ, making this for a time the capital of the empire.

From the foundation of the city to the removal of the seat of government to Sâmarrâ seventy-five years had elapsed, and during this first period the Caliphs held their court in West Baghdad, on the

Arabian side of the Tigris. After the return from Sâmarrâ, and during the second period, which lasted for close on four centuries, East Baghdad on the Persian side of the river became the seat of government; and here the Caliphs built new palaces, a new city with suburbs in the course of time growing up round these. The chief quarter of modern Baghdad also lies on the eastern bank of the Tigris, being the outcome of these suburbs which grew up after the fourth century (the tenth A.D.) round the later palaces of the Caliphs. Every trace of these palaces has now almost completely disappeared, but the city wall built in the fifth century (the eleventh A.D.) to enclose the new suburbs still exists, and this, as will be shown later, is virtually identical with the present wall of Eastern Baghdad.

For a hundred years and more, however, after the time of Manṣûr, these palaces and suburbs not having yet come into existence, East Baghdad consisted of the three northern quarters which lay on the river bank, for the most part outside the limit of the later wall, and above the subsequent site of the palaces, in the region where the village of Mu'aẓẓam now stands. These three northern quarters were called Ruṣâfah, Shammâsîyah, and Mukharrim[1]; they covered a fan-shaped area of ground, which, radiating from the end of the Main Bridge, was bounded by a semicircle sweeping round from the Tigris above the Upper Bridge to the river bank again below the Lower Bridge. Starting from the end of the Main Bridge, two highroads diverged, one going north, the other east, which divided the semicircular area just de-

[1] See Map, No. V.

scribed into three parts; the northern road, towards Mosul, leaving the city limits at the Shammâsîyah Gate, while the eastern or Khurâsân road had its exit at the Khurâsân Gate[1], going towards Persia.

The Mahdî Palace in Ruṣâfah was the nucleus from which East Baghdad developed, and as already described in chapter iii, it was founded by Manṣûr, almost contemporaneously with the Round City, to be the residence of his son and successor Mahdî. It stood near the river bank in the Ruṣâfah Quarter, which last occupied a triangular space of ground bounded on two sides by a great loop of the Tigris, above the Main Bridge, and thus the palace lay to the north-west of the bridge. Ruṣâfah on the land side was bounded by the great northern highroad, this dividing it from the Shammâsîyah Quarter, which occupied the triangle between the two great highroads already spoken of as going north and east from the head of the Main Bridge. The limit of the Shammâsîyah Quarter on the third side to the north-east was the city wall going up from the Khurâsân Gate to the Shammâsîyah Gate on the river bank, the Baradân Gate opening halfway between the two. The Mukharrim Quarter lay to the south of the Shammâsîyah, being divided from this last by the eastern or Khurâsân road. The Mukharrim Quarter was bounded on the west side by the Tigris from the Main Bridge down to the Lower Bridge; while on the third side the limit was the quadrant of the city wall going from the

[1] This Khurâsân Gate of East Baghdad must not be confounded with the gate of the same name in the Round City, which opened on the Main Bridge of Boats. The Khurâsân road, within the city, ran between the two.

Khurâsân Gate to the Gate of the Tuesday Market on the river at the Lower Bridge, the Abraz Gate to the south-east lying about halfway between the two.

On the Tigris bank, immediately below the Gate of the Tuesday Market, lay the grounds of the uppermost of the three later palaces of the Caliphs, namely the Firdûs, and below this came the gardens of the Ḥasanî and the Tâj Palaces. These three palaces, as already mentioned, came in after times to be surrounded by suburbs and then by the new town wall, which at the present day forms the boundary of the city of East Baghdad; but as fixing the southern limit of the three older or northern quarters (these having now almost entirely disappeared), it is to be noted that both the Abraz Gate and the Gate of the Tuesday Market in the Mukharrim Quarter stood within the area afterwards enclosed by the wall round the later palace suburbs, so that the lower part of the old Mukharrim Quarter overlapped the upper part of the region occupied by modern Baghdad[1].

A hundred years after the time of Manṣûr, and about the middle of the period of half a century when Sâmarrâ was the capital, the interval of a year occurred during which Baghdad was once again the abode of the Caliph, or rather of one of the Caliphs, for there were two rival Commanders of the Faithful throughout the year 251 (A.D. 865), one in Sâmarrâ, the other in Baghdad. The latter was Musta'în, who, in consequence of a revolt of the Turk bodyguard, fled for his life from the palace at Sâmarrâ, where Mu'tazz, his cousin, was immediately made

[1] See inset plan to Map No. I.

Caliph in his stead. Musta'în, with his adherents, travelled down the Tigris, seeking refuge in Baghdad; and here, on the appearance of the pursuing army from Sâmarrâ, Musta'în proceeded to entrench himself in Ruṣâfah, which became his headquarters and the centre of the defence.

The siege which followed lasted a year, and was the second of those celebrated in the history of Baghdad, the topography of the city being somewhat changed by the circular wall which Musta'în then built to defend the eastern and western quarters. In West Baghdad the position of the upper and the lower limits of the wall are known, but the course followed by the remainder of the semicircle unfortunately is not specified. The upper end began on the Tigris bank at the Gate of the Zubaydah Fief, above the Harbour of the Ṭâhirid Trench; and the wall met the river again below at the palace of Ḥumayd, at some distance above the Lower Harbour of the 'Îsâ Canal. Between these two points the semicircle probably followed first the line of the Ṭâhirid Trench as far west as the Anbâr Gate, thence crossing to include within its sweep the quarter of the Muḥawwal Gate, and finally coming down the left bank of the 'Îsâ Canal, but not including the Lower Harbour: this at least is what may be gathered from the accounts of the siege. The wall round East Baghdad completed the circle, beginning on the Tigris bank opposite to the palace of Ḥumayd, immediately below the Lower Bridge of Boats. Passing by the Gate of the Tuesday Market, it came to the Abraz Gate on the south-east, thence curved north and west, the wall here being pierced by the Khurâsân and Baradân Gates, till the upper end of the semicircle was reached on the Tigris bank at the Shammâsîyah Gate opposite to the Upper Harbour, here the semicircle on the west side had started[1]. The wall, therefore, included within its circuit the three Bridges of Boats crossing the Tigris.

The description which Ya'ḳûbî has left us of Eastern Baghdad is unfortunately not so full as that which he has written of the western city, and we have to rely on Ibn Serapion for most of the details of the Mukharrim, Shammâsîyah, and Ruṣâfah Quarters. Ya'ḳûbî, however, though he does not mark the relative positions of the various fiefs in East Baghdad which he enumerates, does give a brief list of the highroads which traversed the three northern quarters within the line of Musta'în's wall, which last had been built a quarter of a century only before the time when Ya'ḳûbî wrote. These roads were five in number, not counting the great Khurâsân road going from the Main Bridge eastward to the Khurâsân Gate; and they enable us fairly well to understand the course of the canals described by Ibn Serapion. Of the five roads, two traversed Ruṣâfah, namely the 'straight' road to the palace and mosque of Mahdî, and the road of the Khuḍayr Market, which must have led to the Upper Bridge of Boats. Next came the great northern highroad leading to the Shammâsîyah Gate, and then the road to the Baradân Gate. The road from the Lower Bridge of Boats up the Tigris bank into the Mukharrim Quarter is the last road mentioned by Ya'ḳûbî, this of course being on the south side of the great Khurâsân

[1] Ibn Maskuwayh, 580; Tabari, iii. 1551.

highway, which it probably ran into not far from the Main Bridge, opposite to where the northern road diverged[1].

Before proceeding to describe the various quarters of East Baghdad, it will be convenient to summarize the account given by Ibn Serapion of the canals which traversed this half of the great city, and crossed the highroads which Ya'ḳûbî has mentioned. These canals were all derived indirectly from the Nahrawân, the main canal of the east bank, which starting under the name of the Ḳâṭûl of the Chosroes, branched from the Tigris at Dûr, about one hundred miles above Baghdad. Following a much straighter course than that taken by the river, the Nahrawân attained a length of over 200 miles, and finally rejoined the Tigris at Mâdharâyâ, about one hundred miles below Baghdad. About halfway down the Nahrawân, and somewhat to the northward of due east from Baghdad, the great canal traversed Nahrawân Town, and this was the point where the Khurâsân highroad from Baghdad crossed it, going east into Persia. From the Nahrawân Canal, two transverse canals or rivers, named respectively the Khâliṣ and the Nahr Bîn (or Nahrabîn), flowed westwards to the Tigris, the first joining the river above Baghdad, the second below it; and all the canals of Eastern Baghdad were offshoots which ramified between the Khâliṣ and the Nahr Bîn.

The Khâliṣ left the Nahrawân probably at a point near the town of Bâjisrâ, and flowed into the Tigris at Râshidîyah, a little above Baradân, the town about three leagues due north of Baghdad

[1] Ya'kubi, 253.

which gave its name to the city gate. The Nahr Bîn, on the other hand, left the Nahrawân Canal a short distance above the town of Nahrawân, and flowed out into the Tigris about two leagues below Baghdad at the village of Kalwâdhâ. Hence it was from the Khâliṣ that the northern quarters of East Baghdad were watered, while the suburbs to the south were traversed by the Nahr Bîn offshoots.

From the Khâliṣ a canal branched, running south, called the Nahr-al-Faḍl, which flowed into the Tigris near the Shammâsîyah Gate, in the upper part of East Baghdad. Immediately before reaching this gate, however, two canals, which subsequently uniting formed a loop, branched together from the Faḍl Canal, these supplying Ruṣâfah and the Shammâsîyah Quarters. One, called the Canal of the Wall, went round outside the quadrant of the city wall from the Shammâsîyah Gate past the Baradân Gate to the Gate of Khurâsân; here it was joined by the second, called the Mahdî Canal, which having entered the city at the Shammâsîyah Gate, first threw off a channel that went into Ruṣâfah, and next curving eastwards to the Khurâsân Gate, passed out through this, flowing into the Canal of the Wall. Outside the town their united waters were further augmented by the inflowing of the Ja'farî Canal (or Nahr-al-Ja'farîyah), an offshoot from the parent stream of the Nahr Faḍl, from which it had branched at some distance to the north of the Shammâsîyah Gate; and the stream of the Ja'farî Canal, through either the Canal of the Wall or the Mahdî Canal, flowed back into the Nahr Faḍl, from which it had originally derived its waters[1].

[1] Ibn Serapion (p. 23) is surely mistaken in representing the Mahdî

Coming now to the Mukharrim Quarter and the palaces in the southern part of East Baghdad, these were watered by the Mûsâ Canal and its offshoots, the Nahr Mûsâ being a derivative of the Nahr Bîn. Not far from the right bank of the Nahr Bîn, and lying at some distance outside the walls of East Baghdad, there was a great palace of the Caliph Mu'taḍid, called Ath-Thurâyâ (the Pleiades), which will be more fully noticed in a later chapter. The Mûsâ Canal bifurcated to the west from the Nahr Bîn above the Palace of the Pleiades, through which it flowed, and after irrigating the palace gardens passed out to the place known as the 'Divide,' where its waters parted to form three canals.

The canal to the right, or the western branch, which retained the name of the Nahr Mûsâ, had the longest course of the three; its many branch canals ramified through the Mukharrim Quarter, which its main stream also traversed, and curving round this district, crossed the road going down from the Main Bridge to the Gate of the Tuesday Market, and finally flowed out into the Tigris at the Garden of Zâhir, some distance to the south of the bridge-head. The second or midmost canal from the Divide was called the Nahr Mu'allâ; it entered the city at the Abraz Gate, and passing out again near the Gate of the Tuesday Market, flowed into the Tigris at the uppermost of the palaces of the

Canal as flowing *out* of the Faḍl Canal at the Shammâsîyah Gate. If water flowed down the Ja'farî, the Mahdî Canal must have flowed *into* the Nahr Faḍl, as did also the Canal of the Wall, for the two combined could only serve to discharge the waters of the Ja'farî Canal back into the Nahr Faḍl, with which it thus formed a loop.

Caliphs, known as the Firdûs. Ibn Serapion gives no special name to the third or lowest canal from the Divide, but for convenience it may be called the Canal of the Palaces. Turning off to the south, it watered the grounds of the two palaces of the Caliphs—called respectively the Ḥasanî and the Tâj—flowing out finally into the Tigris, immediately below the Tâj Palace.

Thus, to recapitulate, Eastern Baghdad, in its northern quarters, was watered by the ramifications of the Mahdî, Ja'farî, and Wall Canals, these forming a great loop taken from the Nahr Faḍl, a derivative of the Khâliṣ; while the southern quarters were traversed by the three canals from the Divide of the Mûsâ Canal, which was itself a derivative of the Nahr Bîn: both the Khâliṣ and the Nahr Bîn being offshoots from the great Nahrawân Canal[1].

Before proceeding to describe the eastern quarters in detail, it will be convenient to state in the present chapter what is known of the various bridges of boats which crossed the Tigris, forming the lines of communication between the eastern and the western halves of the great city.

The Tigris at Baghdad, where the river is on an average more than 250 yards wide, has never been spanned (at least in Moslem times) by any structure more permanent than a bridge of boats. Such a bridge is in Arabic generally known under the name of *Jisr*, in distinction to a masonry bridge of arches called a *Ḳanṭarah*, such as was built to cross a canal. Bridges of boats are, of course, easily broken up and shifted up or downstream to meet the needs of traffic, but in the earlier times, and

[1] Ibn Serapion, 19 to 23.

as late as the middle of the fifth century the (eleventh A. D.), there appear to have been three such bridges (Upper, Main, and Lower) permanently set for crossing the Tigris, and the positions of these do not appear to have materially varied, all three having been included within the line of walls (described p. 172) built by Musta'în. From the earliest times the middle or Main Bridge was traversed by the great eastern highroad that led from the Khurâsân Gate of the Round City of Manṣûr to the Khurâsân Gate in the city wall of the three northern quarters. The Main Bridge had at its western end the Khuld Palace and the great review ground, while the arched gate called the Bâb-aṭ-Ṭâḳ was at the eastern end of the bridge, this opening directly into the great market street of East Baghdad, from which the chief thoroughfares branched.

The second or Upper Bridge crossed immediately below the Upper Harbour to the Shammâsîyah Quarter, being reached from the western side by the highroad which left the Round City at the Syrian Gate, traversing the Ḥarbîyah Quarter. At the eastern end of the Upper Bridge was the Bridge Gate (Bâb-al-Jisr), which is often mentioned during the two earlier sieges of Baghdad, namely under Amîn in the year 198 (A. D. 814), and in the time of Musta'în in 251 (A. D. 865), on which latter occasion it is reported that this Upper Bridge, then consisting of twenty boats, was set on fire by the enemy and entirely destroyed. After the middle of the fourth century (the tenth A. D.) the great Palace of the Buyids was built in the Shammâsîyah, occupying the region on the eastern bank, to which the Upper Bridge more immediately gave access.

The third or Lower Bridge—which Ya'ḳûbî calls the first bridge (Al-Jisr-al-Awwal) and Mas'ûdî (apparently) 'the new bridge'—according to Khaṭîb had originally been laid down by Manṣûr at the time when he built the Khuld Palace in 157 (A.D. 774). It is described as starting from near the Barley Gate on the west side, which must have stood near the lower end of the Khuld Gardens on the road coming from the Ḥarrânî Archway, from which point the bridge crossed to the Mukharrim Quarter, within the Gate of the Tuesday Market, from whence, as Ya'ḳûbî describes it, the road coming over from Western Baghdad went up the Tigris bank before reaching the Pitched Gate. Thus the western end of the Lower Bridge must have been moored at a point immediately below the mouth of the Ṣarât Canal, in the quarter afterwards known as the Tustarîyîn, but its exact position depends on that of the Barley Gate, the site of which is somewhat uncertain.

Besides these three permanent bridges of the early period, there was a fourth bridge of boats temporarily established by the Caliph Amîn, which is described as 'double,' and which crossed the river considerably below the Lower Bridge. This was called the Zandaward Bridge, and probably led to the palace which Amîn had built for himself near the Zandaward Monastery, at the place which in after times came to be occupied by the Kalwâdhâ Gate of later Eastern Baghdad[1].

[1] The name in the MSS. of Khatib is spelt *Zandarûd*, but this appears to be a clerical mistake for *Zandaward*, which will be described in a later chapter. Ya'kubi, 248, 254; Mas'udi, ix. 4; Khatib, folios 107 a, b; Tabari, iii. 906; Ibn-al-Athir, vi. 193; vii. 97, 115.

In the days of Hârûn-ar-Rashîd and his more immediate successors, when plots and rebellions were rife in the empire, the bridges of boats were used as convenient places for public executions; here great offenders were crucified, and the heads of rebels were exposed on the poles as a warning to passers-by. Incidentally, we thus have frequent mention in the chronicles of these bridges. In the reign of Hârûn, for instance, when Ja'far the Barmecide had fallen from power and been put to death by the Caliph, his body, after being divided into three parts, was gibbeted on stakes set up in the middle of each of the three bridges. Again, during the reign of Mu'taḍid in the year 280 (A. D. 193), the dead body of Shamîlah was crucified 'between the two bridges of Western Baghdad'; and according to Mas'ûdî the heads of other rebels were also exposed in this same year 'on the bridge.' In 283 (A. D. 896) it is reported that the scaffolding, bearing the roadway above the boats forming the Upper Bridge, suddenly gave way under the press of people, and more than a thousand deaths followed from those who, falling into the water, were drowned. Lastly, not to mention other instances, in the year 289 (A. D. 902) Waṣîf the Eunuch, who had revolted some eight years before, was finally captured, and after being brought a prisoner to Baghdad had suddenly died in prison; by order of the Caliph Mu'taḍid his body was partially embalmed in resin, and then surmounted by the decapitated head was exposed on the bridge, where it remained gibbeted for over ten years, until at length, during a tumult, it was taken down and tossed into the Tigris[1].

These three Bridges (Upper, Main, and Lower)

[1] Ya'kubi, *History*, ii. 510; Mas'udi, viii. 142, 143, 170.

appear to have existed, with only temporary interruptions, down to the middle of the fourth century (the tenth A. D.), when the period of the Buyid supremacy began. Shortly after this, however, the Upper Bridge was dismantled, for both Iṣṭakhri in 340 (A. D. 951), and Ibn Hawḳal in 367 (A. D. 978), report that only two bridges of boats existed in their day, and Khaṭîb mentions that the Upper Bridge, near the Maydân of Mu'izz-ad-Dawlah the Buyid, had before his time been brought down the river to be moored between the review ground and the Bâb-aṭ-Ṭâḳ, in other words it was set to form part of the Main Bridge. With the ruin of the Ruṣâfah Quarter, the Upper Bridge, which crossed from the Ḥarbîyah to the Shammâsîyah, would naturally have fallen out of use, coming to be dismantled; and thus in 450 (A. D. 1058), when Khaṭîb wrote his history of Baghdad, there were, as he says, only two bridges of boats, namely the Main Bridge at the Bâb-aṭ-Ṭâḳ of the Khurâsân highroad, and the Lower Bridge, which he describes as beginning at the Mashra'at-al-Ḳaṭṭânîn (the Wharf of the Cotton-merchants).

The position of the Lower Bridge appears to have been slightly shifted several times during the earlier half of this century. Khaṭîb says that in 448 (A. D. 1056) it had been moored between the Mashra'at-al-Ḥaṭṭâbîn (the Woodcutters' Wharf) of East Baghdad and the Mashra'at-ar-Rawâyâ (the Wharf of the Water-jars) of the western city; but that in the year 450 it had been removed to the position which he describes, opposite the Wharf of the Cotton-merchants. Khaṭîb further informs us that the Lower Bridge, as early as the year 383 (A. D. 993), had already been temporarily moored at the Cotton-merchants' Wharf, but that soon after this date it had been dismantled, and then, until the year 448, there had been only the Main Bridge in use. Of these various wharfs, however, nothing further appears to have been recorded, and it is hence impossible to fix the various positions that the Lower Bridge occupied. Thus throughout the earlier half of the fifth century (the eleventh A. D.) only the Main Bridge was in use, as Khaṭîb reports, and this is confirmed by what is said in the chronicle of a riot which took place during the reign of the Caliph Ḳâim in 422 (A. D. 1031), when the (single) bridge giving communication between the eastern and western halves of the city had to be cut, in order to separate the contending factions of Shî'ahs and Sunnîs who inhabited, respectively, Karkh and the quarters of East Baghdad[1].

Khaṭîb wrote in the middle of the fifth century (the eleventh A. D.), and in the second half of this century great changes took place in East Baghdad, which will be fully described in subsequent chapters. These changes resulted in the building of the city of Baghdad as we now see it, for the three older northern quarters of Ruṣâfah, Shammâsîyah, and Mukharrim, with their city wall, having fallen to ruin, new suburbs sprang up round the palaces of the Caliphs during the reign of Muḳtadî, and in 488 (A. D. 1095) his successor Mustaẓhir surrounded these

[1] Istakhri, 84; Ibn Hawkal, 165. In Khatib compare the British Museum MS., No. 1507, folios 107 a, b, with the Paris MS., No. 2128, folios 36 a, b, which in many cases gives better readings. Ibn-al-Athir, ix. 285 *bis*. Khatib derived his information about the bridges from Abu 'Alî ibn Shâdhân, who died in 420 (A. D. 1029), and from Hilâl ibn al-Muḥsin, who died in 448 (A. D. 1056).

new suburbs by a wall, virtually identical with the one which now encloses modern Baghdad. The bridges of boats which had given access to the three northern quarters were naturally out of position for the new town, and probably before the close of the fifth century (the eleventh A. D.) a single bridge of boats at the palaces of the Caliphs was established. This Palace Bridge is mentioned by the writers of the sixth century (the twelfth A. D.) and by Yâḳût at the beginning of the following century in such terms as to lead to the conclusion that it was identical in position with the single Bridge of Boats now in existence.

The first mention of the Palace Bridge appears to be that found in the account written by the epitomist of Ibn Hawḳal, more than a century after the date of Khaṭîb, namely about the year 568 (A. D. 1173), who states that there was in his day but one bridge, consisting of boats held together by iron chains, which served as the communication between the eastern and the western parts of the city. Nearly a score of years later, when Ibn Jubayr visited the city in 580 (A. D. 1184), this bridge had been recently carried away by the floods, and the people, instead of resetting the moorings of the pontoon boats, had taken to the custom of crossing the Tigris in skiffs. Ibn Jubayr writes that both night and day the passage was thus made by men and women alike, who took great amusement therein. Referring to the earlier years of the sixth century (the twelfth A.D.), he adds that before his date there had been two bridges in use, namely the one at the palace of the Caliphs, which had been so recently carried away, and a second above this (doubtless the older Main Bridge opposite the 'Aḍudî Hospital), but that even with both these passages for crossing the river on foot, the number of those wishing to pass over had always been so great that the boatmen were constantly employed ferrying the people over in their skiffs. In this matter Khaṭîb, in the previous century, has already remarked on the very profitable business done by boatmen of Baghdad, and he gives his authority for the statement that in the time when Muwaffaḳ (brother of the Caliph Mu'tamid) was governor of Baghdad—he died in 278 (A.D. 891)—there were 30,000 of the boats called *sumayrîyah* then in use, the toll at the rate of three pieces of silver for each skiff producing 90,000 dirhams daily, a sum amounting to between £3,000 and £4,000.

From what Ibn Jubayr writes, and from several incidental notices in the works of Yâḳût, it appears that the western end of this Bridge of Boats crossing to the palaces of the Caliphs must have been moored on the Tigris bank in the quarter of the 'Îsâ Palace, which was on the left bank of the Lower Harbour, at the mouth of the 'Îsâ Canal. Along the right bank, on the southern side of this harbour, lay the Ḳurayyah Quarter, and this (as expressly stated by Ibn Jubayr) also was not far distant from this bridge, which according to Fakhri was restored, or rebuilt, by the Caliph Ẓâhir in the year 622 (A.D. 1225), a deed rendered famous by the panegyrics of his court poets. This bridge, as already said, was probably first set up at the close of the fifth century (the eleventh A.D.), but it is curious to find that Balâdhurî (a writer of the middle of the third century A.H.), describing the conquests of the Moslems in Mesopotamia after the death of the

Prophet, states that the Arab troops at this date crossed the Tigris by a bridge of boats moored in front of Ḳaṣr Sâbûr (the Palace of Sapor), which, he adds, 'stood in the place where nowadays the Ḳaṣr 'Îsâ stands.' It is evident, therefore, that in the times of the Persian monarchs a bridge of boats had existed at the very spot where the later Bridge of the Palaces was established nearly five hundred years after their time[1].

Immediately prior to the Mongol siege of Baghdad in 656 (A. D. 1258) the bridge in front of the palaces of the Caliphs must have been dismantled, for Musta'ṣim and his people shut themselves up in East Baghdad, evacuating the western quarters, which were forthwith occupied by the army that Hûlâgû sent to cross the Tigris above the city. After the sack, however, the bridge at the palaces was restored, as also (possibly at a later date) one of the upper bridges, for when Ibn Baṭûṭah visited Baghdad in 727 (A. D. 1327) he found two bridges of boats, one opposite the palaces, and the other higher up, which probably occupied the position of the older Main Bridge at the 'Aḍudî Hospital. These bridges, Ibn Baṭûṭah adds, were constructed 'like the one at Ḥillah,' and this he has described on a previous page as 'a bridge laid on boats connected together and so ordered that they stretch from one side of the river to the other, being held by iron chains that are attached on either bank to great piles driven firmly into the ground.' The bridge of boats which at the present day spans the Tigris at Baghdad, according to the traveller Ker Porter,

[1] Ibn Hawkal, 163, note *e*; Ibn Jubayr, 226, 227; Khatib, folio 108 b; Yakut, iv. 839; Mushtarik, 350; Baladhuri, 249; Fakhri, 379.

measures 670 feet from bank to bank; Abraham Parsons, on the other hand, gives the length as 871 feet, the roadway being carried over thirty-five pontoon boats; and it seems probable that this modern bridge, as already stated, occupies the position of the one described by Yâḳût shortly before the Mongol siege [1].

[1] Ibn Batutah, ii. 97, 105; Ker Porter, *Travels*, ii. 255; Parsons, *Travels*, 118.

CHAPTER XIV

RUṢÂFAH

The foundation of Ruṣâfah. The Mosque and Palace of Mahdî. 'Askar-Mahdî and the Causeway. The Shrine of Abu Ḥanîfah. The Cemetery of Khayzurân. The Tombs of the Caliphs. Later history of the Mosque of Mahdî. The two highroads in Ruṣâfah. The Straight Road and the Road of the Maydân. The Khuḍayrîyah Quarter and Market. The Upper Bridge of Boats.

OUR authorities differ in regard to the date of the foundation of Ruṣâfah. Ya'ḳûbî, the earliest of these, gives the year 143 (A.D. 760) as that in which Mahdî began to erect buildings here: but at this time his father Manṣûr had not yet laid the foundations of Western Baghdad. The more generally accepted account gives the date of 151 (A.D. 768), in the month Shawwâl of which year the Caliph Manṣûr with all his nobles went out from the new city to receive Mahdî, the heir-apparent, on his victorious return from Khurâsân at the head of the army. The Caliph had assigned the eastern Tigris bank, opposite the Round City, to the troops for a camping-ground, and here in anticipation of his son's coming he had caused a palace to be built.

The question of these various dates is not very material, and probably the difference arises from the fact that the great mosque of Ruṣâfah may have been founded as early as 143, while the palace and the houses and fiefs that came to surround it were only begun when Mahdî returned from his Persian expedition. The historian Ṭabarî reports that Manṣûr caused his son to camp in Ruṣâfah with his army, in order to keep the heir-apparent safely at arm's length; and further to be able, should need arise, promptly to quell any feuds that might break out among his Arab troops in the garrison of the Round City—these being of the rival Yamanite and Muḍarite tribes—by aid of the Persian soldiers from Khurâsân, who thus camping apart would be more entirely under the orders of the Caliph. The building of Ruṣâfah was not completed till the year 159 (A.D. 776), that is to say in the second year after Mahdî had succeeded to the Caliphate. The great mosque by all accounts had been the first building to be erected in Ruṣâfah, the palace coming later; and as a consequence, it is especially noted that the Ḳiblah point (towards Mecca) of this mosque was more exactly oriented than the Ḳiblah in the great mosque of the Round City, which had had to conform to the plan of the previously built Palace of Manṣûr, on which it abutted; and further, the Ruṣâfah Mosque was larger and more beautiful than the mosque of the City of Manṣûr[1].

Near the mosque stood the palace, generally

[1] According to Yakut (iii. 279) the Ruṣâfah Mosque was also called Ash-Sharkîyah, or 'the Eastern,' from a village of this name that had originally occupied its site, and which, in time, came to be included in part of Ruṣâfah.

called the Ḳaṣr-al-Mahdî after its founder. One authority, however, states that the Palace of Ruṣâfah was built by Hârûn-ar-Rashîd, more probably it was only restored by him, or possibly he had enlarged the buildings of his father. The Palace of Mahdî was originally surrounded by a wall with a ditch, and close to it was the Maydân or Great Square. The gardens surrounding it were watered by the Mahdî Canal; and part of these grounds are mentioned under the name of the Bustân Ḥafṣ (the Garden of Ḥafṣ) with the pool (Birkah) into which the waters of one branch of the Mahdî Canal were discharged. From the description of this canal and of the roads through Ruṣâfah, we may conclude that the palace and gardens lay near the Tigris bank, while on the land side stood the mosque, and the Maydân was beyond this again, near the road leading to the Upper Bridge[1].

The new quarter was at first known as 'Askar-al-Mahdî (Mahdî's Camp), but Ar-Ruṣâfah (the Causeway) became its more general name, this last having reference presumably to a causeway which had carried the road across the swampy ground formed within the loop of the Tigris by the inflowing streams which, after being canalized, supplied the waters of the Nahr Mahdî. The ground here lay at a lower level than that on the other bank of the Tigris, where the City of Manṣûr was built, the difference amounting to from two to three ells, as was shown by the levels run in order to settle this point, which had become matter of dispute between the Caliph Mu'taṣim and his Wazîr, Ibn Abî Dâûd.

[1] Istakhri, 83; Ya'kubi, 251; Tabari, iii. 322, 364, 365, 366; Ibn Serapion, 23; Yakut, ii. 783.

But though low-lying as compared with the west bank, Ruṣâfah and all Eastern Baghdad, which spread behind it and to the southward, lay well above the ordinary level of the Tigris flood. Iṣṭakhri in the fourth century (the tenth A.D.) further declares that the habitations of Eastern Baghdad, as well as the gardens of the later palaces of the Caliph, derived their water entirely through the canals brought from the Nahrawân (as described in the previous chapter), seeing that except for a small quantity that was raised for irrigation purposes from the Tigris by water-wheels (Dûlâb), water was not obtainable from the river bed, the level there being too low [1].

In the earlier accounts Ruṣâfah is described as standing on the eastern Tigris bank, opposite and as it were balancing the City of Manṣûr on the western side, which last it equalled in area. Writing in the fourth century (the tenth A.D.) Ya'ḳûbî enumerates in great detail the various fiefs which Mahdî had granted to his nobles in the space round the Palace of Ruṣâfah, and these fiefs covered the lands to the north-east and south, which afterwards were occupied by the quarters of Shammâsîyah and Mukharrim. Adjacent to the Ruṣâfah Mosque, and somewhat above it towards the river bank, stretched the great cemetery, where in after times stood the tombs of the later Abbasid Caliphs, while further to the north again was the tomb of Abu Ḥanîfah

[1] Khatib, folio 78 b; Istakhri, 84. 'Ruṣâfah' was a name common to many places where there had been 'causeways'; Yakut in his *Mushtarik* mentions eleven. There was another town of this name in Mesopotamia, near Wâsiṭ (see Ibn Serapion, p. 45), but perhaps the most celebrated Ruṣâfah after that of Baghdad was the Ruṣâfah near Cordova, built by 'Abd-ar-Rahmân, the first Amîr of the Spanish Omayyads.

the Imâm, forming the centre of a quarter to which in after times it gave its name.

The Imâm Abu Ḥanîfah was the founder of the Ḥanîfites, the earliest of the four orthodox sects of the Sunnîs. As has already been mentioned, he aided Manṣûr in the building of Baghdad, and dying shortly after this, namely about the year 150 (A.D. 767), was buried in what came afterwards to be known as the Cemetery of Khayzurân, to the north of Ruṣâfah. Muḳaddasi saw his tomb here in the year 375 (A.D. 985), and describes this as having recently had a portico (*Ṣuffah*) added to it by one of the learned men of the day named Abu Ja'far az-Zammâm. A century later, in 479 (A.D. 1086), when the Saljûḳ Sultan Mâlik Shâh, with the Wazîr Niẓâm-al-Mulk, were in Baghdad, they visited the shrine of Abu Ḥanîfah, over which, in 459 (A.D. 1067), a dome had been built. Shortly before this also a college was founded, adjacent to the shrine, for the teaching of Ḥanîfite law, by one of the Saljûḳ Secretaries of State to Alp Arslân, the father and predecessor of Mâlik Shâh [1]. The traveller Ibn Jubayr found this dome still standing when he visited Baghdad in 580 (A.D. 1184); it was a white cupola, rising high in the air, and he adds that the shrine had given its name to the surrounding suburb. This quarter of Abu Ḥanîfah Ibn Jubayr describes as occupying in his day the uppermost part of Ruṣâfah, far outside the city limits, as these had

[1] Hamd-Allah, on the other hand, says that this 'high building' was the work of the Mustawfi-al-Mamâlik or Provincial Treasurer, named Sharaf-al-Mulk Abu-Riḍâ, who had been in the service of Mâlik Shâh. See the British Museum MS. of the *Nuzhat*, Add. 16736, folio 148 b; but this passage is wanting in other MSS., and in both the printed and the lithographed texts of the *Nuzhat*.

then come to be by the building of the new wall (by the Caliph Mustaẓhir) round the suburbs of the palaces.

Yâḳût, in the next century, speaks of the mosque of Abu Ḥanîfah as adjoining the tombs of the Caliphs at Ruṣâfah, and Ibn Baṭûṭah, who visited Baghdad in 727 (A.D. 1327), describes the shrine (Zâwiyah) of Abu Ḥanîfah, stating that a dole of food was here distributed daily to all comers—this, says Ibn Baṭûṭah, being the only place in Baghdad where, at that time, such charity was still maintained. The tomb of Abu Ḥanîfah was visited in the middle of the last century by the traveller Niebuhr, whose description will serve equally well for the shrine seen at the present time. It stands in the village of Mu'aẓẓam, so called, says Niebuhr, from the name Al-A'ẓam, 'the Venerated' or 'Honoured,' the title which the Sunnîs have given to Abu Ḥanîfah. The village is situated a half-hour distant to the north of the present city gate, called the Bâb Mu'aẓẓam, and it lies on the east bank of the Tigris, opposite to the tombs of the Kâẓimayn on the western side. From a topographical point of view the shrine of Abu Ḥanîfah is of much importance, since it is one of the few places now extant in East Baghdad which date from the Caliphate of Manṣûr[1].

The Cemetery of Khayzurân, in which this tomb of Abu Ḥanîfah was the most important shrine, was called after Khayzurân (Bamboo-stem), wife of the Caliph Mahdî, and the mother of his sons Hâdî

[1] Mukaddasi, 130; Ibn Jubayr, 228; Ibn-al-Athir, x. 37, 103; Ibn Khallikan, No. 775, p. 83; Yakut, ii. 783; Ibn Batutah, ii. 112; Niebuhr, ii. 240. This suburb of Abu Ḥanîfah must not be confounded with the suburb of Ḥanîfah (or of Abu Ḥanîfah) in Western Baghdad, near the Ḥarîm of Ṭâhir, already described, p. 117.

and Hârûn-ar-Rashîd. There had been a graveyard here belonging to the Magians, already before the foundation of Baghdad, and this became the first Muslim cemetery of the eastern city, the tomb of Ibn Isḥâḳ, the earliest biographer of the Prophet Muḥammad, being among its notable shrines [1].

Between the shrine of Abu Ḥanîfah and the Ruṣâfah Mosque stood the buildings erected over the tombs of the later Caliphs of the Abbasid dynasty. Their graves, it would appear, were still to be seen here as late as the year 727 (A.D. 1327), a list of thirty-two Caliphs being then given by the traveller Ibn Baṭûṭah, who asserts that each tombstone at this time still bore the name of the Caliph who lay buried beneath. It is, however, difficult to understand how this could have been the case, since when the Mongol army sacked Baghdad in 656 (A.D. 1258) the city was set on fire, and the tombs of the Caliphs are expressly stated to have all been burnt [2]. Further, Ibn Baṭûṭah could not possibly have seen in Ruṣâfah the graves of Mahdî and of Hâdî, as he asserts, for they had been buried far away from Baghdad; while the eight Caliphs from Mu'taṣim to Mu'tamid, whose names also occur

[1] Khatib, folios 113 a, b, 116 a, b; Marasid, i. 378. It is worth noting that Yakut nowhere mentions the Khayzurân Cemetery by name, though he frequently refers to the tomb of Abu Ḥanîfah. The cemetery of the Ḳuraysh, as already described in chapter xii, lay on the *western* bank of the Tigris, opposite Ruṣâfah, and adjoining the Kâẓimayn shrines. From some confusion, however, the name of the Ḳuraysh Cemetery after the middle of the sixth century (the tenth A.D.) is by some authorities applied to the Ruṣâfah graveyard in East Baghdad, which lay round the shrine of Abu Ḥanîfah.

[2] Rashid-ad-Din, 308. Perhaps, however, they were subsequently restored by order of Hûlâgû, as is stated to have been the case with the great mosque of the Caliph's Palace and the shrine of the Imâm Mûsâ at the Kâẓimayn.

in his list, were those who lived at Sâmarrâ, where each was buried in the gorgeous sepulchre which his successor caused to be built. Hence the list which Ibn Baṭûṭah gives can only be exact for the later Caliphs. After their return from Sâmarrâ, however, the Abbasids from Muʿtaḍid onwards were (with a few exceptions) buried in either East or West Baghdad; and, beginning with Râḍî and Mustakfî, the sepulchres of fourteen Caliphs occupied the courts outside the Ruṣâfah Mosque, which, from the middle of the fourth century (the tenth A. D.) onwards, came to be a city of the dead, standing aloof from the neighbouring inhabited quarters. The penultimate Caliph Mustanṣir, between the years 623 and 640 (A.D. 1226 and 1242), surrounded the cemetery by a strong wall built of burnt bricks; and at this time the royal tombs were of imposing appearance, being kept in good repair, the rents of certain lands having been allotted for the pay of custodians and the expenses of up-keep [1].

[1] Ibn Batutah, ii. 111; Marasid, i. 472. The list of the tombs of the Caliphs buried in Baghdad is given by Yakut in one article (ii. 783), and those buried at Sâmarrâ in another (iii. 22). The details, however, are not quite exact, as a reference to Ibn-al-Athir and other authorities proves, and the following list may serve to correct these inaccuracies. Of the thirty-seven Abbasid Caliphs, the first fifteen, as the annalists remark, were none of them buried inside Baghdad. The Caliph Saffâḥ, the founder of the dynasty, was buried in his palace at Anbâr; Manṣûr died on the pilgrimage, and was buried at the well called Bir Maymûn in Arabia; Mahdî died while on the march from Baghdad into Media, at the village called Ar-Radhdh, in the province of Mâsabadhân, and was buried there under a walnut-tree; Hâdî was buried in the garden of ʿÎsâbâd, a village owned by his brother ʿÎsâ in the suburb outside Eastern Baghdad (not technically included within the city limits), the exact position of which, however, is unknown; Hârûn-ar-Rashîd died and was buried at Ṭûs or Meshed in Khurâsân; in regard to the unfortunate Amîn, after being decapitated in the garden outside the Anbâr Gate of West Baghdad, the

The destruction wrought by the catapults during the second siege of Baghdad, in the time of Musta'în, resulted in the depopulation and rapid decline of Ruṣâfah. A generation later came the building

trunk of his body was probably at first temporarily buried there, his head having been sent to Mâmûn in Khurâsân, and the subsequent tomb of Amîn in the Kâẓimayn has been described in chapter xii; his brother Mamûn was buried at Tarsus in Cilicia, having died on a military expedition against the Greeks. The next eight Caliphs from Mu'taṣim to Mu'tamid all lived at Sâmarrâ, and there lay buried, with the exception possibly of Musta'în, who, after the disasters of the second siege of Baghdad, was taken down the river to Wâsiṭ and put to death, it being uncertain if his body was brought back to Sâmarrâ for burial. After the return of the Caliphate from Sâmarrâ, Mu'taḍid, the sixteenth Caliph, was the first to be buried within the walls of Baghdad. He and his three sons, the Caliphs 'Alî Muktafi, Muḳtadir, and Ḳâhir, as also his grandson Muttaḳî, were all buried in West Baghdad in the Ṭâhirid Ḥarîm. Râḍî, the twentieth Caliph, the predecessor (and brother) of Muttaḳî, was the first of those buried at Ruṣâfah, but his tomb lay apart from the later royal sepulchres, which, lying all close together, began with that of the twenty-second Caliph Mustakfî, who died some years after being deposed in 334 (A.D. 946). For the next three centuries, with three exceptions, all the succeeding Caliphs, being fourteen in number, were buried at Ruṣâfah, the three exceptions being: the twenty-ninth Caliph Mustarshid, killed in battle in 529 (A.D. 1135) near Hamadân, and buried outside Marâghah; his son Manṣûr Râshid, deposed in 530 (A.D. 1136), afterwards slain in Khûzistân and buried outside Isfahân; and the thirty-third Caliph Mustaḍî, who was buried in 575 (A.D. 1180), in the Ḳaṣr 'Îsâ Quarter of West Baghdad, near the Lower Bridge. Where Musta'ṣim, the last of the Abbasid Caliphs, was laid to his rest, the contemporary chronicles do not state, but if we are to believe Ibn Batutah, and give credit to the statement that the tombs of the Caliphs were restored after the Mongol invasion, his tomb also was among those of his ancestors in Ruṣâfah. Ibn-al-Furat, folio 118 b, states that in the year 647, on the 20th of Sha'bân (November 29, 1249), the daughter of the Caliph Musta'ṣim died, and she was buried in the Dâr-al-Ḥasan 'of the Golden Palaces' (Ad-Dâr-al-Mudhahhabah), dirges being composed by the court poets on this event. It is uncertain what palace is here meant, for the Ḥasanî Palace can hardly have been standing at this late date, and the Ṭâhirid Ḥarîm (in West Baghdad) was already a ruin at the beginning of the seventh century A.H., when Yakut wrote.

of the new palaces of the Caliphs on the river bank a mile or more below this, and the great mosque at Ruṣâfah, in little over two centuries after its foundation, now stood solitary among ruins, surrounded by the graveyards of Eastern Baghdad. It remained in use, however, during six centuries as a congregational mosque for the Friday prayers, since all our authorities name it as one of the three great mosques of East Baghdad; and as late as 727 (A.D. 1327), three-quarters of a century after the Mongol invasion, Ibn Baṭûṭah mentions it as yet standing, though apparently at the present day no traces are visible of the ancient structure [1].

Ruṣâfah, at the close of the third century (the ninth A.D.), when this was still one of the three populous northern quarters of East Baghdad, is described by Ya'ḳûbî as traversed by two thoroughfares, which must have started from the neighbourhood of the Khurâsân Road and the eastern end of the Main Bridge. The first of these thoroughfares was that in which stood the Palace of Mahdî and the great mosque, and it is stated that this was 'a straight road' (*Ṭarîḳ mustaḳîm*). Most streets in an oriental city, as is well known, are much the reverse of straight, and hence it seems not improbable that this road followed the line of the original 'causeway' from which Ruṣâfah had derived its name. The second thoroughfare was

[1] Ibn Batutah, ii. 111. Probably excavations made in the tract of land to the south of the present village of Mu'aẓẓam might bring to light the foundations of the old Ruṣâfah Mosque; also, possibly, traces of the palace of Mahdî. This last, according to Khatib (folio 77 b), was, unlike the rest of Ruṣâfah, built of burnt bricks, as doubtless also was the mosque; and such bricks would not have entirely crumbled to dust even after the lapse of eleven centuries.

that passing to the east of the Maydân or Great Square of Ruṣâfah, which appears to have opened on the land side of the palace and mosque. On this road stood the palace of the Wazîr Faḍl, son of the Chamberlain Rabi', who have both been mentioned in a previous chapter, and near this again was the Ḳaṣr of Umm Ḥabîb, the daughter of Hârûn-ar-Rashîd. This palace, according to Yâḳût, overlooked the roadway which he calls the Shâri'-al-Maydân (the Road of the Square), and its lands had been granted in fief to the Princess Umm Ḥabîb, after the death of the Chamberlain Rabi', by her half-brother the Caliph Mamûn. In later times the palace served as a dower-house for the daughters of the reigning Caliph, and finally its grounds came to be annexed to those of the neighbouring Palace of Mahdî in Ruṣâfah.

Yâḳût describes the Road of the Maydân as communicating directly, on the south, with the road going to the Tuesday Market on the further side of the Mukharrim Quarter, while to the north it gave access to the Shammâsîyah Quarter. The upper part of the road of the Maydân was known as the Khuḍayr Market, where in the days of Ya'ḳûbî Chinese goods and other rarities were exposed for sale. This market is often referred to as the Khuḍayrîyah, and at a later time water-jars were sold here. Subsequently it was called the Khaḍariyyîn Quarter (other spellings of the name also are given), and not far off was the shrine of Abu Ḥanîfah, firewood being sold near this at a place on the river bank. In early days a mosque stood here called the Masjid Khuḍayr, and there was the Road of Skiffs (Ṭarîḳ-az-Zawârîḳ) on the Tigris bank, by which the quarter of the Khuḍayr Market probably had its line of communication with the Upper Bridge of Boats. In this neighbourhood also must have been situated the Palace of Waḍḍâḥ, built under the superintendence of a man from Anbâr of that name, by order of the Caliph Mahdî, which is described as standing near Ruṣâfah.

The exact position of the eastern end of the Upper Bridge, crossing the Tigris from the Ḥarbîyah Quarter to the Shammâsîyah Quarter and Ruṣâfah, is nowhere given, but from many incidental notices this must have been at a point not far below the Shammâsîyah Gate. Here the bridge end was closed by a gate often referred to during the Musta'în siege under the name of the Bridge Gate (Bâb-al-Jisr), and the highroad of the Ruṣâfah Quarter, passing through this, traversed the Upper Bridge to the palace of the Ṭâhirid Ḥarîm on the western bank [1].

[1] Baladhuri, 295; Ya'kubi, 253; Tabari, iii. 367; Yakut, ii. 290, 403, 453; iii. 231; iv. 108, 123; Marasid, i. 357; Ibn-al-Athir, vi. 114, 115.

CHAPTER XV

THE SHAMMÂSÎYAH QUARTER

The great Northern Road. The Road of the Bridge and Sûḳ Yaḥyâ. The Road of the Mahdî Canal and Sûḳ Ja'far. Palaces of Ad-Dûr. The Barmecide Fiefs. Sûḳ Khâlid and the Ḳaṣr-aṭ-Ṭîn. Dâr Faraj. Dayr Darmâlis and Dayr Samâlû. The Shammâsîyah Gate. Three Gates Quarter. Mâlikîyah Cemetery. The Shrine of Vows. The Palace of Mûnis. The Baradân Road and Bridge. Barmecide Houses and the Ḥuṭamîyah. Dâr-ar-Rûm: the Christian Quarter. The Dayr-ar-Rûm or the Nestorian Monastery. The Jacobite Church. Other Christian Monasteries in West and East Baghdad. Christian Festivals in Baghdad. The Nestorian Missionary to China. The Market of Naṣr and the Iron Gates. The Palace of Abu-n-Naṣr near the Baradân Bridge.

THE Shammâsîyah Quarter lay on the east side of Ruṣâfah, and from this it was divided by the great northern road, which, turning off at the head of the Main Bridge, went to Mosul up the left bank of the Tigris. This road passed out from East Baghdad by the gate called the Bâb-ash-Shammâsîyah; it was known in the lower part as the Road of the Bridge (Ṭarîḳ-al-Jisr), here being the market quarter called the Sûḳ Yaḥyâ; in its upper part, near the Shammâsîyah Gate, it took the name of the Road of the Mahdî Canal, from the watercourse which flowed along it, and here lay the market called the Sûḳ Ja'far. Between the upper and the lower part the road traversed the place named Ad-Dûr (the Palaces), which Yâḳût describes as having stood at no great distance from the shrine of Abu Ḥanîfah, though when Yâḳût himself wrote in the year 623 (A.D. 1226) Ad-Dûr had long since become a complete ruin.

During the greater part of the reign of Hârûn-ar-Rashîd, when the Barmecides[1] were at the height of their prosperity, Yaḥyâ with his sons Faḍl and Ja'far had continued to live in their houses on the Square (Raḥbah) of the Khuld Palace in West Baghdad (probably the Review Ground), but some time before his tragic death Ja'far had begun to build himself a palace at Ad-Dûr, though he did not live to take up his residence there. The fiefs granted to the Barmecides in East Baghdad appear to have stretched from Ad-Dûr on the high-road of the Shammâsîyah Gate, across to the road going toward the Baradân Gate, where, as will be mentioned presently, other of their palaces occur. Muḳaddasi in 375 (A.D. 985) refers to Sûḳ Yaḥyâ,

[1] The Barmecides were of Persian origin, from Balkh. Khâlid ibn Barmak had been one of the Wazîrs of the first Abbasid Caliph Saffâḥ, and in the reign of Manṣûr he was made Governor of Mosul. His advice to that Caliph, in the matter of the Sassanian Palaces at Madâîn, has been mentioned in chapter ii. In the next generation his son Yaḥyâ became Wazîr on the accession of Hârûn-ar-Rashîd, who for many years left the government of the empire almost entirely to him and his son Faḍl. Ja'far, the other son of Yaḥyâ, was more especially the boon companion of the Caliph, and during seventeen years the Barmecides were thus supreme both in the government offices and in the palace. From their many fiefs in the Shammâsîyah, it seems probable that the market street called Sûḳ Ja'far and the Nahr Faḍl, as the upper part of the Mahdî Canal was called, were named respectively after the two sons of the Wazîr Yaḥyâ.

adding that behind it was a tomb which adjoined the shrine of Abu Ḥanîfah. This market, according to Ya'ḳûbî, took its name from a certain Yaḥyâ, son of Al-Walîd; Yâḳût, on the other hand, states that it was named after Yaḥyâ ibn Khâlid the Barmecide, Wazîr of Hârûn-ar-Rashîd, and this last was doubtless the popular attribution.

Nearer to the Shammâsîyah Gate was the Market of Khâlid the Barmecide, Wazîr of the first Abbasid Caliph Saffâḥ and father of Yaḥyâ just mentioned. Afterwards the Ḳaṣr-aṭ-Ṭîn (the Clay Castle) occupied its site, built either by Yaḥyâ or by his son Faḍl (for Yâḳût in different passages mentions the one and the other as the founder), and this castle is frequently referred to during the second siege of Baghdad in 251 (A. D. 865) in the time of Musta'în. In the seventh century (the thirteenth A. D.), when Yâḳût wrote, the Ḳaṣr-aṭ-Ṭîn had fallen so completely to ruin, that its exact position even was matter of doubt, but from what Ṭabarî states incidentally when relating the events of the second siege, it must have stood very near the Shammâsîyah Gate. After the fall of the Barmecides their various fiefs passed into the possession of Zubaydah, wife of Hârûn-ar-Rashîd, and during the reign of Mamûn, when Zubaydah had fallen from power, they were granted to Ṭâhir, from whom they were inherited by his descendants, the various Ṭâhirid princes and governors. Immediately above Sûḳ Yaḥyâ, and doubtless also on the road leading up to the Shammâsîyah Gate, was a palace called the Dâr Faraj, after Faraj a Mamlûk (slave) of a certain Hamdûnah, concubine of Hârûn-ar-Rashîd, who had manumitted her. Faraj also became the freedman of the Caliph, and his palace is described as being one of the finest in this quarter[1].

The Shammâsîyah Gate, which stood at the upper end of the road, occupied the north-western extremity of the city wall which enclosed the Shammâsîyah Quarter. Shammâsîyah has the meaning of Deaconry (*Shammâs*[2] signifying 'a deacon' in Arabic), and the place originally had been occupied by several Nestorian or Jacobite monasteries, two being especially celebrated, namely the Dayr Darmâlis and the Dayr Samâlû. In the early days of the Abbasid Caliphate the Samâlû Monastery occupied a considerable tract of ground beside the river, stretching in the direction towards Baradân; near it ran the Mahdî Canal (or the Nahr Faḍl), and there was an extensive cane-brake in its vicinity where wild-fowl were shot. The Dayr is described as a magnificent edifice, inhabited by many monks, and it took its name from Samâlû, a town of the Armenian frontier, which Hârûn-ar-Rashîd had captured in the expedition of the year 163 (A.D. 780)[3]. The Caliph caused the whole population of this place to be transported to Baghdad, for by the terms of the capitulation it had been stipulated that none of the families were to be separated, and

[1] Ibn Serapion, 23; Ya'kubi, 253, 254; Mukaddasi, 130; Ibn Kutaybah, 193; Tabari, iii. 1561; Yakut, ii. 522; iii. 195, 200; iv. 114; Mushtarik, 184.

[2] A borrowed word, from the Syriac *Shamosho*. See Fränkel, p. 276. For the position of these monasteries see Plan No. VII.

[3] The Byzantine chronicler Theophanes (i. 453) mentions the siege of this place by the Caliph Aaron (as he calls him). It lay in the Armeniac Theme, and he writes the name Σημαλοῦος, but what place now represents this fortress is an unsolved problem in the historical geography of the Byzantine Empire, and the Arab historians unfortunately offer no indications for fixing the site.

they were settled on the lands to the north of East Baghdad, where was built the monastery which afterwards went by the name of their native place. With the lapse of time the monastery fell to ruin, and the author of the *Marâṣid*, who wrote about the year A. D. 1300, states that all trace of its buildings had then long since disappeared.

The land in this neighbourhood was a low-lying tract near the mouth of the Faḍl Canal, which ran into the Tigris above the Shammâsîyah Gate, as has already been described. This tract is often spoken of as the Ṣaḥrâ or Plain of the Shammâsîyah, also as the Raḳḳah, a term especially denoting lands that are covered by the overflow of a river. During the siege of Baghdad in the reign of Musta'în, the assailants had their main camp in this plain of the Shammâsîyah, and many doughty deeds took place before the Shammâsîyah Gate, which was defended by great catapults set on the city walls[1]. Outside the Shammâsîyah Quarter to the north-east and east, where, according to Ya'ḳûbî, the highroad to Nahrawân and Persia finally left the city limits, was the suburb frequently mentioned in the accounts of the first siege of Baghdad—during the reign of Amîn—as also during that of Musta'în, and it was called Three Gates (Thalâthah Abwâb)[2].

[1] Tabari, iii. 1551, 1559; Yakut, ii. 659, 660, 670; iii. 317; Marasid, i. 432; Baladhuri, 170; Ibn Serapion, 23.

[2] Ya'kubi, 269. Invariably written without the article; hence it cannot have any reference to the three great city gates of Shammâsîyah, Baradân, and Khurâsân. Mas'udi, vi. 443; Tabari, iii. 1576. Probably near the Three Gates was the village called Bâb-ash-Shâm, 'the Syrian Gate,' of which the author of the Marasid (i. 112) writes that in his day, namely about the year 700 (A.D. 1300), this was the name of a small hamlet in the Khâliṣ district standing at no great distance from Ruṣâfah.

Musta'în, profiting by the experience of the former siege, in 251 (A. D. 865) caused all the houses lying between the city wall of the Shammâsîyah and this place to be demolished, in order that the assailants might not find shelter here for the attack. The houses of Baghdad, therefore, in those days stretched as far north as the Three Gates; but all this quarter suffered greatly during the Musta'în siege, and falling to ruin in the next century, the whole of this site afterwards came to be occupied by the palaces of the Buyid princes.

Outside the Baradân Gate, which stood next to the Shammâsîyah Gate on the south-east, stretched the Mâlikîyah Cemetery, called after a certain 'Abd-Allah ibn Mâlik, who was the first person to be buried here. The Mâlikîyah is mentioned as late as the year 530 (A. D. 1136), when the Saljûk Sultan Mas'ûd, who was then besieging Baghdad, pitched his camp at this place. This, the third of the Baghdad sieges, and which lasted for two months, ended in the deposition of the Caliph Manṣûr Râshid[1], but no details of the siege operations are recorded. 'Abd-Allah ibn Mâlik, from whom the graveyard had taken its name, is probably the captain of the guard who was a special favourite of Khayzurân, the wife of the Caliph Mahdî. During the reign of her son Hârûn-ar-Rashîd this 'Abd-Allah became Governor of the Palace and Chief of Police, and on one occasion commanded the troops sent on an expedition against the Greek frontier. The Mâlikîyah was also known as the Baradân Cemetery, and near this was the chapel (Muṣallâ) especially

[1] Not to be confounded with Hârûn-ar-Rashîd. Khatib, folio 114 a; Ibn-al-Athir, ix. 26; Mas'udi, vi. 269, 308.

set apart for the prayers of the festival at the close of Ramaḍân Fast.

Here stood a tomb called the Ḳabr-an-Nudhûr (the Sepulchre of the Place of Vows), where, according to the popular belief, votive offerings having been made, the prayers of the Faithful were invariably granted, and Khaṭîb gives an edifying anecdote relating how 'Aḍud-ad-Dawlah the Buyid prince here obtained the accomplishment of his desires. The grave is said to have been that of a descendant of the Caliph 'Alî, namely of a certain 'Abd-Allah or 'Ubayd-Allah, great-grandson of 'Alî Zayn-al-'Âbidîn (the fourth Shî'ah Imâm). He having been enticed to this lonely place by the emissaries of one of the Abbasid Caliphs, met his death by falling into the pit which had been dug for this murderous purpose and artfully covered over, the unfortunate man remaining buried alive under the earth thrown in by those who were lying in wait. This Sanctuary of the Vows, Yâḳût, writing in the seventh century (the thirteenth A. D.), describes as still standing, being situated about half a mile beyond the city wall of later East Baghdad. The author of the *Marâṣid* adds that originally the streets of the Ruṣâfah suburbs had extended beyond this chapel, though of course in his time all this district had long fallen to ruin, and by the year 700 (A. D. 1300) the tomb was standing far out in the plain, half a league distant, he says, from the houses of the town [1].

The Buyids became masters of Baghdad in the year 334 (A.D. 945), and their buildings in this region will be described in a subsequent chapter; but in the latter

[1] Khatib, folio 114 a; Yakut, iv. 28; Marasid, ii. 385.

years of the preceding century a great palace was erected immediately outside the Shammâsîyah Gate by Mûnis, the general of the armies of Muḳtadir, and it was near the Shammâsîyah Gate that this unfortunate Caliph met his death at the hands of the insurgent troops.

The Baradân Road divided the Shammâsîyah Quarter into two halves, forming the line of communication between the Baradân Gate and the head of the Main Bridge. Ya'ḳûbî refers to it under the name of 'the Road to the Left,' namely from the Khurâsân Road, and it must have turned off this somewhat lower down than the bifurcation of the great northern road leading to the Shammâsîyah Gate. On the lower part of the Baradân Road had stood the houses of Khâlid the Barmecide and of his son Yaḥyâ, with those of the latter's two sons Faḍl and Ja'far. These houses probably lay to the left hand of the road, on the western side, being connected at the back with the Sûḳ Yaḥyâ occupying part of the adjacent road to the Shammâsîyah Gate, as has already been described. Above the Barmecide houses came the Baradân Bridge (Ḳanṭarah Baradân), where the road crossed the Mahdî Canal not far from the Baradân Gate, and near here had been a fief granted by Mahdî to another Barmecide called Abu 'Ubayd Mu'âwiyah of Balkh. The Baradân Bridge had been built by a certain As-Sarî ibn al-Ḥuṭam, who had owned land, building a palace here, and whose name was likewise preserved in that of a village near Baghdad, which having been his property was called Al-Ḥuṭamîyah.

The triangle enclosed by the line of the city

wall and the highroads of the Baradân and Khurâsân Gates, was traversed by the lower part of the Mahdî Canal, on which stood first the quarter called the House of the Greeks, then the Market of Naṣr, and below this the Iron Gates, near the point where the Mahdî Canal bifurcated, one branch flowing back to Ruṣâfah, while the other continued along the Khurâsân Road to the Khurâsân Gate. The Dâr-ar-Rûmîyîn, more generally called the Dâr-ar-Rûm (the House of the Greeks), was the Christian Quarter of mediaeval Baghdad, which existed down to the time when Fakhri wrote, namely the year 700 (A. D. 1300). Its position is approximately fixed by Ibn Serapion, who describes the course of the Mahdî Canal as given in the preceding paragraph, Yâḳût also speaking of this quarter as situated in the neighbourhood of the Shammâsîyah Quarter and at no great distance from the tombs of the Caliphs in Ruṣâfah [1]. In the usage of mediaeval Arabic, the name *Rûmîyîn* or *Rûm* (representing the Romaioi or Greeks) had come to be used for the Christians in general, whether Greek or Latin [2], and the Dâr-ar-Rûm was thus the common name for the Christian Quarter in Baghdad. The Christians in Mesopotamia, who were subjects of the Abbasid Caliphs, belonged for the most part to the two heterodox churches of the Jacobites and

[1] Ibn Serapion, 23; Fakhri, 190; Yakut, ii. 662, 783; iii. 317. By an oversight *Dâr-ar-Rûm* has been omitted in the index to Yakut.

[2] The Spanish Moslems, for instance, call their Christian fellow countrymen Ar-Rûm. An excellent summary of the political and religious condition of the Christians who inhabited the dominions of the Abbasid Caliphs is given in Kremer, ii. 172 to 176. See also Gibbon, *Decline and Fall*, chapter xlvii; and for the Nestorian bishoprics of Asia, Sir H. Yule, *Cathay*, pp. lxxxviii, ccxliv.

the Nestorians, but the dominant sect was that of the Nestorians, and hence their patriarch (or Catholicos) had the right of residence in Baghdad, a privilege which the Jacobites had always sought in vain to obtain.

In the Christian Quarter of the Dâr-ar-Rûm was the church and the great monastery called the Dayr-ar-Rûm. This, according to Yâḳût, had been founded in the reign of the Caliph Mahdî, that is to say between the years 158 and 169 (A. D. 775 and 785), at which time certain Greek prisoners of war, having been settled in this part of Baghdad, the Greek House was built by them with a church in its immediate neighbourhood. This church, either from its origin or by subsequent arrangement, belonged exclusively to the Nestorians; it was very large, being solidly constructed and beautifully ornamented, and in the monastery (*Dayr*) which was subsequently built on the eastern side of the Church, the Catholicos (the word was corrupted by Arabs into Al-Jâthilîḳ) had his cell or dwelling-house. Between the church and monastery a door of communication existed, through which, on the festivals and when Holy Communion was to be celebrated, the monks could pass to and fro. The buildings of the original Greek House are described as standing at some distance apart from the church and monastery; and they would appear to have covered a considerable area, for within the compass of the walls was a broad court surrounded by porticoes.

The author of the *Marâṣid* remarks that 'among the Christian sects, no one of the one sect will pray in the church of the other sect,' and he continues that for this reason the Jacobites had their own particular church in Baghdad, situated near the great church of the Nestorians, this Jacobite church being especially remarkable for the number of wonderful pictures shown there, which, with some other works of art that it contained, caused the place to be much visited by strangers.

In all ordinary circumstances the Christians appear to have enjoyed complete toleration in Baghdad under the government of the Caliphs, for besides these two churches with the great Monastery of the Dayr-ar-Rûm, they possessed many other lesser monasteries in different quarters of the city. Thus in Karkh, on the western side of the Tigris there was the Monastery of the Virgins in the fief of the Christians, which has already been mentioned; also the Dayr Durtâ and the Dayr-al-Ḳibâb upstream, beyond the Zubaydîyah Fief; while in the Ḳaṭrabbul District to the northward of the Round City stood the monastery called the Dayr Ashmûnâ, after the founder, whose body lay buried here. The festival of Ashmûnâ was celebrated on the third day of the month Tishrîn I, corresponding with October, and this monastery, being a very pleasant place of resort, was much visited by the people of Baghdad. Its exact position is not given, but it was at no great distance from the northern suburbs.

In addition to the foregoing, Yâḳût mentions two other monasteries as of Western Baghdad, though again from the lack of precise information the position of neither the one nor the other of these can be exactly fixed. One was the Dayr Midyân, lying on the bank of the Karkhâyâ Canal, which the author of the *Marâṣid* says was also known as the Dayr Sarkhîs (this last name being probably a clerical error for *Sarjîs*, i.e. the Monastery of Sergius), and this is described as a fine place, much frequented by pleasure-seekers from the city. The other monastery in the vicinity of West Baghdad was the Dayr-ath-Tha'âlib (the Monastery of the Foxes), and concerning the position of this there was much dispute. Some authorities state that it stood nearly two miles distant from Baghdad, on the Kûfah highroad towards Ṣarṣar, and near the village of Ḥârithîyah; while according to others the Monastery of the Foxes was the building that stood near the shrine of Ma'rûf Karkhî, and hence was either to be identified with the Dayr-al-Jâthilîḳ (the Monastery of the Catholicos or Patriarch), being merely its other name, or else was a second monastery which had stood alongside of it.

In Eastern Baghdad five monasteries are mentioned by Yâḳût in addition to the great Dayr-ar-Rûm of the Christian Quarter. Upstream were the two monasteries outside the Shammâsîyah Gate, namely the Dayr Darmâlis and the Dayr Samâlû, which have already been noticed; while in the district immediately to the north of this, near the village of Mazrafah, was the Dayr Sâbûr (the Monastery of Sapor), '*very populous, pleasant, and with many gardens.*' Likewise near Mazrafah and at some four leagues distant from Baghdad stood the Dayr Jurjis (the Monastery of St. George) with numerous gardens and fine fruit-trees, of which Yâḳût speaks as one of the pleasantest places to visit in this quarter of the city. Also in East

Baghdad, but downstream, below the southern quarters which surrounded the palaces of the Caliph, was the monastery called the Dayr-az-Zandaward, lying near the Âzaj Gate which will be mentioned in a later chapter. Its gardens had been celebrated for the oranges and grapes grown here, 'the best in all Baghdad,' Yâḳût states; but when the author of the *Marâṣid* wrote, about the year 700 (A. D. 1300), both the gardens and the Monastery of Zandaward had entirely disappeared, its site being then occupied by the houses and streets of New Baghdad.

The account which Yâḳût gives of these monasteries is in the main derived from the work of Shâbushtî, who composed his *Kitâb-ad-Diyârât* (the Book of the Monasteries) in Egypt, and who died about the year 390 (A. D. 1000)[1]. Many of these establishments, by the year 623 (A. D. 1226), when Yâḳût wrote, would appear to have already fallen to ruin, their monks having died or dispersed, but in the days of Yâḳût the gardens of the monasteries still for the most part remained, and are noted by him as 'pleasant places' whither the people of Baghdad went on festival days. The author of the *Marâṣid*, however, writing in the year 700 (A. D. 1300), and therefore after the Mongol siege, in almost every case, having epitomized the notice

[1] The MS. of this work (lacking the first thirteen folios) exists in the Berlin Library, under the No. 8321, which MS. Ahlwardt in the Catalogue has in error ascribed to Abu-l-Faraj Al-Isfahânî, the author of the *Fihrist*. It is to be hoped that before long this important MS. may be published by Mr. F. J. Heer, who in his recent work (*Die historischen und geographischen Quellen in Jacut's Wörterbuch*, p. 88, Strassburg, Trübner, 1899) has given an interesting account of the MS. and its contents.

given by Yâķût, adds that all trace of this or that monastery had in his time disappeared. As already said, there is evidence to show that in former times under the rule of the Abbasid Caliphs, Christians in Baghdad were not subject to any molestation or oppression by the officials of the government. In moments of popular commotion their churches and monasteries doubtless were plundered by the rabble, but the mosques of the Shî'ahs and the Sunnîs alternately had to suffer a like experience, when the mob, in the nominal interests of the one sect or the other, broke loose from all restraint and rioted through the outlying quarters of the great city.

When describing the mother church of the Nestorians near the Dayr-ar-Rûm, Yâķût relates how it was the custom of the Moslems of Baghdad to visit this church on Sundays and on festivals, the crowd then being often very great of those who came to look at 'the young deacons and monks, with their handsome faces'; and he speaks of 'dancing, drinking, and pleasure-making' as matters for which these Dayrs were for the most part visited. Yâķût adds that the Christians in Baghdad were wont to celebrate each of their great festivals at a different monastery; and in his day the most celebrated of these feast days were the four Sundays of the Festival of the Fast (doubtless Easter and the three following Sundays), of which the first Sunday festival was held at the monastery called the Dayr-al-'Âsiyah, the second at the Dayr-az-Zuraykîyah (but neither of these monasteries is elsewhere mentioned), the third Sunday festival being at the Dayr-az-Zandaward, and the fourth at the Dayr Darmâlis; and he adds 'to all these the Christians are wont to assemble, together with many other pleasure-seekers[1].'

As showing the equal footing on which the Christians lived with the Moslems under the Abbasid Caliphs, a translation may be given of the account left us by the Moslem author of the *Kitâb-al-Fihrist*, relating an interview which he had with a certain Nestorian missionary, whom he met in Baghdad during the reign of the Caliph Ṭâi'. The passage, further, is of historical importance as giving the limit in date of the Nestorian missions sent into further Asia; for, as is well known by the Singanfu inscription and other similar documents, Nestorian Christianity had at one time spread throughout the length and breadth of Asia, penetrating into the Chinese empire, and it lay with the chief Patriarch of Mesopotamia to appoint the bishops who resided in India, Central Asia, and the far East. The author of the *Fihrist* states that the missionary he met was a monk, a native of Najrân, which was a Nestorian bishopric of Southern Arabia, and that he met him after his return from a mission to China in the year 377 (A.D. 987). The narrative in the *Fihrist* then continues:—

'Now this man of the people of Najrân had been dispatched some seven years before this date by the Catholicos (or Patriarch of Baghdad) to the land of China, there being sent with him five other men of the Christians, of those whose business it is to attend to the affairs of religion.

[1] Yakut, ii. 616, 643, 650, 659, 660, 662, 665, 666, 670, 680, 695; Marasid, i. 426, 429, 430, 431, 432, 436, 440.

And six years after they had thus gone forth, this monk with one other alone of all that company had returned alive (to Baghdad), whom I met in the Christian Quarter of the Dâr-ar-Rûm behind the church, finding him to be a man in the prime of life with a fine figure, but sparing of words unless he were questioned. So I asked him what had been the cause of his remaining away so long a time, and what reason had brought him back thence, whereupon he recounted to me all the adventures that had befallen him, and what had hindered him in the journey. He said in conclusion that the Christians who had been of old in the lands of China were now disappeared, and that their possessions had perished, so that in the whole land hardly one Christian now remained alive, and though in ancient times the Christians there had possessed a church, this also was now in ruin. And the monk added that when he had at length seen how none remained there of his religion, he had finally returned home, travelling back in less time than it had taken him to perform the voyage out [1].'

On the Mahdî Canal, immediately below the Greek Quarter, was the Market of Naṣr, called after Naṣr the son of Mâlik, of the Khuzâʿah

[1] The description of China, which follows, is very curious, but this is not the place to attempt its translation, and many of the names of Chinese towns and provinces have unfortunately been so corrupted by the copyist of the MS. as to be almost unrecognizable. The text will be found in the *Kitâb-al-Fihrist*, p. 349. The editor, Professor Flügel, has made the mistake in the preface, p. xiv, and his notes, p. 184, of supposing that the Dâr-ar-Rûm, here mentioned, refers to Constantinople: see Kremer, ii. 173, note 2, who rightly points out that it is the Christian Quarter of Baghdad, which is the place intended.

tribe, to whom the Caliph Mahdî had granted these lands in fief. This Naṣr is best known as father of the celebrated ascetic Aḥmad ibn Naṣr, one of the martyrs in the cause of orthodoxy, whom the Caliph Wâthiḳ put to death in 231 (A. D. 846). He had preached against the Caliph, declaring him to be a heretic for denying the dogma that the Ḳurân was 'uncreate'; and for witnessing that the Book of Allah was eternal he suffered death. Khaṭîb, from whom Yâḳût has copied most of his information about these places, adds that there was originally a mosque in the Market of Naṣr, but that this fell to ruin at the time of the second siege of Baghdad, under Musta'în. Khaṭîb further adds that a certain Abu Naṣr Hâshim had bought from As-Sarî [1], the original owner of the fief on the road near the Baradân Bridge, a parcel of land on which Abu Naṣr built himself a palace. This was the finest building in all the neighbouring quarter, at least in the judgement of the Emperor of Constantinople, to whom (so Khaṭîb reports) a drawing representing the various quarters of Baghdad having been submitted, his Majesty pointed out this palace as to his mind the most magnificent. Finally, the Iron Gates (Al-Abwâb-al-Ḥadîd) described by Ibn Serapion as in the Naṣr Market, may possibly be identical with the gate called the Bâb Naṣr, which is mentioned by Ibn-al-Athîr in his chronicle under the year 519 (A. D. 1125) as situated not far from the Shammâsîyah plain, though it is to be remarked that no other writer refers at this late date either to the Naṣr Market or the Iron

[1] See above, p. 206. The name is also written in some MSS. Abu-n-Naḍr Hâshim ibn al-Ḳâsim.

Gates, and it is therefore doubtful whether they existed after the changes effected by the Buyid princes, when these built their palaces in East Baghdad[1].

[1] Ibn Serapion, 22, 23; Ya'kubi, 252, 253; Khatib, folios 88 b, 113 b; Yakut, ii. 783; iii. 207, 317; iv. 187; Marasid, i. 430; Ibn-al-Athir, x. 441.

CHAPTER XVI

THE MUKHARRIM QUARTER

The Khurâsân Road and its Markets. The Bâb-aṭ-Ṭâḳ Gate. The Mûsâ Canal and the Mukharrim. The Zâhir Garden, the Great Road, and the Street of 'Amr the Greek. The Palace of Mu'taṣim. The Long Street, the Palace of Ibn-al-Furât, and the Street of the Vine. The Sûḳ-al-'Aṭsh or Thirst Market. The Market of Ḥarashî and his Palace. The Anṣâr Bridge, the Palace of Ibn-al-Khaṣîb, and the three Tanks. The Great Pitched Gate. The Mukharrim Gate and Road: the Canal to the Firdûs Palace. The Haymarket. Palace of Princess Bânûjah. The Horse Market and its Gate. The Bâb 'Ammâr and the Palace of 'Umârah. The two lower Canals at the Triple Divide. The Mu'allâ Canal. The Bâb Abraz and the Gate of the Tuesday Market. The Canal of the Palaces. The Bâb 'Âmmah. The Mushjîr Fief.

THE southern limit of the Shammâsîyah Quarter was the great Khurâsân Road, which ran from the end of the Main Bridge of Boats eastward to the Khurâsân Gate, whence the highroad went to Nahrawân Town, on the canal of that name. In describing the three northern quarters at the close of the third century (the ninth A.D.), Ya'ḳûbî mentions this Khurâsân Road as the chief market of Eastern Baghdad, where were gathered together all kinds of goods and stuffs and manufactured articles, with by-streets to the right hand and to the left occupied by warehouses of the merchants and the dwellings of the tradesmen. The number of shops in this great market must have been considerable, for, as the result of a fire which occurred here in the year 292 (A.D. 905), more than three hundred shops near the bridge are reported to have been burnt.

In the immediate neighbourhood of the Main Bridge, where the road began, stood the Market of the Goldsmiths (Sûḳ-aṣ-Ṣâghah), and here was the great arched gate, called the Bâb-aṭ-Ṭâḳ, which gave its name collectively to the three northern quarters of Eastern Baghdad, for these are often referred to as the Bâb-aṭ-Ṭâḳ (the Quarter of the Gate of the Archway). This arch had originally formed part of the Palace of Asmâ, daughter of the Caliph Manṣûr, which occupied one side of the roadway, while opposite to it stood the Palace of Prince 'Ubayd-Allah[1], son of Mahdî, the road between the two being known as the Bayn-al-Ḳaṣrayn (the Road between the Palaces). The ground here had originally been granted in fief by Mahdî to his Chief of Police, Khuzaymah ibn Khâzim, whose palace, called the Dâr Khuzaymah, stood at the corner where the road of the Shammâsîyah branched off to the northern gate. In the days of Hârûn-ar-Rashîd the Bâb-aṭ-Ṭâḳ at the bridge head was often used as a meeting-place of the poets, whose works the Caliph delighted to have recited before him, and hence this building had come to be known as the Majlis-ash-Shu'arâ, or the Assembly Hall of the Poets.

The name Mukharrim had been given to the parcel of land here on the Tigris bank long before Baghdad was founded, for during the first century

[1] Khatib, folio 88 a. Yakut, iii. 489, calls him '*Abd-Allah* in error.

of the Hijrah, when the Moslems had recently conquered Mesopotamia, an Arab of that name settled here on a fief granted to him by the Caliph 'Omar. It will be remembered that the Mukharrim Quarter was bounded on the east and south by the city wall of the time of Musta'în, which curved round in a quadrant from the Khurâsân Gate to the Gate of the Tuesday Market, immediately above the Firdûs Palace on the river. The Tigris formed the western boundary of the quarter, and more or less parallel with the river bank ran the Great Road (Ash-Shâri'-al-A'ẓam), leading from the Gate of the Tuesday Market up to the Main Bridge, where, crossing the line of the Khurâsân Road, it communicated with the Shammâsîyah Road and the Road of the Maydân in Ruṣâfah. Through these roads in Ruṣâfah, therefore, the Great Road was the chief thoroughfare from north to south on the eastern side of the river, connecting the Shammâsîyah Gate and the Upper Bridge with the Lower Bridge and the Gate of the Tuesday Market. The name of the Great Road, however, was only applied to that part of the thoroughfare which traversed the Mukharrim Quarter, beginning where the Garden of Zâhir lay along the bank of the Tigris, just below the head of the Main Bridge, and in its upper part the Great Road probably marked the limit of this garden on the east side, the mouth of the Mûsâ Canal being at the lower boundary. The position of the Garden of Zâhir is unfortunately not specifically described, nor is it stated who Zâhir, the original owner of the garden, had been. The accounts, however, clearly indicate that the Zâhir Garden lay on the bank of the Tigris, at the mouth of the Mûsâ

Canal, which flowed through and irrigated the garden after having crossed the Great Road which went down the river side to the Gate of the Tuesday Market; and it seems therefore probable that the garden must have been situated almost immediately below the Main Bridge of Boats. The Zâhir Garden is also mentioned in connexion with the Wazîr of the Caliph Muḳtadir, Ibn Muḳlah, who built himself a palace here—spending, it is said, 200,000 dînârs (about £100,000)—and he annexed some twenty Jarîbs (or seven acres) of the garden, which were included in the precincts of his new palace, the completion of which fell in the year 320 (A.D. 932)[1].

As already described in chapter xiii, the Mûsâ Canal traversed the Mukharrim Quarter from south-east to north-west. It entered the quarter by the Gate of the Horse Market, and after sending off six minor branch canals (which all started from its left bank, flowing towards the river), the parent stream, as mentioned in the last paragraph, ultimately flowed out into the Tigris below the Zâhir Garden. Ibn Serapion states that before reaching the garden, and after crossing the Great Road, the canal traversed the Street of 'Amr-ar-Rûmî (the Greek 'Amr), which it appears likely was a crossroad to the north of the garden. Who this 'Amr was is not given, but possibly he is the individual mentioned by Balâdhurî as having been the freedman of the Caliph Hâdî, who had named him governor of Ḳazwîn in northern Persia[2].

[1] Ibn Serapion, 22; 'Arib, 64, 154, 185. This Zâhir is not to be confounded with the Caliph Ẓâhir.

[2] Ya'kubi, 251, 253; Istakhri, 83; Ibn Serapion, 21, 22; 'Arib, 64, 158; Baladhuri, 295, 323; Mas'udi, viii. 236; Yakut, iii. 232; iv. 441.

In the northern part of the Mukharrim Quarter, on the bank of the Mûsâ Canal, and probably near the Khurâsân Gate, stood the Palace of the Caliph Mu'taṣim, along the southern side of which passed the Long Street (Darb-aṭ-Ṭawîl). This palace had been inhabited by Mu'taṣim between the years 218 and 221 (A.D. 833 to 836), that is to say before he abandoned Baghdad for Sâmarrâ; and it must have fallen to ruin not long after this latter date, for the Mu'taṣim Palace is apparently not mentioned by any authority later than the time of Ibn Serapion, who wrote at the beginning of the fourth century (the tenth A.D.). Just before reaching the Long Street and the Mu'taṣim Palace a canal branched from the Nahr Mûsâ, which, after a short course, reached the garden of the palace built by the Wazîr Ibn-al-Furât, where its waters became lost in irrigation channels. 'Alî Ibn-al-Furât was a statesman well known during the reign of Muḳtadir, whom he served as Wazîr three several times, namely between the years 296 and 312 (A.D. 909 to 924); and along this canal leading to his palace passed the road called the Shâri' Karm-al-'Arsh (or Karm-al-Mu'arrash, as one MS. gives it), which may be translated the Street of the Vine Trellis or of the Climbing Vine.

In this neighbourhood lay the Thirst Market (Sûḳ-al-'Aṭsh), through which the branch canal, now under discussion, took its way shortly after bifurcating from the Mûsâ Canal; and this was one of the chief centres of the Mukharrim Quarter. The market had been built during the reign of Mahdî by Sa'îd-al-Ḥarashî, whose quadrangle and palace, with the market street called after him, will be mentioned presently. The Sûḳ-al-'Aṭsh seems to have fallen early to ruin, for when Yâḳût wrote in the beginning of the seventh century (the thirteenth A.D.), the place where it had originally stood was completely unknown. The original intention of the Caliph Mahdî had been to have called it the Market of Satiety (Sûḳ-ar-Riyy), presumably because it was assumed that 'satiety' for all bodily wants could here be easily attained. It was to have been the rival of the markets of Karkh on the western side, and with a view of taking away trade from these, many merchants were deported from West Baghdad and settled here by the Caliph's orders. The name of Thirst Market, however, was given to it by the people in derision, and this became its permanent appellation. Adjacent to it stood the smaller market called Suwayḳah-al-Ḥarashî, already referred to, with the quadrangle (Murabba'ah) in which stood the palace called the Dâr Sa'îd, this Sa'îd-al-Ḥarashî[1] having been the general whom the Caliph Mahdî dispatched against Al-Muḳanna', the celebrated Veiled Prophet of Khurâsân, whose overthrow, much to the relief of his master, Sa'îd brought about.

To the south of the Palace of Mu'taṣim, and higher up its main stream, the Mûsâ Canal was crossed by a bridge called the Ḳanṭarah-al-Anṣâr, the name of Anṣâr or 'Helpers' having been given to those people in Medina who had aided the Prophet Muḥammad at the time of his flight out of Mecca, and whose descendants in after times still bore this honourable surname. Near this bridge stood the

[1] Ya'kubi, 304; 'Arib, 28, 43. *Ḥarashî* is the true reading, not *Khurshî* (which would mean the Khurâsânian), as given in Yakut, iii. 194; iv. 485.

Palace of Aḥmad-al-Khaṣîbî, commonly called Ibn-al-Khaṣîb, Wazîr in the year 314 (A.D. 926) of the Caliph Muḳtadir[1]; the name of the road which crossed by the Anṣâr Bridge is not given, but it was probably the Road of Sa'd (which will be noticed presently), leading into the Long Street near the Mu'taṣim Palace.

Immediately beyond the bridge three minor canals branched from the Mûsâ Canal, conducting its waters to a like number of tanks, called respectively the Ḥawḍ Dâûd, the Ḥawḍ Haylânah, and the Ḥawḍ-al-Anṣâr, this last after the Helpers, from whom the bridge took its name. The tank of Dâûd lay nearest to the Thirst Market, already described, and it was either called after Dâûd (the Arabic form of David), the son of the Caliph Mahdî, or after one of his freedmen who was the namesake of the prince. The midmost of the tanks was called after Haylânah (Helena), either the favourite concubine of Hârûn-ar-Rashîd, or, according to another version, a slave of the same name who had held the post of Ḳahramânah or Stewardess of the Ḥarîm in the reign of Manṣûr. She is probably identical with the woman already mentioned (p. 146), after whom a suburb and fief in Western Baghdad, near the Muḥawwal Gate, had been named[2].

[1] He was the son of 'Ubayd-Allah, but in accordance with a common custom reverted to the name of his grandfather, Aḥmad ibn-al-Khaṣîb, who had been Wazîr of the Caliph Muntaṣir, in 247 (A.D. 861), at Sâmarrâ. In my notes to Ibn Serapion, p. 282, this palace of Ibn-al-Khaṣîb has been attributed, in error, to the grandfather, who having lived at Sâmarrâ is unlikely to have been the builder of it.

[2] 'Arib, 127; Ibn Serapion, 22; Ya'kubi, 252, 253, 255; Khatib, folio 106 b; Yakut, ii. 362; iii. 194; iv. 485. From the description of the courses of the canals given by Ibn Serapion, it is evident that the Thirst Market lay to the south of the Khurâsân highroad, hence

South again of the Anṣâr Bridge, but further up-stream, the main branch canal of the Mukharrim Quarter bifurcated from the Nahr Mûsâ, leaving it near the gateway known as the Bâb Muḳayyar-al-Kabîr (the Great Pitched Gate), so called from the bitumen or mineral pitch (in Arabic *Ḳîr*) with which it was overlaid. This method of preserving the sun-dried bricks from the effects of damp and rain was of common usage in Baghdad. The bitumen came chiefly from a well lying between Kûfah and Baṣrah, where it rose to the surface of the ground mixed with water. Though originally soft like clay, it soon hardened by exposure, and when plastered on a wall and polished it came to resemble a slab of marble in appearance. It was especially used for lining the hot rooms in the baths, where both floors and walls could thus be rendered watertight; and Yâḳût says there was a large quarter of Baghdad in his day known as Darb-al-Ḳayyâr (the Street of the Pitch-workers), probably identical with the Shâriʻ-al-Ḳay-yârîn (see p. 78) in West Baghdad, mentioned by Ibn Serapion, which took its name from those who were of this trade.

The Great Road of the Mukharrim Quarter, which led up from the Lower Bridge of Boats and the Tuesday Market, by which, according to Yaʻḳûbî, 'one came over from Western Baghdad,' after passing

Yakut (who confesses that no one could, in his day, tell where this market had stood), is certainly wrong in placing it between the Shammâsîyah and Ruṣâfah, and in the immediate neighbourhood of the great Dyke of Muʻizz-ad-Dawlah, which will be described in the following chapter. This last, indeed, must have been separated from the Thirst Market by the whole extent of the Shammâsîyah Quarter. In my paper on Ibn Serapion, p. 283, I have by mistake mistranslated Sûḳ-al-ʻAṭsh as the 'Famine' Market—*'atsh* being, of course, 'thirst,' not 'hunger.'

first along the river bank appears to have bifurcated when it came to the gate known as the Bâb-al-Mukharrim, one branch road turning inland towards the Great Pitched Gate. The branch canal of the Mukharrim Quarter ran down this road to the Mukharrim[1] Gate, where the canal was crossed by an arched bridge, called the Ḳanṭarah-al-'Abbâs, after a brother of the Caliph Manṣûr; and in later times the canal here was known as the Ditch of Al-'Abbâs. A branch, starting from the Mukharrim Gate, flowed off south through a channel dug by the Caliph Mu'taḍid to irrigate the gardens of the Firdûs Palace beyond the town wall; but the main course of the canal, after passing the Mukharrim Gate, turned up north along the highroad of the Mukharrim Quarter (the Great Road), where its waters soon became lost in irrigation channels.

Between the Mukharrim Gate and the Great Pitched Gate, the thoroughfare which, as said, bifurcated from the Great Road, was bordered by the booths of the Hay Market (Ḥawânît-al-'Allâfîn), and at the Great Pitched Gate there turned off the road known as the Shâri' Sa'd-al-Waṣîf, which led towards the Anṣâr Bridge. This road was called after a

[1] The position of the Bâb Mukharrim is difficult precisely to determine. It stood on the canal (Ibn Serapion, p. 22), and lay therefore within the Mukharrim Quarter, and was not a gate in the line of the wall built by Musta'în. Further, from the account of the reception of the Greek ambassadors by Muḳtadir, we learn that the Mukharrim Gate was on the line of the thoroughfare going from the Shammâsîyah Gate down the Tigris to the gate of the palace called the Bâb-al-'Âmmah ('Arib, 64; Khatib, folio 93 b). It seems probable, therefore, that the Bâb Mukharrim stood somewhat to the north of where the Gate of the Sultan (the modern Bâb-al-Mu'aẓẓam) was built at a subsequent date, when the later wall round the quarter of the palaces, which still encloses the eastern city of Baghdad, was erected by the Caliph Mustaẓhir.

certain Sa'd 'the Slave,' possibly the same as Sa'd-al-Khadîm (the Eunuch), who having been originally of the household of Îtâkh the Turk, became the favourite attendant of the Caliph Mutawakkil. On this Street of Sa'd stood the Palace of Ibn-al-Khaṣîb, Wazîr of the Caliph Muḳtadir, already mentioned; and apparently near this was the Market (Suwayḳah) which took its name from Ḥajjâj-al-Waṣîf, who had been a freedman of the Caliph Mahdî.

Further up the Mûsâ Canal, and probably due east of the Great Pitched Gate, was the bifurcation of the uppermost of the six canals which branched from the Nahr Mûsâ, and this had its point of origin near the gate called the Bâb 'Ammâr. It flowed direct to the Palace of Bânûjah, whose name is also written Bânûḳah (meaning Little Bânû or 'Lady' in Turkish), a daughter of the Caliph Mahdî, who is reported to have died young, she having been the first of the Abbasids to be buried in the Khayzurân cemetery outside the Abu Ḥanîfah Suburb. This princess was a great favourite with her father, whom she used always to accompany when he left the capital, and the good people of Baṣrah were on one occasion much scandalized by seeing her ride publicly beside the Caliph Mahdî as he entered their city, she being on this occasion dressed as a page (Ghulâm) in a black tunic and girt with a sword, wearing a man's turban on her head. She is described as having had brown hair and a pleasing figure, its plumpness showing out under her boy's dress; and when she died the Caliph Mahdî mourned for her publicly, sitting to receive the condolence of his nobles as though he had lost one of his sons. Whether her palace lay to the right (north) or to the left (south) of the Mûsâ Canal is not stated, but this branch canal which carried water to its grounds ended here, the stream running dry in the irrigation channels.

The uppermost reach of the Mûsâ Canal, above the branch to the Bânûjah Palace, flowed through the Horse Market called Sûḳ-ad-Dawwâbb (more exactly the Market for the sale of Riding Animals and Beasts of Burden), which was closed by the Gate of the Horse Market at its upper end, and below by the Bâb 'Ammâr. After whom the Gate of 'Ammâr was named is not stated, indeed the only authorities who speak of it are, apparently, Ibn Serapion and 'Arîb; but it is possible that this 'Ammâr may have been a connexion of an individual named 'Umârah, whose palace called the Dâr 'Umârah is mentioned by Yâḳût, quoting from Khaṭîb, as having stood in the Mukharrim Quarter, this 'Umârah being the son of Abu-l-Khaṣîb, chamberlain of the Caliph Manṣûr. In the description left us by Ibn Serapion, the Gate of the Horse Market is the first building mentioned as standing on the Mûsâ Canal, and this probably lay a short distance to the north of the south-eastern limit of the three northern quarters of East Baghdad. Later authorities state that the Mûsâ Canal entered the town very soon after passing out from the grounds of the Palace of the Pleiades, and this Gate of the Horse Market doubtless was in the wall which Musta'în had caused to be built round these quarters at the time of the siege in 251 (A.D. 865)[1].

[1] Ibn Serapion, 21, 22; 'Arib, 17; Ya'kubi, 254; Ibn Jubayr, 130; Ibn Batutah, ii. 106; Khatib, folios 89 b, 90 b, 106 a, 116 a; Yakut, ii. 521; iii. 200; iv. 112; Marasid, iii. 252; Ibn-al-Athir, vii. 65; Ibn

At the Triple Divide, just outside the Palace of the Pleiades, the two other canals from the Nahr Mûsâ branched to the left, southwards, and the upper of the two was called the Mu'allâ Canal. This was so named from Mu'allâ, a freedman of the Caliph Mahdî, afterwards general-in-chief of the forces in the reign of Hârûn-ar-Rashîd, who is celebrated for having held more governments than any of his contemporaries, he having been governor, in turn, of the city of Baṣrah and of the provinces of Ahwâz, Fârs, Yamâmah, and Baḥrayn. The Mu'allâ Canal entered the Mukharrim Quarter by the gate called the Bâb Abraz, which at the beginning of the fourth century (the tenth A.D.) marked the south-eastern angle of the three northern quarters of East Baghdad. After entering the city the canal passed along, between the houses, until it came to the Gate of the Tuesday Market (Bâb Sûḳ-ath-Thalâthah), which at this period marked the southern limit of East Baghdad; and here, leaving the city, the Mu'allâ Canal entered the Firdûs Palace—the uppermost of the three palaces of the Caliphs—and after irrigating its gardens, flowed out into the Tigris close below the palace buildings.

Below the Palace of the Firdûs stood the Ḥasanî Palace (which with others will be more particularly described in a later chapter), and directly to the Ḥasanî Palace flowed the lowest of the three canals from the Divide on the Nahr Mûsâ. After watering the gardens of the Tâj Palace, which lay

Kutaybah, 193; Tabari, iii. 543. In the passage of Ibn al-Athir (vi. 58), corresponding with this last reference to Tabari, the name of the Princess *Bânûḳah* is, in error, given as *Yâḳûtah*, and this mistake has been copied by Kremer, ii. 62.

immediately below the Ḥasanî on the river bank, this third canal finally discharged its waters into the Tigris below the palace gardens. These grounds had been entered by the third canal near the main gateway of the palace garden wall, called the Bâb-al-'Âmmah (the Public Gate), which will be more fully noticed at a later page, but before reaching the gateway, and at some little distance from the Divide, Ibn Serapion writes that the canal passed the Gate of the Fief of Mushjîr (Bâb Ḳaṭî'ah Mushjîr)[1]. This fief must have occupied much of the ground covered by the Rayḥânîyîn Market of later Baghdad, for the place is not mentioned by subsequent writers, but in the beginning of the fourth century (the tenth A.D.) it still bore the name of its original owner. Mushjîr or Mushkîr-al-Waṣîf (the Slave) had been a favourite Turk attendant of the Caliph Mu'taḍid, by whom he was promoted to the command of the army; Mu'taḍid thus requiting a special service rendered to him, for when Mushkîr had been Steward of the Palace to the preceding Caliph Mu'tamid, he had brought about the prompt accession of the nephew (Mu'taḍid) by serving the uncle (Mu'tamid) with a savoury dish of artfully poisoned meat.

Such, at the beginning of the fourth century (the tenth A.D.), before the advent of the Buyids, were

[1] Yakut, iv. 845. In Ibn Serapion (pp. 22 and 279) the name is printed in error *Mûshajîn*. Khatib, folio 106 b, has the right spelling with a final *r*, and compare Tabari, iii. 2121, with Mas'udi, viii. 110. The name is also written *Mûshkîr*, and evidently represents the Persian Mûshgîr (with a hard *g*), meaning 'mouse-catcher,' which is the name of a species of crow, also called *Mûsh-khwâr*, or 'mouse-eater.' The Turk slaves frequently had names (or nicknames) derived from birds, e.g. Tughril, 'Falcon,' Ḳalâûn, 'Duck.'

the three northern quarters of East Baghdad, namely Ruṣâfah, Shammâsîyah, and Mukharrim, which were enclosed by the semicircle of the wall starting from the Tigris at the Shammâsîyah Gate and coming down to the river again at the gate of the Tuesday Market, above the palaces of the Caliph.

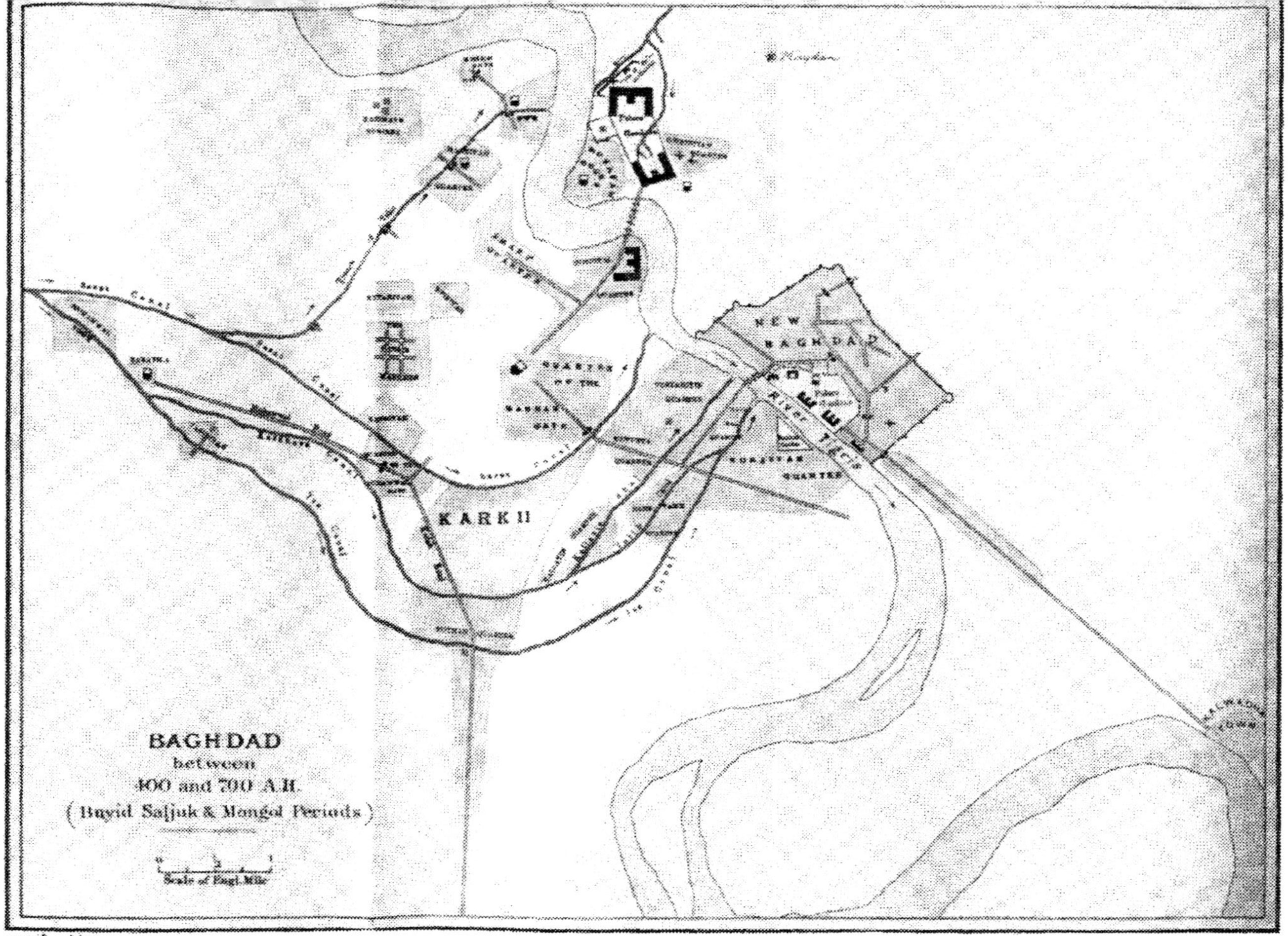

BAGHDAD
between
400 and 700 A.H.
(Buyid Saljuk & Mongol Periods)
Scale of Engl. Mile
NEW BAGHDAD
KARK H
River Tigris

CHAPTER XVII

THE BUYID PALACES

The Palace of Mûnis and the Buyid Palaces. The Dyke of Mu'izz-ad-Dawlah and the Zâhir Garden. The Dâr-al-Mamlakat of Mu'izz-ad-Dawlah. The great Dyke and the Ḳûrij Canal. The Palaces of 'Aḍud-ad-Dawlah. His Garden and the New Canal. Elephants used in Baghdad. The Dâr-as-Salṭanah of the Saljûḳs. Tughril Beg and his marriage ceremony. Demolition of this Palace by the Caliph Nâṣir. The Mosque of the Sultan.

In the early years of the fourth century (the tenth A.D.) the plain outside the Shammâsîyah Gate (as mentioned in a previous chapter) was occupied by the Palace of Mûnis the Chamberlain, who, after governing the Caliphate during most of the reign of Muḳtadir, finally deposed that Caliph in 320 (A.D. 932), and putting him to death in this Palace of the Shammâsîyah, set up his brother Ḳâhir in his stead[1]. The Chamberlain Mûnis, however, was himself disgraced and beheaded by Ḳâhir in the following year, a period of general disorder followed, filling up the reigns of Ḳâhir Râḍî and Muttaḳî, which was finally brought to a close under the Caliph Mustakfî, when in the year 334 (A.D. 946) Mu'izz-ad-Dawlah the Buyid, at the head of his Daylamite troops, became master of Baghdad.

[1] Ibn-al-Athir, viii. 138, 148, 337.

His troops halted at the Shammâsîyah, and the Buyid prince at first took up his quarters in the Palace of Mûnis, which, however, shortly after this must have been demolished to make way for the great palaces of the Buyids. These were erected in the region which is described as bounded by the Zâhir Garden on the lower side, and on the north by the dyke on the Shammâsîyah plain, built under the directions of Mu'izz-ad-Dawlah to prevent the overflow of the canals from the Khâliṣ, which had so often laid this quarter of Baghdad under water. With their grounds the Buyid Palaces must have covered a very considerable area. The southern limit was along the line of the Khurâsân road, while to the right and left the Palaces extended over the space between the Shammâsîyah and the Baradân roads. The Mosque of Ruṣâfah, which was still standing, and the quarter round the shrine of Abu Ḥanîfah, came between the palaces and the river bank, while to the east lay the Christian Quarter of the Greek House, which from the account in the *Fihrist* (given in a previous chapter) of the Nestorian monk who had been to China, evidently was the centre of a populous region of Baghdad as late as the last quarter of the fourth century (the tenth A.D.). In their upper part the Buyid Palaces are described as lying along the Tigris bank, 'opposite to the Farḍah' or Upper Harbour, at the mouth of the Trench of Ṭâhir, on the western bank above the Ḥarbîyah Quarter; while the northern limit of the grounds and gardens was formed by the great Dyke of Mu'izz-ad-Dawlah, which starting from the Tigris bank crossed the Shammâsîyah Plain.

No trace of these palaces now remains, but

Khaṭîb, who wrote a century after the Buyid epoch, and who has left a full description of their palaces, which in his day were already in a state of ruin, always speaks of them as situated above or in the upper part of the Mukharrim Quarter, from which it perhaps follows that some of the palaces lay to the south of the line of the Khurâsân road. In his description the Buyid Palaces are generally referred to as the Dâr-al-Mamlakat (the Palace of the Government), as against the Ḥasanî Palace or the Dâr-al-Khilâfat (the Palace of the Caliphate), where the Caliph reigned, but no longer governed. In this Dâr-al-Mamlakat the various Buyid princes, and after their day the Saljûḳ Sultans, when resident in Baghdad, held their court.

The first Buyid palace to be built was that of Muʿizz-ad-Dawlah, and it is said to have cost thirteen million dirhams, about £500,000 sterling[1]. The great Dyke, already mentioned (called Al-Musannât-al-Muʿizzîyah), the remains of which might still be seen about the year 700 (A.D. 1300), when the author of the *Marâṣid* wrote, was carried across the low-lying plain of the Shammâsîyah, with a view of preventing the waters of the stream, known in later times as the Ḳûrij, from inundating the grounds of the new palaces. Inundations, however, none the less continued to happen, and in the year 466 (A.D. 1074) the dyke was ruptured by a flood in the Ḳûrij, the waters of the Tigris having also risen under stress of the desert wind which kept them

[1] In Yakut, iii. 318, the date A.H. 305 is given for the completion of his palace by Muʿizz; but this must be a mistake, since he only entered Baghdad in 334. It should perhaps be 345 (A.D. 956). Compare also Yakut, iii. 194; and Marasid, ii. 124.

from flowing off, and immense damage resulted in both the eastern and the western quarters of the city. A like inundation is again mentioned by Ibn-al-Athîr as occurring in the year 554 (A.D. 1159). The stream of the Ḳûrij, which did all this damage, would appear to have been identical with, or at least to have followed the line formerly taken by the canal called the Nahr Faḍl, described by Ibn Serapion in the fourth century (the tenth A.D.). Writing in the seventh century (the thirteenth A.D.) Yâḳût mentions further damage which had recently been caused by the overflow of the Ḳûrij, which he writes was a canal that had originally been dug by one of the Chosroes of ancient Persia, being the work of the same king who had excavated the Ḳâṭûl Canal or Nahrawân, from which the Ḳûrij was derived; and this attribution may have some foundation in fact since the name Ḳûrij (or Ḳûraj) is merely the Arabicized form of the Old Persian word *Kûrah*, meaning a canal [1].

Mu'izz-ad-Dawlah died in 356 (A.D. 967), being succeeded by his son 'Izz-ad-Dawlah, who, after he had misgoverned Baghdad during eleven years, was finally deposed by his cousin 'Aḍud-ad-Dawlah, the Buyid ruler of Fârs, and in the year 367 (A.D. 978) this prince entering Baghdad became master of the Caliph and his empire. 'Aḍud-ad-Dawlah was famous for his buildings, among which was the great Hospital in Western Baghdad, which has been already described, and in Eastern Baghdad he enlarged and almost entirely rebuilt the Palace of

[1] See Ibn Serapion, 267; Ibn-al-Athir, x. 62; xi. 164; Yakut, iv. 198; De Goeje, *Histoire des Carmathes* (second edition, 1886), p. 13, note 3.

Mu'izz-ad-Dawlah. This building is named Saray-as-Sulṭân (the Palace of the Sultan) by the Persian author of the *Guzîdah*, who says it was famous as the finest edifice of its age; while of the older palace of Mu'izz-ad-Dawlah nothing was allowed to remain standing but the part called the Bayt-as-Sittînî (the Hall of the Sixty). The land adjacent thereto had originally been granted in fief to Sabuktagîn, Chamberlain of Mu'izz-ad-Dawlah, but this was now taken up by the buildings of the new palace, which consisted of a great court surrounded by porticoes with cupolas built over them, and the western gates of the palace opened on the Tigris bank, opposite the Farḍah or Upper Harbour of the Ḥarbîyah Quarter.

In his new palace 'Aḍud-ad-Dawlah established the hall for the public audience, while the hall of the old Palace of Mu'izz-ad-Dawlah was used as the place of assembly for the Wazîrs. The domed porticoes adjacent were divided off to serve as Dîwâns or offices for the Secretaries of State, while in the Great Court the Daylamites of his bodyguard had their quarters during the summer time. Much is said of the garden which 'Aḍud-ad-Dawlah created beside his palace, and it is reported to have cost a fabulous sum of money. This covered the ground originally occupied by the Maydân or square for polo and horse-racing which Sabuktagîn the Chamberlain had made here, and 'Aḍud-ad-Dawlah had first to spend a considerable sum of money in digging up and carrying away the stones and sand of the Maydân before he could lay down soil suitable for growing trees and plants. The account given by Khaṭîb in his history of Baghdad is, he states, derived from one who had been a witness of the costly changes effected by the Buyid prince; and he describes how all along the Tigris bank, in front of the new palace, the private houses were bought up by order of 'Aḍud-ad-Dawlah, and their walls having been demolished, the space thus obtained after being filled in with soil was planted and added to the new gardens.

The original Maydân of Sabuktagîn was thus doubled in size, the whole site being protected from the inundation of the river by a dyke, presumably forming an extension of the one elsewhere ascribed to Mu'izz-ad-Dawlah. These works alone cost 'Aḍud-ad-Dawlah two million dirhams (£80,000), such being the sum which the prince admitted to have spent when conversing with the writer of the account which Khaṭîb has preserved. For the irrigation of the new garden water-wheels on the Tigris bank were at first set up, but these having proved insufficient, 'Aḍud-ad-Dawlah ordered his engineers to make a channel for bringing water direct from the streams on the north-east of Baghdad, and for this it was found necessary to go as far up as the Khâliṣ river for the head of the new canal[1]. Further, to obtain a level bed a continuous embankment had to be constructed, along the top of which the course of the new canal was dug; then great artificial mounds had to be built up in two places where for some distance the aqueduct was carried many ells above the level of the surrounding plain, and on either side of the long embankment gullies (called *Khawr*) were dug for carrying off the waters in seasons of inundation.

[1] The Khâliṣ flowed into the Tigris some six leagues to the north of Baghdad, near the town of Baradân: see Ibn Serapion, p. 273.

The account goes on to state that for stamping down the soil of this great embankment, as also for demolishing the walls of the houses whose sites were to be used for his garden grounds, 'Aḍud-ad-Dawlah employed elephants. These animals were not unknown in Baghdad during the third and fourth centuries (ninth and tenth A.D.), and the ones now used were probably brought by the Buyids from India. Mas'ûdî, the contemporary historian, frequently mentions elephants in the pages of his chronicle; thus he narrates that in 297 (A.D. 910) Layth, the Saffarid prince, was as a prisoner of war paraded through the streets of Baghdad mounted on an elephant: and the heretic Bâbak at Sâmarrâ in 223 (A.D. 838) was similarly treated, on which last occasion Mas'ûdî states that an immense grey elephant was used, this animal having been originally sent as a present to the Caliph Mamûn by one of the kings of India. The Caliph Manṣûr also is said to have possessed many elephants, which he was fond of employing in state ceremonies, and Mas'ûdî takes occasion to remark that though a mule hated the Bactrian camel exceedingly, he hated an elephant even more, and would behave very disagreeably when forced into the company of these huge beasts, of which behaviour the chronicler gives an amusing instance [1].

When the new canal dug by 'Aḍud-ad-Dawlah reached the city limits, and its channel passed among the houses, the bed was laid in burnt bricks or stone blocks set in concrete of lime; and thus at length a plentiful supply of water was brought to irrigate the gardens of the new palace, the esti-

[1] Mas'udi, iii. 18, 19; vii. 127.

mated cost of these works being set down at five million dirhams, or about £200,000. In addition to the foregoing, we are told that it had been the intention of 'Aḍud-ad-Dawlah to have pulled down the houses occupying the land between the lower portion of the palace and the Zâhir Garden, in order thus to connect the southern part of the new palace with the river bank below Ruṣâfah; but death overtook him before these plans could be fully carried into effect. The palace of 'Aḍud-ad-Dawlah continued to be the official residence of the Buyid princes who succeeded him, and who governed in Baghdad till the middle of the fifth century (the eleventh A.D.). Jalâl-ad-Dawlah, the grandson of 'Aḍud-ad-Dawlah, who became prince in 416 (A.D. 1025), made some additional alterations, and turned the former hall of the Wazîrs into stables for his horses, but the Palace of 'Aḍud-ad-Dawlah otherwise remained intact down to the extinction of his dynasty.

After the fall of the Buyids, their great palace was occupied by Tughril Beg the Saljûḳ, who entered Baghdad in 447 (A.D. 1055) and assumed the reins of government. The southern part of the palaces appears to have been that used by the Saljûḳ Sultans, and these buildings more especially were known as the Dâr-as-Salṭanah[1] (the Abode of the Sultanate). Certain restorations were effected by Tughril in 448 (A.D. 1056), and the contemporary historian Khaṭîb speaks of a great fire which occurred in the year 450 (A.D. 1058), at the moment

[1] In 'Imad-ad-Din, ii. 248, 250, 251, this palace is indifferently named the Dâr-as-Salṭanah, the Dâr-as-Sulṭân, and the Dâr-as-Sulṭânîyah.

when he, Khaṭîb, was writing his history of Baghdad, but the furniture having been removed in time, the walls of the palace were immediately rebuilt, and the whole restored to its former splendour. In this new palace must have taken place the unprecedented espousals of the Abbasid princess, the daughter of the Caliph Ḳâim—a collateral descendant therefore of the Prophet Muḥammad—and Tughril Beg the Turkoman, the nominal vassal, but the real master, of the Caliph. Tughril Beg had commanded a magnificent ceremonial to be arranged for receiving the princess, and the marriage took place in 455 (A.D. 1063), Muslim orthodoxy being much scandalized at such a union, though flattered by the spectacle of Tughril Beg the conqueror of Western Asia, then in his seventieth year, kissing the ground and standing humbly in attendance before the princess his bride, who was seated in state on a throne covered with gold brocade.

The palace of the Dâr-al-Mamlakat—probably the southern buildings of the older Buyid palaces—became at a later date the residence of Mâlik Shâh, the greatest of the Saljûḳ Sultans and the grand nephew of Tughril, when he came to Baghdad in 479 (A.D. 1086) with his minister the Niẓâm-al-Mulk. The later Saljûḳ Sultans also made this palace their abode when in Baghdad, leaving a lieutenant here to govern in their name when they themselves were absent ruling their own people, or engaged in the conquest of neighbouring kingdoms. More than a century thus elapsed; the Saljûḳ power withered away, the rule of the Caliphs becoming a mere shadow of empire in Eastern Baghdad, and finally the palaces of the Buyids and Saljûḳs having fallen almost completely to ruin, these were demolished by the Caliph Nâṣir, who in the year 587 (A. D. 1191) caused the remaining walls to be levelled with the ground[1].

A building which is often mentioned in the chronicles during the last two centuries of the Caliphate was the Jâmiʿ-as-Sulṭân, the third of the great mosques of Eastern Baghdad (the other two being the Ruṣâfah Mosque and the mosque within the precincts of the Palace of the Caliph), where the Friday prayers continued to be said, until the extinction of the Caliphate. The mosque of the Sultan was built by Mâlik Shâh the Saljûḳ, its foundations having been laid in the year 485 (A. D. 1092), and it is said originally to have formed part of the Palace of the Sultanate, namely the Buyid Palace which the Saljûḳs had inherited. The mosque is described as standing between the Garden of Zâhir, which was on the river bank, and the Saljûḳ palace which Yâḳût in several places refers to, incidentally, as lying to the northward 'behind the mosque.' The traveller Ibn Jubayr mentions the mosque in 580 (A. D. 1184), which was about a century after its completion, describing it as standing 'outside the wall of the city,' namely the new town of East Baghdad, which had grown up round the palaces of the Caliphs to the south of the old quarter of the Mukharrim.

Ibn Jubayr adds that he did not know exactly by whom the mosque had been built; it stood contiguous to the Palace of the Sultan, the Shâhîn Shâh (the Great Saljûḳ often bore this title of King of

[1] Khatib, folios 97 a to 98 b. Guzidah, under reign of 'Aḍud-ad-Dawlah, in book iv, section 5; Ibn-al-Athir, x. 15, 103; Yakut, iv. 441.

Kings), who had been ruler of affairs under one of the forefathers of the Caliph Nâṣir, and the mosque, he says, was built by this same Sultan in front of his palace, lying distant about one mile from the Ruṣâfah Mosque. As late as the year 727 (A.D. 1327), when Ibn Baṭûṭah visited Baghdad, the Jâmiʿ-as-Sulṭân was still standing[1], as likewise the Ruṣâfah Mosque and the tomb of Abu Ḥanîfah; and these apparently were the only three buildings of the older Mukharrim and Ruṣâfah Quarters that had survived the Mongol conquest. Of them all only the shrine of Abu Ḥanîfah now remains, the one solitary relic of the three northern quarters of East Baghdad which marks the position of Ruṣâfah.

[1] Ibn Khallikan, No. 750, p. 7; Yakut, iii. 195; iv. 441; Ibn Jubayr, 230; Ibn Batutah, ii. 111.

CHAPTER XVIII

THE PALACES OF THE CALIPHS

The Palaces of Western and of Eastern Baghdad. The Palace of Ja'far the Barmecide; extended by Mamûn. Ḥasan ibn Sahl and his daughter Bûrân. The Ḥasanî Palace restored to Mu'tamid. The Tâj Palace begun: the Firdûs Palace. The Palace of the Pleiades. The Great Mosque of the Palace. The completion of the Tâj. The Shâṭibîyah Palace. The Dome of the Ass. The Wild Beast Park and other Palaces. The reception of the Greek Envoys from Constantine Porphyrogenitus. The Palace of the Tree. The Garden of Ḳâhir. The Peacock Palace. The Hall of the Wazîrs. The burning of the Tâj Palace. Building of the second Tâj. The Gardens of the Raḳḳah.

THE Palace of the Golden Gate, in the centre of the Round City, and the Khuld Palace, on the river bank at the western end of the Main Bridge, have been described in chapter ii, and it was in one or other of these that, when the Caliph Manṣûr was resident in Baghdad, he held his court. His son and successor Mahdî had occupied, during his father's lifetime, the Palace of Ruṣâfah in the northern quarter of East Baghdad, but after succeeding to the Caliphate he went to live in West Baghdad, which continued to be the seat of government during his time, as also during the reigns of his two sons the Caliphs Hâdî and Hârûn-ar-Rashîd.

The earliest of the great southern palaces of East Baghdad, where, during the last four centuries of the Abbasid dynasty, the Caliphs held their court, had originally been a pleasure house, built by Ja'far the Barmecide, brother-in-law and boon companion of Hârûn-ar-Rashîd. It stood in what was then the open country on the Tigris bank below the Mukharrim Quarter, at a considerable distance therefore from Ruṣâfah and the populous northern quarters of East Baghdad. This Palace of Ja'far the Barmecide, which became the nucleus of the great congeries of palaces that afterwards were known as the Dâr-al-Khilâfat (the Abode of the Caliphate), was at first called the Ḳaṣr Ja'farî, but afterwards, having come to be inhabited in turn by Mamûn and by the Wazîr Ḥasan ibn Sahl, it was more generally named the Ḳaṣr Mamûnî or the Ḳaṣr Ḥasanî. In its grounds, after the return of the Caliphate from Sâmarrâ, the great mosque of the palace (Jâmi'-al-Ḳaṣr) was erected, while adjacent to the Ḥasanî, as will be described later, were built two other palaces, namely the Firdûs, upstream, and the Palace of the Tâj, downstream; all three buildings thus standing on the Tigris bank, with great gardens stretching to the back, enclosing many minor palaces within their precincts.

Yâḳût gives us the history of these palaces, and in the first place relates how Ja'far the Barmecide, being much given to wine-bibbing in the company of poets and singers, was frequently reproved by his father Yaḥyâ—at that time Wazîr of Hârûn-ar-Rashîd—for the scandal that he was creating. Ja'far professed inability to alter his ways, but in order to shun the observation of strict Moslems who abhorred wine and singing, he agreed to build himself a palace apart, for the celebration of his joyous assemblies, on the unoccupied lands to the south of the Mukharrim Quarter. Ja'far was at this time still the favourite boon companion of Hârûn-ar-Rashîd, who showed much interest in the building, which was indeed so remarkable for its magnificence, that when all was completed an astute friend advised Ja'far to tell Hârûn that this palace was in reality built as a present for Mamûn, and thus to avoid the well-known jealousy of the Caliph.

Mamûn, the heir-apparent, from the time of his birth had been put under the nominal guardianship of Ja'far, and the Caliph graciously accepting the gift for his son, the new palace, at first called the Ja'farî, came afterwards to be known as the Mamûnî, though it remained exclusively in the occupation of Ja'far until the fall of the Barmecides. After the tragic death of Ja'far, the young prince Mamûn entered into full possession of the palace, and it became one of his favourite places of residence: he enlarged the buildings, added a Maydân or square for horse racing and the Persian game of polo (Ṣuljân), which, according to Mas'ûdî, the Caliph Hârûn-ar-Rashîd had been the first to play in Baghdad, and began to lay out the Wild Beast Park, which afterwards became one of its notable features. Mamûn also built a gate opening on the plain to the eastward, and another through which was brought the branch canal from the Nahr Mu'allâ, as is described by Ibn Serapion; further, he laid out the quarter adjacent, called after him the

Mamûnîyah (which will be noticed more fully in a subsequent chapter), where his attendants and followers built themselves houses; all these alterations in the Ja'farî Palace, according to Yâķût, having been effected during the latter years of the reign of Hârûn, and prior to Mamûn being sent to assume the governorship of Khurâsân with the eastern provinces of the empire.

The Ja'farî or Mamûnî Palace appears to have remained unoccupied for many years after the departure of Mamûn for the east, and it will be remembered how civil war broke out between Amîn and Mamûn shortly after the death of Hârûn-ar-Rashîd, ending in the siege of Baghdad, when Amîn, having evacuated the eastern side, retired first to the Khuld Palace and later to the shelter of the Round City, where he intrenched himself in the Palace of the Golden Gate. The ruin of these two palaces of Western Baghdad appears to have been largely the result of this twelvemonth's siege; though the Khuld suffered less than the other, and when some five years after the death of Amîn, the Caliph Mamûn finally returned to Baghdad, he at first took up his residence on the western side in the Palace of the Khuld, leaving the Mamûnî Palace in the possession of his Wazîr Ḥasan, generally known as Ibn Sahl, who had preceded him to Baghdad as viceroy of 'Irâķ. From the time of his accession Mamûn had been entirely under the influence of the two sons of Sahl—a Persian by birth—one of whom, Faḍl Ibn Sahl, had remained in personal attendance on the Caliph in Khurâsân, acting as his Wazîr, while the brother, Ḥasan, had been sent forward to reestablish the authority of Mamûn in Mesopotamia after the devastation of the civil war. Faḍl lost his life, in Khurâsân, by a palace intrigue, but Ḥasan, after the arrival of the Caliph in Baghdad, established himself firmly in the position of sole Wazîr to Mamûn, and then sought to perpetuate his power by marrying his daughter Bûrân to the Caliph.

The espousals of Mamûn and Bûrân, which were celebrated at the domain of Fam-aṣ-Ṣilḥ, some miles down the Tigris below Baghdad, have passed to a proverb for their splendour, and for the sums spent by Ḥasan Ibn Sahl to do honour to his royal son-in-law. As a slight return for his entertainment, the Caliph after his marriage presented the Mamûnî Palace as a free gift to Ḥasan; and the minister for a time inhabited it, but with much prudence finally made it over to his daughter Bûrân, having in part rebuilt it and added to the grounds. In this palace Bûrân lived her long life—surviving the glories of the reign of Mamûn, and living to see the Caliphate transferred from Baghdad to Sâmarrâ—and to her filial affection, doubtless quite as much as to the restorations effected by her father, is due the fact that the palace from this time onwards was generally known under the name of the Ḳaṣr-al-Ḥasanî (after the Wazîr Ḥasan Ibn Sahl), though later writers still at times refer to it under the name of the Mamûnî, or the Ja'farî Palace.

In 218 (A.D. 833) Mamûn had been succeeded by his brother Mu'taṣim, the last of the three sons of Hârûn-ar-Rashîd who attained the Caliphate, and he, according to one account, inhabited the Palace of Mamûn (namely the Ḥasanî) for some time after his accession. Later, however, he built himself the palace (already described) in the Mukharrim Quarter, to the south of the Khurâsân Gate, living there till the year 221 (A.D. 836), when the excesses of the Turk body-guard, with other events, brought about the removal of the Caliphate to Sâmarrâ. This city, which he partly rebuilt, remained the seat of government for more than half a century, and during the reign of eight Caliphs, though one of these, namely Musta'în, fleeing from Sâmarrâ (as has been mentioned in a previous chapter), came down the river to Baghdad, and there was besieged by the Turk body-guard of his rival the Caliph Mu'tazz. It will be remembered that the headquarters of Musta'în during this siege were in the Palace of Mahdî in Ruṣâfah, the chief attack of the besieging army being directed against the Shammâsîyah Quarter, and the ruin of the three northern quarters of Eastern Baghdad may be dated chiefly from the events of this unfortunate year 251 (A.D. 865). The second siege of Baghdad ended with the death of Musta'în, whereupon Mu'tazz, his cousin, was recognized as sole Caliph, he and the next two puppet Caliphs continuing to live on at Sâmarrâ under the tyranny of the Turk body-guard.

During the Zanj rebellion, which broke out in Lower Mesopotamia during the Caliphate of Mu'tamid—the last of those who lived at Sâmarrâ—the Regent Muwaffaḳ, brother of the Caliph and the actual ruler of the empire, leaving Mu'tamid to reside at Sâmarrâ, came down to Baghdad, and made the older capital his headquarters during the many years that were spent in fighting the rebels. The long residence in Baghdad of the actual ruler of the empire doubtless paved the way for the return of the Caliphs to their original metropolis. This came about shortly after the death of Muwaffaḳ, when Mu'tamid, six months before his own death, finally abandoned Sâmarrâ to take up his permanent abode in Baghdad, which, indeed, he had temporarily visited on more than one occasion. On the death of Mu'tamid in 279 (A.D. 892) his body was taken back to Sâmarrâ for burial among the tombs of his immediate predecessors, but his nephew Mu'taḍid (the son of Muwaffaḳ), who succeeded as Caliph, remained in Baghdad, which during the next four centuries, and until the fall of the Caliphate, became once more the residence of the Abbasids.

It is related by Yâḳût that when Mu'tamid returned to take up his residence in Baghdad, he found Bûrân the widow of Mamûn still alive, and in occupation of the Ḥasanî Palace, where she had continued to live undisturbed after the death of her husband and of her father Ḥasan Ibn Sahl. Mu'tamid, who required a palace to live in, requested Bûrân to remove elsewhere, promising her another palace in exchange, and the request of the Caliph was naturally equivalent to a command. Bûrân pleaded for and obtained a short delay under pretext of arranging her affairs, and forthwith set about putting the palace and its furniture into thorough repair, so that when she finally removed to another house, the Ḥasanî Palace was made over to Mu'tamid in perfect order—Yâḳût describing how its halls were spread with gold-woven carpets and reed matting, its doors hung with needful curtains, and its storerooms filled with all requisite vessels for the service of the Caliph, while in attendance were numerous slave girls and eunuchs.

Mu'tamid, we are told, expressed a due regard for what the widow of his great uncle had done for him, and proceeded to take up his abode in the Ḥasanî Palace, where he died shortly after, as has been said in the last chapter, poisoned by Mushkîr his steward, who saw his advantage in the reign of a new Caliph.

Yâḳût has taken this anecdote about Bûrân from the history of Baghdad by Khaṭîb (as usual, without acknowledgement), but with an important difference, for Khaṭîb gives it as the Caliph Mu'taḍid (nephew of Mu'tamid) who received back the palace from Bûrân (he reigned from A.H. 279 to 289). Khaṭîb thereupon adds that he perforce doubts the authenticity of this anecdote, which he had copied from an earlier author, because Bûrân herself died some years before Mu'taḍid came to the throne. Now Bûrân, who lived to be over eighty, died at Baghdad in 271 (A.D. 884), as is mentioned in another passage by Khaṭîb and confirmed on good authority, that is to say, some eight years before the accession of Mu'taḍid; but if the (unacknowledged) alteration made by Yâḳût be accepted—namely if we read Mu'tamid for Mu'taḍid, and the two names only differ by a single letter—there will be no antecedent improbability in the story reported by Khaṭîb. In the year 270, for instance, the chronicles state that Mu'tamid was on a temporary visit to Baghdad (before he finally settled there in 279), and he might very well on this occasion have received back the Ḥasanî Palace from Bûrân, with all the circumstances related in the anecdote[1].

[1] Yakut, i. 806 to 809; Mas'udi, vii. 65; viii. 296; Ya'kubi, 255; Khatib, folio 92; Ibn Khallikan, No. 119, p. 16; Abu-l-Mahasin, ii. 72.

With the accession of Mu'taḍid and the permanent establishment of the Caliphate in East Baghdad, a new era of palace-building was inaugurated, for this Caliph not only enlarged the Ḥasanî and laid the foundations of the Tâj, but built for himself two other palaces, namely the Firdûs and the Thurayyâ. The Ḥasanî Palace was added to by buildings erected on the Maydân (or Square), which Mamûn had left, and the whole was surrounded by a wall, after a new Maydân had been laid out in the lands to the eastward, where private houses had been pulled down to provide the necessary space. Adjacent to the Ḥasanî, but higher upstream, Mu'taḍid built the Ḳaṣr-al-Firdûs (the Palace of Paradise), at the place where the waters of the Mu'allâ Canal flowed out into the Tigris; and in the gardens of this palace was a lake (as has already been mentioned in chapter xvi) fed by a channel coming from an offshoot of the Mûsâ Canal, at the bifurcation near the Mukharrim Gate. The Firdûs Palace had a gate called the Bâb-al-Firdûs, and apparently at one period the name of the Firdûs was commonly used to denote the Palaces of the Caliph in general, for in Arabic the word *Firdûs* either stands for the Paradise of Heaven (and as such applied to a palace) or may be taken to signify a wild beast park (in Greek παράδεισος), such as was often made, following the ancient Persian custom, in the purlieus of the royal abode.

The Palace of the Pleiades (Ḳaṣr-ath-Thurayyâ), as has been already mentioned in chapter xiii, lay on the Mûsâ Canal two miles distant from the Ḥasanî Palace, and its site must therefore have been outside the later city wall, which was built round the southern quarters of East Baghdad some two centuries later than the time of Muʻtaḍid. The Pleiades were, of course, beyond the precincts of the palace gardens on the Tigris bank, and the Caliph Muʻtaḍid, for his convenience, had this distant palace connected with the Ḥasanî by an underground passage, two Arab miles in length, along which his women and their attendants could pass from the Ḥasanî to the Thurayyâ without appearing in public. According to Masʻûdî, a contemporary authority, the Palace of the Pleiades cost Muʻtaḍid the immense sum of 400,000 dînârs (equivalent to about £200,000), and its grounds are said to have originally covered an area three leagues in extent. The passage-way two miles in length, above mentioned, was vaulted throughout, and ran under the houses and streets which came to be built outside the Palaces of the Caliphs; it long continued in use, only falling to ruin at the time of the first great inundation of Baghdad—presumably that of the year 466 (A. D. 1074), when the bursting of a dyke below the Ḳûrij Canal had laid the whole of the eastern city under water[1].

In addition to the two palaces of the Firdûs and the Thurayyâ, Muʻtaḍid also laid the foundations of the famous Palace of the Crown (Ḳaṣr-at-Tâj), which when completed and enlarged by succeeding sovereigns became in after centuries the chief official residence of the Caliphs. Muʻtaḍid, however, did not live to carry out his plans for the Tâj, and he had even, it was said, countermanded the building in the year 286 (A. D. 899), on his return from the expedition against Âmid in Upper Mesopotamia,

[1] Ibn Serapion, 22; Yakut, i. 808, 924; iii. 871; iv. 846; Khatib, folio 92; Mas'udi, viii. 116; Ibn-al-Athir, x. 62.

for he was led to fear that from its position the Tâj Palace would be invaded by smoke from the neighbouring houses of the city suburbs beyond the wall of the precincts.

In the year 289 (A.D. 902) Mu'taḍid was succeeded by his son 'Alî Muktafî, who, during a reign of six years, carried to completion the works that his father had begun, and built the great mosque for the Friday prayers, within the Palace of the Caliphs. This was known as the Jâmî-al-Ḳaṣr, and was the second of the three great mosques of East Baghdad (the first having been the Ruṣâfah Mosque, and the third the Saljûḳ Mosque of the Sultan, both already described). The ground upon which the palace mosque was built had been previously occupied by the dungeons where Mu'taḍid kept his state prisoners, these being certain vaulted chambers which had originally been used for housing the workmen who built the Ḥasanî Palace. 'Alî Muktafî at the beginning of his reign ordered these vaults to be demolished, and a mosque, intended at first only for his personal use, to be built in their room. This mosque, however, was afterwards thrown open to the people, who, according to Khaṭîb, from an early date took a liking to come hither for their daily prayers, and here they would sit till the close of night, discussing their private affairs. The palace mosque continued in use during the remaining four centuries of the Abbasid Caliphate; at the time of the Mongol siege it was set on fire and partially burnt, but by order of Hûlâgû was afterwards rebuilt, though doubtless shorn of much of its former magnificence; and there is reason to believe that some vestiges of this mosque of the palace are still standing near the ruined minaret of the modern Sûḳ-al-Ghazl (the Thread Market), which with other existing remains will be more fully noticed in the concluding chapter of the present work [1].

Besides building the great mosque, 'Alî Muktafî also completed the Palace of the Crown (Ḳaṣr-at-Tâj), which his father had begun. To obtain the needful materials the Caliph caused the Ḳaṣr-al-Kâmil (the Palace of Perfection), by whom built is not stated, to be demolished; and he also threw down a part of the great White Palace of the Chosroes at Madâin (Ctesiphon), thus still further carrying on the work of destruction which Manṣûr had begun (as related in chapter iii), when he attempted to make use of stones brought from here for the building of Baghdad. In later times the Palace of the Tâj was also apparently known as the Dâr-ash-Shâṭibîyah [2], the meaning of which name is obscure, but it is under this name that it is referred to by Ḥamd-Allah, the Persian writer of the eighth century (fourteenth A.D.). As already stated, the

[1] Khatib, folio 101 a, b; Rashid-ad-Din, 302, 308; Niebuhr, ii. 242.

[2] The name varies in the MSS. of the Nuzhat: the form here given is that found in both the printed text, p. 147, and the lithographed edition of Bombay. The British Museum MS. Add. 7707, gives the reading as *Dâr-as-Salṭanah*, which was the name of the hall of audience in the later, second, Palace of the Tâj (see below, p. 262), besides being more generally applied to the great Saljûḳ Palace, as stated in the previous chapter. Of the Paris MSS., No. 127 of the Bibliothèque Nationale agrees with the printed text, while Nos. 128 and 129 give the reading *Dâr-ash-Shaṭîyah*, which might be translated 'the River Bank Palace.' *Dâr-ash-Shâṭibîyah* would have the unlikely meaning of 'the Xativa Palace,' after the town of Xativa in the province of Valencia in Spain, or (more grammatically) this name might be translated 'the Palace of the woman of Xativa'; but both significations are improbable, and the origin of the name is nowhere explained by the Moslem authorities.

Palace of the Tâj stood on the Tigris bank below the Ḥasanî Palace, and its foundations were supported by a great dyke which projected out into the stream. It was more especially for making this dyke that the ruins at Madâin were used as a quarry, quantities of burnt bricks being dug out from the foundations of the Palace of the Chosroes, while the ancient battlements of its remaining walls were taken down and carried up the river to crown the summit of the Tâj.

This dyke, stretching out into the Tigris, was a special feature of the Tâj Palace, and during the great inundation of the year 466 (A.D. 1074) all the boats of Baghdad were moored for safety under its wall. The main building of the Tâj rose like a 'crown' above this dyke, supported on five vaults or arches, these resting on ten dwarf columns, each five ells (or about 8 feet) in height. 'Alî Muktafî also constructed halls of assembly and divers cupolas in the immediate neighbourhood of the Tâj; one especially was known as the Cupola of the Ass (Ḳubbat-al-Ḥimâr), this being a tower ascended by a spiral stair, of such an easy gradient that the Caliph could ride to the summit on a donkey trained to an ambling gait. Thus without fatigue he could enjoy the view over the surrounding country, for the height of this tower is described as very great, and in plan it was semicircular. A proof of the immense extent of the buildings erected by 'Alî Muktafî may be deduced from the report given by the contemporary Mas'ûdî, that this Caliph, at his death, left nine thousand riding-animals, to wit horses, mules, and swift dromedaries, which were all housed within the palace stables.

The next Caliph, Muḳtadir, brother of 'Alî Muktafî, who began his reign in 295 (A. D. 908), added considerably to the buildings round the Tâj, establishing a Wild Beast Park in the grounds stretching between the Palaces of the Tâj and the Thurayyâ on the Mûsâ Canal. A general idea of what the Palaces of the Caliph had come to be at this time is to be gained from the description which Khaṭîb has left us of the reception granted to the Greek ambassadors sent by Constantine Porphyrogenitus to Baghdad in 305 (A.D. 917)[1]. The envoys, on their arrival, had been lodged in the upper part of East Baghdad, and later they were brought in state by the Great Road from the Shammâsîyah Gate, through the Mukharrim Gate to the Bâb-al-'Âmmah (the Public Gate) of the palace precincts, troops in double line keeping the road for the whole of this distance. Before being introduced to the presence of the Caliph, who received them in the Palace of the Tâj, the envoys were shown over the various buildings within the precincts, and these at the date in question are said to have numbered twenty-three separate palaces.

Entering through the hall of the Great Public Gate, the envoys were taken first to the palace known as the Khân-al-Khayl (the Riding House), which is described as for the most part built with porticoes of marble columns. On the right side of this house stood five hundred mares with saddles of gold or silver, while on the left side stood five hundred mares with brocade saddle-cloths and long head-covers; and each mare was held by the

[1] Translated in full in the *Journal of the Royal Asiatic Society* for January, 1897, p. 35.

groom wearing a magnificent uniform. Beyond this palace, after passing through various corridors and halls opening one into the other, lay the Park of the Wild Beasts, with separate houses for the various kind of wild animals, entered from the park, where all the beasts would herd together, or come up close to the visitors, sniffing and eating from their hands. The elephant-house was near this, in which were kept four elephants, caparisoned in peacock silk brocade; and on the back of each sat eight men of Sind, and javelin-men with fire. Then in another palace there were one hundred lions, fifty to the right hand and fifty to the left, each lion being held by its keeper, for about its head and neck were iron chains; and in diverse neighbouring gardens there were other elephants and lions, also giraffes and hunting-leopards, which were all duly brought out for the inspection of the Greek ambassadors.

Among the most famous buildings erected by Muḳtadir was the Palace of the Tree (Dâr-ash-Shajarah), so called from the tree made of silver, weighing 500,000 dirhams (or about 50,000 ounces), which stood in the middle of its palace surrounded by a great circular tank filled with clear water. The tree had eighteen branches, every branch having numerous twigs, on which sat various kinds of mechanical birds in gold and silver, both large and small. Most of the branches of the tree were of silver, but some were of gold, and they spread into the air carrying leaves of divers colours, the leaves moving as the wind blew, while the birds through a concealed mechanism piped and sang. On either side of this palace, to the right and left of the tank, stood life-sized figures in two rows, each row consisting of fifteen horsemen, mounted upon their mares, both the men and the steeds being clothed and caparisoned in brocade. In their hands the horsemen carried long-poled javelins, and those on the right appeared to be attacking their adversaries in the row of horsemen on the left-hand side. It is further stated that in the time of Muḳtadir the halls of the Palace of the Firdûs were hung round with ten thousand gilded breastplates; and in a neighbouring corridor that was 300 ells in length, were ranged on stands ten thousand other pieces of armour and arms, to wit, bucklers, helmets, casques, cuirasses, and coats of mail, with ornamented quivers and bows.

Near the Firdûs stood the palace called the New Kiosk (Al-Jawsaḳ-al-Muḥdith), which lay in the midst of gardens. In its centre was a tank made of tin-plate (*Raṣâṣ Ḳal'î*), round which flowed a stream in a conduit also of tin plate, which is described as being more lustrous than polished silver. This tank was 30 ells in length by 20 across, and beside it were set four magnificent pavilions with gilt seats adorned with gold embroidery of Dabîḳ work. Round this tank extended the garden, with lawns wherein grew dwarf palm-trees to the number of four hundred, the height of each being 5 ells (about 8 feet), the entire trunk of the trees, from root to spathe, being enclosed in carved teak wood, encircled with gilt copper rings. These palms bore full-grown dates, and by careful cultivation, in almost all seasons, the fresh ripe fruit might be found on their branches. In the garden beds also were melons of the sort called Dastabûyah, and of many other species besides[1].

Probably within the precincts of the Tâj Palace and near the river bank had been the beautiful little garden laid out by the Caliph Ḳâhir, brother and successor of Muḳtadir, where (according to Mas'ûdî, a contemporary, who probably had himself visited the place) the unfortunate Ḳâhir, after his deposition, was received in audience by his nephew the Caliph Râḍî. The description of the little garden, as follows, is taken from the history of Mas'ûdî, called the *Meadows of Gold*, when relating the interview:—'Now the Caliph Ḳâhir had made in a certain one of the courts of the palace a garden about a Jarîb (or a third of an acre) in extent, which he had planted with orange-trees brought from Baṣrah and 'Omân, of such kinds as have been imported from the lands of India. And these trees having become interlaced, the fruits thereof hung like stars, red and yellow, in among the branches, while round and about various kinds of shrubs were planted with sweet-smelling herbs and flowers. Further, in this same court were kept many species of birds, such as turtle-doves and ring-doves, blackbirds and parrots, all of which had been brought thither from foreign countries and far-off cities, so that the garden was in the extreme beautiful, and the Caliph Ḳâhir, who loved to drink wine, had been wont to hold his assemblies in this place.'

In after days the Palace of the Tree (Dâr-ash-Shajarah), built under Muḳtadir as already described, was used as a state prison by later Caliphs, who, as a measure of precaution, kept their nearer rela-

[1] 'Arib, 64; Khatib, folios 93 b to 96 a; Yakut, ii. 251.

tions here in honourable confinement, duly attended by numerous servants and amply supplied with every luxury, but forbidden, under pain of death, to go beyond its walls. In the neighbourhood were also other palaces, for during the fourth century of the Hijrah (the tenth A.D.), after the Buyid princes had become masters of Baghdad, the Caliphs being no longer allowed to take any part in the government, spent much of their spare time building magnificent kiosks within the precincts of the royal domain. Thus the Caliph Muṭî', who reigned from 334 to 363 (A.D. 946 to 974), erected the Peacock Palace (Dâr-at-Tawâwîs); also the Murabba'ah and the Muthammanah Palaces (to wit the Square and the Octagon House); possibly too the palace called the Dâr Shirshîr, the situation of which is unknown; and at this period, when the palaces of the Caliphs may be considered to have attained their utmost extent and splendour, it is recorded that a certain treasurer of 'Aḍud-ad-Dawlah was wont to say that the house of the Caliph in Baghdad covered ground equalling in extent the whole city of Shîrâz, the chief town of Fârs, and the capital of his master the Buyid prince.

A century and a half later than the time of the Buyid supremacy—when Sultan Sanjâr, the last of the great Saljûḳs, was the protector of the Caliphate—the Caliph Mustarshid, who reigned from 512 to 529 (A.D. 1118 to 1135), added the great hall to the Tâj Palace, which was used for the reception of the Wazîrs, who, at the chief festivals, came to offer their congratulations to the Caliph. This hall went by the name of its gateway, and was called the Bâb-al-Hujrah (the Privy Chamber

Gate), and here Mustarshid and the succeeding Caliphs were wont to sit in state, bestowing robes of honour on their favourites and on the ministers appointed by the Saljûḳ Sultan to govern Baghdad and the province of Mesopotamia [1].

In the long list of the Abbasid Caliphs there are two (whose reigns are separated by an interval of two and a half centuries) who figure in our transliteration under the similar titles of Muktafî and Muḳtafî. The first, 'Alî Muktafî, who began his reign in 289 (A.D. 902), has his name spelt with an ordinary *k*, while the name of the last, Muḥammad Muḳtafî, who ascended the throne in 530 (A.D. 1136), is spelt with the dotted *ḳ*, and for greater distinction their personal names have been given in these pages with the title. In the reign of the first, 'Alî Muktafî, the Palace of the Tâj was completed; in the reign of the last, Muḥammad Muḳtafî, it was burnt to the ground—this occurring in the year 549 (A.D. 1154), when the building having been struck by lightning, took fire, which continuing to burn unchecked during nine days, both the Palace of the Crown and the adjacent Dome of the Ass were reduced to ashes. The Caliph Muḥammad Muḳtafî immediately commanded that the Dome of the Ass should be rebuilt on the original plan, but dying before his orders could be carried to completion, the building was stopped by his successor, and thus remained in an unfinished state till the year 574 (A.D. 1178), when Mustaḍî, his grandson, had the half-built walls demolished.

Their foundations Mustaḍî ordered to be made

[1] Yakut, i. 809; ii. 520, 521, 524; iv. 34; Khatib, folios 92 a, b, 93 a, b; Ibn-al-Athir, x. 62; Marasid, i. 112, 383; Mas'udi, viii. 225, 336.

level with the top of the great dyke on which the older Palace of the Tâj had stood, and causing the charred ruins also of this palace to be dug up, the space thus obtained was used in part for the great court of the new, or second, Palace of the Tâj, which Mustaḍî now proceeded to build. This new Tâj stood somewhat higher up the river bank than where Mu'taḍid had built the first palace; but it overhung the river like the original building, and is described as standing partly on the great dyke, round and under which the waters of the Tigris flowed. The main building, which rose to a height of 70 ells (about 105 feet) above the water level, was vaulted, the lower story like the first Palace of the Tâj being supported on five great arches, springing from a like number of marble columns, while in the centre a sixth column supported the central point of the vaulting on which the building rested.

On the western bank of the Tigris, in the Karkh Quarter and opposite the Tâj Palace, there were in these later times large and very beautiful gardens, where the Caliphs were wont to land when they crossed the river; and these pleasure grounds of the Caliph were known as the Gardens of the Raḳḳah, a name which, as already mentioned, is used to denote any low-lying plain subject to inundation from the river floods. The second Palace of the Tâj was the chief glory of the latter days of the Caliphate; in one of its halls the new Caliph, on his accession, was wont to receive from his subjects the oath of allegiance, sitting under the principal dome at a window that looked out on to the Great Court, and this part of the palace appears to have been more especially known as the Dâr-as-Salṭanah (the Hall of the Sultanate), a name which, as already mentioned, had possibly been also given to the earlier Palace of the Tâj[1].

[1] See above, note 2 to p. 253; Yakut, i. 809; ii. 804; Marasid, i. 193.

Map VIII. To face page 263

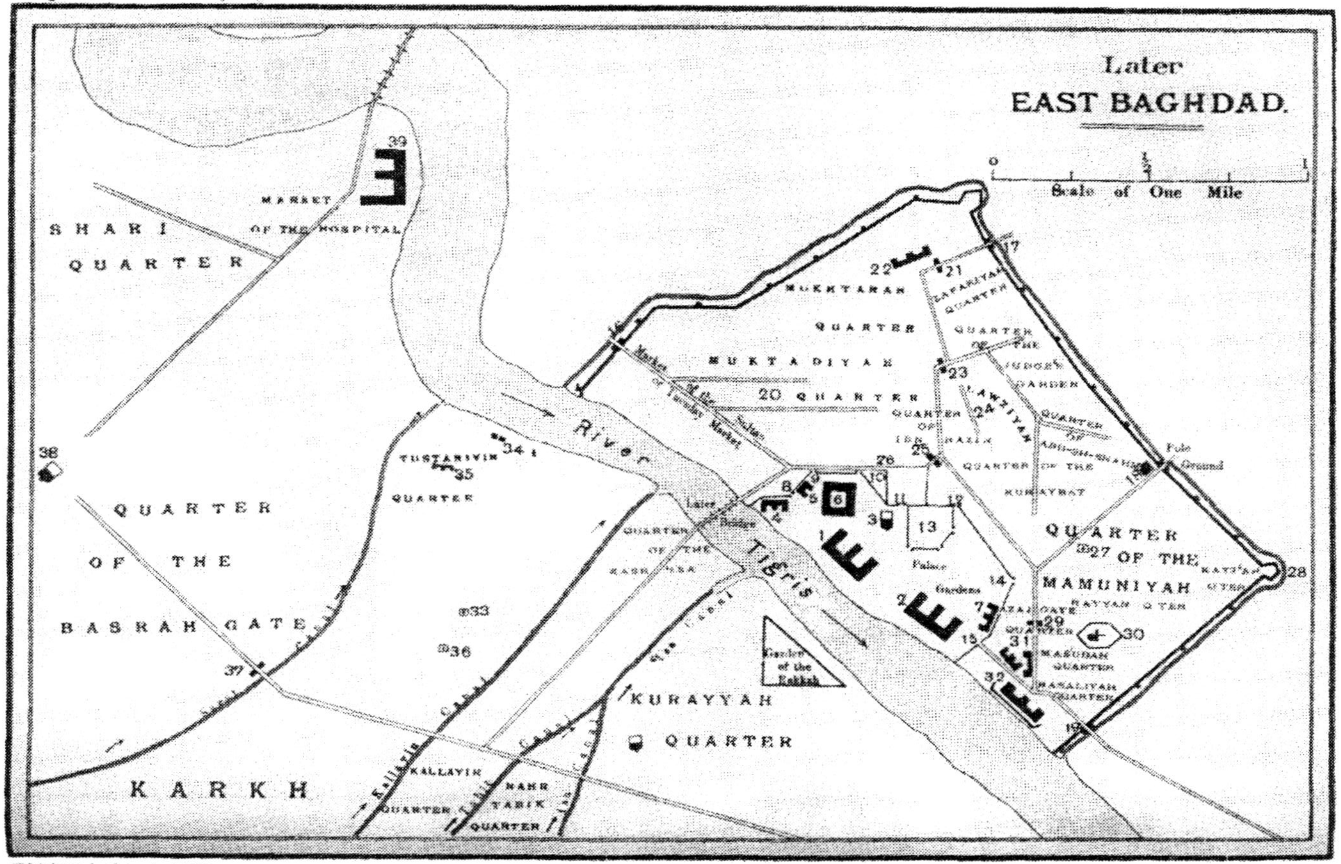

B.V. Darbishire 1900

REFERENCES TO MAP No. VIII.

1. The Ḥasanî Palace.
2. The Tâj Palace.
3. The Mosque of the Caliph.
4. The Mustanṣirîyah College overlooking the Wharf of the Needle-makers.
5. Palaces of the Princess.
6. The Rayḥânîyîn Palace.
7. Palace of the Maydân Khâliṣ.
8. Gate of the Willow-tree.
9. Gate of the Date Market.
10. The Badr Gate.
11. The Nubian Gate.
12. The Public Gate.
13. Outer Precincts, with the three Gates called Bâb-ad-Duwwâmât, Bâb 'Ullayân, and Bâb-al-Ḥaram.
14. The Garden Gate.
15. Gate of Degrees.
16. Gate of the Sultan (Modern Bâb-al-Mu'aẓẓam).
17. Gate of Khurâsân or Bâb-aẓ-Ẓafarîyah (Modern Bâb-al-Wusṭânî).
18. The Ḥalbah Gate and the Belvedere (Modern Bâb-at-Talism).
19. Gate of Kalwâdhâ or Bâb-al-Baṣalîyah, later called Bâb-al-Khalaj (Modern Bâb-ash-Sharkî).
20. Street of Bricks and Darb-al-Munîrah.
21. Abraz Gate of older Wall and Cemetery of the Wardîyah.
22. The Tâjîyah College.
23. Archway of the Armourers.
24. Street of the Canal.
25. Archway of the Artificer.
26. The Great Square and the Perfumers' Market.
27. Tomb of Abd-al-Ḳâdir Gîlânî.
28. The Persian Bastion.
29. The Azaj Gate.
30. The Zandaward Monastery.
31. The Bahâîyah and the Tutushî Hospital, in the Tutush Market.
32. The Niẓâmîyah College, Wharf, and Market.
33. The Tomb of Ma'rûf Karkhî.
34. The Barley Gate (Bâb-ash-Sha'îr).
35. Palace of 'Aḍud-ad-Dîn the Wazîr.
36. Shrine of 'Awn and Mu'în (site of the Modern Tomb of Zubaydah).
37. The Baṣrah Gate.
38. The Mosque of Manṣûr.
39. The Hospital of 'Aḍud-ad-Dawlah.

CHAPTER XIX

THE PALACE GATES AND ADJOINING QUARTERS

The Precincts, called the Ḥarîm or Ḥaramayn, and its Wall. The Quarters of the Mu'allâ Canal. The Town Wall. Gates of the Palace. The Bâb Gharabah and the Bâb Sûk-at-Tamr. The Needlemakers' Wharf: the Palace of the Cotton Market. The Palaces of the Princess, Dâr Khâtûn and Dâr-as-Sayyidah. The Mustanṣirîyah College. The Palace Mosque. The Badr Gate and Palace. The Elephant House. Market of the Perfumers. Other Markets round the Square of the Mosque. The Rayḥânîyîn Palace. The Dargâh-i-Khâtûn and the Libraries. The Nubian Gate and the Great Cross of the Crusaders. The Public Gate. Gates of the Palace Suburbs and the Garden Gate. The Gate of Degrees. General arrangement in the later Palaces.

THE Palaces of the Caliphs, the more important of which have been mentioned in the foregoing chapter, consisted of a great complex of buildings, which, with their gardens and courts, occupied an area nearly a square mile in extent, surrounded by a great wall with many gates. This area of the Palaces is generally referred to by Yâḳût in the seventh century (the thirteenth A.D.) under the name of the Ḥarîm, which may be translated the Precinct or the Sanctuary; while Ḥamd-Allah in the succeeding century speaks of it as the Ḥaramayn, another form of the same word, but in the dual, hence meaning the Double Sanctuary, this name probably having reference to the inner and the outer precincts.

It is uncertain by whom the great wall round the palace-area was built. Mu'taḍid, the first Caliph to reside permanently in Baghdad after the return from Sâmarrâ, when he enlarged the Ḥasanî (as already mentioned), at the close of the third century (the ninth A.D.), is said to have surrounded this palace by a wall, which in part may be identical with the wall which Yâḳût describes in the beginning of the seventh century (the thirteenth A.D.). This last, however, enclosed all the Palaces in a semicircular sweep, it began at the Tigris bank above the gardens and came down to the river again below the Tâj, and in this were the gates to be mentioned presently.

Outside the precincts and surrounding the Palaces of the Caliphs on the north, east, and south (the Tigris occupying their western side), stretched the later quarters of East Baghdad, which dated from the middle of the fifth century (the eleventh A.D.), and these quarters were enclosed by the city wall, with its four gates (one to the north, two to the east, and one to the south), which thus followed a line more or less parallel with the inner wall surrounding the Palaces.

The city wall and gates will be described in the following chapters, when the outlying suburbs of Eastern Baghdad come to be dealt with; for we have first to notice the inner wall which encircled the Palaces of the Caliphs, with those quarters of the city which stood more immediately adjacent to the gates of the palace. Yâḳût describes the palace precincts as in his time covering ground to an extent equalling a third part of the whole city of East Baghdad, being divided from the town quarters by the inner wall pierced with seven gateways. These were, three to the north, then near the north-east corner the two main gates of the palace precincts, below which for the space of a mile the wall had no gateway except the small garden gate, till finally the lowest gate was reached which opened to the south, close to the Tigris bank, and below the Palace of the Tâj[1].

The uppermost of the gates in the palace wall was the Bâb-al-Gharabah, which took its name from a *Gharabah* or Babylonian willow-tree which grew here. On the Tigris near this gate was the Mashra'at-al-Ibrîyîn (the Wharf of the Needle-makers), which probably lay close to the eastern end of the later Bridge of Boats, and this wharf is often mentioned in connexion with the next gate in the palace wall, called the Bâb Sûḳ-at-Tamr (the Gate of the Date Market), which must have opened at no great distance from the Bâb-al-Gharabah. The Date Market Gatehouse was a high-built structure which gave access to a palace within the precincts, called the Ḍâr-al-Ḳuṭunîyah (the Palace of the Cotton Market), and this building also overlooked the Needle-makers' Wharf. Yâḳût states that in his day this gate and the adjacent palace were both closed, the gateway having been walled up in the early part of the reign of the Caliph Nâṣir, that is to say shortly after the year 575 (A.D. 1180).

Within the precinct wall, near the Gharabah Gate, were two palaces called the Dâr Khâtûn and the

[1] Ibn Serapion, 22; Nuzhat, 147; Yakut, ii. 255.

Dâr-as-Sayyidah (both names signifying the Palace of the Princess), which had belonged to the daughter of the Caliph Muḳtadî, who reigned from 467 to 487 (A.D. 1075 to 1094); but both these palaces were demolished when the Dâr-ar-Rayḥânîyîn, which will be mentioned presently, came to be built. Adjacent to the Date Market Gateway was the palace of the same name, which lay within the precincts but overlooking the Wharf of the Needle-makers outside, and in front of this were terraces occupied by the sellers of dried fruits. These merchants more especially had their shops in that part of the town which lay immediately to the north of the Palaces, where the roads passing through these quarters converged on the northern gate of the city wall (as will be more particularly described in the next chapter), the main thoroughfare being that of the Tuesday Market, leading to the Gate of the Sultan[1].

Within the precincts, and, as seems probable, immediately south of the Gharabah Gate (occupying some of the area formerly covered by the older Ḥasanî Palace, for one of its walls was washed by the Tigris stream), stood the great College of the Mustanṣirîyah. Of this college the ruins still exist, while of the adjoining Palaces of the Caliphs hardly a trace remains; but unfortunately, as the college was only completed in 631 (A.D. 1234), no mention of it occurs in Yâḳût, who had finished his great geographical dictionary shortly before this date, and therefore we do not know for certain on what grounds of the older precincts the college was actually built. Mustanṣir was the penultimate Caliph of the house of 'Abbâs and the father of

[1] Yakut, ii. 255, 519, 520; iii. 783; Marasid, i. 383; v. 408.

Musta'ṣim, whom Hûlâgû put to death, and this Madrasah of the Mustanṣirîyah was founded by him with a view to supplant and eclipse the celebrated Niẓâmîyah College (to be described in chapter xxi), which Niẓâm-al-Mulk had built nearly two centuries before.

We are told that in outward appearance, in stateliness of ornament and sumptuousness of furniture, in spaciousness and in the wealth of its pious foundations, the Mustanṣirîyah surpassed everything that had previously been seen in Islam. It contained four separate law-schools, one for each of the orthodox sects of the Sunnîs, with a professor at the head of each, who had seventy-five students (Faḳîh) in his charge, to whom he gave instruction gratis. The four professors each received a monthly salary, and to each of the three hundred students one gold dînâr a month was assigned. The great kitchen of the college further provided daily rations of bread and meat to all the inmates. According to Ibn-al-Furât there was a library (Dâr-al-Kutub) in the Mustanṣirîyah with rare books treating of the various sciences, so arranged that the students could easily consult them, and those who wished could copy these manuscripts, pens and paper being supplied by the establishment. Lamps for the students and a due provision of olive oil for lighting up the college are also mentioned, likewise, storage places for cooling the drinking-water; and in the great entrance hall (*Aywân*) stood a clock (*Ṣandûḳ-as-sâ'ât*, 'Chest of the Hours,' doubtless some form of clepsydra), announcing the appointed times of prayer, and marking the lapse of the hours by day and by night.

Inside the college a bath house (Ḥammâm) was erected for the special use of the students, and a hospital (Bîmâristân), to which a physician was appointed, whose duty it was to visit the place every morning, prescribing for those who were sick; and there were great store-chambers in the Madrasah provided with all requisites of food, drink, and medicines. The Caliph Mustanṣir himself took such interest in the work of the institution that he would hardly let a day pass without a visit of inspection; and he had caused a private garden to be laid out, with a belvedere (Manẓarah) overlooking the college, whither it was his wont to come and divert himself, sitting at a window—before which a veil was hung—and which opened upon one of the college halls, so that through this window he could watch all that went on within the building, and even hear the lectures of the professors and the disputations of the students.

A century after its foundation, Ibn Baṭûṭah, who visited Baghdad in 727 (A.D. 1327), dilates on the magnificence of the Mustanṣirîyah College, which had fortunately escaped destruction during the Mongol siege; and he describes it as situated at the further end of the Tuesday Market (Suḳ-ath-Thalâthah), which was the commercial centre of Baghdad in his days. The law-schools in the Mustanṣirîyah were then still frequented by students of the four orthodox Sunnî sects, each sect or law-school having its separate mosque, and in the hall the professor of law gave his lectures, whom Ibn Baṭûṭah describes as 'seated under a small wooden cupola on a chair covered by a carpet, speaking with much sedateness and gravity of mien, he being clothed in black and wearing a turban; and there were besides two assistants, one on either hand, who repeated in a loud voice the dictation of the teacher.'

The Persian geographer Ḥamd-Allah, writing a dozen years later than Ibn Baṭûṭah, also refers to the Mustanṣirîyah Madrasah as the most beautiful building then existing in Baghdad; and it appears to have stood intact for many centuries, for the ruins of the college, as already mentioned, still exist, occupying a considerable space of ground immediately below the eastern end of the present Bridge of Boats. Mustanṣir likewise restored the great mosque of the palace (Jâmi'-al-Ḳaṣr), originally built by the Caliph 'Alî Muktafî (see p. 252), and Mustanṣir set up four platforms (*Dikkah*) on the right or western side of the pulpit, where the students of the Mustanṣirîyah were seated and held disputations on Fridays after the public prayers. The remains of this mosque also exist, at the present day occupying part of the Sûḳ-al-Ghazl (the Thread Market), at some little distance to the eastward of the ruins of the Madrasah. When Niebuhr visited Baghdad in 1750 he found that the ancient kitchen of the Mustanṣirîyah College was clearly to be recognized, being used in his day as a weighing house; and Niebuhr copied here the inscription which gives the name and titles of the Caliph Mustanṣir, with the statement that this Madrasah had been completed in the year 630 (A.D. 1233). A similar inscription (also extant) was seen by Niebuhr in the ruined mosque, with the date of 633 (A.D. 1236), doubtless when the restoration by Mustanṣir was finished, for, as already said, the foundation walls in all probability are far older than this date, and belong to the great mosque of the Palace of the Caliph [1].

The third gate in the palace wall, which opened at no great distance to the eastward beyond the two gates of the Willow Tree and of the Date Market, was called the Bâb-al-Badrîyah or the Bâb Badr, from the Market of Badr that lay immediately outside, where had stood the Palace of Badr, the favourite and all-powerful minister of the Caliph Muʻtaḍid. This Badr had originally been a slave of the Caliph Mutawakkil, who had given him his freedom, and Badr rapidly rose to the command of the armies under Muʻtaḍid, during whose Caliphate Badr came to be considered as the chief man of the state, and among other matters superintended the restoration of the Mosque of Manṣûr in Western Baghdad, as related in chapter iii. He fell a victim, however, to the jealousy of ʻAlî Muktafî, son and successor of Muʻtaḍid, and Badr was put to death in the year 289 (A.D. 902). The Bâb Badr had formerly been called the Bâb-al-Khâṣṣah (the Privy Gate), but it had changed its name after the Palace of Badr came to be built.

Yâḳût mentions that the Bâb Badr had been closed since the time of the riots during the reign of the Caliph Ṭâiʻ—that is to say since the year 367 (A.D. 978), when ʻAḍud-ad-Dawlah the Buyid made himself master of Baghdad—but Yâḳût also asserts that the Caliph Ṭâiʻ restored this gate, and that opposite to it had stood the Dâr-al-Fîl (the Elephant Palace), which the belvedere (Manẓarah)

[1] Kazwini, 211; Abu-l-Fida, *History*, iv. 471; Abu-l-Faraj, 425, 442; Ibn-al-Furat MS., folios 20 b, 21 a; Ibn Batutah, ii. 108; Nuzhat, 148; Niebuhr, ii. 241; Jones, 312.

of the gate overlooked. The Caliph Ṭâi' afterwards demolished this Dâr-al-Fîl and turned its site into a burial-ground; this was at the close of the fourth century (the tenth A.D.), and from what Yâķût writes it would seem that in his day, namely at the beginning of the seventh century (the thirteenth A.D.), the ancient Badrîyah Gate and the Badr Palace had both disappeared[1]. Half a century before the time of Yâķût, however, the Bâb Badr was in existence, and the traveller Ibn Jubayr passed through it to reach a court of the mosque, within the Palace of the Caliph, where he heard a notable sermon preached on the 15th day of the month Ṣafar, 581 (May 18, 1185); further, he mentions the belvedere or upper chamber overlooking this court, and states that the Caliph Nâṣir with his sons sat at the window of this belvedere to listen to the sermon.

Immediately outside the wall of the palaces, and beginning at the Badr Gate, was the street known as the Market of the Perfumers (Sûķ-ar-Rayḥânîyîn), which was overlooked by the palace of the same name (Dâr-ar-Rayḥânîyîn) standing inside the Ḥarîm wall[2]. The Market of the Perfumers led directly

[1] Yakut is certainly in error (i. 444) in stating that the Badr Gate was in the vicinity of the Bâb-al-Marâtib of the palace wall and of the city gate called Bâb Kalwâdhâ, since the first of these, and the nearer of the two to the Bâb Badr, must have been at least a mile distant from it. Further, the author of the *Marâṣid* is equally in error (i. 112) in describing the Bâb Badr as having been built by the Caliph Ṭâi', seeing that it took its name from the favourite minister of that Caliph's great-grandfather.

[2] *Rayḥân*, which in Mesopotamia and the East generally meant the Basil plant, in Spanish-Arabic was especially used for the Myrtle; and it has passed into modern Spanish, where *Arrayan* is the common name for myrtle, e.g. the *Patio de los Arrayanes* or 'Court of Myrtles' in the Alhambra of Granada.

into the square before the great mosque of the palace (Jâmi'-al-Ḳaṣr), which last, as has already been said, lay immediately within the precincts adjacent to the Bâb Badr, or rather between it and the next gate called the Bâb Nûbî.

The Market of the Perfumers—where sweet-basil (Rayḥân) and other flowers were sold—was at one time a place of considerable importance, and diverging from it were many minor market streets. In one of these the weavers of palm baskets (As-Safaṭîyîn) had their shops, twenty-four in number, with a caravanserai known as the Khân 'Âsim, and twenty-three other shops adjacent thereto. The perfume-distillers (Al-'Aṭṭârîyîn) also had their market near here with forty-three shops, and close by were the sixteen workshops of the drawers of gold wire, while from this roadway led the Sûḳ-aṣ-Ṣarf (the Market of the Money-changers), the whole forming a network of thoroughfares lying round the great square of the palace mosque, to the north of the Gate of Badr and the Nubian Gate (Bâb Nûbî).

A considerable portion of the original Market of the Perfumers was thrown down during the alterations effected by the Caliph Mustaẓhir between the years 503 and 507 (A.D. 1109 to 1113), when he demolished the Dâr Khâtûn and the palace built by his sister near the Gharabah Gate, known as the Dâr-as-Sayyidah, and having bought up part of the site of the Market of the Perfumers, he caused part of the street here to be removed. A large area was thus rendered available, and a new palace was built, which overlooking the remainder of the Perfumers' Market, was known as the Dâr-ar-Rayḥânîyîn, taking its name from the adjacent market. It formed a great quadrilateral building, surrounding a court which measured 600 ells (about 300 yards) square, the centre being occupied by a garden, and within the circuit of the new palace there were more than sixty halls (Hujrah). One of these was known by the Persian name of the Dargâh-i-Khâtûn (the Lady's Palace); it stood in the part nearest to the Nubian Gate (which will be described presently), and this palace was afterwards inhabited by the Princess Fâṭimah, granddaughter of Mâlik Shâh the Saljûḳ, and wife of the Caliph Muḥammad Muḳtafî, whom she espoused in 534 (A.D. 1140). She is said to have been a learned princess, and appears to have exercised some influence on the political complications of the time; she died in this Dargâh-i-Khâtûn in 542 (A.D. 1147) before her husband, and was buried by him in the tombs of the Caliphs at Ruṣâfah.

Half a century after the foundation of the great Palace of the Rayḥânîyîn, the Caliph Mustanjid, grandson of Mustaẓhir, in the year 557 (A.D. 1162) built the Manẓarah (belvedere), which overhung the Market of the Perfumers close to the Bâb Badr; this probably being the belvedere mentioned in the year 581 by Ibn Jubayr, where he saw the Caliph Nâṣir sitting in state to hear the sermon in the palace mosque, as has already been described. The later Caliphs appear to have spent much of their time in the Palace of the Rayḥânîyîn; and in the garden of the great court, at no great distance behind the belvedere, Musta'ṣim, the last of the Caliphs, built two Treasuries or Libraries for his books. These were still standing intact after the

Mongol siege, for about the year 700 (A.D. 1300) the author of the *Marâṣid* describes them, adding, however, that in his time the greater part of the adjacent palace was in ruin, and that the grounds had become a wilderness, where nothing grew, but the plants that had run wild of the former garden of the Caliph [1].

In the palace wall to the east of the Bâb Badr were the two main gates of the precincts, called respectively the Bâb-an-Nûbî (the Nubian Gate) and the Bâb-al-'Âmmah (the Public Gate). The Nubian Gate was also called the Bâb-al-'Atabah (the Gate of the Threshold), this being the name more especially for its inner portal, which, as the nominal threshold of the abode of the Caliph, was solemnly kissed by all ambassadors of foreign potentates who came to Baghdad. The 'threshold' was a block of white marble, like a column, laid across in front of the inner gateway. It was probably under this stone that the Caliph Nâṣir caused the great cross of the Crusaders to be buried, which Saladin had sent him as a present. The cross, which is described as being of immense size, and as having been held in high honour by the Christians, fell into the hands of the Moslems, with much other booty, at the battle of Ḥaṭṭîn in 583 (A.D. 1187), when Saladin overthrew the power of the Franks in Palestine. From the battlefield the cross had first been taken as a trophy to Damascus, whence in the year 585 (A.D. 1189) it was brought to Baghdad, where, says the chronicle, the Caliph ordered it 'to

[1] Yakut, i. 444; ii. 255, 519; iv. 665, 666; Marasid, i. 382; iii. 162; Mas'udi, viii. 114, 161, 218; Ibn Jubayr, 223; Ibn Khallikan, No. 703, p. 20.

be buried under the threshold of the Bâb-an-Nûbî, with a small part thereof projecting forth, this same being of brass, but gilt, which the people passing over would tread under foot, spitting thereon; and thus it was done on the 16th of the month Rabî' II of that year' (June, 1189)[1].

The Bâb-an-Nûbî at one period must have been used as the principal gateway of the Palaces, and more than half a century before the reign of the Caliph Nâṣir, at the time of the riots which broke out at Baghdad in the year 520 (A.D. 1126), when the Caliph Mustarshid was fighting against Sultan Maḥmûd the Saljûḳ, the chronicle states that the Nubian Gate was the only one allowed to remain open in the palace precincts, all others having been blocked or locked up by the orders of the Caliph. The most frequently mentioned, however, of the gates of the palace was the Bâb-al-'Âmmah—meaning the Gate of the Commonalty, or the Public Gate—which was also known as the Bâb 'Ammûrîyah. Its huge iron gates are said to have been brought to Baghdad by the Caliph Mu'taṣim from the city of Amorium in Asia Minor, which city he had stormed and burnt to the ground during his celebrated campaign of the year 223 (A.D. 838) against the Byzantine Emperor Theophilus. The Bâb-al-'Âmmah would appear to have been the original entrance to the grounds of the Ḥasanî Palace; it is mentioned by Ibn Serapion, and the Canal of the Palaces entered by it, after passing the Gate of the Fief of Mushjîr (as described in chapter xvi), the site

[1] Abu Shamah, ii. 82, 139. This reference I owe to Professor Lane-Poole. Some curious details are given as to the earlier history of this great cross.

of which must have been afterwards taken up by the Perfumers' Market.

Within the Ḥarîm wall and occupying the space between the Nubian Gate and the Public Gate were suburbs inhabited by the lowest orders of the Baghdad populace, being closed off from the adjacent palace precincts by an inner wall, in which opened three chief gateways, besides posterns. These gates of the inner wall, as described by Yâḳût at the beginning of the seventh century (the thirteenth A.D.), were first the Bâb-ad-Duwwâmât (the Gate of Tops, such as children play with), next the Bâb 'Ulayyân (which may mean the Hyaena Gate), and thirdly the Bâb-al-Ḥaram (the Gate of the Sanctuary).

Returning to the Bâb-al-'Âmmah, the wall of the precincts ran thence for about a mile, first south-east, and then south-west, before it reached the Bâb-al-Marâtib near the river bank, and in this long stretch was only one opening, namely the Bâb-al-Bustân (the Garden Gate). Outside the wall near this gate began the quarter known as the Mamûnîyah (which will be described in chapter xxi); and the Garden Gate was remarkable for its Manẓarah (belvedere), which overlooked the Place of Sacrifice, where, on the 10th of the month Dhu-l-Ḥijjah, on the occasion of the greater festival which closed the pilgrim season, the victim was solemnly sacrificed.

The lowest of the gates in the precinct wall, and probably opening near the Tâj Palace, was the Bâb-al-Marâtib (the Gate of Degrees), which is described as having been one of the finest and best built of those giving access to the Ḥarîm. Yâḳût adds that in the old days its warder had always been a person of importance, and the Gate of Degrees stood at a distance of two bow-shots, or a couple of hundred yards, from the Tigris bank. Such were the gates in the palace wall surrounding the Ḥarîm or Sanctuary, as described by Yâḳût, who explains that though the royal precincts were chiefly occupied by the numerous Palaces of the Caliphs, various minor quarters were also included within the walls, these being inhabited by the personal attendants of the sovereign and many of the great officers of state. Access to the actual Palace of the Caliph, and his private parks and gardens, was only gained by passing an inner wall, which on the land side entirely surrounded the royal residence, and cut it off from all intrusion from the city quarters; but egress from the palace gardens was kept free on the river side, where the Tigris for nearly a mile formed the boundary of the precincts [1].

From the description summarized in the preceding pages, it is evident that at the time when Yâḳût wrote both the Firdûs Palace and the Ḥasanî had long since disappeared, having fallen to ruin probably before the beginning of the fifth century (the eleventh A.D.). The site of the Firdûs, immediately to the south of the Gate of the Tuesday Market of the old Mukharrim Quarter (mentioned by Ibn Serapion), probably lay some distance outside the wall of the palaces which Yâḳût has described. The ground where the Ḥasanî had formerly stood appears to have been occupied at the close of the fifth century (the eleventh A.D.) by the palaces which stood near the three Gates of the Willow Tree, of the Date

[1] Ibn Serapion, 22; Yakut, i. 451; ii. 255; Mushtarik, 130; Ibn-al-Athir, x. 449; Fakhri, 276.

Market, and of Badr, opening in the north wall of the precincts, where in later times the Mustanṣirîyah College and the great Palace of the Rayḥânîyîn came to be built.

To attempt any exact plan of the Palaces of the Caliphs is of course impossible, but from all that has come down to us it seems probable that the ancient minaret at the present day standing in the Thread Market (Sûḳ-al-Ghazl), at a considerable distance from the ruins of the Mustanṣirîyah College, and which bears an inscription of the Caliph Mustanṣir, was only restored, not built by him, being, as already said, a part of the great palace mosque erected by the Caliph 'Alî Muktafî. In the latter days of the Caliphate the area of the Ḥarîm, or precincts, as described by Yâḳût, would appear to have contained two chief palaces, one, the New Tâj, which stood on the river bank rather above the site of the first Palace of the Tâj (described by Ibn Serapion), and secondly, the Palace of the Rayḥânîyîn, lying at some distance from the Tigris and below the Mustanṣirîyah College. To the eastward stood the great palace mosque, at the north-east angle of the Ḥarîm walls, and of this building the minaret in the Sûḳ-al-Ghazl is now the sole remaining vestige.

CHAPTER XX

THE QUARTERS NORTH OF THE PALACES

The wall of East Baghdad and its four Gates. The Bâb-as-Sulṭân and the Sultan's Market. Streets of the Tuesday Market. Quarters built by Muḳtadî after the Inundation. The Road of the two Archways. The Street of the Canal. The Ḳarâḥ Ibn Razîn and the Muḳtadîyah. Mukhtârah Quarter and the Bâb Abraz. College of the Tâjîyah and the Wardîyah Cemetery. The Bâb Ẓafar and the Ẓafarîyah Quarter. The Quarter of the Judge's Garden and other quarters called Ḳarâḥ.

THE modern city of Baghdad, on the east bank of the Tigris, is surrounded on three sides by an ancient wall, pierced by four gateways, one of these bearing an inscription set up there by the Caliph Nâṣir. During the reign of this Caliph Baghdad was visited by Ibn Jubayr, and the description he has left of the city wall, with four gates, makes it certain that the present wall is virtually identical with the one which Ibn Jubayr described in 581 (A.D. 1185), three quarters of a century before the Mongol siege.

This wall, according to the Persian historian Ḥamd-Allah, was first erected by the Caliph Mustaẓhir, and the chronicle of Ibn-al-Athîr confirms the fact under the record of events of the year 488 (A.D. 1095). Three-quarters of a century after this, the Caliph Mustaḍî repaired or rebuilt the wall, as recorded in a contemporary account written by the anonymous epitomist of Ibn Hawḳal, and Ibn-al-Athîr gives us the exact date of this restoration, namely the year 568 (A.D. 1173). The epitomist of Ibn Hawḳal, after mentioning that in his own day the Nahr Muʿallâ Quarter (which is the name both he and Yâḳût give to the suburbs round the palaces forming new Baghdad) was surrounded by this strong and high wall, states that outside the wall was a deep ditch connected with the Tigris above and below, and that water thus flowed round the whole city. The epitomist further adds that at this period the more ancient northern quarters of East Baghdad had already fallen totally to ruin, with the exception of the outlying suburb round the shrine of Abu Ḥanîfah and the great mosque at Ruṣâfah (as described in chapter xiv), and that the only populous quarters in his day were those lying immediately outside and surrounding the Palaces of the Caliphs.

A dozen years after this the traveller Ibn Jubayr, who visited Baghdad in 581 (A.D. 1185), describes with much minuteness the city as he found it, and as already said especially mentions the town wall with its four gates, which enclosed the suburbs that had grown up round the palaces during the preceding century. The four gates will be more fully noticed in the following pages when speaking of the several quarters to which they gave egress, but briefly to name them as described by Ibn Jubayr and by Ḥamd-Allah the Persian geographer, they were these. In the north wall, (i) the Gate of the Sultan, now called the Bâb-al-Mu'aẓẓam; in the east wall, (ii) first the Ẓafarîyah Gate, which the Persian author calls the Khurâsân Gate, and which is now known as the Bâb-al-Wusṭânî, and next (iii) the Ḥalbah Gate, at the present day shut up and called the Gate of the Talisman, from the inscription of the Caliph Nâṣir, already mentioned; lastly, to the south, (iv) the Baṣalîyah Gate, referred to during the Mongol siege by the Persian writers as the Gate of Kalwâdhâ, and which Ḥamd-Allah calls by the curious title of the Bâb-al-Khalaj, this at the present day being known as the Eastern Gate (Bâb-ash-Sharḳî)[1].

The description given by Ḥamd-Allah, writing in the year 740 (A.D. 1339)—three-quarters of a century, therefore, after the Mongol siege—exactly corresponds with what is found at the present day. The city wall, he says, was built of kiln-burnt bricks, the ditch outside being lined with these bricks likewise, and the wall extended in the form of a semicircle, measuring 18,000 paces round, going from the Tigris bank above the city to the river

[1] Nuzhat, 147, and Guzidah, under reign of the Caliph Mustaẓhir; Yakut, iv. 845, and Ibn Hawkal, 164, note *e*; Ibn-al-Athir, x. 172; xi. 260; Ibn Jubayr, 231; Jones, 310. On p. 309, Commander Jones in the matter of the age of the present walls, states his opinion that 'in all probability [the Gate of the Talisman, rebuilt in 618 or A.D. 1221], is of later construction than may parts of the foundation of the wall, for they bear the impress of age, and exhibit, moreover, the open brick and mortar work peculiar to the older *Masannehs*—a name applied to substantial embankments of masonry, built principally as water defences, on which the fortifications are raised. The foundation of the Baghdad walls may therefore date from the third century of the Hejireh.' In point of fact, they date from the fifth century, equivalent to the eleventh century A.D.

again below the southern quarters[1]. The great Palace of the Buyids, and of the Saljûḳ Sultans who succeeded to their power, as has already been shown in chapter xvii, lay to the north of the new city, covering part of the ground formerly occupied by the Shammâsîyah Quarter; and in front of this palace stood the great mosque called the Jâmiʿ-as-Sulṭân, from which a road went southward, entering the city by the single gate in the north wall called either the Bâb-Sûḳ-as-Sulṭân (the Gate of the Sultan's Market) or simply the Bâb-as-Sulṭân (the Sultan's Gate).

This gateway is frequently mentioned by the Persian historians in their accounts of the siege of Baghdad by the Mongols. At the present day the Bâb-al-Muʿaẓẓam occupies its site, being so called from the shrine of Abu Ḥanîfah the Imâm, which lies some distance to the north of it, and standing in a position to the westward of the former Palaces of the Sultan. Immediately within the gate, and going down towards the Palaces of the Caliphs, was the market called Sûḳ-as-Sulṭân, at the lower end of which came a street named the Darb-al-Munîrah, in the immediate neighbourhood of the Muʿallâ Canal. Another street also mentioned by the same authority (Yâḳût) as situated on this canal is the Darb-al-Ajurr (the Street of Kiln-burnt Bricks), and this in the early part of the seventh century (the thirteenth A.D.) was the centre of a populous quarter. A hundred years later, when Ibn Baṭûṭah visited Baghdad in 727 (A.D. 1327), the main thoroughfare

[1] The printed text of the Nuzhat, p. 147, gives the number as 15,000 Gâms or paces; the London and the Paris MSS., however, all give 18,000 Gâms, as also the lithographed text, p. 135.

across these markets had reverted to the older name of the Street of the Tuesday Market[1], which, beginning within the northern gate in the city wall, came down to the wall of the Palaces of the Caliph, and next passing through the Market of the Perfumers (Sûḳ-ar-Rayḥânîyîn), communicated with the square in front of the great mosque of the palace.

The quarters surrounding the Palaces of the Caliph to the eastward, away from the Tigris bank, and to the southward towards the town of Kalwâdhâ downstream, for the most part were included within the lines of the city wall, though there were suburbs beyond the Bâb-aẓ-Ẓafarîyah to the north-east, as also beyond the Bâb-al-Baṣalîyah to the south, otherwise called the Kalwâdhâ Gate. These eastern and southern quarters were the latest to be built in East Baghdad, and dated in the main from the reign of Muḳtadî, after whom one quarter—the Muḳtadîyah—was named. This Caliph was the contemporary of Mâlik Shâh, the founder of the Mosque of the Sultan, already described in chapter xvii, and of his famous Wazîr the Niẓâm-al-Mulk, who built the College of the Niẓâmîyah, which stood on the southern side of the palaces; and Muḳtadî was father of the Caliph Mustaẓhir, who built the city wall.

The reign of Muḳtadî, therefore, which lasted from the year 467 to 487 (A.D. 1075 to 1094), and of his son, witnessed a considerable extension to the area of East Baghdad. The city had been to some extent left in ruins at the end of the previous reign of Ḳâim, when in the year 466 (A.D. 1074) the whole eastern district was laid under water through

[1] Yakut, i. 59; ii. 564; Ibn Jubayr, 231; Rashid-ad-Din, 283; Ibn Batutah, ii. 108.

the bursting of the great Mu'izzîyah Dyke of the Ḳûrij Canal. The Tigris at the time had been in flood, and further a strong wind from the desert had thrown back the waters, which, it is reported, rose so high as to reach even the roofs of the houses. The calamity was the more terrible from its having occurred in the darkness of the night, and an immense number of people perished by the sudden falling in of the walls which had been undermined by the rising torrent. The new quarters planned by Muḳtadî replaced the ruins that had been thus caused by the floods, and extended round the older Mamûnîyah suburb, which had adjoined the Palaces of the Caliphs to the south-east, being described by Yâḳût as curving down from the line of the Mu'allâ Canal on the north-east, back to the Tigris bank on the south; and, as already stated, these suburbs during the succeeding reign of Mustaẓhir were enclosed by the line of the new city wall.

From the square of the palace mosque a thoroughfare running northward, parallel with the Mu'allâ Canal, led past the ancient Abraz Gate (in the former wall of the Mukharrim Quarter) to the Bâb-aẓ-Ẓafarîyah in the new city wall. This thoroughfare is known as the Road of the Two Archways (Shâri'-al-'Aḳdayn), namely the Archway of the Artificer ('Aḳd-al-Muṣṭani') and the Archway of the Armourers ('Aḳd-az-Zarrâdîn). Leaving the square of the great mosque of the palace (Raḥbah Jâmi'-al-Ḳaṣr) at the north-east corner, the road, after a short distance, came first to the Archway of the Artificer, which is described by Yâḳût as being 'a great gate in the midst of the city,' and after passing through it the highway bifurcated. To the right the road led down to the Mamûnîyah Quarter and the gate called the Bâb-al-Âzaj, which will be described in the next chapter, while to the left the main thoroughfare continued north, following the line of the Mu'allâ Canal.

The Mu'allâ Canal here ran in a conduit, partly underground, and to the right of it was the Road of the Canal (Darb-an-Nahr). The main thoroughfare, after skirting the canal for the distance of a bowshot (say somewhat less than a hundred yards), next reached the quarter called the Ḳarâḥ Ibn Razîn, a place of considerable extent, since to cross it was 'a good horse gallop [1],' by which a distance of about half a mile may be indicated.

The Road of the Canal, already mentioned, also led into this quarter, through which passed the

[1] On several occasions Yakut makes use of the terms 'bowshot' and 'horse gallop' to mark short distances, but he nowhere explains what length these measures represented, and the dictionaries give no aid in the matter. A 'bowshot' or 'arrow flight' (*ghalwah* or *ramyah-sahm*) may approximately be estimated at somewhat less than a hundred yards, but the term was used vaguely and often meant any distance up to a quarter of a mile or even more. Thus Idrisi (p. 144) speaks of the Island of Rawḍah, near Cairo, as being two miles long (which it is) and 'a bowshot' across, it measuring in point of fact about 500 yards in breadth. Again, Ibn Jubayr (p. 50) describes the Sphinx as lying 'a bowshot' distant from the Great Pyramid, and the space which separates the two is at least 350 yards. Lastly, the Hellespont at Abydos is described as 'a bowshot' across (Kitâb-al-'Uyûn, p. 26; Abu-l-Fida, p. 200), and the distance is, in reality, over three-quarters of a mile. A 'horse gallop' (*shawṭ-al-faras*) may be estimated at about half an Arab mile or 1,000 yards. Thus Yakut (i. 263) in describing Alexandria speaks of the Pharos as standing opposite the harbour on the point of the island, which last lay out to sea 'a horse gallop' distant from the mainland. The island is now joined to the coast by the silting up of the old harbour, but judging by the present maps, half a mile would be a fair estimate of the distance which formerly was covered by the sea.

Street of the Nut Market (Darb-al-Lawzîyah). To the north-west of the Ḳarâḥ of Ibn Razîn stretched the Quarter of the Muḳtadîyah, already referred to, which was named after its founder the Caliph Muḳtadî, while beyond the Ibn Razîn Quarter to the north stood the Archway of the Armourers, which could be closed by a gate. This was sometimes called the New Archway, but it came to be known as the 'Aḳd-az-Zarrâdîn, they being the smiths or armourers who forged coats of mail, and who lived near this part of the roadway.

The word Ḳarâḥ, which occurs in connexion with the name of many different quarters in this part of the city, is explained by Yâḳût as signifying *a garden* in the Baghdad dialect; with the lapse of time, however, these 'gardens' coming to be built over, the term Ḳarâḥ continued in use as the name of the new suburb. The Muḳtadîyah[1] Quarter, which as already mentioned lay on the north-western side of the Ḳarâḥ of Ibn Razîn, is one of those which suffered most during the second of the great inundations of Baghdad, namely that of the year 554 (A.D. 1159), on which occasion all the upper part of the city was for a time again laid under water; and Yâḳût reports that little beyond mounds of mud covering the ruins of former buildings remained visible, after the river had subsided, to mark the position of the various submerged quarters,

[1] The name Muḳtadîyah is by mistake printed Muḳtad*ir*îyah in Yakut, i. 774, and the Marasid, i. 185; the right reading, however, is given both in a note to this last as an alternative reading, and in the text of Yakut, iv. 45. From the chronicle of Ibn-al-Athir, x. 156, there can be no doubt that Muḳtadî, who died in A.H. 487—and not Muḳtadir who was killed in A.H. 320—was the Caliph who built this Quarter.

which extended all the way from the Muḳtadîyah down past the Mamûnîyah Quarter, and to the Âzaj Gate to the south-east of the palaces.

Beyond the second of the two archways, that of the Armourers, described above, the thoroughfare again bifurcated; the road to the right (turning eastward) led to the quarter called the Ḳarâḥ-al-Ḳâḍî (the Garden of the Judge), while to the left the main thoroughfare continuing northward first traversed the Mukhtârah Quarter, and then came to the old gate, formerly opening in the wall of the Mukharrim Quarter, called the Bâb Abraz[1]. At the beginning of the seventh century (the thirteenth A.D.), when Yâḳût wrote, the gateway of the Bâb Abraz—which name he gives under the corrupt form of Biyabraz or Bayraz—had long been in ruin, and the cemetery called the Wardîyah then lay beyond it. The Bâb Abraz is first mentioned by Ibn Serapion, in the early part of the fourth century (the tenth A.D.), and, as will be remembered, it was then the limit of the three northern quarters of East Baghdad to the south-east, opening in the wall of the Mukharrim Quarter, where the Mu'allâ Canal entered the city. Yâḳût also gives this gateway the name of the Bâb Bîn, derived evidently from the canal called the Nahr Bîn, from which the Mu'allâ Canal (through the Nahr Mûsâ) originally took its waters[2].

Near the Bâb Abraz, during Saljûḳ times, namely

[1] Ibn-al-Athir, x. 62, 156; xi. 164; Yakut, i. 807; ii. 564; iv. 45, 46, 440; Marasid, iii. 252.

[2] Unless the Mûsâ Canal, from the Nahrawân, had become silted up by the thirteenth century A.D., Yakut (iv. 845) must be mistaken in saying that the waters of the Mu'allâ Canal are derived from the Khâliṣ.

about the year 482 (A.D. 1089), stood the college called the Madrasah-at-Tâjîyah, built by Tâj-al-Mulk, chancellor of Sultan Mâlik Shâh, and during this period the cemetery of the Bâb Abraz was used as the burial-place of many persons of note. This cemetery, otherwise known as the Wardîyah, extended beyond the Abraz Gate, to the left of the roadway, and the thoroughfare thence passed directly to the gate of the town wall called the Bâb Ẓafarîyah. Round this gateway lay the Ẓafarîyah Quarter, which took its name from the Ḳarâḥ or Garden of Ẓafar, lying outside the quarter, its original owner Ẓafar[1] having been one of the chief servants of the Caliph, though of which Caliph, or when Ẓafar flourished, is not stated. From the details given of its position there can be little doubt that the Bâb Ẓafarîyah of Ibn Jubayr and Yâḳût—which Ḥamd-Allah a century after the Mongol invasion names the Bâb Khurâsân (and some MSS. give it as the Gate of the Khurâsân Road)—is identical in position with the modern Bâb-al-Wusṭânî, which, as already stated, is the north-east gate in the present city wall, through which passes the high-road to Persia and Khurâsân.

Returning once again within the city limits, it will be remembered that the thoroughfare after passing through the Archway of the Armourers bifurcated, and the main road to the left has just been described. The branch to the right led eastward from the Armourers' Gate for the distance of an arrow flight

[1] In the printed text of Ibn Jubayr, p. 231, line 8, the name of this gate is spelt Bâb-aṣ-Ṣafarîyah (with an initial *Ṣâd*, in place of Ẓâ), but there can be little question that Ẓafarîyah is the right reading, as given in Yakut and Ibn-al-Athir in the passages quoted below.

(or about one hundred yards), reaching a point where the road again bifurcated. To the left, eastward, it led straight to the quarter called the Ḳarâḥ-al-Ḳâḍî (the Judge's Garden), while to the right and south of this the branch road gave access first to the place called the Ḳarâḥ of Abu-sh-Shahm, and next to the quarter known as Al-Ḳubaybât (the little Domes). Of the founders of these various suburbs nothing is known, but Yâḳût adds that the four quarters called after the Ḳarâḥs, or Gardens, of Ibn Razîn, Ẓafar, Al-Ḳâdî (the Judge), and Abu-sh-Shahm, were each in his day standing apart like so many separate hamlets; also they were well built, populous, and spacious quarters, each having its own mosque and market streets[1].

[1] Ibn Serapion, 22; Yakut, iii. 587; iv. 45, 845, 920; Marasid, ii. 388, 393; iii. 252; Ibn-al-Athir, x. 120; Nuzhat, 147.

CHAPTER XXI

THE QUARTERS EAST AND SOUTH OF THE PALACES

The Mamûnîyah Quarter. The Ḥalbah Gate and its Inscription. The Persian Fief and the Burj-al-'Ajamî. The Ḳaṭî'ah Quarter and the Rayyân. The Bâb Baṣalîyah or Gate of Kalwâdhâ. The township of Kalwâdhâ. Palace of the Kalwâdhâ Raḳḳah. The Âzaj Gate. Ḳarâḥ Juhayr, the Zandaward Monastery: the Maydân and Mas'ûdah Quarters. The eastern Ḳurayyah and the Niẓâmîyah College. The Bahâîyah and the Tutushî Hospital. The later Tuesday Market.

THE quarters just described lay immediately within the city wall, between the Ẓafarîyah and the Ḥalbah Gates, and to the east of the thoroughfare known as the Street of the Two Archways, which was the left-hand branch at the first bifurcation outside the Archway of the Artificer. The right-hand branch at this bifurcation led south through the Mamûnîyah Quarter to the gateway within the city, known as the Bâb-al-Âzaj, and thence to the Bâb-al-Baṣalîyah, which opened in the lowest part of the city wall beyond the Baṣalîyah Quarter.

The Mamûnîyah Quarter, as already stated in chapter xviii, owed its name to the Caliph Mamûn, whose attendants had built their houses here on lands adjacent to the palace afterwards called the

Ḳaṣr Ḥasanî. In general terms the Mamûnîyah Quarter may be described as including the whole of the space between the wall of the Palaces of the Caliph near the original Ḳaṣr-al-Ḥasanî, and the gate in the city wall called the Bâb Ḥalbah, and it extended down to the Âzaj Gate within the city on the south, while on the north it was bounded by the various Ḳarâḥs to the east of the highroad of the two archways. The Mamûnîyah included many minor quarters, and all these are said to have suffered considerable damage during the great inundation of the year 554 (A.D. 1159); the Mamûnîyah, however, must have been subsequently rebuilt, for in the middle of the next century, Hûlâgû, on entering Baghdad after the great siege, took up his abode here, prior to visiting the Palaces of the Caliphs.

At the end of the main street crossing the Mamûnîyah was the Bâb Ḥalbah, the gate in the city wall described by Ibn Jubayr in 581 (A.D. 1185), and which is also frequently mentioned in the accounts of the Mongol siege. This gate was the next, on the south, to the Bâb Ẓafar, and it is the present Bâb-at-Talism, or the Talismanic Gate, which still bears the inscription set up here by the Caliph Nâṣir, referred to above. This inscription states that the gate which it adorns was built and restored by 'the Imâm Abu-l-'Abbâs Aḥmad An-Nâṣir-li-Dîn-Allah, ... and the termination of the work was in the year 618,' that is to say A.D. 1221. It is said that this gateway was in former times known as the White Gate, and it is at the present day walled up, having been closed since A.D. 1638, when Sultan Murâd IV, the Turkish conqueror of Baghdad, entered in triumph through its portals[1].

Near the Ḥalbah Gate was the belvedere called the Manẓarat-al-Ḥalbah, which is described as standing at the further end of the market which traversed the Mamûnîyah Quarter. The word *Ḥalbah* signifies 'a racecourse' or 'hippodrome,' and outside this gate, before the city wall had been built, was the place commonly used for playing the game of Ṣuljân or polo. When the Saljûḳ Sultan Mâlik Shâh visited Baghdad in the year 479 (A.D. 1086), the chronicle mentions that he rode from his palace of the Dâr-al-Mamlakat to this part of the town, and played polo here in the early part of the day on which he made his state visit to the Caliph Muḳtadî.

Not far from the Ḥalbah Gate, and to the south-east, was the Ḳaṭî'at-al-'Ajam (the Persian Fief), near which was the great bastion in the wall, so often mentioned during the Mongol siege under the name of the Burj-al-'Ajamî (the Persian Tower). It was against this point that Hûlâgû directed the storming party to make their main attack, and Baghdad fell when the 'Ajamî Tower had been taken. Although apparently the name has now gone out of all memory, there can be no doubt that the ancient Burj-al-'Ajamî is the present great corner bastion at the eastern angle of the city wall, now known as the Angle Bastion (Tâbiyah-az-Zawîyah). In the accounts of the siege the Persian Tower is described as lying between the Ḥalbah and the Kalwâdhâ Gates, and the Ḳaṭî'at-al-'Ajamî (the

[1] Niebuhr, ii. 240; Rawlinson, *Encycl. Brit.*, s.v. *Baghdad*; Ker Porter, ii. 263; Jones, 309. Tavernier (i. 239), who was in Baghdad in 1652, names it 'la Porte Murée.'

Persian Fief) would thus have occupied the space within this angle of the city wall. The Persian Fief gave its name to the Ḳaṭî'ah Quarter, which was one of those built by the Caliph Muḳtadî; and in the seventh century (the thirteenth A.D.) it is described by Yâḳût as being a suburb that was like a separate hamlet, while contiguous to it and towards the Mamûnîyah lay another quarter called the Rayyân, which the same authority mentions as one of the most populous to be seen in his day in East Baghdad.

In the account of the city wall given by Ibn Jubayr in 581 (A.D. 1185), the gate which opened to the south near the Tigris bank is called the Bâb-al-Baṣalîyah, and the Baṣalîyah Quarter is one of those mentioned in Yâḳût as having been built by the Caliph Muḳtadî in this part of the city. The name of the Bâb-al-Baṣalîyah, it is true, does not occur in either Yâḳût or in the Persian accounts of the Mongol siege; but the Kalwâdhâ Gate, which Yâḳût expressly states lay contiguous to the Baṣalîyah Quarter, is frequently referred to, and since no Bâb Kalwâdhâ is mentioned by Ibn Jubayr, it may be safely assumed that his Baṣalîyah Gate, opening in the direction of the Kalwâdhâ township, is identical with the gate afterwards known as the Bâb Kalwâdhâ. One of the Mongol generals had his headquarters before the Kalwâdhâ Gate during the great siege, and it was here, after Baghdad had fallen, that Musta'ṣim, the last of the Abbasid Caliphs, was brought out and made to stand as a suppliant in the presence of Hûlâgû, in whose camp not far from this gate the Caliph subsequently met his death.

This Başalîyah or Kalwâdhâ Gate is evidently the one which Ḥamd-Allah, writing in the middle of the eighth century (the fourteenth A. D.) and eighty years after the Mongol siege, calls the Bâb-al-Khuluj, which may mean the Gate of the Canals (plural of *Khalîj*), but the reading is uncertain, and the name unfortunately does not appear to be mentioned by any other authority[1]. At the present day this gate is known as the Bâb-ash-Sharkî (the Eastern Gate), but in the last century, when Niebuhr in 1750 visited Baghdad, it was known, he reports, under the Turkish name of the Karolog Ḳapi, probably a corruption of Karâñliḳ-Ḳapi, meaning the Gate of Darkness[2], but this name also has apparently now fallen out of use. The name of the Bâb Kalwâdhâ frequently occurs in the chronicle of Ibn-al-Athîr. During the troubles of the year 535 (A.D. 1141), the Caliph Muḥammad Muḳtafî

[1] The printed text of the Nuzhat, p. 147, also the lithographed edition, p. 135, both give *Bâb Khalaj*, without vowels, and omitting the article. The MSS. of the British Museum give the readings *Bâb-al-Khalaḥ* and *Bâb-al-Khala'* (the last with *'ayn* in place of final *jîm*); the Paris MSS. give *Bâb-al-Khalaj*, or *al-Halaj*, or *al-Khalaḥ*. The reading *Khuluj* (in the plural) is only tentative, because this at any rate gives a meaning, but it is to be noted that *Khalîj*, though the common word for a canal in Egypt and the west, does not appear to be commonly used in this sense in Mesopotamia, where the term *Nahr* is always employed both for a river and a canal. Possibly, if the true reading be *Khalaj*, the appellation may be taken from the well-known Turk tribe of that name, whom Istakhri (p. 245) has described, and who at a later time (A.D. 1290 to 1320), under the name of the Khiljî Sultans, became the second Muslim dynasty of India who ruled at Dehli. It must be noted, however, that there is no historical evidence connecting the Khalaj Turks with any gate of Baghdad.

[2] I owe this explanation to Professor E. G. Browne. Tavernier (i. 239) speaks of it in 1652 as the 'Cara Capi, la porte noire,' which confirms the above etymology.

caused both this and the Ẓafarîyah Gate to be temporarily blocked up; and in the account of the inundation of the year 604 (A.D. 1208), it is stated that the suburb round this gate came to be much imperilled by the overflow of the ditch outside the city wall, on which occasion the Caliph Nâṣir caused the mouth of the said ditch on the Tigris to be closed by a temporary dam, which should prevent the influx of the river water.

Kalwâdhâ, it will be remembered, was an important township on the eastern Tigris bank, about a league below Baghdad, the site of which is occupied by the modern village of Gerârah. Ibn Hawḳal, as early as the year 367 (A.D. 978), relates that though Kalwâdhâ had a Friday mosque of its own, and was therefore to be considered as a separate township, it might almost be counted as forming part of Baghdad, for in his day the houses were continuous along the river bank from below the Palaces of the Caliph to Kalwâdhâ. Near where the Kalwâdhâ Gate came to be built in later days, there had stood a Kiosk belonging to the pleasure-loving Caliph Amîn, outside which, in the year 198 (A.D. 814), was encamped one part of the army then besieging Baghdad in the name of the Caliph Mamûn. At the date in question the later Palaces of the Caliphs (in East Baghdad) were represented by the single palace of the Ḳaṣr Ja'farî only, begun by Ja'far the Barmecide in the reign of Hârûn-ar-Rashîd, and Amîn had later on built himself this pleasure-house in the adjacent Raḳḳah or swamp of Kalwâdhâ. This place came to be known as the Ḳaṣr Raḳḳah Kalwâdhâ, and it was to reach his new Kiosk from the west bank that Amîn laid down the Zandaward Bridge of Boats which has been mentioned in chapter xiii [1].

Ibn Jubayr, in the year 580 (A.D. 1184), after describing the town wall with its four gates, adds that besides these there were many other gates within the city, built for shutting off the various market streets and quarters. One of the chief of these inner gateways was the Bâb-al-Âzaj (the Gate of the Portico or Gallery), standing in the southern part of the Mamûnîyah Quarter. Although the exact position of the Âzaj Gate in relation to the Gate of Degrees in the palace wall and the Baṣalîyah Gate of the town wall is not given, it must have stood within this last, and it gave its name to the surrounding quarter. The Bâb-al-Âzaj is frequently mentioned by both Yâḳût and Ibn-al-Athîr in connexion with the Niẓâmîyah College, the Tutushî Hospital, and the various suburbs adjacent to the Mamûnîyah, namely the Quarter of the Persian Fief, the Maydân, the two Mas'ûdah Quarters, the Rayyân, and the Dayr-az-Zandaward. The Quarter of the Bâb-al-Âzaj was on three occasions partly burnt down, namely in the years 440, 467, and 551 (A.D. 1048, 1075, and 1156), and the fire in most cases extended to the neighbouring Mamûnîyah Suburb.

Near the Bâb-al-Âzaj lay the 'garden' or quarter known as the Ḳarâḥ Juhayr, and also in this neighbourhood stood the old convent called the Dayr-az-Zandaward, this Zandaward having been originally

[1] Yakut, i. 655, 807; ii. 884; iv. 142, 665; Marasid, i. 314; iii. 33; Rashid-ad-Din, 282, 298, 300; Ibn-al-Athir, x. 103, 156; xi. 51; xii. 184; Abu-l-Faraj, 474, 475; Ibn Hawkal, 165; Tabari, iii. 868, 951; Jones, 310.

a canal of the Kalwâdhâ district, which also gave its name to the Bridge of Boats mentioned in a preceding paragraph. The convent has already been referred to in chapter xv, and its gardens were celebrated in the time of Yâḳût for the oranges and grapes grown here, the latter being reported to have been the finest of all the districts round Baghdad. The Maydân Quarter, which gave its name to one of the neighbouring Palaces of the Caliph in the Ḥarîm called the Ḳaṣr Maydân Khâliṣ, lay close to the Âzaj Gate; the quarter may have received its name from the Maydân or square originally laid out near this by the Caliph Mamûn when he rebuilt the Palace of the Ḥasanî, as described in chapter xviii, but nothing else is recorded of it. In this same neighbourhood stood the two small Quarters both called Al-Mas'ûdah, after a slave-girl of that name, who was of the household of the Caliph Mamûn. One of these Mas'ûdah Quarters was within the Mamûnîyah, while the other, through which passed the thoroughfare called the Darb-al-Mas'ûd, stood on part of the endowed lands ('Aḳâr) belonging to the Niẓâmîyah College. Adjacent to this was the Ḳurayyah Quarter of East Baghdad (the Ḳurayyah of West Baghdad has been described in chapter vi), which is mentioned by Yâḳût as lying near the Palaces of the Caliphs[1].

The celebrated College of the Niẓâmîyah was named after its founder Niẓâm-al-Mulk—Wazîr in turn of the two Saljûḳ princes Alp Arslân and Mâlik

[1] Yakut, i. 232, 476, 826; ii. 598, 665; iv. 122, 398, 528, 714; Marasid, i. 314, 431, 519; ii. 97, 393, 433; Ibn-al-Athir, ix. 376; x. 67; xi. 143. Khatib, folio 107 b, for *Zandaward* gives *Zandarûd*, and the Paris MSS. confirm this reading, which Wüstenfeld also cites as an alternative from other MSS. of Yakut (v. 198).

Shâh, also the friend and patron of the astronomer-poet Omar Khayyâm. The college was founded in 457 (A.D. 1065), and opened two years later, being especially established for the teaching of the Shâfi'ite school of law. Among its more celebrated lecturers was the great theologian Ghazzâlî and Bahâ-ad-Dîn (better known with us as Bohadin the biographer of the Saladin), who was under-lecturer during four years in the Niẓâmîyah. Close to the Niẓâmîyah was another college called the Bahâîyah, near which again stood the hospital called the Bîmâristan Tutushî, opening on the market called the Sûḳ Tutush, which went from the Niẓâmîyah to the Âzaj Gate. This hospital and market were built by Khamârtakîn, who had originally been the slave of Tâj-ad-Dawlah Tutush, one of the sons of the Saljûḳ Sultan Alp Arslân, and he died in the year 508 (A.D. 1114). A century later, in the time of Yâḳût, all these buildings were still in good repair, and from numerous incidental notices it seems clear that the Niẓâmîyah College stood between the Bâb-al-Âzaj and the Tigris bank, not very far from the Baṣalîyah Gate of the town wall, and on the road leading to this gateway from the Gate of Degrees in the wall round the Palaces of the Caliphs.

The traveller Ibn Jubayr attended prayers in the Niẓâmîyah on the first Friday after his arrival in Baghdad; this was in the year 581 (A.D. 1185), and he describes it as the most splendid of the thirty and odd colleges which then adorned the city of East Baghdad. Already in 504 (A.D. 1110), and only a score of years after the death of Niẓâm-al-Mulk, this college had been thoroughly repaired. Ibn Jubayr further reports that in his day the endowments derived from domains and rents belonging to the college amply sufficed both to pay the stipends of professors and to keep the building in good order, besides supplying an extra fund for the sustenance of poor scholars. The Sûķ or market of the Niẓâmîyah was one of the great thoroughfares of this quarter, and it is described as lying adjacent to the Mashra'ah or wharf, which proves that the college must have stood near the Tigris bank. Opposite to this, on the western bank of the river, in the Karkh Quarter lay the Ķurayyah suburb of West Baghdad, which, as has already been pointed out, must not be confused with the other Ķurayyah suburb adjacent to the Niẓâmîyah.

When Ibn Baṭûṭah visited Baghdad in 727 (A.D. 1327), namely three-quarters of a century after the Mongol siege, the Niẓâmîyah College was still standing and in good repair. He describes it as situated in the middle of the great market street of East Baghdad, then generally known as the Tuesday Market (Sûķ-ath-Thalâthah), near the upper end of which stood the Mustanṣirîyah College, as described in a preceding chapter. This long street must have followed a serpentine course round the ruined wall of the Palaces of the Caliphs, going up from the Kalwâdhâ Gate on the south, to the Bâb-as-Sulṭân on the north-west, where the original Tuesday Market had stood in the days of Ibn Serapion. Writing a dozen years later than Ibn Baṭûṭah, Ḥamd-Allah, the Persian historian, briefly alludes to the Niẓâmîyah, which he calls 'the mother of the Madrasahs' in Baghdad. This proves that down to the middle of the fourteenth century A.D. the college was still standing, though at the present time all vestiges of it have disappeared, as indeed appears already to have been the case in the middle of the last century, for Niebuhr found no traces of the Niẓâmîyah to describe in his painstaking account of the ruins in the city of Caliphs, as these still existed at the time of his visit[1].

[1] Ibn Khallikan, No. 410, p. 112; No. 599, p. 114; No. 603, p. 119; No. 852, p. 131; Ibn Jubayr, 220, 231; Yaḳut, i. 826; iv. 85; Ibn Batutah, ii. 108; Nuzhat, 148; Ibn-al-Athir, x. 38.

CHAPTER XXII

RECAPITULATION AND AUTHORITIES: EARLY PERIOD

Five periods of Abbasid History. The First Period begins. Ṭabarî and the first siege of Baghdad. Growth of Western and of Eastern Baghdad. Civil war between Amîn and Mamûn. Baghdad besieged by Ṭâhir and Harthamah. Death of Amîn; Mamûn in Baghdad. Mu'taṣim removes to Sâmarrâ. The Second Period begins. The second siege of Baghdad under Musta'în. City walls built. Baghdad again the Capital. Ya'ḳûbî and Ibn Serapion. The first systematic description of the city. Mas'ûdî and his history called *The Golden Meadows*.

I PROPOSE in these concluding chapters to sum up in chronological order the topographical information which has been set out in detail in the preceding pages, and the occasion may serve to name in turn the authors to whose writings we are indebted for the knowledge that has enabled us to reconstruct the plan of mediaeval Baghdad[1]. From its foundation by the Caliph Manṣûr to its capture by Hûlâgû the Mongol, the history of the city is that of the Abbasid Caliphate, and the events accompanying its rise and fall will perhaps be better understood if the five centuries that elapsed during this long period be divided into five rather unequal parts, repre-

[1] References to authorities are, for the most part, now omitted, these having been fully given in the previous chapters.

ıting, as it were, so many acts in the great drama the history of Islam.

These five divisions are:—(1) the period of the great Caliphs, from the foundation of the dynasty in 132 (A.D. 750) to the death of Mamûn in 218 (A.D. 833); (2) the period during the tyranny of the Turkish body-guard, ending in 334 (A.D. 946), when Mu'izz-ad-Dawlah the Buyid prince became master in Baghdad; (3) the period of the Buyid supremacy; (4) followed by the Saljûḳ supremacy, beginning with Tughril Beg, who entered Baghdad in 447 (A.D. 1055), and ending with the death of Sultan Sanjâr, the last of the great Saljûḳs in 552 (A.D. 1157); (5) lastly, the period of decline and fall, which ended with the Mongol conquest, the sack of Baghdad in 656 (A.D. 1258), and the death of the last Abbasid Caliph Musta'ṣim[1].

In so far as the history of Baghdad itself is concerned, the first period of course only starts with the date of the foundation of the Round City by the Caliph Manṣûr, namely about the year 145 (A.D. 762), closing with the death of Mamûn, as already said, or in other words, the period begins with the reign of the grandfather of Hârûn-ar-Rashîd, and ends with the life of the second of his sons who attained the Caliphate. These seventy and odd years form the most brilliant epoch of Moslem history; the Caliphs were then great warriors and sovereigns, and the fact is significant that, with the sole exception of Amîn, no Caliph during this period died in Baghdad. Their tombs lie scattered over the length and breadth of the empire[2]—from the pilgrim road

[1] See the Chronological Table given before chapter i.

[2] See note [1] to p. 194.

near Mecca to Ṭûs in Khurâsân, or the gate of Tarsus in the north-west—for the burial-place of the Caliph was where he had died, on the road, so to speak, journeying in the affairs of Islam.

For this first period we have unfortunately no written contemporary authorities, but for the topography of Baghdad an event of much importance is the first siege of the capital in the year 198 (A.D. 814), when (as will be remembered) Amîn, son of Hârûn-ar-Rashîd, defended himself during eighteen months against the generals of his brother Mamûn. The detailed narrative of this siege, taken down from the accounts of eye-witnesses and reduced to system, has been transmitted to us in the pages of the great chronicle of Ṭabarî. In this the incidental mention of places attacked or defended during the siege operations enables us to fix the position of many points left vague in the two great systematic descriptions of Baghdad which belong to the following century, composed respectively by Ya'ḳûbî and Ibn Serapion, from whose writings, chiefly, the plan has been reconstructed.

It will be remembered that Baghdad as founded by Manṣûr was a circular city or burg four miles in circumference, having four equidistant gates with a triple wall, which in concentric circles enclosed the great palace and mosque of the Caliph standing in the middle of the wide central area. Before the death of Manṣûr in 158 (A.D. 775), however, the city had already spread far beyond these modest limits. Suburbs had grown up along the highroads starting from each of the four gates, and these suburbs, together with East Baghdad or Ruṣâfah, founded at almost the same time as the Round

City, but on the other bank of the Tigris, covered ground measuring five miles across in length and in breadth.

Thus, beginning at the Baṣrah or south-eastern gate of the Round City, one highroad went down-stream along the river bank, having the Sharḳîyah Quarter on the one hand near the Tigris, and the great Karkh Quarter on the other side, inland; and this last with its markets is described as stretching for nearly two leagues southward of Baghdad. The Karkh Quarter on the side furthest from the river was bordered by the highroad running south, which was the Pilgrim Way leading to Mecca. This was known as the Kûfah Road (from the city of that name where the Euphrates was crossed), and this highway started from the bifurcation outside the Kûfah Gate at the south-western part of the Round City. Beyond the square at this gate two high-roads began, namely the Kûfah Road south, bordering Karkh as just described, and the Muḥawwal Road west, passing through the town of Muḥawwal on the 'Îsâ Canal to the city of Anbâr on the Euphrates. From the Syrian Gate, in the north-western part of the Round City, a thoroughfare also went westward, called the Anbâr Road, which passing first through the Ḥarbîyah suburb to the Anbâr Gate, and there crossing the bridge over the Trench of Ṭâhir, finally struck into the Muḥawwal Road at a point beyond Muḥawwal town, having thus far kept along the northern bank of the 'Îsâ Canal.

Beyond the suburb at the Kûfah Gate, and lying westward of the Round City, were the various suburbs of the Muḥawwal Gate on the highroad to the town of that name; while north of the Syrian Gate stretched the Ḥarb Quarter or the Ḥarbîyah, occupying all the ground upstream above the Round City; beyond which, again, began the cemeteries afterwards known as the Kâẓimayn. Outside the north-eastern or Khurâsân Gate of the Round City, the Caliph Manṣûr had built his palace, called the Khuld, lying to the right or south of the road leading to the Main Bridge of Boats across the Tigris; and on the further side of the river stood the palace and suburb of Ruṣâfah. This lay to the northward of the bridge end, and it had the Shammâsîyah Quarter beyond it eastward, stretching from the river bank opposite the Ḥarbîyah Quarter to the gate of East Baghdad opening on the Persian high-road, which was called the Khurâsân Gate of the Eastern City, while to the south of the Main Bridge lay the Mukharrim Quarter.

During the reign of Mahdî, son and successor of Manṣûr, Ruṣâfah grew to rival West Baghdad in the extent and magnificence of its various palaces and market streets. Round the palace and mosque which Mahdî had built, his attendants and their followers received grants of lands, and just as the Round City had come to be encompassed by the suburbs in which stood the fiefs of the nobles belonging to the court of Manṣûr, so Ruṣâfah during the eleven years' reign of Mahdî became the centre of a town of palaces built by the next generation of courtiers. In the year 170 (A.D. 786), when the reign of Hârûn-ar-Rashîd began, the three eastern quarters of Ruṣâfah, the Shammâsîyah, and Mukharrim, formed nearly as great a city on the east side of the Tigris as did the city of Manṣûr with its suburbs on the west side. The Caliph still lived in the Khuld Palace, and nominally the Dîwâns or offices of government were in the Round City; but his Wazîr Ja'far the Barmecide had built himself a palace on the eastern Tigris bank below the Mukharrim Quarter (which palace subsequently formed the nucleus of the later palaces of the Caliphs), and much of the business of state was now transacted in Eastern Baghdad under the supervision of Ja'far.

The fall of the Barmecides shed a gloom over the later years of the reign of Hârûn-ar-Rashîd, and after the death of the great Caliph, the rivalry which had ever existed between his two sons—Amîn, whose mother was the Abbasid Princess Zubaydah, and Mamûn, the son of a Persian bondwoman—promptly flamed up into civil war. The Caliphate belonged by right of birth to Amîn, but Hârûn had named Mamûn next in the succession, and meanwhile had made him governor for life of Khurâsân and the whole eastern half of the empire. On the death of his father Amîn had succeeded peaceably to the throne, and at first remained inactive at Baghdad, but before long he precipitated the inevitable crisis by naming his own son Mûsâ heir-apparent, thus attempting to deprive Mamûn of the succession. Mamûn promptly took up arms in defence of his rights, and causing his brother Amîn to be solemnly deposed in all the mosques of Persia, Syria, and Arabia, where the governors were all partisans of Mamûn, his armies advanced through Persia on Lower Mesopotamia for the siege of Baghdad.

Amîn meanwhile having lost all power even in

'Irâḳ, had shut himself up in the capital, and Mamûn, who preferred to remain safely in far-off Khurâsân, had given the command of the invading force to two of his generals, namely Harthamah, who was to attack Baghdad from the east, and Ṭâhir (subsequently founder of the Ṭâhirid dynasty of Khurâsân), who, crossing the Tigris at Madâin (Ctesiphon) into Lower Mesopotamia, was to march up the great Kûfah road and thus invest the city from the western side. The accounts in Ṭabarî name the exact positions of the troops. Harthamah, on the eastern side, after defeating the army which Amîn had sent to oppose him at Nahrawân, established his headquarters on the hither side of the canal called the Nahr Bîn, probably near the spot where the Palace of the Pleiades was afterwards built, and there fortified his camp with a wall and a ditch. His right wing was before the Shammâsîyah Gate on the river bank above the city, while his left wing occupied a pleasure palace lately built by Amîn in the plain or Raḳḳah of Kalwâdâ below the city. At this date Eastern Baghdad had no town wall, but the townspeople built barricades to block the roads at their exit from the city, and from gate to gate the line of houses and garden walls served as the outer line of defence.

On the western side Ṭâhir established his headquarters in the garden outside the Anbâr Gate, where the Anbâr Bridge crossed the Trench that went by his name, and he forthwith began his attack on the outlying suburbs of this side. The houses in the Ḥarbîyah Quarter were in great part destroyed by his catapults (Manjanîḳ), and the ruin effected is described as extending from the Tigris bank at the

Baghîyîn Quarter round past the Syrian Gate to the Kûfah Gate and the line of the Ṣarât Canal. Fire completed the destruction begun by the catapults, the great mills at the junction of the two Ṣarât Canals were in part destroyed, and all the suburbs from the Quarter of Ḥumayd along the Karkhâyâ Canal are stated to have been laid in ruins. The siege dragged on from month to month, and the inhabitants of the city meanwhile suffered horribly. The Princess Zubaydah, widow of Hârûn-ar-Rashîd, was driven out of her palace in the fief near the Ḳaṭrabbul Gate, and joined her son in the Round City, which, with the Khuld Palace and the suburbs to the south along the river bank, became the last refuge of Amîn and the garrison.

Little by little the line hemming them in was drawn tighter, and all attempts to break through failed. A great fight took place in the Kunâsah Quarter, and the garrison attempted a sally in the neighbourhood of the Darb-al-Ḥijârah (the Street of Rocks), beyond the Muḥawwal Gate, on which occasion Ṭâhir came near to lose his life, but the besieged, after performing prodigies of valour, were again driven back. In order to facilitate the dispatch of reinforcements to and from the army under Harthamah on the eastern river bank, Ṭâhir had moored a new bridge of boats across the Tigris above Baghdad. He now ordered a general attack to be made by Harthamah on the east side, and here, when the Khurâsân Gate had been stormed, the besiegers soon gained possession of the whole of East Baghdad. The siege had begun before the end of the year 196 A.H., and it was in the beginning of 198 that Harthamah having thus become master of

Ruṣâfah, the Shammâsîyah, and Mukharrim—the three quarters forming that half of the city which lay on the Persian side of the Tigris—proceeded to cut the Main Bridge of Boats, and thus isolate the Round City and its defenders.

Meanwhile in Western Baghdad, when it was seen that the defence was failing, the merchants had begun to parley, and the troops of Amîn were ever deserting in increasing numbers. Ṭâhir could now occupy the quarters on the southern side of the Round City, namely the Sharḳîyah, with Karkh and its great markets; further, he had succeeded in destroying the two masonry bridges—the Old Bridge and the New—over the Ṣarât Canal, by which the highroads from the Kûfah and Baṣrah Gates passed out into the suburbs. The unfortunate Caliph Amîn now retired, with his mother Zubaydah, to the Palace of the Golden Gate in the Round City, egress to the Tigris being still preserved through the Khuld Palace and its gardens; but here the river bank was already commanded by the catapults of Harthamah, whose troops had occupied the whole eastern side, and Ṭâhir was closely investing the walls of the Round City. His lines, we are told, ran from the Tigris at the foot of the Khuld Gardens, up the Ṣarât Canal past the Baṣrah Gate to the Kûfah Gate, and thence turned north back to the river, after blocking the Syrian Gate, the Tigris bank being regained immediately above the Khuld Palace.

The end could not long be delayed. The Khuld Palace on the river had to be deserted by its garrison, becoming untenable from the shower of stones shot by catapults which Harthamah had planted in the Mukharrim Quarter; whereupon Amîn, with his mother and those few troops who still stood by him, retired within the ruined city of Manṣûr, shutting himself up in the Central Palace of the Golden Gate. Before long, this too becoming untenable, Amîn, driven to surrender and fearing Harthamah less than Ṭâhir, set out in secret, and embarked, to cross the river to the camp of the besiegers on the east side. By ill chance, or through treachery, the boat was overturned, and the luckless Amîn, after swimming back to the western bank for shelter, was taken prisoner by the enemy's troops, and forthwith put to death in the garden near the Anbâr Gate by order of Ṭâhir, that general sending the head of the deposed Caliph to Mamûn in Khurâsân as a proof that the war was now really at an end[1].

The reign of Mâmun, who some months after these events arrived in Baghdad, witnessed the rebuilding of the half-ruined capital. The Round City, however, would appear never to have recovered from the effects of the siege, and Mamûn, when resident in Baghdad, for the most part lived in the Barmecide Palace below the Mukharrim Quarter on the east bank, which (as described in chapter xviii), after having been greatly enlarged by the Wazîr Ḥasan Ibn Sahl, was subsequently known as the Ḥasanî Palace. On the death of Mamûn and the accession of his brother Mu'taṣim, the riots caused by the Turkish body-guard ultimately forced that Caliph to betake himself to Sâmarrâ, which now became the capital of the Caliphate. Here Mu'taṣim, and after his death six Caliphs in turn,

[1] The details of the first siege will be found in Tabari, iii. 864 to 925.

reigned and built palaces, while successive captains of the guard controlled the affairs of the empire at their pleasure. This was the second period in the history of the Abbasids, namely that of the long tyranny of the Turkish guard, which only came to an end with the advent of the Buyid princes. While the Caliphs thus lived at Sâmarrâ, Baghdad was under the rule of governors, for the most part Ṭâhirids, for Ṭâhir, after bringing Amîn to his death, had prudently retired from court to live as a semi-independent prince in Khurâsân, and during this period, when the Caliphs were the puppets of the body-guard in Sâmarrâ, diverse members of his family in succession occupied the chief provincial governorships throughout the Abbasid dominions.

The period of fifty-eight years, during which the Caliphate had its seat at Sâmarrâ, was interrupted in 251 (A. D. 865) by the episode of the flight to Baghdad of the Caliph Musta'în, who made the attempt, unsuccessfully, thus to escape from the tyranny of the Turkish guard. Then followed the second siege of Baghdad, of about a year's duration, by an army dispatched from Sâmarrâ in the name of a cousin, the rival Caliph Mu'tazz, whom the captain of the guard had set up in the place of Musta'în. During this second siege Baghdad was defended by Muḥammad ibn 'Abd-Allah, a grandson of Ṭâhir who had besieged the city rather more than half a century before; but it was Ruṣâfah or East Baghdad that now became the headquarters of the defence, not West Baghdad with the Round City, as had been the case in the time of Amîn. For the details of this siege, also, we are indebted to the pages of Ṭabarî, who possibly himself witnessed some of the incidents that he describes, since he must have been nearly thirty years of age at the date in question.

As soon as Musta'în had safely reached Ruṣâfah, he ordered the governor, Muḥammad the Ṭâhirid, to block the roads coming in from Sâmarrâ by cutting the dykes of the canals above Baghdad, and he next set to work to surround both the eastern city and the western with walls. As already said, the Caliph fixed his headquarters in Ruṣâfah, and on the east side the new wall began at the Shammâsîyah Gate on the Tigris bank above the Palace of Mahdî. Sweeping round through a quarter-circle, by the Baradân Gate to the Khurâsân Gate at the exit of the highroad to Persia and the east, the wall thus enclosed the Ruṣâfah and Shammâsîyah Quarters; then curving back through another quarter-circle, it included the Mukharrim Quarter and came to the Tigris again at the Gate of the Tuesday Market. In West Baghdad the wall began above at the Gate of the Fief of Zubaydah, thus including the Upper Harbour, and passing to the Ḳaṭrabbul Gate followed up the line of the Trench of Ṭâhir, probably as far as the Anbâr Gate, for this and the Bâb-al-Ḥadîd (the Iron Gate) are especially mentioned during the siege operations. From the Trench the wall curved down in a great semicircle, enclosing the City of Manṣûr and part of Karkh, until it joined the Tigris again beyond the Baṣrah Gate, below where the Ṣarât Canal had its outflow at the Palace of Ḥumayd. The exact line followed by the wall between the upper part of the Ṭâhirid Trench and the Palace of Ḥumayd is not given, but it probably followed the line of one of the

Karkh canals, and we are told that a ditch was dug outside the wall wheresoever no canal already existed. The total cost of these fortifications is reported to have amounted to 330,000 dînârs or gold pieces, a sum equivalent to about £160,000.

The main attack on the part of the besieging troops was from the north, being directed against the Shammâsîyah Gate on the east side, and opposite this on the west bank, against the Ḳaṭrabbul Gate. Further Ṭabarî mentions that along the wall of the Fief of Zubaydah and the Trench the defenders greatly harassed their opponents by stones from the Manjanîḳs or catapults erected over various other gateways. After many months' blockade and several battles, a general assault was finally ordered by the Sâmarrâ captains, and all down the line, from the Yâsirîyah Quarter and the Anbâr Gate on the west, to the Khurâsân Gate at the eastern extremity of the Shammâsîyah Quarter, a stubborn defence was made, until the Upper Bridge of Boats having been set on fire, the outer defences were at length carried. The end followed rapidly. Musta'în, being driven out of Ruṣâfah, became a prisoner, and was forced to abdicate; before long he met his death at the hands of his captors, and the Turkish guard thereupon returned victorious to their nominal sovereign Mu'tazz in Sâmarrâ[1].

It has been pointed out that the ruin of Western Baghdad, and especially of the Round City, had resulted from the first siege in the time of Amîn; it may be added that the three northern quarters of East Baghdad (Ruṣâfah, Shammâsîyah, and Mu-

[1] The details of the second siege are given in Tabari, iii. 1553 to 1578.

kharrim) only in part ever recovered the effects of this second siege, which had resulted in the death of Musta'în. The Turkish body-guard had for the time triumphed, but before another thirty years had elapsed events occurred which caused Sâmarrâ to be deserted by the Caliphs, and Mu'taḍid (nephew of Mu'tazz), who succeeded to the throne in 279 (A.D. 892), permanently re-established the Caliphate in the older capital. Settling in East Baghdad, he laid the foundations of the great complex of palaces which stood on the Tigris bank below the Mukharrim Quarter, forming the Ḥarîm or Precinct, which was afterwards known as the Dâr-al-Khilâfah (the Abode of the Caliphate). These Precincts ultimately became the nucleus of the later city, which in time developed from the line of suburbs that spread round the land side of the great palaces. This new town was walled in at a subsequent date, and at the present time still exists, on the east bank of the Tigris, as the modern city of Baghdad.

It is to the writers who flourished during the last quarter of the third century (the ninth A.D.), namely Ya'ḳûbî, Ibn Rustah, and Ibn Serapion, that we owe our first, and indeed our only systematic descriptions of Baghdad. Ya'ḳûbî begins by the Round City as it was originally founded in the reign of Manṣûr, and then passes on to a detailed account of its suburbs, concluding with a brief notice of the three eastern quarters of Ruṣâfah, Shammâsîyah, and Mukharrim. The description of the canals given by our next authority, Ibn Serapion, supplements Ya'ḳûbî, enabling us to plot out his topography, and Ibn Rustah adds some few additional details, but the critical examination of these three authorities need not detain us now, since having formed the basis of matters discussed in earlier chapters of the present work, their accounts have already been fully reviewed. Points of detail are in many instances supplemented by incidental notices, under the various years, occurring in the volumes of the great chronicle of Ṭabarî already mentioned, and thus the earlier desçriptions can be filled in and confirmed.

A matter that must be noted in connexion with these and the following accounts of Baghdad, is the curiously arbitrary way in which the Arab geographers for the most part speak of the position of the City of Manṣûr in relation to the points of the compass, and to the system of canals and roads that surrounded it. They assumed that the Tigris held its course entirely from west to east, and hence lay to the *north* of the City of Manṣûr; further, that the Ṣarât Canal (coming from the Euphrates) ran in a direction from south to north before flowing out into the Tigris, and thus passed to the *east* of the Round City. On these suppositions, which a glance at the map will show only can agree very partially with the facts of the case, all the topographical descriptions are based. Thus the Bâdurâyâ district is invariably spoken of as lying east of the Ṣarât, while the district of Ḳaṭrabbul was to the west of this stream; we, on the other hand, should rather have said that these districts (respectively below and above the Round City) lay to the south and north of the Ṣarât. Again, Ya'ḳûbî in describing the suburbs near the Muḥawwal Gate states that along the Ṣarât, going upstream *south* (we should say *west*), there are certain fiefs lying to the *westward* (we should say *north*) of this canal, and the City of Manṣûr as a whole was considered by him to have occupied its *western* bank. This arbitrary view of the matter, in regard to the main points of the compass, must account for the reference made by Mas'ûdî to the Bâb-al-Ḥadîd (the Iron Gate) on Ṭâhir's Trench, which he says was a gate of Baghdad that opened 'towards the south'; the explanation being that the Trench here curves away after leaving the Ṣarât, and hence the gates along its upper course were described as opening 'towards the south,' because the Trench, which bifurcated from the Ṣarât, was held to flow west before turning north to flow into the Tigris in a parallel course with its parent stream[1].

To complete the list of our earliest authorities it remains to be mentioned that, besides his work on geography (giving us the detailed description of Baghdad), Ya'ḳûbî also wrote a history, which he finished in the year 260 (A.D. 874), and dating from rather more than half a century later, we have the celebrated work called *The Meadows of Gold* by Mas'ûdî. From the pages of both these historical works, as from the chronicle of Ṭabarî already mentioned, innumerable small details may be gleaned regarding the topography of Baghdad, which, though incidental and fragmentary, are often invaluable for fixing minor points, as may be inferred from the number of times these authors have been quoted in the notes of all the earlier chapters of this work.

[1] Instances are too numerous for reference in full, but the following will be sufficient to prove what is stated above. Ya'kubi, 244; Mukaddasi, 120; Mas'udi, vi. 482; Yakut, i. 640; Marasid, ii. 486.

CHAPTER XXIII

RECAPITULATION AND AUTHORITIES: MIDDLE PERIOD

The building of the Palaces in East Baghdad. The Third Period begins. The Buyid Supremacy: their Great Palace: the Dyke of Mu'izz-ad-Dawlah and the Hospital of 'Aḍud-ad-Dawlah. Iṣṭakhrî and Ibn Ḥawkal. Muḳaddasi. Decline of the Buyids. The Fourth Period begins. The Saljûḳs. The History of Baghdad by Khaṭîb. Area of East and West Baghdad. New Baghdad and the Wall of Mustaẓhir: the Saljûḳ Mosque. The Sieges of Baghdad in the reigns of Manṣûr Râshid and of Muḥammad Muḳtafî. Period of decay: the Persian poet Khâḳânî. Benjamin of Tudela. Ibn Jubayr. Yâḳût. Many separate walled Quarters. The Mustanṣirîyah College and the Ḥarbâ Bridge. Ibn Khallikân.

THE half century which followed on the return of the Caliphs to Baghdad, and which preceded the advent of the Buyids, witnessed the building of the great palaces (including the Mosque of the Caliph) in the southern part of East Baghdad along the river bank. These palaces, it will be remembered, lay immediately to the south of the Gate of the Tuesday Market in the city wall which Musta'in had built, and East Baghdad before long was thus almost doubled in area. During the transition period, the older wall which went in a semicircle round the three northern quarters of Ruṣâfah, Shammâsîyah, and Mukharrim, must either have been purposely destroyed, or else allowed to fall to ruin, for the new quarters, which ultimately sprang up round the Palaces of the Firdûs, the Ḥasanî, and the Tâj, in part overlapped the Mukharrim. In the early years of the fourth century (which began A. D. 912), the walls of the City of Manṣûr in West Baghdad had likewise fallen to complete ruin, as also the two Palaces of the Golden Gate and the Khuld, the ground here as time went on being taken up by the new quarters that came to surround the Baṣrah Gate and the gate known as the Bâb-al-Muḥawwal, on the great highroad leading west towards Anbâr from the Kûfah Gate of the Round City.

The Turk body-guard, since the return of the Caliphs from Sâmarrâ, had lost all power, and in 334 (A. D. 946) the third of the periods into which it has been found convenient to divide the history of the Abbasids began, its outset being marked by the advent of the Buyid Prince Mu'izz-ad-Dawlah in Baghdad. The period of the Buyid supremacy lasted for rather more than a century, and was characterized by the erection of many fine buildings in the capital of the Caliphate. The Buyid princes were Persian by descent and Shî'ah by sympathy; they had subjugated both Mesopotamia and the region now known as Persia, where various members of the family occupied the provincial governments, while from this date onward the prince, who was recognized as head of the house, as a rule made Baghdad his residence, and from this centre of authority controlled the Caliph, and in his name sought to dominate all Eastern Islam.

The Buyid princes built their palaces in East Baghdad (as related in chapter xvii), on the ground formerly occupied by the Shammâsîyah and part of the Mukharrim Quarter; and these palaces, which their successors the Saljûḳ princes took over and enlarged, were known by the general name of the Dâr-as-Salṭanah (the Abode of the Sultanate). They were begun under Mu'izz-ad-Dawlah, the Buyid who especially had entitled himself to the lasting gratitude of the people of Baghdad by erecting the huge dyke which, when kept in repair, prevented the inundation of the city by the flooding of the streams flowing out into the Tigris at the Shammâsîyah lowlands. At a later date, his nephew and successor 'Aḍud-ad-Dawlah built the hospital in West Baghdad on the ruins of the Khuld Palace, and this for three centuries was a school of medical science, which became famous throughout the East under the name of the Bîmâristân 'Aḍudî (the Hospital of 'Aḍud-ad-Dawlah).

During the century of the Buyid supremacy we have the first three names in the long list of our Arab geographers, namely Iṣṭakhrî, Ibn Hawḳal, and Muḳaddasi, each of whom has devoted some paragraphs of his work to a succinct description of Baghdad. The geography of Iṣṭakhrî, who wrote in 340 (A.D. 951), was re-edited and enlarged by Ibn Hawḳal in 367 (A.D. 978); but as regards Baghdad, the two accounts are practically identical, except for a very few minor details. Both mention East Baghdad as almost entirely taken up by the palaces; in the first place, by the Palaces of the Caliph or Ḥarîm (the royal Precincts), these extending in the southern part with their gardens as far down as the Nahr Bîn, two leagues distant from the centre of the town; and secondly, by the Palace of the Buyid Sultan in the upper part of the city—the walls of these two sets of palaces being described as rising above the Tigris bank in a continuous line, which extended from the Shammâsîyah Quarter downstream for a distance of about five miles. Opposite the Shammâsîyah of the eastern side lay the Ḥarbîyah Quarter in West Baghdad, and below this stood Karkh, which further at this time gave its name in general parlance to all that half of Baghdad which lay on the western bank; East Baghdad being still known as the Ruṣâfah side, or as the Quarter of the Bâb-aṭ-Ṭâḳ, from the great arched gate of this name at the head of the Main Bridge.

Iṣṭakhrî mentions three great Friday mosques as in use at his date, namely the Mosque of Ruṣâfah and that of the Palace of the Caliph in East Baghdad, with the old mosque of the City of Manṣûr in West Baghdad; while Ibn Hawḳal (a quarter of a century later) adds a fourth, which had come into use by his time, namely the Mosque at Barâthâ, on the road to Muḥawwal Town, originally a shrine dedicated to the Caliph 'Alî, whom the Shî'ahs more especially hold in honour. In Kalwâdhâ also, down the river on the east side, there was at this date a great mosque which might rightfully be considered as belonging to Baghdad, seeing that the houses of the eastern city were continuous from below the Palaces of the Caliph to this outlying township. Both Iṣṭakhrî and Ibn Hawḳal—in spite of the numerous magnificent palaces—especially note and deplore the ruin which had already befallen many quarters formerly flourishing; thus Iṣṭakhrî writes that all the road between the Main Bridge and the eastern Khurâsân Gate had in former days been occupied by houses, but that in his time these were for the most part already in ruin.

In Western Baghdad Karkh is said still to be the most populous and best preserved quarter, and here the merchants who lived at the Yâsirîyah suburb had their houses of business. Iṣṭakhrî then proceeds to give a detailed account (copied without acknowledgement by all subsequent authorities) of the 'Îsâ Canal flowing through Karkh, which was navigable for boats from the Euphrates to the Tigris, many unnavigable branch canals, namely the Ṣarât and other minor channels, ramifying throughout the adjacent quarters. The extreme breadth across both halves of the city (East and West Baghdad) Iṣṭakhrî gives at five miles (the same as the length given for the palace walls along the eastern river bank), and his account concludes with the remark that the gardens of the Palaces of the Caliphs and others in East Baghdad were almost entirely irrigated by water-channels derived from the Nahrawân Canals (whose courses have been carefully described by Ibn Serapion), since, according to Iṣṭakhrî, the Tigris ran at too low a level for its waters to be brought into these gardens, except by the mechanical contrivance of the water-wheel, called Dûlâb, which (says he) involved much labour.

The account of Baghdad written by Muḳaddasi in 375 (A.D. 985) is less interesting than might have been expected from the other portions of his excellent and original work. He mentions few topographical details, but after expatiating on the many advantages of position and climate which Manṣûr gained by selecting this particular site for his capital, passes on to lament the present ruin of the great city, which he fears would soon rival Sâmarrâ in its state of chronic insurrection and infamous misrule. In Karkh, on the west bank, he describes the Fief of Rabi' as the most populous quarter, and states that on this side were to be found most of the markets and fine houses spared by the general decay. He speaks of the hospital lately built by 'Aḍud-ad-Dawlah opposite the Bridge of Boats leading to East Baghdad; and in this other half of the city the best preserved quarters were, he says, those lying round the Bâb-aṭ-Ṭâḳ (the great Arch at the Bridge-head) and near the Dâr-al-Amîr, namely the Palace of the Buyid Princes recently built over part of the Shammâsîyah Quarter.

'Aḍud-ad-Dawlah had died in Baghdad during the year 372 (A. D. 982), a short time before Muḳaddasi wrote this description, and he was buried (as all good Shî'ahs should be) at Mashhad 'Alî, the celebrated shrine on the Euphrates where the grave of the Caliph 'Alî was said to have been made. After the death of 'Aḍud-ad-Dawlah the Buyid power declined, and a period of internecine war followed, which only ended in 447 (A. D. 1055), when Tughril Beg the Saljûḳ, after suppressing the last Buyid prince, became master of Baghdad. With him begins the period of the Saljûḳ supremacy (the fourth period in the history of the Abbasids), which lasted about a century, and is celebrated for the acts and deeds of Alp Arslân and Mâlik Shâh. The Saljûḳs were of the Turk race (the Buyids had been Persians), and unlike their predecessors, the Saljûḳ princes for the most part did not reside in

Baghdad, but maintained here a deputy in their stead. He acted as their Lieutenant-Governor of Mesopotamia, and resided permanently at Baghdad, occupying the Buyid Palace now generally called the Palace of the Sultan. In other words Baghdad, during Saljûḳ times, was no longer even nominally the seat of government in Islam.

Dating from the earlier years of the Saljûḳ period we have the *History of Baghdad*, a work written by Khaṭîb in 450 (A. D. 1058), which still unfortunately remains in manuscript. It is full of interesting details in regard to the origin and position of the various buildings in both the western and eastern quarters of the city, and much of it has been copied, without any acknowledgement, by later compilers such as Yâḳût. This work of Khaṭîb contains, for instance, the account of the Greek embassy to Baghdad of the year 305 (A. D. 917[1]), with the description of the Palaces of the Caliphs in the time of Muḳtadir, and though the book is in great part merely a compilation, it is a compilation at first hand citing authorities, which is more than unfortunately can be said of most of the work of later writers.

The century of the Saljûḳ supremacy witnessed the great expansion of East Baghdad, for during the reign of Muḳtadir suburbs were found and grew up round the Palaces of the Caliph which were afterwards surrounded by the city wall in the time of Mustaẓhir. As showing the wide extent of the

[1] See *J. R. A. S.*, 1897, p. 35. The full name of the writer is Aḥmad ibn 'Alî al-Khaṭîb al-Baghdâdî, and the name *Khaṭîb*, meaning the 'preacher,' has been adopted for reference in these pages merely for convenience of brevity.

town on both banks of the river, even before this reign Khaṭîb reports that when he lived at Baghdad there were six great mosques where the public prayers were said on the Friday. These were, four in West Baghdad: namely the Mosque of Manṣûr in the Round City, the Mosque of the Ḥarbîyah Quarter, that of the Fief of Zubaydah, and the Mosque of Barâthâ halfway to Muḥawwal on the 'Îsâ Canal; while in East Baghdad there were but two Friday mosques, namely the Mosque in Ruṣâfah and that which the Caliph 'Alî Muktafî had built in the palace—for the Jâmi'-as-Sulṭân was of later date than the time of Khaṭîb[1].

Khaṭîb also gives some important data concerning the area covered by the houses of Baghdad in his day, confirming what has been told us in the previous century by Iṣṭakhrî, to the effect that the city had then already extended over an area of land measuring five miles across in breadth and width. The statements found in Khaṭîb are reckoned in terms of the Jarîb, a land measure which was a square of sixty ells side. Adopting twenty-three inches as the mean of the various estimates for the length of the Dhirâ' or ell, three Jarîbs and a third may be taken as equivalent to our acre, or in other words ten Jarîbs are equal to three acres, and the English square mile would contain 2,133 Jarîbs[2].

Coming now to the statements made by Khaṭîb, we find that three valuations of the area of the city at different epochs are recorded. The earliest dates

[1] Khatib, folio 103 a; and for what follows see folio 108 a, b.

[2] For this estimate of the Jarîb compare Mawardi, p. 265.

from the time when Muwaffaḳ, brother of the Caliph Mu'tamid, was in Baghdad—presumably therefore about the year 270 (A. D. 884)—during the Zanj rebellion, while the Caliphs still resided at Sâmarrâ. It is reported that East Baghdad at this time covered 26,250 Jarîbs, West Baghdad covering 17,500 Jarîbs, of which total the cemeteries counted for seventy-four Jarîbs. These figures give an area of about 12⅜ and 8¼ square miles respectively for the two halves of the city, east and west, or twenty-one square miles in total, the cemeteries occupying rather more than twenty-two acres of this space.

Next, at some date nearer to the time of Khaṭîb, which is not specified, but when Baghdad had once more become 'the Abode of the Caliphate,' the numbers recorded are 27,000 Jarîbs for East Baghdad, and for the older city on the western bank, at one time 26,750 Jarîbs, but at another time 16,750 Jarîbs—unless indeed the higher of these figures be regarded as merely a clerical error for the lower, though as against this supposition it is to be remarked that each figure is cited and vouched for by Khaṭîb on a separate authority. These figures work out as the equivalent of 12¾ square miles for East Baghdad, and for the lower estimate of the western city, somewhat under eight square miles. In round numbers 20½ square miles for both sides at this lower estimate for West Baghdad, while the sum total would come up to about twenty-five square miles if we accept the higher figure.

These calculations cannot of course be regarded as very exact, but the Arabs were, for their time, skilful land surveyors, practising the art for fiscal assessment and for the laying down of the irrigation canals. Further, as above noted, these figures tend to confirm the estimate already given by Iṣṭakhrî, which at five miles across, length and breadth, would give twenty-five square miles for the square, and $19\frac{1}{7}$ square miles for the area of a circle with this diameter[1]. How much Baghdad has decreased since the times of the Caliphs is made evident by the fact that at the present day East Baghdad is computed to cover an area of 591 acres, while in West Baghdad the remains known as the Old Town comprise only 146 acres, giving a total for both sides which is equivalent to rather over one square mile and a sixth, this diminished area being now surrounded by walls whose circuit is estimated at about five miles.

The Saljûḳs, as already said, had inherited from their predecessors, the Buyids, the great palace and government offices called the Dâr-as-Salṭanah in the upper part of the eastern city. On the south side of this Mâlik Shâh founded the great Saljûḳ mosque known as the Jâmi'-as-Sulṭân, while at about the same time his Wazîr Niẓâm-al-Mulk built and endowed the Niẓâmîyah College on the land by the Tigris bank below the Palaces of the Caliph. These buildings both date from the reign of the Caliph Muḳtadî, in whose time also many new quarters were laid out to the north and east of the Palaces of the Caliphs, which quarters before long came to form the new town of East Baghdad. In

[1] For the length of the side of the Jarîb, namely sixty ells, Khatib uses the term *Ḥabl*, meaning 'a cord,' or 'rope,' which apparently is not given in this special sense in our dictionaries, and it may therefore be worth noting.

488 (A.D. 1095), at the beginning of the reign of the next Caliph, Mustaẓhir, this new city, lying about a mile below the Saljûḳ Palaces, was surrounded by a wall pierced by four gates, which wall (as proved by the gateways) is identical in its main lines with the present town wall of modern Baghdad.

The Caliphate, even before the beginning of the Saljûḳ period, had already sunk into political insignificance, and the Caliphs now having much spare time and considerable revenues employed their energies in palace building. It is indeed mainly to this period that the great Ḥarîm or Precinct, as their residence came to be called, owed its magnificence, as described in the pages of Yâḳût. He mentions in particular the great Rayḥânîyîn (the Palace on the Perfumers' Market), and the second Palace of the Crown (Ḳaṣr-at-Tâj), both of which were built at the close of the Saljûḳ period.

In the year 530 (A.D. 1136), under the Caliph Manṣûr Râshid (not to be confounded with Hârûn-ar-Rashîd), Baghdad sustained a third siege, of only two months' duration, however, by an army under command of Sultan Mas'ûd the Saljûḳ. The Sultan, who had pitched his siege camp at the Mâlikîyah, effected a complete blockade of the city, for the Governor of Wâsiṭ sent him up reinforcements in boats which effectually shut the river exit, while the populace, taking advantage of the troubles, rose in insurrection against the Caliph, plundered the quarters of the western city, and sacked the palace of the Ṭâhirid Ḥarîm, where it is said they gained an immense booty. After a blockade of fifty days the Caliph Manṣûr Râshid finally fled to Mosul, and was there forced to abdicate, his uncle Muḥammad

Muḳtafî being set up in his place, and Sultan Mas'ûd retired with his army eastward[1].

A fourth siege took place twenty-one years later, during the reign of the Caliph Muḥammad Muḳtafî, whose relations with Sultan Muḥammad, nephew and successor of Sultan Mas'ûd aforesaid, had become so strained in A. H. 551 that the Saljûḳ Sultan, marching into 'Irâḳ, appeared with his army before the walls of Baghdad in the month Dhu-l-Ḳa'adah of that year (January, 1157 A.D.). The Caliph forthwith shut himself up in East Baghdad, where a great store of munitions and provisions, by his orders, had been brought together. The city walls were well provided with catapults and mangonels, the towers being garrisoned by crossbowmen. Further, barges, also carrying crossbowmen and catapults, were set to patrol the Tigris—where the bridges of boats had been taken up—in order more thoroughly to guard the riverside of the eastern city.

Marching down the great Khurâsân road, Sultan Muḥammad effected a junction with his Lieutenant, the Governor of Mosul, and himself crossed the Tigris above Baghdad. The attack was then begun in two divisions, namely from the western quarter and from the north-east, where part of the army occupied the great Palace of the Saljûḳs outside the city wall. Upstream, above Baghdad, Sultan Muḥammad had already spanned the Tigris by a new bridge of boats, thus conveniently to connect the two portions of his army. His own headquarters were on the Ṣarât Canal, but from time to time he crossed to the Saljûḳ Palace of the

[1] The details of the third siege of Baghdad are given by Ibn-al-Athir, xi. 26.

eastern side in order to urge on the siege operations. In East Baghdad the city walls were already closely invested by his troops, in spite of frequent sallies from within the town, and the besiegers were shortly after their arrival reinforced from Ḥillah, Kûfah, Wâsiṭ, and Baṣrah. In spite of numbers, however, the siege made but little progress, and at the end of two months the Sultan found that his advanced positions had come to be so much harassed by the mangonels of the townspeople, that he was forced to shift his headquarter camp and retire westwards to the line of the Nahr 'Îsâ. His troops had more than once directed their attack against the river front of East Baghdad, where there was no city wall, only the line of the great palaces of the Caliph and the garden walls; but here the assailants were easily beaten off by the Baghdad people, and already they had lost many of their best men.

Meanwhile, in the month Ṣafar of 552 (March, 1157 A.D.), the Ḥajj caravan from Mecca arrived on its return journey, and the pilgrims were much scandalized at the spectacle of the Commander of the Faithful being assaulted in his own capital by the Saljûḳ Sultan. Further, in the course of the last two months the Caliph had successfully turned the arts of diplomacy against his adversary, and Sultan Muḥammad in addition to the ill success of the siege, now found himself threatened by treason at home, where a relative was intriguing to supplant him in his capital city of Hamadân. Thus matters went rapidly from bad to worse, and in the following month of Rabî' I (April), after having been rather more than three months fruitlessly encamped before Baghdad, Sultan Muḥammad in despair of success precipitately raised the siege. He had to recross the Tigris by his new bridge above the Saljûķ Palace before setting out for Hamadân with his body-guard and personal followers, and his retreat was so ill organized that he came near to lose all his baggage on the passage of the bridge. The people of Baghdad, immediately on hearing of his departure, had come pouring out of the city; they forthwith stormed and sacked the great Saljûķ Palace, the gates of which they tore off, burning all the furniture within its precincts, and then suddenly advancing, cut the communications between the body-guard of the Sultan and the main portion of his army, which had remained encamped in West Baghdad. Sultan Muḥammad, however, only delaying to recover his personal baggage, hastened his retreat along the Khurâsân highroad towards Hamadân, and the remainder of his army, under the command of the Governor of Mosul, though still in force on the western bank, finding that they were thus abandoned by their master, promptly retired north on Mosul, without any further molestation from the besieged.

The details of this siege, of which the foregoing is a condensed account, are graphically related by the contemporary historian 'Imâd-ad-Dîn of Isfahân, who was in Baghdad at the time, and took the occasion to indite a congratulatory ode to the Caliph Muḥammad Muķtafî on the success of his arms. The account, it is true, adds little to our topographical knowledge, but in the dearth of contemporary writers it is not without interest[1]. A notice of the third siege, that of the year A.H. 530, as also very succinctly of this fourth

[1] 'Imad-ad-Din, ii. 246 to 255; Ibn-al-Athir, xi. 140.

siege of the year A. H. 551, are likewise recorded under their respective dates in the chronicle of Ibn-al-Athîr, who becomes our best general authority for Baghdad after the beginning of the fourth century (the tenth A. D.)—when Ṭabarî and his continuator 'Arîb have closed their annals—and this chronicle carries us down to the year 628 (A. D. 1230), namely to the reign of the father of the last Abbasid Caliph of Baghdad.

The Saljûḳ supremacy may be said virtually to have come to an end with the death of Sultan Sanjâr, the last of the great Saljûḳs, in 552 (A. D. 1157); after which began the fifth and last period in the history of Baghdad, which was characterized by the almost complete political insignificance of the Abbasid Caliphs; and finally the Caliphate, after a century of this dotage, ended with the Mongol invasion under Hûlâgû in 656 (A. D. 1258). During this period the Caliphs were chiefly occupied in pulling down and rebuilding ephemeral palaces, and with laying out gardens within the Ḥarîm walls, all of which futilities appear to have greatly impressed the Persian poet Khâḳânî, who visited Baghdad in 550 (A. D. 1155), on his pilgrimage to Mecca. He has left us a very rhetorical description (useless, unfortunately, for topographical purposes) of what he saw in 'the Abode of the Caliphate': the gardens, he says, are the equal of those of Paradise; the waters of the Tigris, which are only comparable in their pellucidness to the tears of the Virgin Mary, flow round past the Karkh Quarter, and the river surface is everywhere covered with boats which Khâḳânî likens to the cradle of Jesus for their grace of build. With a good deal more in this style of bombast, and avoiding any detailed description of the town or its palaces, Khâḳânî concludes his poem with a long panegyric of the Caliph Muḥammad Muḳtafî and of the various learned persons whom he saw in Baghdad[1].

Benjamin of Tudela, the Jewish traveller, visited Baghdad a few years after the time of Khâḳânî, approximately in 555 (A. D. 1160), but his narrative gives us little topographical information, since his attention is wholly directed to enumerating the settlements of his co-religionists in Babylonia. He states, however, that in his time the Caliph only left his palace once a year, namely on the great feast day at the close of the Ramaḍân Fast, when setting forth in procession he visited the mosque near the Baṣrah Gate, which same Benjamin of Tudela says was the metropolitan mosque of the city. The Jâmi' of the old Round City of Manṣûr is evidently the place here designated; but it may be questioned (comparing this with the account left us by Ibn Jubayr a quarter of a century later) whether either the Caliph Muḥammad Muḳtafî or Mustanjid really maintained the seclusion of which Benjamin of Tudela speaks[2].

The graphic descriptions of Baghdad given by the Spanish Arab Ibn Jubayr, who visited Baghdad in 581 (A. D. 1185) are a complete contrast to the futilities of the Persian poet Khâḳânî. Ibn Jubayr was then on his way back from Mecca, and came up the great Kûfah highroad from the south, having

[1] Khakani, p. 91. I have to thank my friend Professor E. G. Browne of Cambridge for the loan of this work, which I should otherwise have failed to see.

[2] Benjamin of Tudela, i. 97.

crossed the Euphrates at Ḥillah by the bridge of boats recently established here by the Caliph Nâṣir for the convenience of the pilgrims, who formerly had had to cross the great river in a ferry. Leaving the Euphrates, Ibn Jubayr passed through the town of Ṣarṣar on the canal of that name, and entered Baghdad on the third day of the month Ṣafar, corresponding in that year to the middle of May, alighting in the suburb of West Baghdad called the Ḳurayyah, which lay over against the Niẓâmîyah College of the eastern city.

Ibn Jubayr devotes many pages to the account of what he did and saw during the fortnight of his sojourn in the capital of the Caliph Nâṣir, whom he had the honour of seeing on more than one occasion. He describes West Baghdad as being for the greater part in ruin. Its four most populous quarters were: first, the Ḳurayyah Suburb near the Bridge of Boats, the best built in the first instance and the least dilapidated; next to this was Karkh, surrounded by its own wall; and above was the Quarter of the Baṣrah Gate (for what remained of the Round City had now come to be known by the name of its south-eastern gateway), with the great Mosque of Manṣûr, still used for the Friday prayers; lastly, the quarter called the Shâri' (the Highroad), along the Tigris bank above the 'Aḍudî Hospital, the market of which connected the Shâri' Quarter with the Suburb of the Baṣrah Gate. Other but less populous quarters of West Baghdad were the Ḥarbîyah, the highest on the river bank, and adjacent thereto the 'Attâbîyah, noted for the manufacture of the 'Attâbî (tabby) silk and cotton stuffs named after it. Further, Ibn Jubayr saw the tomb of

Ma'rûf Karkhî near the Baṣrah Gate Suburb, and the shrine of the Imâm Mûsâ in the great cemetery to the north (known now as the Kâẓimayn), this last being surrounded by the graves of many distinguished and holy personages.

Across the river in East Baghdad, opposite the Kâẓimayn, was the quarter round the tomb of Abu Ḥanîfah, lying above Ruṣâfah and its great mosque, and round this last were seen the sepulchres of many other holy men, and more celebrated still the tombs of the Caliphs. At a considerable distance below Ruṣâfah came the Palaces of the Caliph, covering an area estimated at more than a quarter of the whole of the eastern city, and the royal precincts were encircled by the various palaces of the Abbasid nobles, 'so to speak, imprisoned in their grandeur.' Ibn Jubayr was much struck by the beauty of the gardens in this quarter; but he remarks that the markets of East Baghdad were none the less almost entirely supplied by the produce of the lands under cultivation on the opposite or western bank. There were three great mosques for the Friday prayers in use in East Baghdad when Ibn Jubayr was there, namely the Mosque of the Caliph within the palace; the Mosque of the Sultan, which lay outside, to the north of the Gate of the Sultan in the city wall, in front of the Saljûḳ Palaces; and, lastly, the Ruṣâfah Mosque, which stood (he says) a mile distant from the Mosque of the Sultan aforesaid, in the neighbourhood of the shrine of Abu Ḥanîfah.

In the whole of Baghdad Ibn Jubayr further counted eleven mosques where the Friday prayers were said, and of Ḥammâms or hot baths, so many that none could tell their number, one person assuring him that there were over two thousand, and he adds that in these the halls were so finely plastered with bitumen, brought from Baṣrah, that the visitor imagined the walls to be lined with slabs of black marble. Of colleges—'each more magnificent than a palace'—over thirty were to be counted, the greatest being the Niẓâmîyah, which had been recently restored. Lastly, Ibn Jubayr describes the city wall with its four gates, which went in a semicircle round East Baghdad, from the Tigris bank above, to the river again below the city quarters; and this wall, as already said, is virtually identical with the present wall round modern Baghdad, for one of the extant gates still bears an inscription set up by the Caliph Nâṣir, who was reigning when Ibn Jubayr visited Baghdad.

Towards the close of the reign of this same Caliph Nâṣir, and about the year 623 (A.D. 1226), Yâḳût wrote his great *Geographical Dictionary* (the articles arranged in alphabetical order), which forms perhaps the greatest storehouse of geographical facts compiled by any one man during the Middle Ages. He knew Baghdad intimately, having been brought up there, but wrote at a distance, compiling uncritically, and hence in minor points of detail he is sometimes guilty of egregious blunders. His description of the Palaces of the Caliph is invaluable, but his statements concerning the relative positions of places and quarters in Baghdad, especially in regard to the points of the compass, are both vague and contradictory. If we were without the works of his predecessors, it would be impossible, following his accounts alone, to draw up any consistent plan of Baghdad; but with the earlier systematic descriptions of Ya'ḳûbî and Ibn Serapion to fall back on, enabling us to correct his frequent minor errors, the plan of the city having thus been laid down gains a fullness of detail that would be unattainable without the information contained in the long series of articles in his Dictionary.

He describes (under various articles) West Baghdad as consisting in his day of a number of separate quarters, each enclosed by its own wall. Thus the Ḥarbîyah in the northern part of West Baghdad lay 'like a separate walled town,' nearly two miles distant from the remainder of old Baghdad, and it was surrounded by many waste lands. The Ḥarbîyah included several minor quarters, and to the west of it lay the separate townships of the Chahâr Sûj (Four Markets), of which the 'Attâbîyah (noticed already by Ibn Jubayr) was the best known part. South of the Ḥarbîyah stood the old mosque of Manṣûr, which was included in the Quarter of the Baṣrah Gate, this gate, as already said, having given its name to all that still continued to be habitable of the Round City. The Karkhâyâ Canal, according to Yâḳût, had disappeared, but the great merchants' quarter of Karkh remained standing 'a horse gallop' (or about half a mile) distant from the Baṣrah Gate Quarter, and the population of this last being of the orthodox Sunnî faith were the rivals of the Karkh people, who were all bigoted heterodox Shî'ahs.

Adjoining Karkh, and on the Tigris bank, was the Ḳurayyah and the Quarter of the Ḳallâyîn Canal, where fried meats were sold, also the Ṭâbiḳ Canal Quarter, which in the time of Yâḳût had been recently burnt down; and hence, as he says, these were already for the most part merely so many rubbish heaps. The quarter round the Muḥawwal Gate, lying inland from Karkh, and inhabited by Sunnîs who were always at feud with their Shî'ah neighbours, appears to have still retained some of its former opulence; while the town of Muḥawwal, a league beyond the outer suburbs of West Baghdad, was populous and famous for its excellent markets. The Shûnîzîyah Cemetery lay to the south of Karkh, while to the north of the Ḥarbîyah extended the great burial-ground round the shrine of the Imâm Mûsâ, afterwards known as the Kâẓimayn.

On the eastern bank, the centre of population was the great Palace of the Caliph, described as occupying a third part of the whole area of the city; all round this lay a network of markets and streets extending to the city wall, and in places going beyond it. Outside and at some distance to the north of this wall was Ruṣâfah with its mosque surrounded by the tombs of the Caliphs; while upstream, beyond this again lay the quarter named after the shrine of Abu Ḥanîfah, with its own market; and these two outlying suburbs, with the neighbouring Christian quarter, called the Dâr-ar-Rûm (House of the Greeks), were all that remained habitable in the time of Yâḳût of the older part of the eastern city, which formerly had consisted of the three great quarters of Ruṣâfah, Shammâsîyah, and the Mukharrim.

Yâḳût, it will be seen by the dates, describes Baghdad for us as the great city stood immediately prior to the Mongol invasion; and the only building of note erected after his time by the Caliphs was the Mustanṣirîyah College. This was built by Mustanṣir, the father of the last of the Abbasids, and the description of it is given in the contemporary chronicle of Abu-l-Faraj. The ruin of this college still exists, and at some distance from it stands the minaret of a mosque also inscribed with the name of this same Caliph. No mention, however, of Mustanṣir having built a mosque occurs in the chronicles, and (as stated in a previous chapter) it seems probable that these remains of the so-called Mustanṣirîyah Mosque are in reality those of the far older mosque of the palace (built by 'Alî Muktafî more than three centuries before), which Mustanṣir having restored, caused to be ornamented with the inscription now bearing his name. It may be added that besides these buildings in the city of Baghdad, Mustanṣir also constructed the magnificent stone bridge of four great arches over the Dujayl Canal near the town of Ḥarbâ, as is mentioned by the historian Fakhri, the remains of which still exist and have been carefully described by Captain Felix Jones, R.N.[1]

In the dearth of authorities for the last centuries of the history of Baghdad, the great Biographical Dictionary compiled about the year 654 (A.D. 1256) by Ibn Khallikân is a very useful work of reference. He was a native of Arbela, near Mosul in Upper Mesopotamia, and though he does not appear himself to have visited Baghdad, he was evidently well acquainted with the history of its public buildings. From incidental remarks in the various biographies we often gain information—concerning the later buildings especially—which is lacking in

[1] Fakhri, 380. Jones, 252, where two drawings of this bridge will be found, also the copy of the inscription by Mustansir which it bears, dated the year 629 (A.D. 1232).

the meagre chronicles of this period; thus his article on Mâlik Shâh is our only authority for the fact that this prince was the founder of the Jâmi'-as-Sulṭân, the great Friday mosque of the Saljûḳs in East Baghdad, outside the Palace of the Sultan. Ibn Khallikân died at Damascus in 681 (A. D. 1282), a score of years after the Mongol sack of Baghdad; but of these recent events he maintains a discreet silence in his dictionary, which deals with the notable personages of the past age only, and we have to fall back on Persian histories for details of the great siege.

CHAPTER XXIV

RECAPITULATION AND AUTHORITIES: FINAL PERIOD

The Fall of Baghdad: the Mongol invasion. Persian Histories: the Ṭabaḳât-i-Nâṣirî, Rashîd-ad-Dîn, and Waṣṣâf. Details of the Mongol siege. Death of the last Caliph Musta'ṣim. The Marâṣid-al-Iṭṭilâ'. Summary of history of Baghdad since the Mongol siege. Ibn Baṭûṭah, the Berber. Ḥamd-Allah, the Persian. The tomb of 'Abd-al-Ḳâdir of Gîlân. Modern descriptions of Baghdad: Tavernier and Niebuhr. The so-called tomb of Zubaydah. The Plan of mediaeval Baghdad and of the modern city. Excavations required to discover the sites of the three ancient Mosques.

FOR the details of the fall of Baghdad and the great siege by Hûlâgû the Mongol, we have to consult, in the main, the works of Persian historians, since Ibn-al-Athîr closes his chronicle with the year A.H. 628, and neither Abu-l-Faraj nor Abu-l-Fidâ affords much information on this subject. Indeed, of the Mongol siege in the seventh century A.H., we know far less than we do, thanks to Ṭabarî, of the first siege in the time of the Caliph Amîn in the second century A.H.

The Persian history called the Ṭabaḳât-i-Nâṣirî, which was written shortly after 658 (A.D. 1260), is a contemporary authority for the times of Hûlâgû, and this with the information found in the work of

Rashîd-ad-Dîn, also written in Persian, which was finished in 710 (A.D. 1310), provides a fairly clear account of the siege operations[1]. After overrunning and devastating Western Persia, the Mongol armies poured down the great Khurâsân road from Ḥulwân, the main body marching direct on East Baghdad. A considerable detachment, however, had been sent upstream, with orders to cross the Tigris at Takrît, thence to make a sweep round, and after capturing Anbâr on the Euphrates, these troops were to approach West Baghdad by the line of the 'Îsâ Canal.

The Mongol forces were led by Hûlâgû (grandson of Changîz Khân) who commanded the centre division in person, and he pitched his camp to the east of Baghdad, the siege beginning in the middle of Muḥarram of the year 656 (January, 1258). His main attack was directed against the 'left of the city'—to one coming from Persia—namely the Burj 'Ajamî (the Persian Bastion) and the Ḥalbah Gate. The right wing of the Mongol army lay before 'the breadth of the city,' that is, on the north side, facing the gate of the Market of the Sultan, or the Bâb-as-Sulṭân; and the left wing was encamped before

[1] Another almost contemporary writer is Waṣṣâf, the historiographer of Ghâzân the Îl-Khân of Persia. He was born at Shîrâz in A.D. 1263, five years, therefore, after the Mongol siege of Baghdad, and must have known personally many of those who had taken part in this famous event. His history was composed in the year 700 (A.D. 1300), and I have gone through the pages of this work which are devoted to Hûlâgû and the siege, but have been unable to glean a single fact not already mentioned by Rashîd-ad-Dîn; the bombastic style in which Waṣṣâf writes being indeed but ill adapted for conveying any precise topographical information. Fakhri is a contemporary Arabic authority; he wrote in the year 700 (A.D. 1300), and had been in Baghdad, but his account of the siege gives few topographical details.

the Kalwâdhâ Gate at the southern extremity of East Baghdad. The detachments that had previously been sent north across the river, after defeating the armies of the Caliph Musta'ṣim on the right bank of the Tigris, took up their positions in two attacks, one near the 'Aḍudî Hospital at the upper (older Main) Bridge of Boats, while the second had its siege camp below this to the southward, probably near the lower bridge opposite the Palace of the Caliph, and outside the quarter known as the Ḳurayyah.

On the western bank, the lower camp of the Mongols is variously described as having been pitched at the place called Dûlâb-i-Baḳal (in the Persian history of Rashîd-ad-Dîn), or at the Mabḳalah (according to Abu-l-Faraj), the former name meaning 'the water-wheel of the vegetable (garden),' and the latter 'the kitchen garden,' both terms reminding us of the older Dâr-al-Battîkh (Fruit Market), which stood, according to Ibn Serapion, in this part of West Baghdad[1]. The Ḳal'ah or Citadel, which is also mentioned by Rashîd-ad-Dîn when describing the attack on the west side, presumably has reference to what in the thirteenth century A.D. still remained standing of the old fortifications of the Round City of Manṣûr.

The siege operations, pushed to the uttermost by Hûlâgû outside the city, were but too well seconded by treachery within the walls of Baghdad, for both Karkh and the quarter round the shrine of the Imâm Mûsâ in the Kâẓimayn were inhabited by Shî'ahs, who to prove their abhorrence of the Sunnî Caliph corresponded traitorously with the infidel

[1] See above, p. 85.

enemy. After a blockade of about fifty days, a great assault was ordered at the Persian Bastion south of the Ḥalbah Gate, and East Baghdad being taken by storm, the Caliph Musta'ṣim was finally brought out prisoner with his family and lodged in the Mongol camp. Shortly afterwards Hûlâgû on entering the city took up his residence in what Rashîd-ad-Dîn calls the Maymûnîyah (the Monkey-house), doubtless a designed corruption for the name of the Mamûnîyah Quarter, which lay on the side of East Baghdad nearest to what had been the headquarter camp of the Mongols.

The sack of Baghdad which followed lasted forty days, during which time a large proportion of the inhabitants were butchered in cold blood; while a conflagration which destroyed the Mosque of the Caliph, the shrine of Mûsâ-al-Kâẓim, and the tombs of the Caliphs at Ruṣâfah, besides most of the streets and private houses, completed the ruin of the city. The death of the Caliph Musta'ṣim, and of his sons, followed close on these events—the details of their 'martyrdom' are variously given in different authorities, who, however, agree as to the main facts—and then the Mongol hordes passed on to further conquests and fresh plunder; Hûlâgû leaving orders that the great Mosque of the Caliph and the shrine of Mûsâ in the Kâẓimayn should be rebuilt[1].

[1] A full description of the fall of Baghdad, carefully put together from all available sources—Arabic, Persian, and Turkish—will be found in Sir H. Howorth's *History of the Mongols* (iii. 113 to 133). For the death of the Caliph Musta'ṣim the well-known account given by Marco Polo (i. 65), which is confirmed by the Chronicle of Ibn Furât, his contemporary, is presumably true in the main facts. See a paper in the *J. R. A. S.* for 1900, p. 293, by the present writer.

The state of ruin to which Baghdad was reduced by the Mongol sack is clearly indicated, half a century later, in the *Marâṣid*, an epitome of Yâḳût's *Geographical Dictionary*, which was composed about the year 700 (A.D. 1300) by an anonymous author. This book gives a summary of the facts detailed in the more voluminous work; but in addition, the epitomist, when treating of places personally known to him, constantly supplies emendations for correcting Yâḳût, and states how matters stood in his own day. Hence, though primarily only an epitome of a compilation, the *Marâṣid* has for Baghdad and Mesopotamia the value of an authority at first hand. The author's description of Baghdad city is graphic and terse. After referring to the ruin brought about by a long succession of plundering armies—Persian, Turk, and Mongol—each of which had in turn wasted the goods and houses of the former inhabitants, he concludes with the following paragraph:—

'Hence nothing now remains of Western Baghdad but some few isolated quarters, of which the best inhabited is Karkh; while in Eastern Baghdad, all having long ago gone to ruin in the Shammâsîyah Quarter and the Mukharrim, they did build a wall round such of the city as remained, this same lying along the bank of the Tigris. Thus matters continued until the Tatars (under Hûlâgû) came, when the major part of this remnant also was laid in ruin, and its inhabitants were all put to death, hardly one surviving to recall the excellence of the past. And then there came in people from the countryside, who settled in Baghdad, seeing that its own citizens had all perished; so the city now is indeed other than it was, its population in our time being wholly changed from its former state—but Allah, be He exalted, ordaineth all[1].'

The history of Baghdad, from the date of the Mongol invasion (A. D. 1258) to the present time, may be summed up in a few paragraphs: in fact, from having been the real or nominal capital of Islam Baghdad now became merely the chief town of the Province of Arabian 'Irâḳ.

The descendants of Hûlâgû, the Îl-Khâns, after governing Persia and Mesopotamia for something less than a century, were succeeded by the Jalayrs in Mesopotamia, Shaykh Ḥasan Buzurg, chief of the line, making Baghdad his residence in A. D. 1340. In A. D. 1393 Timur occupied Baghdad, remaining there a couple of months, and on his departure left orders to his lieutenant, Mîrzâ Abu Bakr, to rebuild the city, which had then fallen for the most part to ruin. After the death of Timur, Sultan Aḥmad the Jalayr in part recovered possession of his dominions, but in A. D. 1411 the dynasty gave place to the Ḳara-Kuyunli, the Turkomans of the 'Black Sheep,' who occupied Baghdad till they were in turn dispossessed, in A.D. 1469, by the rival clan of the Aḳ-Kuyunli or 'White Sheep' Turkomans.

In A. D. 1508 the troops of Shâh Ismâîl I of Persia took Baghdad from these Turkomans: but the Persians gave place to the Ottoman Turks in A. D. 1534, when the general of Sultan Sulaymân the Magnificent conquered the city. In A. D. 1623, under Shâh 'Abbâs the Great, the Persians, through the treachery of Bakîr Aghâ the Janissary, once more became masters of Baghdad; but a few years later, in A. D. 1638, they were again driven out, when

[1] Marasid, i. 163.

Sultan Murâd IV conquered the city. And since this date Baghdad has been the residence of the Turkish Pasha of Mesopotamia.

Our latest Arab authority for Baghdad is Ibn Baṭûṭah, the Berber, whose travels may rival those of his contemporary Marco Polo in extent. In his book he takes Ibn Jubayr as his model, and he cites long passages from the work of his predecessor; but unfortunately does not always state quite clearly whether what Ibn Jubayr had described in 581 (A. D. 1185) was what he, Ibn Baṭûṭah, had still found existing in Baghdad at the date of his own sojourn there in the year 727 (A. D. 1327). This vagueness of statement at times militates against the value of his work from a topographical point of view. Ibn Baṭûṭah, however, describes some buildings of a later date than Ibn Jubayr; the Mustanṣirîyah College, for example, indicating where this stood in Eastern Baghdad, and hence, since its ruins still exist, enabling us to add another fixed point for connecting modern Baghdad with the plan of the city in the times of the Caliphs. Further, Ibn Baṭûṭah (unless indeed in this he is merely servilely copying his predecessor Ibn Jubayr), appears to have been the last authority who saw the three great mosques of the older capital still standing:—namely the Mosque of Manṣûr in West Baghdad, and the Ruṣâfah Mosque on the eastern side, lying one mile distant from its neighbour the Mosque of the Saljûḳ Sultan. At the present day, these three buildings seem to have entirely disappeared, as also all vestiges of the 'Aḍudî Hospital, which in the fourteenth century A. D. was a ruin standing on the right bank of the Tigris, at the place where the older Main Bridge of Boats had crossed the river to Ruṣâfah.

The last Moslem authority for Baghdad is the Persian historian and geographer Ḥamd-Allah, surnamed Mustawfî (the Treasurer), who was the contemporary of Ibn Baṭûṭah, the Berber. He wrote an Universal History called the *Tarîkh-i-Guzîdah* (the Choice Chronicle) and a work on Geography called the *Nuzhat-al-Ḳulûb* (the Heart's Delight), the later work having been completed in the year 740 (A.D. 1339). Ḥamd-Allah describes Baghdad, both east and west, as in his day surrounded by walls. The eastern city wall had four gates, and from the river bank above to the river bank below, followed a semicircle measuring in circuit 18,000 paces. The western suburb, which as a whole was called Karkh, had two gates in its wall, and this wall measured 12,000 paces in its semicircular sweep. The description of Ḥamd-Allah is thus virtually identical with that given by Ibn Jubayr, his predecessor by two centuries, and in the matter of the walls corresponds with what is now found to exist in modern Baghdad. Ḥamd-Allah does not give names to the two Karkh gates, but the four gates in East Baghdad are named, and they may be easily identified with those mentioned by Ibn Jubayr, and are identical with the four that still exist under other names at the present day.

Ḥamd-Allah especially describes the shrines of Baghdad; namely the Kâẓimayn with the tomb of Ibn Ḥanbal and the tomb of Ma'rûf Karkhî on the west bank; and on the eastern side the shrine of Abu Ḥanîfah. These, for the most part, exist at present, and in his day also, though no trace of them now remains, the tombs of the Caliphs might still be seen in Ruṣâfah, standing apart by themselves like 'a little town.' He is also one of the first to mention the shrine of 'Abd-al-Ḳâdir of Gilân, which is a noted place of pilgrimage in modern Baghdad; this 'Abd-al-Ḳâdir being the celebrated founder of the Ḳâdirîyah sect of dervishes—one of the most widespread religious orders of Islam—who dying at Baghdad in 651 (A. D. 1253) was buried there a few years before the Mongol siege.

Coming down to modern times, one of the earliest travellers who has described Baghdad (giving also a rough plan) is the celebrated French jeweller J. B. Tavernier, who, on his way to and from India, travelled through Mesopotamia in 1632 and again in 1652. His notice of Baghdad is of the latter date, to wit a few years after the Turkish conquest under Sultan Murâd IV.

His description and plan show that the city was then much what it is now, except that the area within the walls was then less given up to ruin. On the eastern bank of the Tigris, the town was surrounded by its wall of burnt brick, some three miles in total circumference, with bastions at intervals, having a deep ditch without. The area covered by houses measured some fifteen hundred paces in length by seven or eight hundred paces in breadth. The wall was pierced (as at the present day) by four gates: namely 'Maazan Capi,' the gate leading north-west to the Mu'aẓẓam Shrine; then two gates in the length of the wall on the north-eastern side, each of which Tavernier has marked as 'porte murée,' these being the present Bâb-al-Wusṭânî and Bâb-at-Talism, which last is still closed as by order, it is said, of Sultan Murâd IV;

finally, the gate to the south-east downstream now known as the Bâb-ash-Sharḳî, which Tavernier names 'Cara Capi' or the Black Gate.

At the Bridge-head also was a gateway called 'Sû Capi' or the Water-Gate, and the Bridge of Boats led across to the suburb of West Baghdad, described as 'le Faubourg dans la Mésopotamie[1].'

A hundred years after the time of Tavernier Baghdad was visited by Carstein Niebuhr, then on his way home after his celebrated journey in Arabia. He passed through Mesopotamia about the year 1750, and has left a description of Baghdad, the accuracy of which modern authorities confirm in every point: noting all the remains of the ancient city that then could be with certainty identified, most of which are also again mentioned in the *Report* of Commander Felix Jones, written in 1857.

What may be seen here at the present day is as follows. The seat of the Turkish provincial government is in the Eastern City on the Persian side of the Tigris, and the old wall surrounds the town on the land side, pierced by the four ancient gateways, one of which, the Bâb-at-Talism (the Gate of the Talisman), as already stated, bears the inscription of the Caliph Nâṣir. The ruins of both the Mustanṣirîyah College and the mosque exist, and not very far from this last stands the shrine of 'Abd-al-Ḳâdir of Gilân, which, as already said, dates back to the last days of the Caliphate.

Above the city, on the eastern Tigris bank, stands the tomb of the Imâm Abu Ḥanîfah in the village now known as Al-Mu'aẓẓam, and on the western bank, opposite this, Niebuhr especially mentions

[1] Tavernier, i. 230–239.

that the sepulchre of the Imâm Ibn Ḥanbal (more correctly of 'Abd-Allah Ibn Ḥanbal) had formerly existed, but that shortly before his visit in 1750, this tomb had been carried away by the floods of the Tigris. On the western bank also, but above the Mu'aẓẓam village of the east side, is the Shî'ah shrine of the Kâẓimayn, some of the buildings of which may date from the times of the Caliphate; but of the Round City of Manṣûr apparently nothing remains—unless it be the Kûfic inscription bearing the date 333 (A.D. 945), which Sir H. Rawlinson describes as existing in this Quarter in the Convent (Takiyeh) of the Bektash Dervishes.

What is now called the Old Town on this western bank, occupies part of the site of the older Karkh suburb, as is proved by the tomb of Ma'rûf Karkhî which still exists, standing at some distance outside its western gate, and this has been a much venerated shrine since the date of his death in the year 200 (A.D. 816). Niebuhr mentions as situated in this same neighbourhood the tomb of a certain Bahlûl Dânah, whom he describes as having been a relative and boon companion of the Caliph Hârûn-ar-Rashîd, the gravestone bearing for date the year 501 (A.D. 1108). This personage apparently is not noticed by any other authority, and Hârûn-ar-Rashîd, in point of fact, had been dead more than three centuries at the date inscribed on the tomb.

In regard to the so-called tomb of Zubaydah, which now lies a little to the south of that of Ma'rûf Karkhî, the facts cited in the Chronicle of Ibn-al-Athîr (see above, p. 165) are wholly against the assumption that this was the place of her burial. The older authorities, who mention the neighbouring shrine of Ma'rûf, make no allusion to any tomb near here of the celebrated wife of Hârûn-ar-Rashîd; further, in the Chronicle just named, it is distinctly stated that Zubaydah was buried in the cemetery of the Kâẓimayn, lying near the river bank some three miles to the north of the picturesque monument which apparently has for the last two centuries borne her name. Niebuhr, who describes the tomb as it stood in the last century, gives the text of the Arabic inscription which in his day adorned it. In this it is set forth that 'Âyishah Khânum, daughter of the late Muṣṭafâ Pâshâ, and wife of Ḥusayn Pâshâ, Governor of Baghdad, was buried here in Muḥarram of the year 1131 (November, A.D. 1718), her grave having been made in the sepulchre of the Lady Zubaydah, granddaughter of the Abbasid Caliph Manṣûr, and wife of Hârûn-ar-Rashîd, the date of whose death is correctly given as having occurred in the year 216 (A.D. 831).

To this information Niebuhr adds the statement that the tomb of Zubaydah had been restored when the Turkish Khânum was buried here, some thirty years before he visited Baghdad, but by whom the monument was originally built appears to have been then unknown. Sir H. Rawlinson, who lived for many years in Baghdad, writes that the tomb of Zubaydah was first erected in A.D. 827, corresponding with A.H. 212; but this would be four years before the date of her death as recorded on the unimpeachable authority of Ṭabarî, and Sir Henry gives no authority for his statement. He also, apparently, entertained no doubts as to the present monument being the resting-place of this princess, so famous both in the chronicles and the *Thousand and One Nights*;

though this attribution, as already stated, is entirely negatived by the earlier authorities. Indeed, as far as is known, the first mention of this building being considered to be the tomb of the Lady Zubaydah appears to date from the eighteenth century only, when in A.D. 1718 Ḥusayn Pâshâ buried his wife here, in what at that time he was told had been the sepulchre of the famous Abbasid princess [1].

In conclusion a few paragraphs may serve to explain how the attempt has been made, in the preceding chapters, to lay down the limits of mediaeval Baghdad on the plan of the modern city. The landmarks are, of course, the few ancient vestiges that still remain to mark the sites of buildings mentioned during the times of the Caliphs; and starting from the plan of the present walled city on the east bank of the Tigris, we have to work backwards to the Round City of Manṣûr on the western bank, of which no trace now exists.

It will be remembered that East Baghdad of the present day has four gates, and there appears to be

[1] For illustrations representing the so-called tomb of Zubaydah, and the shrine of Ma'rûf Karkhî, see Jones, 311. It is possible that this modern tomb of Zubaydah may be the building described in the twelfth century A.D. by Ibn Jubayr, and which Ibn Batutah saw in A.D. 1327 standing near the highroad outside the old Baṣrah Gate (Ibn Jubayr, 227; Ibn Batutah, ii. 108). The tomb within this shrine then bore an inscription stating that 'Awn and Mu'în were buried here, two of the descendants of the Caliph 'Alî, son-in-law of the prophet Muḥammad. In the fourteenth century A.D. this same shrine is described as a beautiful building, within which was the gravestone lying under a spacious dome-shaped monument. It would seem not unlikely that in the course of the next three centuries, the inscription having become illegible, and all memory of these Alids long forgotten, popular tradition may have fixed on this tomb as that which had been built over the remains of the celebrated wife of Hârûn-ar-Rashîd, more especially since her real sepulchre in the Kâẓimayn probably did not survive the Mongol siege, and the subsequent conflagration.

no reason to doubt that these, with the town wall, are identical in position with what is described by Ibn Jubayr as existing in A.D. 1185; further, the ruins of the Mustanṣirîyah College and the ancient minaret of the Mosque of the Caliph still mark the upper limit of the palace precincts, which, lying within an encircling wall on the river bank, originally occupied about a third of the area of the present walled town. Another fixed point on this eastern side is the existing shrine of Abu Ḥanîfah, which, we are told, stood immediately above the Ruṣâfah Mosque; the Quarters of Ruṣâfah and Mukharrim lying between this point and the wall of the present town, one beyond the other on the Tigris bank. Above the Abu Ḥanîfah Shrine was the Upper Bridge of Boats, while the Shammâsîyah Gate and suburb stretched back from the river, and to the north of the Mukharrim Quarter.

The Shammâsîyah Quarter of the east bank lay opposite the Ḥarbîyah Quarter of Western Baghdad; and this suburb spreading out below the tombs of the Kâẓimayn enclosed in a great semicircular sweep the northern side of the Round City of Manṣûr. The present Kâẓimayn Shrine is the landmark fixing the upper limit of West Baghdad, and its position in regard to the City of Manṣûr is clearly set forth in the old accounts. The position of the City of Manṣûr and of its four gates is fixed, within certain narrow limits, by the facts stated as to its size:—its four equidistant gates having been a mile apart one from the other, while that known as the Khurâsân Gate opened on the river and the Main Bridge. The Main Bridge-head, on the eastern side, was below Ruṣâfah and above Mukharrim, these two quarters being divided by the great eastern highroad that went along the south side of the Shammâsîyah from the Main Bridge to the Khurâsân Gate of the (upper) eastern city.

The site of the Ruṣâfah Mosque must have been in the loop of the Tigris above the Main Bridge, for the palaces of the Buyids and Saljûḳs afterwards stretched from the river bank above the shrine of Abu Ḥanîfah to near the river bank again at the Zâhir Garden in the Mukharrim Quarter immediately below the bridge. Here the great Mosque of the Sultan was afterwards built by Mâlik Shâh, which stood a mile distant from the older Ruṣâfah Mosque, and it lay at a considerable distance outside the upper gate of the wall of later (and modern) Eastern Baghdad. This gate of the later wall appears to be almost identical in position with the more ancient gate of the Tuesday Market, the lowest in the line of the older wall which had surrounded the three Northern Quarters of Mukharrim, Shammâsîyah and Ruṣâfah; for this older wall of the Northern Quarters went from below the Lower Bridge inland to the Abraz Gate (which we know from Yâḳût stood within the area of the modern city) and thence going up past the Khurâsân and Baradân Gates rejoined the river bank again at the Shammâsîyah Gate, some distance above the shrine of Abu Ḥanîfah, over against the Kâẓimayn on the west bank. The line of this older wall can only be traced approximately by plotting in the various roads and gates mentioned, but its general course is clearly indicated by many incidental references.

In Western Baghdad a fixed point is the present shrine of Ma'rûf Ḳarkhî, which we are told lay outside the Baṣrah Gate of the Round City; and the positions of the Baṣrah and Kûfah Gates—lying a mile apart one from the other, and opening on the highroads going, respectively, south to Kûfah, and down the Tigris bank—are fixed within narrow limits by the Ma'rûf Shrine. The present Bridge of Boats, which crosses the Tigris opposite the remains of the Mustanṣirîyah College, is almost certainly identical in position with the bridge mentioned by Ibn Jubayr and Yâḳût as starting from the Ḳaṣr 'Îsâ Quarter, which was separated by the Lower Harbour, at the mouth of the 'Îsâ Canal, from the Ḳurayyah Quarter. The positions of these two quarters in regard to the Baṣrah Gate of the Round City are thus fixed; and the Ḳurayyah Quarter lay opposite the Niẓâmîyah College in Eastern Baghdad, which stood near the Tigris bank between the Palaces of the Caliphs and the city wall at the Kalwâdhâ Gate, which last is now known as the Bâb-ash-Sharḳî of modern Baghdad.

The courses of the 'Îsâ Canal, the Ṣarât, and the Trench of Ṭâhir, with their numerous branches, also the site of the town of Muḥawwal, of which apparently nothing now remains, are all fixed, within narrow limits, by a line drawn from the point where the Nahr 'Îsâ left the Euphrates below Anbâr to the mouth of this canal, where its waters poured into the Tigris at the Lower Harbour immediately below the Palace Bridge and opposite the Mustanṣirîyah College. Further, the curves followed by the 'Îsâ Canal and the Ṣarât, with their connecting watercourses, have to be laid down so as to carry these round the circle of the City of Manṣûr, which, with the Ḥarbîyah Quarter, lay between the Ṣarât and the Trench of Ṭâhir; due account being taken of the network of waterways described by Ibn Serapion which thus enveloped the Round City to the south, west, and north, while the Tigris bank marked its eastern limit.

Such, in brief outline, is the method that has been followed in constructing the accompanying plans; the details are filled in from the incidental mention by many authorities of the relative positions of places; and that in their general lines these plans are fairly exact appears to be proved by the plotting-out, where various minor points from diverse authors all work into the places indicated by the two contemporary descriptions of Ya'ḳûbî and Ibn Serapion. But though the relative positions of most of the important places are thus fixed on more than one authority, the actual positions on the modern map are still to be sought, and these can only be ascertained when excavations shall have been made, bringing to light the ruins of the Mosque of Manṣûr in the western city, and of the Ruṣâfah Mosque on the eastern bank, with the great Mosque of the Sultan a mile distant from it. Some traces of these great mosques must surely be extant, for they were built of kiln-burnt bricks or tiles, which do not quickly perish, and all three were still standing in the fourteenth century A.D., when Ibn Baṭûṭah visited Baghdad.

INDEX

E. B. refers to places in Eastern Baghdad.
W. B. refers to places in Western Baghdad.

FINIS

OXFORD
PRINTED AT THE CLARENDON PRESS
BY HORACE HART, M.A.
PRINTER TO THE UNIVERSITY

Printed in the United States
126096LV00002B/11/A

9 781417 947805